Three sheets to the wind

Pete Brown writes about beer and other drinks for a variety of publications, and runs a drinks marketing consultancy. He thinks he may have the best job in the world. He lives with his wife in North London, in a house which always has lots of empties outside on the day the recycling people come around.

For more information about beer, visit the author's website
www.pete-brown.co.uk

By the same author

Man walks into a pub
A sociable history of beer

Three sheets to the wind

*One man's quest for
the meaning of beer*

PETE BROWN

MACMILLAN

First published 2006 by Macmillan
an imprint of Pan Macmillan Ltd
Pan Macmillan, 20 New Wharf Road, London N1 9RR
Basingstoke and Oxford
Associated companies throughout the world
www.panmacmillan.com

ISBN-13: 978-1-4050-4987-0
ISBN-10: 1-4050-4987-1

1 3 5 7 9 8 6 4 2

A CIP catalogue record for this book is available from
the British Library.

Typeset by SetSystems Ltd, Saffron Walden, Essex
Printed and bound in Great Britain by
Mackays of Chatham plc, Chatham, Kent

A toast

To Liz and to Chris,
the most considerate travelling companions.

And to the kindness of strangers.

Three sheets to the wind – The sheet is the rope attached to the clew of a sail used for trimming sail. If the sheet is quite free to flap without restraint, the sheet is said to be 'in the wind', and 'a sheet in the wind' is a colloquial nautical expression for being tipsy. Thus to have 'three sheets to the wind' is to be very drunk.

Brewer's* Dictionary of Phrase and Fable, Millennium Edition

---

*   Funnily enough.

Contents

ix

Contents

Acknowledgements

'It's my round . . .'

When I wrote *Man Walks into a Pub* I had to thank various friends for their general support, and the British Library for letting me in, and that was pretty much it. This book is very different. It simply could not have been written without the active involvement of a huge number of people around the world who gave up their time and treated me to sometimes astonishing hospitality. Such is the nature of the international beer community that several of them have become firm friends since.

There are well over a hundred people whose help I truly appreciate – the people who responded to cold emails to set up visits and interviews for me; the people who got friends of friends to give up their valuable time; the people who showed me around pubs and breweries and told me all about their countries and lives, and spoke English to me because I couldn't speak anything else – space does not permit a full list, and I owe each and every one of you at least a pint.

But the following deserve special mention because this book truly would not have happened without them: Andrew Arnold, Shirley Braithwaite, Chris Crabb, Dermot O'Donnell, David Downie, Deborah Hale, John Harley, Alec and Gill Highnam, Tom and Kirsten Highnam, Takeshi Kato, Adam Kirby, Philip Malpass, Cian Molloy, Declan Moore, Philip Van Munching, Matthew Murray, Miyoko and Nick Ohki, Garrett Oliver, Billy Quinn, Angus Robinson, Jonny Stancill, Alan Milius Thomsen, and last only in alphabetical order, The Wade.

Thanks must also go to the world's brewers, large and small, with particular mention to Asahi Bridgeport, Carlsberg, Diageo, Inbev, Carlton United, the Malt Shovel Brewery, Sprecher Brewery, Budweiser Budvar, SAB Miller, and The Munich Tourist Office

Thanks to Jason Cooper, not only for commissioning and editing the book, but for suggesting I write it in the first place. To Chris Gittner, for chaperoning me through some of Europe's finest drinking dens. And to my wife Liz, who not only kept me alive and sane and fed throughout the long writing months, after all the travel was done, but also selflessly followed me through some of the most beautiful and exotic cities in the world, often with only a credit card to keep her company. True love recognizes no borders.

Finally, this book is also dedicated to both Terry McEwan and Jane Highnam, for embodying the meaning of *gemutlichkeit*, the *craic*, *hygge* and *la chispa*.

1

'Just the one'

London

'Fancy a pint?'
  'Yeah. When?'
  'Tonight? About five thirty?'
  'Yeah, all right. Just the one, though. Can't be too late.
Tuesday night.'
  'Course not. Same here. Half five then.'
  'Cheers.'
  'Cheers.'
  And that's how it starts.

'Fancy a pint?'
  It's an innocent enough question. As invitations go, it's one
of the most appealing I can imagine that involves remaining
fully dressed. Every time someone asks me if I fancy a pint,
it seems like a remarkably good idea, one that never loses its
sheen as an original, inventive, exciting concept.

But often there's more to this little phrase than meets the ear. Usually, when we ask someone if they fancy a pint, we're asking if they would like more than one. Sometimes, the pint proposer will make this clearer by inserting an important extra word, asking, 'Do you fancy a *quick* pint?' which seems to imply that your companion only wants to spend a brief time in the pub but of course means the exact opposite.*

And there's more to 'Fancy a pint?' than traditional English understatement. One of the best running gags in *The Fast Show* was the bloke who found himself in an endless succession of crap situations being bored to tears of futility until he eventually looks into the camera and implores, 'Anyone fancy a pint?' He's asking if we'd like to join him in escaping the meaningless dirge that makes up most of our everyday lives. If you're working with someone and they suggest going for a pint, it means let's move this relationship on to a different level; let's finish with all the bullshit for today and go and speak to each other as equals, with our guard lowered. It could mean we need to talk, but I don't want to make it too heavy. It can mean a good friend thinks it's about time you caught up, or an acquaintance wants to talk to you about something in particular, something that requires your help or point of view, or something they think you should know about or discuss.

So when Simon, my ex-boss, phones me and says, 'Fancy a pint?' I know he's not just lonely and looking for a drinking

---

* Even if the proposer doesn't realize this, what they mean is let's stop whatever we're doing now quickly, and spend a long time in the pub. It might not even mean that at the time, but that's what it always ends up meaning.

buddy. He's a popular bloke, and if all he wanted was an escort to the pub he wouldn't have to phone me. He wants to talk to me about something. I don't know what yet, because used in this sense, 'Fancy a pint?' always carries a little bit of intrigue with it, a frisson, and that's something Simon has always been very good at building. So when I accept this particular offer, I have no reason to suspect that the first pint of this ordinary Tuesday is going to lead to an awful lot more than just a second or third. This is a pint that will have far-reaching consequences, a pint that will change my life, a pint that will cost me a lot more than the price of a late cab home.* But to be fair, Simon doesn't know this either. I doubt he'd have phoned if he did.

In the fifth century BC, the Chinese philosopher Lao-tzu said, 'A journey of a thousand miles begins with a single step.' I'm sure Lao-tzu would also agree that the longest pub crawl starts with a single pub. That pub is the Stabbers.

The Stabbers is one of several pubs in Knightsbridge whose main reason for existence seems to be to mess cruelly with the heads of tourists who expect every doorway on one of London's swankiest streets to lead to an absolutely fabulous consumer paradise. The Stabbers isn't really called the Stabbers of course; it's got a much nicer name than that. But none of the regulars can remember what it is, even though it's written in nice gilt lettering above the door. It's nicknamed the Stabbers precisely for the worst-case scenario you might imagine. The Stabbers is the pub where the help in all those exclusive stores gather to give the servility a rest when they're

---

* About a thousand times more, to be exact.

off duty. In other words, it's a locals' pub, but one that just happens to be in the middle of one of the most exclusive shopping streets in the world. You can see how misunderstandings might happen. Even accounting for the decor.

The Stabbers is the kind of pub that elevates 'in need of refurbishment' from a mumbled estate agent's phrase to a bona fide interior design style. Last year it closed for several weeks, during which time the sound of hammering and sawing could be heard from within, yet when it reopened, it was exactly the same as before, down to the spirals in the carpet that may or may not have once been part of the original design.

It's dark in the Stabbers. It takes a few seconds for people's eyes to adjust from the outside. Sitting at the bar, you can watch the tourists walk in, and you can see the hope and happiness drain from their faces.

I need to stress here that neither I nor Simon drink in the Stabbers – or anywhere else in Knightsbridge for that matter – by choice. Simon works in the soon-to-be-demolished Bowater House, a 1960s office block that squats like a giant, evil spider over the entrance to Hyde Park across the road. The building is home to a group of advertising and marketing companies I used to work for, and for whom Simon still does, for the time being.

'So, are you busy?' asks Simon, returning from the bar with our second pints. (The first ones went quickly while we were catching up on who's shagging who across the road – not gossiping, you understand, just catching up.)

'I am,' I nod, 'too busy. I don't have any free time at all.'

'Would you like to do some work for us?' asks Simon.

'Of course. I'd love to.'

A year ago I finished writing my first book, *Man Walks into a Pub: a sociable history of beer*. I used to work on beer advertising at the agency across the road, and my job developed into an obsession to find out more about why we drink the beer we do, the way we do. I managed to finish the book and sell it to a publisher while I was still working full time, which meant writing for a couple of hours before going to work, writing all evening when I got home, and writing all weekend for about eight months.

A few months ago the book was published. While it's never going to cause J.K. Rowling or Dan Brown any sleepless nights, it's selling better than anyone expected. I decided to give up full-time work so I could write some more without having to eat breakfast, lunch and dinner at my desk and lose touch with all my friends, but there are few writers who can make a living from writing full time, and I'm not one of them. So my new plan is to spend half my time writing, the other half as a freelance consultant to the ad agencies and clients I used to work for. It seemed like a good plan – until I developed freelancers' paranoia.

When you're working freelance, if someone offers you work, you take it. You're never offered work more than a few weeks in advance, so no matter how busy you are, you live in absolute certainty that when this contract finishes, no one is going to offer you another one. And if you are foolish enough to tell someone you're too busy, they'll have to find someone else to do the job. And that person might be better than you, or cheaper, or tell better jokes, or buy his round more diligently, and then they'll phone him first next time they need someone and you will never work for anyone ever again.

So I'm not spending more time writing at all; I'm spending

more time working. And the fact Simon asked me for a pint to offer me yet more work is very good news indeed.

We watch an American couple laden with Harvey Nichols bags walk in and spot Smiffy and Shabby, a couple of the regulars, at the bar. They look around as if searching for someone who can offer an explanation and, finding none, they quickly turn and leave.

'We need you to go to Prague,' says Simon.

'Wow. What, on my own?'

'No, there's a few of us going. We'd like you to run a brainstorming session with us and our client over there. They sell chocolate and we're coming up with some ideas for them. We thought you'd be good as a fresh pair of eyes. Help us decide if our ideas are any good or not.'

'Sounds great,' I say. We talk through some of the details. It's sorted: we're going to Prague next week, with an overnight stay.

I've never been to Prague before. I'm thrilled to be going, but I'm also a little nervous. That may sound ridiculous, but my flash of panic when I thought Simon might want me to go to a former Soviet Bloc country on my own betrays a shameful secret for someone of my generation: I am a crap traveller.

It's not that I don't want to travel and see more of the world. When Simon said, 'We need you to go to Prague,' the panic was balanced by a fleeting belief that I was James Bond, being briefed on a new mission by M. It's just that I haven't travelled much, so I remain generally incompetent at it, and I never seem to be able to get around to rectifying that.

I first really became aware of people visiting foreign places when I went to university. My new mates would spend their summers inter-railing around Europe or enrolling with

BUNAC to become handlers at North American summer camps. Some went backpacking around Asia and came back wearing ethnic clothes and telling stories about Afghan tea and interesting gourds. Back home in Barnsley my old, non-uni mates, who were now working and driving cars, were going on Club 18–30 holidays to the Mediterranean. They came back with stories of the exoticism of the food, the beer, the women and, especially, the effect some of these discoveries had on the contents of their arses. Meanwhile, I passed the long summer breaks back home in a village where pit closures had removed not only most of the jobs, but also the whole point of the community, and got deservedly laughed at in Barnsley Job Centre when I asked if there were any summer jobs for students. Or I stayed in St Andrews, my university town, becoming more deeply involved in the student union and working behind the bar in our favourite pub, the Niblick, my skinny frame blissfully unaware of the impact this would ultimately have.

So I never Travelled like my friend Allan – travellers often pronounce the word with a capital T – who, after graduation, did peace studies in America during the first Gulf War, almost died of the irony, and recuperated by going to Central America to teach English, where huge floods washed his village clean away, and he had to climb trees when he wanted to go to the toilet, finding a comfortable branch at a safe height from which to do his business.

I never Travelled like my friend Alistair, who started at St Andrews after spending a year in Pakistan. The habit of haggling over everything from big scarves to the price of a pint didn't endear him to the local barmen, and he achieved the dubious fame of being regarded as tight even by his fellow

Scots. After graduation he went to teach English in Cairo. Three years later, the day he left his apartment to return home, he was clearing out his room and realized that if he'd had his bed where his wardrobe had been, he'd have woken up to a view of the pyramids every morning.

I just assumed that these people could do this because they possessed skills I didn't. Skills like being able to start conversations with people you don't know. Like being able to walk into a travel agent. I got nervous going to visit my mate Steve in Luton. I didn't board a plane until I was twenty-two years old.

Since then I have failed to visit places like Guatemala or Mauritius, even Ibiza. I haven't trekked. I haven't backpacked. I haven't eaten anything I can't pronounce. All my travel has been strictly lower case, safely looked after either by holiday reps or office PAs. I hear they don't even let you into university these days unless you've caught dysentery in Phuket or planted mango trees in Kerala. I'm just different. Small children chide me for my naivety about the world and tell me I need to get out more. To some people, Prague may be a city that was interesting ten years ago but is now a mere repository for stag and hen nights, a quick Easyjet hop for a boozy weekend. To me it's as exotic as Zanzibar.

Of course, I don't say any of this to Simon. For a responsible, professional bloke in his mid-thirties, it would be like admitting I can't drive.*

As we're finishing our second pints, Kiran and Caroline, two girls from the agency, bustle into the pub. You can tell they're from the agency even if you don't know them, because

---

* I can't drive, by the way.

their faces actually light up when they enter the Stabbers,
Bowater House being the only place in Knightsbridge next to
which the Stabbers has a nice atmosphere. It would be rude
to refuse their offer of another pint.

'How's the book?' asks Kiran.

'It's all right, thanks.'

'We saw you on telly,' says Caroline. 'They called you a
beer expert.'

'Can we have your autograph? Can we touch you?'

'Watch it; I'm too important now to sit here and take
cheek from you.'

'We know. You're a beer expert.'

'Tell us something amazing about beer, beer expert.'

'When was beer invented?'

'Buy my book. It's in there.'

'Can't we have free copies?'

'No.'

'What's the difference between lager and bitter?'

'Buy my book.'

'Why do pubs close so early?'

'Buy my book.'

'Why do we drink pints when everyone else around the
world drinks smaller measures?'

'Buy— Actually, you know what? I don't know the answer
to that one.'

'What? Call yourself a beer expert?'

'No, I don't. The telly calls me a beer expert.'

'You are starting to look like a beer expert.'

'When are you going to grow a beard?'

'Are you wearing sandals?'

'That's exactly the kind of image and attitude to beer I'm

trying to challenge and you both bloody well know it. I'm not just talking about real ale, even though it's a fantastic drink and there's no logical reason why it's not one of the hippest drinks there is apart from that bloody nerdy stereotype—'

'He's off again.'

'Can't you ever talk about anything other than beer for more than five minutes?'

'You *asked* me about it!'

'Yeah, but we didn't want you going on about it all night.'

'All night? What do you— Fine, let's talk about something else. What are you working on just now apart from the chocolate?'

'You don't really want to know. You're just saying that. You just want to talk about beer.'

'I honestly don't.'

'Ah, the beer expert,' announces Shabby, shuffling over to our table from his tourist-scaring position at the bar. Given that he's been able to see me sitting here for the last hour or so, I wonder briefly why he waited until the two young women arrived before coming across to say hello.

'Shabby was wondering,' says Shabby, 'what you have to do to get to be a beer expert. Because if it's about drinking a lot of it, I daresay you're sitting on Shabby's title.'

'It's more about reading about it and researching it, Shabby.'

'So are you saying Shabby's not a beer expert?'

Just as I'm about to attempt to leave, more old friends arrive from the agency. I start to feel control of my evening slipping away.

*

10

Total sobriety is not a natural human state. Throughout human history all societies, without exception, have used some form of intoxicating substance, and alcohol is by far the most common. There is evidence of beer and wine making as far back as 7000BC, and the likelihood is that it started even earlier.

Why do we drink? Simple: because it makes us feel better.

In 2002 Oxford's Social Issues Research Centre compiled a review of over 5,000 books, journal articles, conference proceedings, abstracts and research papers, backed up by an extensive online search of university and government libraries and databases around the world, and consulted Professor Dwight Heath, professor of anthropology at Brown University. Heath has spent over thirty years researching the effects of alcohol, and acts as a consultant to people like the World Health Organization and the International Centre for Alcohol Policies.

They concluded that alcohol can make you cheerful, calm, friendly, lazy, peaceful, animated, euphoric, sentimental, generous or tender. This isn't news; the Aztecs referred to their drink pulque as *centzonttotochtli*, which means four hundred rabbits, a comment on the wide array of effects it could have. In countries such as the UK and the US we believe the most common effects are to make drinkers more violent or sexually permissive, but in fact, what the SIRC report shows is that by far the most common effects – anywhere – are relaxation and heightened sociability.

In the Stabbers we demonstrate this by picking on Olivia, a new arrival from across the road, and discussing how fat her neck is. Olivia has a fat neck in the same way I have a sculpted six-pack. She knows this, but it doesn't stop her from becoming agitated and feeling the need to protest in the strongest possible terms as Fat Neck hovers around her and settles on her shoulders, her latest and only nickname until anyone thinks of a better one, or gets bored of it, whichever comes first.

Even though I've been protesting that I don't really want another one thanks, it's soon my turn to buy a large round. I phone Liz, my wife, to tell her I'll be late home.

'I already gathered that, lovely,' she says. (She's Welsh. And very understanding.)

And so we continue to drink Belgian lager, until it's time to leave and drink Danish lager in a nearby Indian restaurant. In other words, just a typical English night out. Admittedly it's a bit heavy for a Tuesday, but it's little different from what millions of Brits do every week.

Soon I'll know just how similar – and how different – it is from what our peers around the world would do in the same situation.

Prague

'You see,' begins Petr, leaning forward, 'the thing about our country is this. To understand us, you must understand our sense of humour. We take nothing seriously. We make jokes about everything, because we have learned that there is no point looking at the world in any other way.'

Petr is all right. I like his outlook.

'Because if you look at the long history of the Czech people, we have been conquered and beaten and dominated by every nation and empire you can think of. We are a nation of losers. We cannot beat any country in war so as a country, we have learned not to be aggressive – there is no point. We have to be proud of something else. There was the time we beat the Russians in ice hockey to claim the gold medal in the Winter Olympics. There was much dancing and singing that night. We packed Wenceslas Square until dawn. We drank so much beer. That was a party. We showed them that we are a force that cannot be dismissed! Yes, but apart from that – the Russians though, can you believe it – we are proud of our sense of humour. We laugh at ourselves. And we laugh at everyone else.'

Petr and I are having our philosophical chat over lunch in the middle of our day-long meeting. Simon and the others from London have gone off to another room to have a side meeting. Petr is doing his best, not only to make me feel comfortable, but also to give me a crash course in understanding the nature of Czech society.

He continues, over a forkload of fried potato: 'This is the key to understanding the Czech view of the world. We are not an aggressive people. We have learned to laugh at aggressive people.' He pauses, and there's the first twitch of a smile. 'Such as you English, for example.'

Now you hang on a bleedin' minute, pal.

Before I can retaliate – sorry, respond – Jan, who's a mover and shaker in chocolate and gets Petr to design wrappers for him, chips in. 'Ha, yes. The English. I enjoy meeting them on my holidays. I often go to places such as Blackpool.'

It's nice of Jan to change the subject like this, away from something that could have turned nasty. 'Blackpool. That's great,' I say with a cheesy grin, 'I used to Travel there a great deal as a child. Why Blackpool?'

'To watch you fighting each other in the streets.'

Jan chuckles silently, pleased with himself – which is surprising given that he has a girl's name, but I'll wait before delivering this killer blow in our cultural debate. Petr joins in the self-satisfied chuckling. They swap a couple of quick anecdotes in Czech and laugh a little harder.

I'm in a tricky situation now. I'm the only person in the room who doesn't speak Czech. Everyone is speaking English to indulge me. If I upset them, things could become difficult. But at the same time there's national honour at stake. 'Hang on though,' I start, groping towards a defence of my country-men. 'I happen to know that the Czechs drink more beer than anyone else in the world, right?' They nod. 'And mainly it's strong lager.' They nod again, a little too proudly for my liking. 'That means there must be at least as much fighting here on a Friday night as there is in England. Probably more.'

Now it's my turn to look pleased. And I still have the girl's name thing up my sleeve, primed.

They stop laughing and look at me, confused, as if their impeccable grasp of English has momentarily deserted them. I've got them. Tomas, a colleague of Jan, eventually says, 'Pardon?'

'Well,' I say, 'ask anyone in England and they'll tell you that the main reason we fight is that we drink so much. You drink more than we do, so surely you must fight each other at least as much as we do.'

They continue to stare at me, open-mouthed, for several seconds. Then all three erupt into hysterical laughter. They swap glances and roll their eyes in a fashion which I could easily find insulting, but I'm determined to prove them wrong about how violent we are, so instead of kicking it off and teaching them a lesson (never really an option for me in any situation, if we're honest) I do that nervous thing where you kind of pretend to get the joke but make pleading faces for someone to explain it to you at the same time. This was not supposed to happen.

'Drinking beer makes you fight! That is a good one, oh yes!' Jan is almost weeping.

'Can you imagine trying to have a fight after twelve beers?' gasps Tomas. 'Right you – I'm going to fucking kill you – but just wait there a minute, I have to go to the toilet again first! Aargh *haagh*!'

This is the kind of laughter you only ever see in cartoons, laughter that makes people lie on their backs waving their arms and legs in the air, then turn over onto their stomachs and pound the floor, tears squirting from their scrunched-up faces. I didn't think real people laughed like this but Tomas is currently about one guffaw away from it – maybe as little as a chortle.

Petr is out of his chair, just about hyperventilating, doing a mime of a drunk trying to throw punches while tripping over his own jelly-legs. 'You two – stand still so I can hit you! Ahhhh ha ha ha ha ha hoo hoo hoo *haaaaaaaargh!*'

I wait for the laughter to subside a little.

It takes a while.

I fantasize about how great it would be if I could make people laugh this hard when I'm actually *trying* to be funny.

More time passes.

'So,' I say eventually, 'you're telling me that you, the biggest beer drinkers in the world, have honestly never heard of a link between drinking and fighting?'

Tomas recovers first. 'No. Never. *Haaargh!* It's simply not possible. Alcohol doesn't make you fight. It relaxes you. *Hee hee*. Everyone knows that. And anyway, you drink to chill out and have a good time. You spend all that money getting to a state where you are happier. What would be the point of ruining it by fighting?'

And I have to admit, he has a point.

North London

'Who is the odd one out: Pink, Marc Bolan, Jimmy Somerville or Madonna?' shouts Mistress Mel.

'. . . so then they said English people don't fight because they're drunk, they fight because they're violent,' I say, quietly so she can't hear me.

'I don't fight when I'm drunk,' says Chris.

Chris is my best friend. He often disagrees with assertions people make as a kind of reflex reaction. It's how he makes conversation. But this time what he's saying is also true. Chris turns into the pope when he's drunk; he starts blessing people and kissing their hands.

'Generally, I mean,' I say.

'Maybe it's my German ancestry,' says Chris, 'Maybe I'm just better than the rest of you.'

'They said the Germans are violent as well. We're warlike races.'

'No talking at the back there!' We shrink away from Mistress Mel's glare as she continues: 'Next question: in what year were the following records all top ten hits . . .'

'Nineteen eighty-one,' I whisper.

'No. It's eighty-two,' says Chris.

'Do you really think we're just a bunch of frustrated yobs though? I mean, I drink nearly every day and I haven't had a fight since I decided to stop Nigel Bailey picking on me in 1982.'

'Last time I even saw a fight in a pub was that time we were watching the World Cup qualifier – must have been ninety-seven – and the Italian police were beating the shit out of the England fans on telly and then that bloke came into the pub with a portion of chips and everyone just went to take some without thinking and they just flew up into the air and it kicked off,' says Chris. 'Anyway, do you know the answer to that Jimmy Somerville one or not?'

'Haven't a clue.'

'I don't know why I bring you along to this. Call yourself a beer expert?'

'It's a music quiz. What's that got to do with beer? They never ask about beer. And anyway I bring you along. This is my local.'

'Tell me about it. If you'd reciprocate sometimes and come down the Dog and Bell we might bloody win something, but no. Always got to be your trendy north London pubs full of people who take this sort of thing really seriously, hasn't it?'

'Look who's talking.'

I don't know if blokes in their mid-thirties are still allowed to have best friends, but Chris and I have known each other since we were nine years old and there doesn't seem to be much we can do about it. Throughout our entire lives together he has failed utterly to hide a deeply sentimental and romantic heart under a gruff exterior that was cynical way before its time. He's a big lad, and when he comes to our house he takes up an entire sofa, carpets the room with the day's *Guardian*, gets over-competitive about the things he likes and takes the piss mercilessly and unrelentingly about the things he doesn't. Until recently, no one had ever seen him and Phill Jupitus in the same room together, and even now some of our friends insist that was done with mirrors.

'And the final question – who had a hit in 1983 with "Dolce Vita"?'

'Ryan Paris,' I whisper to Chris.

'How come you know all the questions about really crap novelty records?' he says, scrawling on the answer sheet.

'Anyway, I don't call myself a beer expert.'

'You'd like to, though. Ooh, look at me; I'm a beer expert. Send me free beer.'

'But we have got this reputation for binge drinking and causing trouble. I suppose what the Czechs are saying is that beer might be a feature, but drinking can't be the cause of it. I mean, look at continental drinking. Whenever you see pictures of drunk people puking in the streets on a Saturday night, the papers always talk about how we should drink more like they do in France and Spain and Italy, all civilized and laid back and sophisticated. I mean, they don't normally include the Czechs in that because the Czechs drink beer and that makes it a bit more complicated because continental drinking is always about wine. But maybe it's the same.'

'I thought you were supposed to know all this anyway,' says Chris.

I thought so too.

Leaving aside the fact that I wrote a book about beer, if any nation is going to be expert on beery issues, we Brits would like to think it's us. Beer is a cornerstone of our culture. Our real ales are the best beers in the world – surely – and our pubs set the template for global drinking culture. But the Germans, the Czechs and even the Australians claim that they teach the world to drink, and the most unlikely nation in the world – the USA – is claiming with increasing justification that it makes the most interesting beers. Britain is only the eighth biggest beer producer and on a per capita basis there are five or six nations who drink more beer than us, and that's not counting the countries where home brew rules. Does beer mean the same to all these people as it does to us?

'You know what you should do,' says Chris, after filling in the guesses for all the answers we didn't know.

'What?'

'You should go to this conference with Beardie.' Beardie is our mate Steve, who writes the science bit for *The Times Higher Education Supplement*. 'He says it's the first ever world conference on ancient and prehistoric beer. It might be all archaeological, but it is global. Start at the beginning and see if that helps you figure it out. Starting with first principles. There might be all these global beer experts you could ask.'

'Brilliant. When is it?'

'Couple of weeks, I think.'

'Right, I'm definitely going to that.'

'Definitely?'

'Absolutely.'

'Oh. OK. If you're sure.'

'Well, why wouldn't I be?'

'How's your Spanish?'

'Why?'

'The conference is in Barcelona.'

'Oh.'

And that's how it begins. I've finished the chocolate job.

There's no excuse. I can't back down now. But would I have stuck to my resolve if I had known this trip to Barcelona would lead to a 45,000-mile pub crawl through more than four hundred bars in twenty-seven towns and cities in thirteen different countries on four continents? If I knew it would take me to places as far-flung and glamorous as New York, Sydney, Tokyo and Barnsley? If I knew I'd gain over a stone in weight and spend more money in less time than I've ever spent before? Me being such a crap traveller?

Of course I would.

2

'Los Borrachos'

Barcelona

In most of the world's cities 8.30 a.m. on a Monday morning would be the height of rush hour. In Barcelona it feels like the middle of the night. The streets are deserted as Steve Farrar, science writer and beard wearer, and I head up into the Catalonian hills. We feel privileged to see the city like this. The sea is a hazy liquid gold as the sun climbs above it.

The air is fresh and cool, and I've never been less excited about spending the day in a lecture theatre. But we must. We join thirty odd academics – sorry, that should read thirty-odd academics – on the implausibly beautiful campus of Barcelona University for the world's first International Congress on Beer in Prehistory and Antiquity.

Proceedings start with a panel of five academics welcoming us in Catalan. The third speaker, a crumpled man in his mid-sixties, finishes his address and promptly falls asleep while people are still applauding politely.

I wonder what makes an academic study beer, and look around the room for clues. It's quite a mix of people: there are a couple of bearded mountains dressed in black, perhaps what you'd expect a beery academic to look like; a good collection of tweedy middle-aged men, some with tidy beards, some without; but also some very young people and some very, very old ones. The programme suggests a huge array of disciplines – straightforward archaeologists, archaeo-botanists, classicists and historians. The genius of this conference is that beer spans a whole range of ways in which we seek to find out about the past. By bringing all these people together and cross-fertilizing their learning (an unappealing image if you were to see them, but bear with me) there's a chance that we could actually be pushing forward the boundaries of knowledge. When I say 'we', I do of course mean 'they'.

When the speeches in Catalan finally draw to a close, it's announced in English that we can now go and pick up our receiver units for simultaneous translation. This is not the order of events I would have preferred, but at least it's still the first morning.

The first speaker – funnily enough – addresses the conference in English. Dr Patrick McGovern is a celebrated American chemist and molecular archaeologist with a big grey beard and an easy-going manner. His first love is wine, but you can't study the origins of one drink without getting involved with others. Go far enough back, and beer, wine and mead blur into one. He tells us about beerstone, or calcium oxalate. This is a yellowy solid that accrues in vessels in which beer has been kept, and can be dated. In archaeological terms this is a relatively new discovery, and it's leading to new revelations about the origin of brewing. Whereas the consensus on beer is that the earliest evidence dates from Mesopotamia at around 3000 BC, McGovern announces that his team have found traces that date back at least as far as 5400 BC.

Now, this may be the point where you and I part company and you decide that I'm just a sad fanboy, but I can hardly write in my notebook with excitement. It's only the first session, and already we're rewriting the history of beer!

McGovern then shows us fragments from reliefs in the British Museum featuring people drinking wine and beer. While wine is drunk from individual containers little different from wine glasses today, beer is drunk from large communal pots through long, reed-like straws. They needed straws because the husks of the barley were still in the porridgey brew, but why big communal pots? The obvious answer, especially when juxtaposed with the wine drinkers, is that wine has always been the drink of the more affluent while beer was drunk by poorer people. But McGovern shatters this myth as well. In 1957 the 2,700-year-old tomb of King Midas, or perhaps his father Gordius, was excavated in Turkey. Among the finds was the largest set of Iron Age drinking vessels ever found, many cast in bronze and gold. The long straws that people had assumed were reeds were found to be made from gold and silver, inlaid with lapis lazuli and other precious stones. And many of them had traces of beerstone. Communal beer drinking was nothing to do with economy and everything to do with sociability. The longer the straws, the more people can gather around the pot. Beer is still drunk in this way today across large parts of Africa, China and South America.

This confirms what I've always thought – beer is simply the most sociable drink there is. Drinking on your own is, at best, a bit sad. But whereas you might associate wine more strongly with meals and drinking in couples, and spirits with either greater connoisseurship or a desire to get drunker quicker, this evidence confirms that almost the whole point of beer is getting together with your mates in a relaxed, forget-your-worries, just-be-yourself manner.

The big warm glow I get from this gives me the strength to make it through the rest of the morning. As a rule, academics do not count sizzling presentation skills among their awesome talents. One after another, Spanish researchers stand up over the course of two long hours to talk about fragments of pots they have found at various sites in the Iberian Peninsula bearing traces of beerstone. No matter that they've just heard the same thing themselves three times already, each one feels the need to explain what beerstone is, why they were looking for it and why it's so amazing that they found it. People switch back and forth from carousel slides to overhead projector acetates, necessitating one being switched on and the other switched off each time. They haven't rehearsed. The boredom becomes transcendental.

One thing I do take from all this is that Spain has always had a strong brewing culture. This comes as a surprise because Spain is famous for wine and sherry. It's part of that sophisti-cated continental cafe culture that we don't seem to have in the UK, a culture it shares with France, Italy and the rest of Mediterranean Europe. I've struggled to find an existing book on beer that even mentions the country, and most of us would struggle to name a Spanish beer brand. San Miguel, you say? Nice try, but if it came up in a pub quiz tiebreak, I'm afraid you'd lose. It's originally from the Philippines and was first brewed in Spain in 1956. Yes, really. But in total volume terms Spain drinks more beer than any other country in Europe apart from the UK and Germany. In 1950 beer consumption in Spain was only two litres per head per year. In 2003 it had grown to seventy-eight litres, while consumption of wine had halved.

Even among those who are aware of it, the conventional wisdom is that Spain's enthusiasm for beer is relatively recent. The modern beer market is about a century old, founded mainly by German immigrants fleeing domestic unrest in the late nineteenth century. We're learning this morning that there has always been a Spanish beer culture. The Romans found it here, and the wealth of evidence from these digs shows that it was an important activity in every settled community. The Spanish Emperor Charles V (1500–58) was a beer lover. Even though this may have had something to do with the fact that he grew up in Ghent, in Flanders, that doesn't change the fact that one of his first laws was a beer purity statute, and his courtiers set up the first commercial breweries in Spain.

This is all astonishing stuff, but anyone who understands Spain properly would warn you not to be surprised by anything here. This is a country that won't be pinned down that easily. The Iberian Peninsula ends only a few miles from the start of Africa, and is cut off from the rest of Europe by the Pyrenees. Culturally and geographically, no one would disagree that Spain is part of Europe, and Alexandre Dumas' famous declaration, 'Africa begins at the Pyrenees,' is often taken out of context. But Spain does go its own way, often confusing people who think they have its measure. During his Iberian campaign against Napoleon, the Duke of Wellington said, 'In Spain, two plus two does not always equal four.' More recently, famous British anthropologist Julian Pitt-Rivers added, 'Every country and society is different, but Spain is a bit *more* different.' The Spanish may not define themselves through beer the way Germans, Belgians, Danes or Czechs do, but they do drink an awful lot of it. I'm looking forward to getting out of the lecture theatre and seeing what a country looks like that drinks so much beer almost without seeming to notice.

But there's still a long time to go before that can happen. The speeches drone on. The low monotone of the interpreter doesn't help. A group that dug at the Valle de Ambrona gives us a DVD of their dig, and they seem inordinately pleased with themselves. Several people involved in the other digs seem to be getting agitated by their performance. When the session is opened up for questions, the seething tension gives way to a full-blown strop. Now this is more like it! One of the other diggers deliberately misunderstands the Ambrona lot and accuses them of wrongly claiming that they have found the earliest evidence of brewing in the world. I was only half-listening to a stuttering translation, and even I know they said nothing of the sort, but this is merely an excuse for a fight, which takes us all the way into lunch.

In the afternoon Max Nelson, a Canadian classicist, takes the stage. He's the first speaker not to mention beerstone. Better than that, he uses a mixture of references from Greek, Roman and northern European texts, leavened by an outrageous degree of common-sense conjecture, to suggest a wholesale rewrite of beer's story.

Beer historians usually maintain that the knowledge of brewing beer as we know it came from the Middle East into Europe via the Greek and Roman empires, or perhaps sea-going Phoenician traders. That's what I wrote in *Man Walks into a Pub*. Max Nelson says there is no actual evidence to support this. He then points out that the whole European beer tradition is fundamentally different from the historic Middle Eastern one. The Egyptians and Mesopotamians baked grain into loaves which could be stored before being used for brewing and kept beer in amphorae, clay jars. By contrast, in Europe we have always brewed using straightforward grains rather than loaves and kept beer in wooden barrels. Add in the fact that beer has always been considered a second-class beverage compared to wine – a product of Greek and Roman attitudes – and Nelson's conclusion is that beer as we know it today is the result of a direct lineage indigenous to Europe which has nothing to do with the Middle East.

This proves to be a rare highlight. Twelve hours after the opening speeches, we finally start winding up. There's an evening reception hosted by Moritz, a German-style Pilsner about to relaunch in Catalonia. Free beer no longer feels like a perk; it's a right. The first one goes down without touching the sides. Refreshed, Steve and I wander among groups of academics. They all share a deep love of beer which goes beyond their respective fields of study. Most of them brew their own. A very intense Englishwoman and an earth-mother type from Florida talk passionately about malting their own grain over open fires. For fun.

The essence of what the academics do is scenario-building: you have various fragments of evidence in place, and you use these to sketch in your best supposition of the missing details between them. The more pieces you have, the more accurate your overall picture will be. I listen to one cluster mull this over. A very distinguished-looking eastern European gentleman, whom I have so far overheard conducting fluent conversations in Spanish, French and English, nods vigorously and spits with real venom, 'Some archaeologists have too much imagination!' flicking his eyes towards Max Nelson as he does so. But by meeting and comparing notes across disciplines in this way, some of the gaps are being filled literally as we (all right, they) speak.

I find Jordi Juan Tresserras, one of the conference organizers, and ask him why the conference is being held in Barcelona. Is it to highlight Catalonia's undervalued role in the study of beer?

'Those guys from the Ambrona dig. They started making so much noise about what they had found. Them and their DVD. What they found was no big deal. We had found the same stuff years ago.'

I wait for him to continue, but he seems to have finished. He sees I don't quite understand.

'We wanted to set the record straight.'

'So . . . you organized the first ever conference on ancient and prehistoric beer – a global event – just to sort out a rivalry between two local digs?'

'Not just two! Everybody had already found what those guys claimed was new!'

'Oh. OK.' There doesn't seem to be anything else to say.

Back in town, Steve and I meet up with Chris. I'm not ruling out the possibility that Chris's suggestion I attend this conference was more about giving him half an excuse to come to Spain than it was to sort out my beer conundrum. Over the years he has visited Spain about twelve times and developed an insatiable appetite for its geography, its people, its art, its culture, its approach to life, and especially its food and drink, which burns almost as brightly and fiercely in his heart as the crush he developed on Nigella Lawson that we started to get a bit concerned about a few years ago. In Britain many people have a particular image of Spain – lobster-pink, high rise and drunken – but Spaniards talk about *Las Españas*. There's more than one Spain, and the one that Chris loves is the one that enchanted Hemingway and Orwell rather than good old Ryan Paris, Black Lace and Sylvia Vrethammar.* He's probably been spending the day in cafes and bars pretending to be a European intellectual, or maybe just reading the paper over a beer.

We head down La Rambla, the mile-long pedestrian walkway that's the compulsory starting point for any tourist. Off to the left of La Rambla is El Barri Gòtic, Barca's old town, a maze of tiny alleyways, every now and again opening out into squares, some ornate, others run-down. You never know what you'll find around the next bend. There is a lifetime's worth of bars in here: tourist traps, excellent tapas, theme pubs and dives. It's after 10 p.m. and we need to work fast. We order our first *cervezas*.

In the global language of beer, there are essentially two different words for the beverage: beer, *bier, birra, birru* (Japan) and even *pivo* (central and eastern Europe) all share a common root. *Cerveza* or *Cerveja* dates back to the Roman empire. When the Romans first arrived in northern Europe they were dismissive of beer, with Caesar writing a poem in which he argued that the grain-based beverage smelled of goat, but they eventually acquired a taste for it, even building their own breweries. They regarded the beverage as a gift from Ceres, the

---

* The woman who had a huge hit in 1974 with *Y Viva España*. Apparently she was Swedish. 'There is more to me than just *Y Viva España*,' she said mistakenly at the time of her hit.

goddess of agriculture, and ultimately came to revere it as a potion that imparted strength, *vis*, to the drinker, so *cerevisia* was literally a gift of strength from the goddess. Praise indeed from a bunch of wine drinkers.

Every bar serves a few dishes of tapas. The local specialities seem to be crusty bread assaulted by suicidal tomatoes and green peppers known as *pimientos de Padron*. These are without doubt the highlight of any cuisine I've experienced, thanks to their sheer entertainment value. They are small, sweet and fried, served heavily salted in batches of twenty or so. But the catch is that every now and again you'll get one that's fiery hot – a chilli pepper – indistinguishable from the rest until you bite into it. Locals reckon the ratio of hot ones is about one in ten, but with the various plates we have in different bars it varies anywhere between one in five and one in twenty. Even the intensity of the heat is variable, and sometimes you can't be sure. Several times conversation is interrupted by one of us saying something like, 'I think I might have got the . . . *oh, fucking HELL!*' before urgently draining a beer, eyes bulging.

The next day I rise late and realize it would be pointless to go straight back to the conference; I'd just sleep through the morning round. Steve files his copy from the hotel, and we head into town for lunch.

Just off La Rambla is the Mercat de la Boqueria, allegedly Europe's biggest food market. It's stunning to look at and almost intoxicating to be in. Several of the market stalls turn out to be bars where you sit on high stools and order beer and tapas, which are prepared inches away as you watch. The whole place is packed, but we manage to squeeze in at Kiosko

Universal, a big corner stall which has draft Estrella on the bar and advertises various plates in scribbled English on blackboards above our heads. I order a plate of 'mixted fish' and watch as fresh seafood is tossed on a hotplate, squirted with lemon-flavoured olive oil and sprinkled with salt and chopped parsley. Langoustines sit twitching and waving in a bowl on the bar top in front of us. When they hit the hotplate they vainly arch their backs away from the heat, which makes me feel bad until they're put in front of me along with clams, prawns, sardines and the best squid I've had in my life. I'll have another cold beer with it, thanks.

I linger at Kiosko Universal until the last possible moment, then go to face the afternoon lectures. Most of the presentations are dire, but we do learn that the cocoa plant was originally cultivated to make a form of chocolate beer, a fact that somehow has the potential to inspire new levels of unity among men and women across the world.

Finally, we're wrapping up. Despite my struggle to stay awake, it seems the conference has had way more interest than anyone expected. There is a real burst of activity in uncovering evidence of ancient brewing and replacing some of the supposition in the story with fact. There are rumblings about a follow-up conference in two years. But now it's time for the Roman Feast. This is the highlight. The university has used all its archaeological expertise to create the food and drink enjoyed here 2,000 years ago. We wander over to the courtyard to try it out.

Toga-clad staff are waiting for us and place a crown of leaves on each of our heads as we enter. We crowd around a table where an enormous array of herbs and spices is laid out. I've heard before that Roman cooking closely resembled Thai food today, and here's the proof. This selection has been assembled from old records of recipes and analysis of jars, and includes cumin, cardamom, mustard seeds, rosemary, ginger, garlic and fish sauce.

The food is laid out in terracotta dishes on a bright red tablecloth, looking simultaneously familiar and alien. Menus handed to us on scrolls tell us that we're looking at toasted chickpeas, hard-boiled quails' eggs seasoned with oil marinated in salt of Apicius, fragrant cheese sauce, olive pâté with aromatic herbs, pumpkin with 'seasoning common in ancient Rome' and bread, accompanied by re-created ancient beer, mead and wine.

The ancient beer is served flat and cool and has an earthy aroma, something musty and a bit dead, like a damp cellar. But after a few sips it's not as unpleasant as I first thought. It's very easy to believe that this is what people were drinking two or three thousand years ago; different from beer today but recognizable as beer nevertheless. It's a satisfying moment, here in the middle of a beer quest across Europe, to go back through time as well, right to the beginning.

Suddenly there's a commotion at the entrance to the courtyard. A second later a hundred middle-aged women, none of whom have ever been inside the conference lecture theatre, fill the space. As one they sidle up to the table, pause, then on some invisible signal attack. The plates of quails' eggs are grabbed and stripped in seconds. This is a clever strategy – the quails' eggs are the only items served on individual plates. Once they've seized these, they have a surface on which to pile up the other delicacies originally intended as finger food, to be grazed at gently. But these women are professional buffetologists, and they're too clever for that. Armed, they fan out around the table.

I hover behind the advance party, one row back from the spread. They don't seem to be in any hurry to move on, and it gets quite physical. Middle-aged Catalan women tend to be quite short and stumpy, and they use this to their advantage. They must be the spouses of the academics (though if they all are, the evidence suggests Catalonian professors are allowed two wives each) and some knowledge of ancient crafts seems to have rubbed off on them, such as how barbed arrow- and spearheads work. With their low centres of gravity and sharp minds, they dart in under your shoulders, then inflate, sticking out their elbows to prevent you getting past them, fastening themselves in place while they gorge. Consequently, despite having been here first, I remain one row back as rank after rank zips under me, until the table has been stripped bare.

The harpies disappear as quickly and strangely as they arrived, leaving me to attempt to put a meal together from the dregs in the overturned bowls. The few bits I salvage are delicious. A very elderly academic glares at me with pure hatred and disgust over his full plate, which one of the harpies must have got for him. I have no idea what I'm doing to upset him; my conference badge is clearly visible so I have as much right to the food as he does, which is more than can be said for the harpies.

There are a few clumps of academics left, but they are starting to drift off. Those that remain are deep in highly specific conversations about smooth malting floors, or oxalate, or seed distribution, and there isn't much room for a generalist, especially one with a notebook and camera.

And there the evening's story could have ended. It so nearly does, and possibly should have. Just before I leave I decide to grab one more mug of beer, just to see if I can figure it out. It's a *Sliding Doors* moment: in one reality I drift back to the hotel, have a beer or two with Chris and am in bed around one-ish. In another I'm in La Raval, a district on the east side of La Rambla which was described by Jean Genet in the 1920s as 'a multitude of dark, dirty, narrow streets' where 'no one would have dreamed of cleaning his room, his belongings or his linen'. It doesn't seem to have changed a bit. In a dilapidated square that hasn't seen pavement cafe culture for a long time, amid a smattering of glum-looking prostitutes, stands Bar Marsella, a shabby, unassuming place that was once the haunt of Genet himself. Its speciality was and still is locally made absinthe.

The bar itself is suffused with a fiery glow that radiates from every surface. Ornate chandeliers hang low from a patched-up, mottled ceiling which hasn't seen fresh paint for at least fifty years. Century-old whisky and gin bottles sit in padlocked, mirror-backed cabinets around the room. One wall is dominated by an ancient mirror painted with an ad for *absenta*, and for the first time I make a connection between absent and absinthe. I've never had absinthe before, but this seems like the perfect place to give it a try.

I'm with Chris, Max Nelson the American classicist, a giant Swedish medieval historian and home brew freak, a mad Mexican doing a PhD in York and a pair of unlikely looking Irish field archaeologists who introduce themselves as Declan and Billy. They're here filming the conference, finding out more about beer because they just may have found evidence of brewing in Ireland that predates any yet found in northern

Europe. But they each have a sardonic gleam in their eye that makes me wonder if they're not conducting some kind of blag or reality TV wind-up.

Half of us are still wearing our laurel wreaths, and some of us seem a little too attached to them. Absinthe and ancient beer combine to powerful effect, and soon it's two thirty and we're in the square outside a bar quickly pulling down its shutters and sliding bolts across its doors. Billy decides to go to sleep on a filthy mattress in the street while those of us with cameras take pictures of him with an eerie sense of calm purpose. The Swedish giant strides off towards his hotel. Billy and Declan insist that Chris and I come to Galway so they can 'get us pissed in the west of Ireland', and finally I understand what makes such a diverse collection of academics come together to study beer.

'Course, this is not proper Spanish drinking,' says Chris as we trudge back to our hotel.

'What? What do you mean?'

'I mean, I love Barcelona, but the bars close early compared to other places, and they don't do free tapas. No, if you want to see real Spanish drinking we need to go to Madrid.'

'Why didn't you say that?'

'I just did.'

'I'd better phone Liz and tell her I'll be late home then.'

Madrid

I've decided that the key to beating this crap traveller thing is to recognize that cities are like dogs: you have to show them who's boss at the very start of your relationship. If the city owns you, you lead a confined existence within it. This is what happened to me when I travelled on business: you're sealed off in an environment of airport–taxi–hotel–taxi–restaurant–taxi–hotel–taxi–office–taxi–airport. You never really *connect* with the city.

But if you take on the city and face it down at the start, if you show you're not scared, it rolls over and opens itself up to you. The best way to do this, I now realize, is to use public transport. This gets you right in at the same level as the locals, forces you to interact with them, and gives you a rough idea of the city's layout and where you are within it. By the time you've completed your first journey, you feel like you know the ropes.

Chris looks at me pityingly when I propose this. 'I just thought we'd get the metro to the hotel cos it's cheaper,' he says. 'It's only Madrid, not bloody Bogota.' And he stomps off to the ticket machine.

If you were here about 500 years ago, you would have thought this was the last place on earth to build a great city. We're on a 650-metre-high plateau 300 kilometres from the sea, in a place that endures scorching summers and freezing winters. But if you were King Felipe II, you would have seen things differently. Spain is about twice the size of the UK, and this spot is its geographical centre. Felipe moved the royal court here in 1561, and caused a capital city to be custom-built around him. In a country obsessed by regionalism, he was making a strongly worded statement about unification, centralization and strong leadership. Look at a map of Spain now, and all the main roads radiate out from this central hub.

We find our hotel in a busy street just south of the city

centre and almost get no further. Next door to an unassuming-looking tapas bar nestles a narrow kebab shop, spit turning behind the counter, and I'm just searching for the right comment when I spot a gleaming silver beer font on the bar counter. In design, the best ideas are often the simplest, and this is no exception: a kebab shop that sells draught beer. I become emotional, and start looking for an estate agent.

Chris pulls me gently away, and we stop for lunch in the Plaza Puerto del Moros (Gate of the Moors), a nearby square dominated by a massive sixteenth-century church flanked by fields of outdoor cafe tables. It's just midday, and we feel a little odd after a bone-jarringly early start this morning, but a quick look around the busy square reveals that 90 per cent of the cafe patrons are sipping *cañas*, small glasses of beer. It would be rude not to join them.

Spain is still fiercely regional in its outlook. The country is divided into seventeen *autonomías*, each with its own government, budget and cultural ministry. And many of them have their own beer. Ask for a beer in southern Spain, and you'll simply be given a Cruzcampo. Ask for the same in the north, and you'll get a San Miguel. Over in Catalonia, it's Estrella Damm. Here, it's Mahou. Red and white signs advertising the brand perch outside the door of almost every bar in Madrid. I'd hazard that there's not a great deal of difference between the beers, but fierce brand loyalty is another expression of regional identity.

Our Mahou arrives in ice-frosted glasses with a good inch of thick, creamy head, and an accompanying dish of soft, sweet olives. The beer tastes amazing: very smooth, not too bitter or too sweet, delicate but definite.

In his *Complete Guide to World Beer*, Roger Protz devotes

just over one of his 240 pages to Spain's beers, which it has to share with Portugal. This is one page more than Michael Jackson's *Beer Companion*, which features a map entitled Beer Regions of Europe that doesn't even have the Iberian Peninsula on it: a curious insult to the millions of beer drinkers who live here. Of course, as these writers would be quick to point out, beers such as Mahou lack the character and finesse of their northern European counterparts, but they are perfect for the country and its climate. Life is simpler in southern Europe, and it's appropriate that the beer is too.

There is a danger that we're falling into that rose-tinted holidaymaker trap that encourages you to take a bottle of your favourite tipple back home with you only to find it tastes foul as soon as you open it under familiar lead-grey skies. But no, this beer is good. I'm sure of it. If you look up Mahou on www.bottledbeer.co.uk, a beer rating website, you'll see that it describes Mahou, not inaccurately but perhaps a touch pejoratively, as 'nondescript . . . fairly light-tasting (i.e. bland). A bog-standard pseudo-pilsner, although refreshing on a hot day.' The reaction this has provoked among visitors to the site is extraordinary. Amid three pages' worth of comments, Darren declares, 'Anyone who knows beer, knows it does not get much better than this fine beverage.' 'I saw my boyfriend get down on his knees and pray to a Mahou lorry!!!' says Sue. 'Mahou rocks. Spent 4–5 days in Madrid a few weeks ago. The quality of this beer is so, so good. Creamy head above a refreshing lager that is neither too sweet nor dry. The best lager I've tasted,' says Anthony. You can argue that these people don't really appreciate good beer, but I have neither the desire nor the courage to do so.

The only thing that could improve my Mahou is a ham sandwich. By the time we attract the waiter's attention to order one, we need another beer as well. And then we start to relax.

The square is full of quiet conversation, underscored only by birdsong and the occasional sound of a distant motor scooter. For the centre of a capital city, it's very quiet and peaceful indeed. Maybe . . . maybe too quiet. With an aggressive *blart*, a saxophonist appears from nowhere. Replete in candy-striped shirt and cheeky hat, he plays something that sounds like the Benny Hill theme tune, only with an undercurrent of menace. He uses the acoustics of the church walls to great effect, and renders any attempts at conversation futile. He finishes, and the sound of birdsong re-emerges uncertainly. He seems to be threatening to play some more unless we give him some money. We don't, but other people do, so he compromises by moving to the next cafe, then the next, each still in earshot, the same tune over and over. Back on his first pitch, an accordionist appears, signalling it must be time for us to move on.

Several bars later, probably in the tartan-walled, bullfight-showing Irish theme pub we find on a corner of the busy Plaza San Miguel, we decide it would be a good idea to continue our push for authenticity by popping back to the hotel for a siesta. On the way back, most of the bars we passed earlier are closed. Dramatically closed. Not just with the door locked and a sign saying something like 'Back in an hour', but shuttered and boarded up as if they have gone away for the summer.

We surface again at around 8.30 p.m. I wonder what's for

breakfast before realizing it's still Friday, then wonder how I've managed to acquire jet lag after a two-hour journey that doesn't cross any time zones. This calls for a beer.

At 9 p.m. the streets are busier than they have been all day. The many cobbled squares are full of people from eighteen to eighty standing outside bars, sipping *cañas* and talking animatedly. Beer is everywhere you look. Where you might see a newspaper kiosk or hot dog stand in Britain, there's a beer tap here. It's been claimed that Spain has more drinking establishments than the rest of the EU combined – almost certainly no longer true since the accession of ten new member states, but the point is still made. And yet drunkenness is simply not a feature of everyday life. The reason there are all these bars is that alcohol is fully integrated into society, and beer is just another drink. Over 40 per cent of adults say they have a beer with lunch. Madrid itself allegedly boasts 100,000 bars, one for every hundred of the population. This is because *madrileños* love going out, not to get drunk but simply to spend their leisure time – whether that involves eating, reading, watching a bullfight on TV – in the company of other people.

Dwight Heath, the world's foremost authority on the anthropology of drinking, tells a story about the town in Spain he visited every year for twenty years, where the men spent most of Sunday in the local bar drinking steadily, with children running around freely. One year he goes back to find a sign in the window saying children under sixteen are not allowed. When Heath asks about this, the barman gestures to a new electronic games machine in the corner. 'It's that damned machine. Sure it makes money, but not only is it noisy, we have to look out for the kids. Those games are addictive, you know.'

Madrid is a city of beautiful architecture punctuated by tiny slivers of bars. Felipe II designed the Plaza Major, the main square, himself. It remains the heart of the city, accessed by stepped corridors, and once inside you can only gaze up at the rows of balconies. It's stunning, like the central courtyard of a huge palace. And yet even here, among the big tourist-trap terrace cafes, there are tiny bars with just enough room for a fridge and a counter which will just about accommodate a beer font and a bowl of olives, maybe a plate of ham and no more than two stools. Most of them are filled by groups of two or three men, drinking beer, arguing furiously, dropping olive stones and small paper napkins at their feet, before moving on to the next bar a few yards away and repeating.

This is the perfect beer-drinking culture. The only problem is that it's dying. European integration means that regulations, and ultimately habits, are becoming uniform across the continent. For generations Spain, Italy and France have kept this healthy drinking culture alive by ensuring there is no mystique or naughtiness associated with alcohol. Children have a little wine mixed into their water with meals, and as they get older, the concentration of wine becomes stronger. Because the first experience of drinking is in the home, by the time kids are eighteen and going out to bars, there's nothing big and clever about it. But things are changing. This freer, healthier relationship with drink belongs to a time when these countries were rural and relaxed. As they become closer to the industrialized north, alcohol is increasingly seen as a problem. And if you start to see it this way, it becomes a self-fulfilling prophecy. Young Spaniards are starting to have their first drinking experience with peers rather than families, and are adopting Anglo-Saxon drinking patterns as a result: a recent survey shows that over half of all Spanish sixteen-year-olds claim to have been drunk at least once. As a result, there is increasing pressure for opening hours to be curtailed and access to drink to be limited. Even Madrid is succumbing to the pressure – tonight the bars will start closing around 1 a.m., unthinkably early by *madrileño* standards.

All the more reason to enjoy it while it lasts. We stand at the top of Cava Baja, a narrow street running off the square we were in earlier, and gaze along several hundred yards in which every single doorway is a restaurant or bar. The differences between bar, tapas bar and restaurant are fuzzy and not always obvious. Take away the high-end restaurants with their white tablecloths and place settings, and the rest form an unruly, gregarious jumble, some of which offer a cursory *ración* to go with your beer, while others are nationally renowned for a particular dish.

We eventually go for La Chata, on the basis that the whole front is covered in glazed tiles painted with Madrid street scenes from a century ago. Inside, the walls are crowded with pictures of famous matadors and their more notable adversaries. Huge hams hang from the ceiling. Every drink comes with a free bowl of olives and chorizo. When Chris goes briefly off-piste and orders a gin, it's bigger than any of the beers we've had so far.

We move on through the night, and everywhere we go beer is so ubiquitous, it's invisible. Several places are even called *cervecerías* – literally beer shops. The menus in most bars don't even list the beer they stock, and yet the vast majority of patrons are drinking it. It's just beer: like air or water, it's so vital you don't even notice it.

If La Chata was festive, El Madrono must be all Spain's

Christmases come at once. The bar is on a corner, and every available inch of tiling of both outside walls is covered with faithful reproductions of the best the Prado gallery across town can offer. Inside, pride of place is given to *Los Borrachos*, a painting by Velásquez. The literal translation of this title is *The Drunkards* but because the eponymous revellers seem to be having a good time and not hurting anyone, the English-speaking art world has decided that what Velásquez really meant to call it was *The Feast of Bacchus*, because that sounds a bit more classy. The Roman god of wine and creativity sits in the centre, surrounded not by other creatures of myth but by partygoers from Velásquez's own time. Bacchus, slightly distracted, is looking away while crowning one of the drunkards with a laurel wreath. The rest of the lads look on, most gazing adoringly at Bacchus through beer goggles, while one seems to be reaching out to try to nick the crown from his pal.

Clearly this captured the reality of drunken behaviour in Velásquez's time, but there's nothing like that going on now. The bar is busy and voices are loud, but they're animated rather than screaming. There are still seats to be had at the bar, and not because people have fallen off them. Bright, laminated colours leap out from the tiles wherever you look, and *Los Borrachos* holds its own in the middle of countless other old works. If this isn't where the expression 'a night on the tiles' originated, it should be.

Everywhere we go we are given free tapas: olives, bread, crisps – a hearty plate of stew in el Madrono – and quite often chorizo. The freebie nature of tapas and the popularity of very fine chorizo within it supports the theory that this wonderful cuisine started out as a way of keeping the flies out of your beer. *Tapa* literally means lid, and many people argue that it was originally a bit of bread that sat on top of your glass, which acquired the odd topping over time as bar owners realized how well a nice bit of salty meat stoked people's thirst. Happily munching plate after plate of local delicacies, Chris and I are simply succumbing to a local variation of a big international beer-drinking rule: wherever you drink beer, salty snacks are not far away. In Britain it's crisps. In the United States it's peanuts or nachos. In Kenya it's a chopping board piled high with freshly slaughtered and barbecued goat meat. You take a slice between your fingers and dip it into one of the mounds of salt at each corner of the board – seems like a very different custom when I describe it like that, but the principle is the same – salty snacks. Here it's chorizo.

We could easily spend an evening drinking beer and eating heartily without paying for a single morsel of food. But we're English, and we feel obliged to order something extra out of politeness, even though we're not that hungry, because of all the free samples. So we do end up occasionally consulting the menus.

Conscious that I'm a member of possibly the last monolingual population in Europe, I don't want to sound like one of those Brits who believes everyone else should learn English, but I'm probably going to. Most bars offer English translations of their menus. I only know a handful of Spanish words so I have to consult these translations. And the problem is, they read as if they have been translated not by someone who has an incomplete grasp of English, but by someone who doesn't really understand Spanish – me, for instance.

For example, they translate *jamón* into English as ham. A vaguely literate Brit could sort of figure that out for himself.

But *jamón de jabugo* is 'translated' as jabugo ham. That's the kind of thing we used to do when we bullshitted vocabulary tests at school when we hadn't revised. *Tomates*: it's hardly worth the ink copying it over to the English column and inserting the extra o, is it? And yet other terms are dragged kicking and screaming into English against their best interests. I know what *tortilla* is, and it sounds so much less appetizing if you call it a slice of fried egg and potato cake.

The real issue here is that when it comes to food, Spanish is simply a superior language. *Bocadillo* is just a great word, one that you want to say out loud all the time, which is possibly why Chris and I are eating so many of them. It makes the word sandwich, the very idea of it, pathetically lame. *Bocadillos* are obviously going to taste better. In English, prawn is occasionally used as a derogatory term. You could never imagine anyone doing that with *gambas*. *Huevos rancheros* makes eggs sound almost good enough to eat, a dish that needs to be saddled up and ridden into the sunset. And *patatas bravas*? They speak for themselves. Chunks of fried potato slathered in a fiery tomato sauce, the very name sounds like the kind of food The Clash would have eaten.* This is a country of cowboy food. Masculine food. The simple act of ordering it puts hairs on your chest, and translations into namby-pamby English undermine its power.

As the night goes on, olive stones, toothpicks and paper napkins gather in drifts at the brass foot rails under each bar. It's half eleven, then midnight, and people stay up, energetic, good-humoured but definitely not pissed, wankered or bollocksed – nowhere close. And everyone is still drinking beer.

---

* Specifically, in the period from *London Calling* to *Combat Rock*.

There's a connection here. It's obvious that beer is about something quite different from intoxication, and that there is no link between the availability of it and the likelihood of getting drunk. If you can drink as much as you want, whenever you want, why would anyone drink beer if their main aim was to get drunk? You can get the same volume of gin for the same price if that's what you're after.

The Spanish don't have many words to describe drunkenness. This is a culture where getting drunk to the point of losing control is, in the words of one Spanish anthropologist, 'considered barbarous, disgusting, ridiculous and a blot on a man's honour'. Most people out tonight would say that they have only been drunk once or twice in their lives. But they do freely admit to drinking enough to alter their mood. This is the concept of *saber beber*, proper drinking, to the state of *alegre*, merry or high. They also refer to this state as *la chispa* – literally, the spark – and regard it as quite separate from drunkenness. It's the state where you have drunk enough to loosen up and feel more lively, definitely affecting your brain and probably your ability to drive safely, but you're still some way off losing physical coordination, starting to slur and stagger. Somehow the Spanish manage to get to this state and then pace their drinking so they maintain it – not sobering up and not getting any drunker. The only words we have for it in English are merry or tipsy, which come loaded with effeminacy. Usually, Brits describe it as 'a bit pissed', a phrase which recognizes that, for us, it's a brief stage on a journey somewhere further, even though this is probably the best part of the night – the part when you feel clever and relaxed, when the banter and flirtation is at its best. It never occurred to me before now that there might be three separate quite distinct states of sobriety – sober, *la chispa* (what we might call buzzed) and drunk.

It's already starting to feel a little bizarre to me that back home we drink pints. In one bar when we ask for *dos cervezas*, the barman places our accents (God knows how) and reaches for pint glasses even though everyone else is drinking *cañas*. We stop him, take the smaller measures, and feel no uncertainty about our masculinity in doing so. We see two pissed people all night, and they turn out to be the tail end of an English hen party. Compared to the typical seven pints and a curry, the staggered (as opposed to staggering) *cañas y tapas* buzz feels very right.

At around one thirty the bars start to close up. The nightclubs are just getting going. If we wanted to stay out all night on principle it would be no problem, but the big, mixed crowd is winding down and going home. We're tired. We've had our fill. But while a club might be pushing it, we do fancy a nightcap. We decide it has to be the Holy Place, the Kebab Shop that Serves Draught Beer, mere sleepwalking distance from our hotel. Perfect, apart from the fact that metal shutters slide down over the door as we approach. But the little tapas bar next door is still open.

Now, this is exactly what we were looking for. A TV plays in the corner, as manic and incomprehensible as 'Channel 9' from *The Fast Show*. The fact that the TV sound is competing with a CD of Tom Jones's greatest hits makes it even more difficult to work out what's going on. The barman, all flowing grey hair, bushy moustache and expansive gestures, is a pure archetype of the 'continental' bar owner. Language notwithstanding, he's straight from central casting of British TV ads for Stella Artois, an unaltered fixture for the last hundred years. He obviously knows everyone else personally; evidently, they are all regulars. We are the only tourists here.

We're looking at the tapas menu, unsure what to order, when our host approaches us, slaps us warmly on our backs and says something that ends with the word *jamón*. It doesn't matter how much *jamón* you eat of an evening, it always sounds appetizing, and he's so welcoming and makes it sound like such a good idea that we simply nod. He scuttles – no, I'm not being patronizing, that's definitely the right word – into the corner behind the bar. Was that a cackle of glee? No, it couldn't have been. We're just tired. But out of the corner of my eye I feel, rather than see, him rubbing his hands together and dancing a little jig. I look at him properly; he's taking a cloth cover from a leg of ham which is held fast in a special contraption, and starting to shave off slices.

Most of the bars we've been in so far have a huge leg of ham on a fixture like this. Bolted into a vice, trotter sticking up in the air, the leg is held fast while the choicest bits are carved off. More legs hang waiting from the ceiling, small plastic cones at the bottom to catch the grease slowly sweating out. This is how ham should be served, and Chris and I resolve that when we have made our respective fortunes, when we each have kitchens with acres of worktops, breakfast bars and every imaginable implement hanging on racks from the ceiling, we're coming back for *jamón*-leg-holding contraptions. We'll even find out what the cool, elegant, Spanish name is for them.

The *jamón* tastes fantastic – salty and fruity and smoky and more ham-like than any ham I've ever had before. It's so full of flavour, it must have been aged for a very . . . long . . . time . . . probably a really . . . expensive . . . process . . .

The bastard.

I grab the menu. Across two pages, every plate costs between three and eight euros. Every one, that is, apart from the last item right at the bottom of the last page: *Jamón de Bellota*, twenty euros a plate. Do we want some ham? Yes, mate, of course we'd like some ham. Thank you very much. I ask for the bill. There, grinning up at us, are two plates of *Jamón de Bellota*. Our new friend, who shall henceforth be known as the Hamburglar, beams at us from behind the bar.

He may be a devious git, but that doesn't necessarily make Hamburglar a bad man. The ham was excellent after all, probably worth every cent. It's not his fault if we didn't know what we were ordering. And after his windfall he's feeling generous. He gives us each a complimentary glass of luminous greeny-yellow stuff, which we know must be downed in one according to the unwritten International Code of Drinking. He follows this up with a complimentary tapa. At a guess it's something's liver, ground up and smeared on bread. Clever. We need some more of the fluorescent stuff – no longer free – to get rid of the taste of it. And from there the evening follows a sadly predictable course.

This is not a normal hangover. This is something life-threatening, with a yellowy-green tinge.

After rising late, I'm being dragged through the Rastro, the Sunday morning flea market, and I'm not enjoying it as much as I should. I know that Madrid is an atmospheric city, far more romantic (in the poetic sense of the word – I'm here with Chris, remember) than somewhere obvious like Paris. And anything you can imagine is for sale on one of the stalls lining the steep, cobbled streets and squares: books, antiques, knock-off designer gear, military surplus, second-hand clothes, and for some reason thousands of spoons. But I'm not interested. I think I might be suffering from scurvy. I just want a nice sit-down and a glass of orange juice.

After the markets, we trudge through narrow streets, up and down short, steep slopes between tall, pastel-painted buildings. Windows are shuttered against the sun, each with its own tiny wrought iron balcony. A dog or cat dozes on every fifth one, or gazes down at us dispassionately, or barks with shrill pretend fierceness, fooling no one. A year after the start of the Iraq War, every other balcony flies rainbow peace flags or white sheets painted with the words *No a la Guerra*.

Just as I'm about to cry with desperation for a seat and some liquid, we finally arrive at our lunchtime destination. The Plaza Santa Ana is one of Madrid's most popular drinking spots. One side of the gently sloping square consists entirely of *cervecerías*. Here, beer is celebrated rather than simply drunk. Cervecería Santa Ana displays beer bottles from around the world in glass cases flanking its two wide entrances. *Cervecería Alemana* is a German *Bierkeller* and was Hemingway's local. Next door is Naturbier, Madrid's only brewpub, which creates its own range of organic beers in coppers at the rear of the bar. Each of these places has a broad, busy terrace outside on the pavement. We leap (all right, shuffle with intent) for the nearest available table.

The waiter makes his way past our table carrying a tray of six beers balanced on the upturned palm of one hand, the glass-handled mugs frosted, the condensation just starting to run. They look like sunlight in a glass, and all thoughts of orange juice go out of the window.

I feel better after the first beer, delighted when I see that there are dishes that include vegetables on the menu, this being a slightly classier and more touristy spot than the backstreet *cervecerías* we've been trawling. I order gazpacho to start, and it's sucked in through my mouth, nose and skin pores before the bowl has touched the table. My body sings with every mouthful. Colour starts returning to my cheeks. I calm down a bit, have a salad to follow, and I'm feeling much better. Time for another one of those beers.

Much, much later, after a brief excursion away from beer to explore the Prado gallery, and after many more wonderful bars, we find ourselves having to face up to the fact that it's time for our final drink in Madrid. We head back to *Cervecería La Fuentecilla*, or as we now refer to it, Hamburglar's Place. It couldn't really be anywhere else, especially as the Kebab Shop that Serves Draught Beer is closed again. Perhaps it's merely a myth, a symbolic exhibit, a postmodern extension of this city's many excellent art galleries. The idea of it is probably better than the reality anyway. But this is a disaster – the door to Hamburglar's is also locked, even though it's still well before midnight! Chris and I look at each other, distraught. But suddenly our cheeky moustachioed friend is here, all bustling aprons, unlocking the door, ushering us in and making a show of recognizing us, trying to hide the cartoon dollar signs flashing in his eyes. We're regulars now. Of course we are; that's why we came back. He makes us feel like regulars, and it's the most thrilling feeling there is for a beer drinker when it happens in a particular pub for the first time. And we're part of a lock-in.

In the UK lock-ins are a big deal. More than any other form of lawbreaking, the lock-in feels like a collective, noble rebellion by the People against their oppressors. Doors are bolted, curtains drawn, lights dimmed. The remaining drinkers move from their tables to the bar, speaking softly, no one acknowledging that they should have gone home by now. It happens most in rural areas, where there is a thin police presence. I've never been party to one in London. The fact that here Hamburglar is entirely at liberty to lock and unlock his door whenever it suits him does not lessen the thrill we feel. Nor does the fact that he leaps up to unlock the door for every single person who rattles it over the next two hours, be they wizened local or American tourist. You may ask then why he insists on locking the door again after admitting each new guest, but let's not break the spell.

The same Tom Jones CD is playing through the speakers, and it seems like the same telethon is still on the TV. We take the same seats, and he gives us the same gregarious, back-slapping welcome, pouring our beers before we ask. See? I told you. We're regulars now.

Back when I was a student, the pub I worked in, the Niblick, was run by Tony Marini, a man in his mid-twenties who stood five foot four inches tall and was almost super-model skinny. But the brick-shithouse regulars who gave me an endless, seamless stream of verbal abuse from the second I went on duty until we finally threw them out at midnight deferred to Tony without hesitation. He had a still, calm authority that cowed the most troubled heavy boozer, the same aura that characterizes every successful landlord and bar manager around the world.

Hamburglar is from the same mould. If you took a photo-graph of him, he would look like an unremarkable, unassum-ing middle-aged man. But when you're in his presence – and most crucially, when he's looking at you from the business side of a bar – he is a centre of enormous power and charisma. He is omnipotent, all-seeing. He is judge, counsellor, policeman, confidant, and friend. He can make or shatter dreams. But the absolute core of his appeal is that, unlike other types of governor or supreme being, everyone recognizes that he invariably uses his awesome powers on the side of good. These powers can be terrifying to behold (Who can live with the shame of being barred?) so it feels thrilling to be on his good side, like you've been accepted into a gang of cooler, bigger boys. You're happy to go along with anything he says. Come on, you might as well have another beer, what the hell! You're hungry, right? A little snack? Yes, a snack! A bit of ham, yeah? Yeeaah! There you go. Oh, that's forty euros. Cheers!

Great barmen are sorely needed in international politics. They have a record of peacemaking and solving disputes that Kofi Annan would stand up and cheer if only someone would let him know. I'm convinced it wouldn't take more than a single evening to achieve lasting world peace. Look, I'm your mate, and I'm telling you, you're out of order. Trust me. So what we're going to do is, you, sunshine, are going to pull all your settlers out of the West Bank, and as God is my witness (or Allah, mate!) I promise you that he won't throw another rock, because he knows I won't be very happy with him if he does. Can't say fairer than that, can you? Come on, how's about some of this weird fluorescent shit to seal the deal? Mates? Mates. Cheers!

I realize that, from the clay pots and straws onwards, beer drinking in different cultures around the world has developed along broadly similar lines. We're all human after all. Hamburglar's encapsulation of the global essence of the great barman underlines a point made by every anthropologist of drinking: in all societies – every single one – drinking is a social activity.* It helps put people at ease; it gives you something to do with your hands, provides a common focus to start a conversation. In Australia someone who drinks alone is 'drinking with the flies'. Among the Vlach Gypsies of Hungary drinking alone when others are nearby is to symbolically reject a commitment to links with other people. From Japan, the United States, Spain and France to remote tribal communities in Africa and South America, reciprocal giving and receiving – round buying – is used to cement social bonds, and toasting your drinking companions is universal. In most cultures, while mood alteration, relaxation and throwing off inhibition is sort of the whole point, excessive public drunkenness – slurring, falling over, anti-social behaviour – is frowned upon. As a rule, wine is a more formal drink often drunk with food, whereas beer seems to be more democratic and unpretentious. Places where people drink beer may vary, but they always tend to be havens offering an escape from the pressures of the outside world, where you can take time out and enjoy a relationship of equals with your fellow drinkers. In most cultures this puts the drinking place at the heart of the community.

Our glasses are empty and here's Hamburglar refilling them. He says *jamón* under his breath, and he's already walking towards the corner where the family treasure is kept. But this time we're ready for him.

This time we say no.

Hamburglar stops. He turns to face us. I think I see the beginnings of respect in his eyes, a recognition that we are

---

* I found some books and papers – beer academia is habit-forming.

worthy adversaries. He shrugs, gives us our beers and returns to his seat in the corner.

We finish our complimentary olives and crisps. We talk rubbish. And—

'*Patatas bravas?*'

If you've ever read *Dune* by Frank Herbert, you'll be familiar with a technique known as The Voice, used by the Bene Geserit nuns. Following intensive lifelong training, they are able to modulate the pitch and inflection of their voices so precisely that they can be used to compel people to do their bidding. I always thought it was mere science fiction. Until now.

I didn't even hear him come up behind us. '*Patatas bravas?*' He whispers it between our heads. Even with our preparation, this knocks us back. He's been sitting at that table studying us, and he's read us so perfectly, it's chilling. He's looked deep into my soul. He knows about the whole Clash-food thing. And he's offered me what he knows is my heart's desire. Each consonant is a kiss, each vowel a soft, spicy-chip-smelling sigh.

Time slows down, the way people describe it in moments of extreme crisis. I can feel my body language starting to say yes, each fibre of my facial muscles flexing as my eyebrows shoot up in an expression of delight, the back of my neck contracting, my head starting to lift in what is bound to be a rapid, over-eager nod. And somehow I manage to intercept it. The nod becomes a shake, the eager puppy-dog face becomes what I can only hope is a wry, firm but regretful no, rather than a confused, drunken leer. It is a triumph of sheer willpower. And an emphatic testament to the fortifying qualities of already having eaten a huge quantity of *patatas bravas* earlier in the day.

For a second Hamburglar looks confused. And perhaps

the psychic channel he opened between us is still there, but somehow I know with absolute certainty that this is the first time his sales technique has failed since February 1986. But he recovers quickly, acknowledges his defeat with a good-humoured smile. And then he hands us the two very large whiskies he made us order without noticing while he was using the *patatas bravas* as a mere decoy.

The Tom Jones CD ends and starts again, which means we've already been in here for over an hour. Hamburglar goes back to his regulars – sorry, some of his *other* regulars. But as 'What's New Pussycat?' tinkles one more time he saunters past us, casual apart from a rapid flick of the eyes between us and our glasses. We have his measure now. We can see his game.

'*Dos* Ballantyne?'

'*Sí!*'

At various points over the next hour I write the following things in the notebook I've been carrying with me:

These moments when you feel like you've found home . . .

Phantoms from 1970s British TV continue to appear on screen.

The etymology of chicken in a basket. Exoticism of the dish in the 70s. Not on a plate!

And, shamefully,

In an alternate reality I stopped Samantha Fox from becoming a lesbian.

Soon we've drunk all Hamburglar's Ballantyne. He gives us the dregs of the bottle for free and hits us with something else. As a rule, when it comes to whisky Chris refuses to drink any-thing younger than Natalie Portman. But for the Hamburglar he's making an exception. The shutters are down now over the door outside, and as we groan along to 'Green Green Grass of Home' I realize we really are in a lock-in. I'm holding my pencil like a crayon, and Chris is announcing that Hamburglar is now his dad. I decide to abandon my beer quest and my job, and stay here drinking in this bar every night for the rest of my life.

Maybe one day, when I truly am local, I can persuade Hamburglar to put a second CD on the jukebox.

3

'Where you find beer, there you find good life'

The White Hart, north London

'You spawny bastard.'

'No, I'm not.'

'You're a spawny fucking bastard.'

'It's not spawny!'

'It's spawny.'

'It's not as cushy as you think it is, you know.'

'You're a spawny bastard.'

I've been having this conversation a lot recently. Friends, work colleagues, taxi drivers. The old lady who lives next door. They all seem to have the same reaction. They don't seem to be able to appreciate the whole thing from my point of view. Admittedly, Chris expresses his feelings more directly than most.

'I'll admit writing about beer is better than being Bernard Manning's masseur, but it's not all down to luck, you know. And it's not as if it's a holiday.'

'Come on, I'll swap you then. If it's so crap, I'll trade you jobs.'

'Hang on, you can't really say this is my job. I've got to do it *on top of* my job. And it was your idea to go to Spain in the first place.'

'Whatever. So did you get what you needed in Madrid? Do you understand continental drinking now and can we talk about something else?'

'Well, sort of. But what surprised me was that they had decent lager in Spain.'

'So? You're not complaining, are you?'

'No, but ... why? I mean I know why, but why lager? It's everywhere you go. You know, lager accounts for 90 per cent of all beer sold around the world. And it was invented in the Czech Republic. It's funny to think of people everywhere around the world drinking a product that's originally from eastern Europe.'

'Don't change the subject. You're still a spawny bastard.'

'I'm really, really not. Oh, hang on a sec, that's my phone. Hello? Oh, hi, Adrian. What? Blimey. Yes, definitely. No, absolutely. Count me in. Cheers then. See you soon. Bye.'

'Who was that?'

'Er, a bloke called Adrian, from the British Guild of Beer Writers.'

'The *what*?'

'The, um, British Guild of Beer Writers.'

'Aargh ha ha ha ha ha ha ha!'

'So he, er, wanted to know if I'd be interested in an all-expenses-paid trip to the Czech Republic to see the Pilsner Urquell brewery.'

'Oh. You. You. *Bastard*.'

Prague

U Pinkasu is a network of rooms with arched brick ceilings, so that even the levels above ground feel like a maze of cellars or catacombs. An accordion plays jolly folk music from hidden speakers, making me smile involuntarily. It's Wednesday night, it's busy, and every single person in the pub – young and old, male and female – is drinking beer.

There are four of us here from the British Guild of Beer Writers: Adrian Tierney-Jones, Jeff Evans, Tim Hampson and myself. A year ago I was as surprised as anyone that there actually was a British Guild of Beer Writers, but there really is. I was allowed to join after *Man Walks into a Pub* came out, and was delighted to discover that the stereotype I had of beer writers (a stereotype you may perhaps still mistakenly share) was nothing like the reality. After all, you have to bear in mind that these are the beer fans who can actually write. They are articulate and intelligent and can converse on a whole range of subjects other than beer.

The guild doesn't get expenses-paid foreign trips as a matter of course, but this is an interesting situation. Pilsner Urquell, created in Plzeň, Bohemia, in 1842, was the world's first golden lager. There had been plenty of lagers before – brown and black lagers had been popular in neighbouring Bavaria for centuries – and contrary to what Pilsner Urquell now claim, it's reasonable to suppose there were even pale beers before.* But if the

---

* Colour derives from the degree to which the malted barley is roasted during production. There are plenty of pale ales around the world today whose malt is lightly toasted, and while malting temperatures used to be

town's burghers had realized how quickly their new style would be copied around the world, they might have trademarked it earlier, and Pils, Pilsner and Pilsener would now all be variants of one brand name rather than generic terms for the world's most popular beer style. If you enjoy drinking golden lagers – and 95 per cent of us do – then you're either drinking Pilsner Urquell, or a (pale) imitation of it.

For anyone with even a passing interest in beer then, Pilsner Urquell is a brand that should be protected and preserved. Which is why many beer aficionados got very upset when the brewery was bought in 2000 by the brewing giant currently known as SABMiller, home of such imitation pilsners as Miller Lite and Castle Lager. As you might expect, pretty soon everyone was saying the beer wasn't as good as it used to be, even before the new owners modernized the brewery. And cut the lagering time.

OK, time for a brief science bit. Lager is a lot more delicately flavoured than other beers, because lager yeasts are different from ale yeasts. Both create beer by fermenting sugars in the malt. There are simple sugars and more complex ones. Ale yeasts as a rule can't ferment complex sugars so these remain in the beer, giving it more body and flavour. Lager yeasts convert more of the sugars, leaving a thinner liquid, higher in alcohol. A decent lager gets its character from the slow, secondary fermentation that takes place in cold caves or cellars over a period of weeks, hence the name (lager derives from the German for store). If you cut this maturation time, it stands to reason that you're destroying the character of the

---

much harder to control, it's reasonable to assume some people managed this in the past.

beer. So you can understand why some beer writers got upset. SABMiller have invited us to see for ourselves that the beer is as good as ever.

I'm the youngest delegate by about ten years, and I am anxious not to say or do anything that makes my Johnny-come-lately status too obvious – the other three were writing about beer when I was still learning to drink Castlemaine XXXX and thinking it was a sophisticated choice. But thankfully I'm not quite the least experienced person here when it comes to beer. We're joined by Julian, a freelance writer who is just starting some corporate communications work for SABMiller, and Briony, from SABMiller's press office, who's here to look after us.

Alexej Bechtin, a corporate affairs man from SABMiller, is telling us about the pub we're in. 'In 1843, Jakub Pinkus, a great fan of the Pilsner beer, decided to begin selling it in Prague. He was the first. Just one year after Pilsner Urquell was created. It is still the most famous traditional Czech pub. It is where the people gathered to discuss politics and language.'

As part of the Austro-Hungarian empire, Bohemia was settled by millions of German speakers. German was the official language of government and commerce, so language was a political issue. Today, big towns and cities still use both German and Czech names, Pilsen/Plzeň for example. Thanks to this history and to its unpretentious ambience, U Pinkasu now walks a fine line between traditional pub and popular tourist attraction.

The Czechs drink more beer than anyone else in the world. They call it Czech bread. In various places around the world and throughout history beer has been referred to as liquid bread, but the Czechs are saying more than that. It shows how possessive they are about beer, how much it forms a cornerstone of their national character.

Finally our beers arrive, half-litre glass mugs with chunky handles slammed down onto solid, pottery beer mats. The most noticeable thing about the beer is its foamy head – all three inches of it.

'The bigger the foam, the better the beer,' says Alexej. It's just one of those things that divide drinkers around the world. Among Bohemians and Bavarians, the world's lager experts, a big, thick head is the sign of a good beer. Yorkshire drinkers have the same expectation of a decent pint of bitter. That's all I'm saying.

Being beer writers, there's no chink of glasses and quick, deep pull. In this company the correct procedure is to contemplate the beer a little more carefully, looking first at its appearance, then swirling it to get the aroma, before holding it on your tongue to appreciate its fullness of flavour and texture. It's not the kind of thing you should really do down your local unless you want to get laughed at, but with a decent beer it's just as valid an exercise as it is with wine, and yields pleasant rewards.

Pilsner Urquell has a lovely delicate aroma. The first sip is crisp and refreshing. It tastes of lager, but manages to taste more strongly of lager without tasting strongly of alcohol, if that makes sense. In the UK we divide lager into standard and premium solely on alcoholic strength: under 4.5 per cent it's standard; 5 per cent and above, it's premium. Generally speaking, the higher the alcohol content the stronger the flavour, because longer fermentation time increases depth and complexity, but Urquell, undoubtedly a premium lager in any sane definition of the word, is only 4.4 per cent, and yet it's full of flavour. That the Czechs are not as obsessed with alcohol content as we are provides an important clue to their relationship with beer.

As we reach the halfway mark down our first drinks (which doesn't take very long at all, despite all the swilling and tasting) a selection of cheese and meats arrives on our table. They're quite salty and work very well with the beer, creating a powerful appetite. We're going to need it.

Because it is officially the Most Historic Pub in the Czech Republic, U Pinkasu's menu is both very traditional and very informative. It's the size of a broadsheet newspaper, and contains almost as much information. Section after section of dishes feature immense steaks and hearty-sounding goulashes, with the odd salad nudged in furtively in the corner. But if there is a Czech national dish, it seems clear from the menu that it must be dumplings. You would not believe how versatile and varied a dense ball of flour can be.

One of the most appealing things on the menu is the information about opening times on the front: 9 a.m. until 4 a.m., every day. The Czech Republic is a laid-back liberal country, and there are not really any licensing laws to speak of. Pubs open pretty much whenever they want. There's zero tolerance on drink driving – no alcohol in the blood at all – and they sort of try to discourage underage drinking, but that's about it for regulation. Beer is everywhere; it can be bought anywhere – we even passed a hot dog stall in the street on the way here that had a draught Gambrinus font on it.

'The average Czech will drink between five and ten beers a day,' says Alexej. 'It is customary to drink beer with lunch. But not with breakfast.'

Well, maybe not any more, but if he's taking the trouble to spell that out, doesn't that make you suspicious? Someone at SABMiller back in London told me about his experiences as part of the original team which came over to negotiate the purchase of the Pilsner Urquell brewery. 'Our first meeting with the Czechs – it was 9 a.m. – and when we all sat down, the guy chairing the meeting asked what we'd like to drink. We all asked for coffee, so he turned to an assistant and said, "Eight coffees and eight beers."'

Despite drinking so much and being so unconstrained in their access to drink, binge drinking and public drunkenness remain rare among the Czechs. The high per capita consumption comes from the fact that they do it so often, and in such great numbers – women as well as men drink beer. Because of the relaxed legislation, as with Spain, when kids reach eighteen they don't go mad and get drunk. Instead they seem to arrive at legal drinking age with a healthy respect for the stuff. And because drinking is not about youthful rebellion there's no reason to drink less as you get older and settle down. No wonder that a popular Czech proverb is, 'Where you find beer, you find good life.'

The dumplings arrive. Enid Blyton always used to describe feasts so big that tables would groan under their weight. The author probably thought she was using a colourful metaphor, but with Czech dumplings this is literally true. My plate carries four of them, flanking a mountain of purple cabbage in the middle. I cut into one. It's bready, with flecks of ham embedded in it. It's not that these things are hard – they yield unnervingly under the knife, as if drawing you into a trap – they're just so *condensed*. If black holes are formed by a star collapsing in on itself and reaching a point of infinite mass, then this is what happens if the same process is applied to bread. I swear each one exerts a gravitational pull. Light bends as it gets near them. I manage to eat the first one, and worry that my stomach will distend to the floor when I stand up.*

It's after 10 p.m. when we admit defeat and have the remains of our plates hoisted away. It's an early start tomorrow, so after drinking somewhat less than the average Czech on a school night, we waddle back to the hotel, the appropriately named Palace. In my room the lights have been turned low, the sheets have been turned down. Lying on my pillow gazing up at me, giving me a very direct come-on, are two posh chocolates. The dumpling in my stomach moves over obligingly. Exhausted by the struggle to retain critical objectivity about my hosts, I turn in.

Plzeň

The Czech Republic was born on New Year's Day 1993 when, after seventy years together, the Czech and Slovak leaders decided that it would be best for everyone if the two states demerged. Neither leader asked his people's opinion on this, but like everything else thrown at them over the years, the Czechs seem to have accepted their fate with pragmatic good grace.

The Czech Republic consists of two territories: Bohemia and Moravia. Moravia, to the east, has a relatively unsung wine culture, doomed to be eternally overshadowed by the beer of its sister – Bohemia has been synonymous with beer

---

* When I get home, I've gained four pounds in two days.

for centuries. It has also famously given its name to people
who lead an unconventional life, particularly poets, writers
and artists. It seems fitting that beer is such a big part of
Bohemian life, and I had intended to use this tour to explore
the link. But there isn't one really. Bohemian was probably
first used to describe Gypsies travelling through Europe, who
were thought to have originated here.

The Bohemian landscape is suitably dark and mysterious.
Having grown up next to the Pennines, I'm a big fan of
hills. The sea does of course offer the best view you can have
if you get any choice in the matter, but a good range of hills
is a close second. If you're not on the coast and you haven't
got hills, then there's not much point having windows really.
Hills and sea in conjunction, well, I can sit and stare all day.
But in our Pilsner Urquell minibus driving out towards Plzeň
on a bright morning that suggests the possibility of spring for
the first time this year, I realize that hills are even more
impressive when they are thickly coated with trees. Naked
English moorland may have a stark, desolate beauty to it, but
rolling Bohemian woodland suggests real magic and romance.
Especially when we get far enough away from Prague for the
newly-built Ikeas and Tescos to drop away behind us.

Culturally, there's a case for arguing that Bohemia doesn't
really belong with Moravia at all, and should in fact be a
country with its western neighbour, the German region of
Bavaria. The brooding forests stride across the border between
the two countries, and just over in Bavaria they gave birth to
the creepiest childhood fairy tales. Seeing the forests now is
intoxicating in a particular way I hadn't bargained for. The
associations that start swirling around my mind as I gaze out
of the window are things from childhood, things I haven't

thought of for over twenty years: Hansel and Gretel, Narnia, *The Golden Pathway* – a beautiful set of books I used to have which contained colour plates protected by greaseproof paper that I tore out and drew on – and inevitably *The Singing Ringing Tree*.* I start to shake. I feel the colour drain from my face. Think nice thoughts. Think nice thoughts. It's OK ... It's fine ...

Beer.

Apart from the landscape, Czech Bohemia and German Bavaria are also united by a passion for brewing. Both sets of inhabitants of these vast central European forests have been celebrated and feared as great drinkers since Roman times, if not before. With frequent German claims over Bohemia through history and Bavaria's sense of separation from the rest of Germany, it's easy to imagine Bohemia-Bavaria as one country, transcending national boundaries, with a common geography, a common love of beer and passion for brewing it.

---

* When I was a kid the BBC had so little money for children's pro-grammes it used to import them from eastern Europe. A badly dubbed serialization of *Heidi* defines 1970s bleakness for me as surely as the Winter of Discontent does for anyone ten years older. But *The Singing Ringing Tree* ... It's a generational cliché to talk about how we used to hide behind the sofa when *Doctor Who* came on. You couldn't do that with *The Singing Ringing Tree* because the terror was so complete it froze you to your chair and glued your eyelids open and you could only sit there, silently thinking, I want to scream, but I can't. Parents loved it because they thought it kept us quiet, little realizing how much noise we would be making if it were not for the spell being cast. If you are in your thirties, I need say no more. If you're younger and you fancy a laugh, go up to someone you know who is in the right age bracket, say, 'The Singing Ringing Tree' to them, and enjoy the reaction. You may not want to try this in a pub, as the involuntary screaming might get you thrown out.

Indeed, it was a Bavarian who created Bohemia's most cele-brated beer.

Bohemians have always been very serious about beer – the first ever brewing textbook was written by a Bohemian, Tadeas Hajeck, in 1588. The first records of brewing in the country go back to the tenth century and the monks of the Brevnov monastery, at which time the right to brew beer was theirs alone. This changed in the late thirteenth and early fourteenth centuries, when Good King Wenceslas began granting brewing rights to householders in the new towns and cities that were developing.* In 1307 he issued 250 such licences to the burghers of Plzeň, which may be when he first started being associated with Christmas, at least by the lucky burghers.

While Bohemian beer enjoyed a reputation of quality throughout Europe, it could still be variable, as could beer produced anywhere until a giddy rush of modern techniques transformed brewing in the late nineteenth century. But bad brews upset the burghers of Plzeň more than they would most people. In 1838 they declared a crisis after one batch of beer was so bad it was poured down the drain in front of the town hall. The burghers decided to club together and build a new, state-of-the-art brewery, uniting their skills and resources, and stealing as many ideas and resources as they could from the Bavarians.

Martin Stelzer was commissioned to design and build the new Burghers' Brewery. He travelled extensively around Bavaria, where he met the man he knew he wanted as brewmaster. Josef Groll was wonderfully described as 'coarse,

---

* Wenceslas is a real historical figure, more commonly known in the Czech Republic as King Vaclav.

even by Bavarian standards'. According to Professor Eduard Jalowetz, in his catchily titled 1930 book *Pilsner Beer in the Light of Practice and Science*, 'Groll was a simple man without any proper manners and *according to his father*, the rudest man in Bavaria.'* But he knew what he was doing where beer was concerned.

Groll was briefed to recreate a Bavarian-style lager at the new Burghers' Brewery. At the time, brown Bavarian lager was celebrated across Europe, and brewers came to Munich to learn by both study and industrial espionage. It was lager, but it was dark and strong, much richer and more characterful than your average lager today. Groll recruited Bavarian brewing assistants and barrel makers, and brought Bavarian yeast with him. But what came out of the tanks in Plzeň in October 1842 was not Bavarian beer. The burghers were waiting in a state of high anticipation. When they were handed a 'golden beverage with thick snow-white foam . . . the drinkers having tried its sharp delicious taste, welcomed it with such cheers that had never been experienced in Pilsen before.' Bavarian skill had met Czech ingredients. Moravian barley is sweet, Bohemian Saaz hops have little bitterness but a lot of aroma, and the very soft, sandstone-filtered Plzeň water allows these flavours to come through. As Professor Jalowetz says, 'The beer produced was certainly a surprise for everybody including Master Groll. The burghers had planned to build a new brewery to produce beer in the "Bavarian way" and a lucky chance brought a pleasant surprise for all, a new type of beer, not known to anybody then.' Soon Pilsener, or Pilsner,

---

* My italics. Because if your dad says that about you, you have to accept you have problems.

beer was being discussed excitedly throughout the Austro-Hungarian empire and beyond.

Other styles of golden lager would emerge later, but none would capture the imagination like the first. Timing played a big part. Glass had just become affordable for widespread use. Sure, it tasted good, but Pilsner's success demonstrates that the first drink is often with the eye.

In 1845 Josef Groll was fired for being impatient, aggressive, arrogant and rude. Given that they knew all this when they hired him, it seems the real problem was that he treated everyone equally. Behaving like Gordon Ramsay with your staff was one thing. Treating the shareholders the same way, well, that wouldn't do at all.

We arrive at the Pilsner Urquell brewery at around 10 a.m. As a rule, breweries are not lovely to look at – at best they might be interesting or dramatic – but this one strives to be the exception, and is straightforwardly, aesthetically beautiful. The old buildings, painted cream and dark green, have either been preserved or restored, and there's an art deco theme running through the whole site that owes a lot more to pride than functionality.

We're escorted to the boardroom, a magnificent space full of frescoes, mirrors and more art deco flourishes, and are offered beer. 'We call it cold tea,' laughs one of the high-ranking brewery men who pops his head around the door to say hello. Finally, it's time to get down to the serious purpose behind our visit.

Pavel Prucha has worked at the brewery for the last thirty years and spent ten of them as head brewmaster. He now carries the title head of quality assurance. 'It is very unusual for me to drink water,' he says as Alexej introduces us. Mr Prucha starts talking about the brewery in broad, tourist-friendly terms, but after about a minute he has drifted, in a roundabout way, to the topic of quality assurance. The brewery holds a 'special tasting' each month, with a national panel of specially trained taste technicians. All of them know what the ideal flavour profile of Pilsner Urquell is, and they try to match the beer to it. Within this, there is a 'special group of tasters', consisting of seven to ten former brewmasters. Samples are also sent to an independent research institute in Prague. And SABMiller's European headquarters also checks quality on a monthly basis. I don't know about my fellow beer writers, but I take the hint.

After tasting the beer in the most scientific way possible, we tour the brewery. Mr Prucha explains that the driving motivation is to keep the taste profile of Pilsner Urquell identical over time. It was first quantified in 1931 in a logbook which he takes great pride in showing us. It lists a string of measures, some obvious, like ABV, some more obscure, like apparent attenuation, and some that even the beer writers haven't heard of. It's not a question of whether tasters like the beer or not, but whether on an ongoing basis Pilsner Urquell still matches the profile. As the world's first golden lager, there's clearly a sense of duty to preserve it for future generations, a living window into the past. Mr Prucha argues that new technology may change the brewing process, but that he can account for the changes, and the end result can be achieved much more efficiently and consistently. Questions from Tim, Jeff and Adrian soon leave Briony, Julian and me floundering. It comes down to a face-off between Tim and Mr Prucha about the speed of fermentation in conical fermenters compared to horizontal ones. Like the workings of the internal combustion engine or the rubric of the European Constitution, this is one of those topics that, while important, is of little interest to anyone outside a very small group of experts.

Throughout the conversation, Alexej leans in closely to Mr Prucha, watching him intensely, finishing sentences for him and even rephrasing some of his comments. It's the only aspect of the trip that reminds us this is a PR exercise, one that is tightly controlled. I start to think of Alexej as the Enforcer.

For all the arguments, some of us are still convinced that the beer is less characterful than it used to be, and it's clear to me by the time we leave the brewery that this controversy is not going to go away. But without wishing to defend a huge corporation that certainly doesn't need my help, the issue illustrates perfectly a fundamental irony of serious beer appreciation. Pilsner Urquell only came into being because the burghers of the town built a state-of-the-art brewery and hired an innovative brewmaster with a mastery of modern techniques. The beer only survived thanks to the constant application of new technology, from Plzeň's first steam engine to power the brewery to the first burglar alarm to guard the precious yeast. Innovation was curtailed against the brewery's wishes under four decades of communist control. When that rule ended in 1989 it was only natural that the brewery would want to catch up. If you think you produce the world's best Pilsner, you're going to want to make sure you're at least as up to date as your lesser competitors. It's a bit cheeky for us to come in and tell them that we're very glad they modernized for the first 150 years, but from now on we'd rather they didn't. Although I don't know it yet, this point will be made to us much more forcefully in a few hours time.

After lunch in the brewery's new restaurant, a vast 600-seat affair in the old cellars, we say goodbye to Alexej and Mr Prucha and have a brief tour of Plzeň. It has a very impressive church and some pubs only marginally less so, many with intricately painted facades rivalled in grandeur only by the town hall. But the exteriors are about as much as we have time to take in. We're on a tight schedule.

Chyne

Tim has asked if we can stop off in a nondescript Czech village and visit a typical pub, away from the city and the brewery towns, to see how ordinary Czechs drink. So about eight miles outside Prague we pull off the motorway and into the village of Chyne. It's a bleak place, surrounded by brown fields edged with the last stubborn banks of compacted filthy snow and scattered with tractor parts. The road runs along the edge of an industrial railway, and the buildings seem to have been unceremoniously dumped here against their will. I think we'd all like to make a joke about the place to lighten the atmosphere, but we don't want to be disrespectful. So instead we talk about Alexej, the Enforcer.

'I bet he'll be waiting for us outside this pub.'

'Yeah, he probably has a network of secret tunnels across the whole of Bohemia.'

The laughter stops when we pull up outside the pub and, sure enough, there is Alexej, waiting for us. 'This is where I live,' he says, and for a second I almost laugh. But I don't think he's joking. I'm not sure he's capable. He guides us into U Loulu, the village pub, pretending not to have heard our

unkind descriptions of his home nor to understand the significance of our mumbling about the 'Duelling Banjos' music
from *Deliverance.*

'It is a popular village for people who commute into
Prague,' he explains. Well, that's his story. The network of
secret tunnels seems just as likely.

U Loulu is furnished with chipboard and lino – a traditional Czech pub, just like we asked for. The locals don't
seem too pleased to see us, possibly because we're interrupting
what looks like a crucial scene from the locally produced soap
opera playing on the ancient TV set above the bar. We're
shown to a room at the side blocked off from the main bar
area, and the barman brings us a round of Gambrinus at
twelve koruna (27p) each.

It's places like U Loulu, one in every village, that make
Gambrinus the biggest brand in the country. And it's in these
villages that a steady, constant diet of lower-strength beer
makes the Czechs the world's biggest drinkers.

Alexej picks up his narrative about the pub in Czech life,
and I feel bad about thinking of him as the Enforcer. He's
giving up an awful lot of time, and he's a mine of information.
(But where did he get this information from? How did he
obtain it? No, I'm going to stop now.) 'In Czech villages there
are two places that count,' he says, 'the pub and the school.
Each village tries to keep its pub and its school. This means
the community lives.'

The communist state used to control all the pubs, but after
the Velvet Revolution they were given back to the families that
had owned them. They're still family-run today. Under communism, pubs were even busier than they are now. Workers
resentful of the state would start at eight, take a ten o'clock

break, then lunch, then another break, notching up around ten beers through the working day. 'This was referred to as state pretence,' says Alexej. 'The state pays us, and we pretend to work.'

The barman tries to bring more beers to our table, but we have to move on. We're due back in Prague for a meeting with the chairman of the Czech Beer and Malt Association. We hadn't asked for this, and we're not sure why it's on our itinerary. But we're about to find out.

Prague

'*Who does this arrogant Englishman think they are?*'

The chairman's deep, booming voice is almost squeaking under the pressure of his barely suppressed fury. Alexej nods sympathetically. Without looking at us, his body language says, Now look what you've gone and done. You've upset him, you English bastards. He never takes his eyes off the chairman. He looks as though he's aching to mop his brow for him, pat his arm. But even now he's still finishing the chairman's sentences and rephrasing things. He's just doing it in a whisper, so the chairman can't hear him.

Jan Vesely has been chairman of the Czech Beer and Malt Association for twelve years. The association has existed since 1873, but it didn't really have a role under communism. Now it's back, and has been making great progress in improving the quality of Czech beer. Mr Vesely seems to want to get something off his chest, and that's why we're here. When someone asks him about the recent 'Ten Commandments' of proper beer making issued recently by Budweiser Budvar, it all comes out.

Budvar have taken advantage of the changes in Pilsner Urquell's brewing methods to remind everyone that *they* still do things the traditional way. All's fair in marketing warfare, but the launch of the campaign just happened to coincide with the arrival from the UK of Mike Benner, CAMRA's new CEO, who held a press conference in Prague to support the launch of the Ten Commandments and issue a forceful critique on declining standards in Czech brewing brought about by modernization. Mr Vesely dismisses the whole affair as 'a thunderstorm in a teaspoon' but has clearly failed to convince even himself that this is how he truly feels, hence his barely contained explosion just now.

'CAMRA arrive in town and call their press conference without talking to anyone here. They say the quality of our beer is declining. The average man in the street is very upset by this. People have small prides, and one of them is Czech beer. It is clear that CAMRA know nothing of our history!' He stares furiously at the table, his whole face shaking. 'We think our beer is getting better. Fifteen years ago the shelf life was seven days. People used to turn the bottles upside down to check for solids! There were no labels. We used to use rice and sugar. Distribution was centralized. Many districts had the choice of only one beer.'

Mr Vesely then tells us how under communism resources were allocated via a pyramid structure from a central planning committee. Brewers were near the bottom of the pyramid, cash cows with very little investment. In the 1980s they were still working with equipment from the '50s. The only investment available was for beers with export markets to 'hard cash' countries. This meant Budweiser Budvar and Pilsner Urquell. Everyone else had to fight for money.

'In Russia, when a community was felt to deserve a reward, Czech beer was sent in,' he says. 'So in Czechoslovakia people would look around for beer that was meant for export, because this was the only way of being sure of decent beer. Maybe the quality of those beers has stayed the same. But the quality of every other beer has either drastically improved or the beer has disappeared.'

Having said his piece he starts to calm down a little, and tells us about life in the Czech Republic more generally. Even now, comparisons with Russia still feature heavily in his thinking. 'The standard of living may not be changing, but the style of living is. You must understand: we were not starving at the end of communism. Everyone had a car and a place to live. But now it is possible to spend more money, and this has increased the pressure in everyday life. The thing is to show other people what I can afford. The new Russian, he does not want his table cleared, he wants everyone to see how many beers he can afford. In Russia you see people drinking on the streets. Not here. People do not drink beer to drink beer, but to meet people, to make friends.'

Chastened, we leave the chairman's office, and say goodbye to Alexej – we think – for the last time. Perhaps he will be watching us from a distance for the rest of our time here, but chaperone duties are taken over by his colleague, Katerina, who is going to show us around Prague.

It may have become as familiar to British stag nighters as Dublin, Newcastle and Manchester, but in many ways Prague remains beautiful, dramatic and mysterious. Perhaps because of the Czechs' pragmatic attitude to wars, the city has survived centuries of conflict virtually unscathed, and now boasts 600 years' worth of baroque architecture in immaculate condition.

This also means the city retains an ancient street plan which is easy to get lost in. Katerina leads us from busy squares full of brightly lit shops and British city-breakers on the piss, round corners into deserted alleys where you feel like you've suddenly leapt forward to the small hours of the morning, such is the abruptness with which the people, light and noise disappear. In these side streets, cobbles shining under the sparse street lights and tenements looming up on either side, you remember you're in Kafka's city. Then you round the next corner and you're back in – well – *FHM*'s city, I suppose.

Earlier I asked Jan Vesely if there were any problems with English people. 'They are noisy, but they are not really hooligans,' he replied. 'They are not harming our culture. They don't have much contact with other people when they are here.' I was pleased by this, but wondered if he was just being polite: in 2004 the Czech tourism office called for a clampdown on the pissed-up British stag nights that congregate here for cheap beer and sex. The Prague police estimate that 20 per cent of weekend crime in the city is caused by drunken Brits. It's a statistic that you tend not to see in those corners of the British press that talk about the 'threat' posed by economic migrants coming from central Europe to the UK.

We move through the Stare Mesto, the main square of the old town, and into a tight warren of winding alleys that makes the rest of the city look ordered and logical. You could spend all day in here wandering from pub to pub, and many people do. Translated, the pub names sound like inns where travellers seek refuge and find adventure. They're what English pubs would be called if they had all been named by Tolkien: the Black Ox, the Wounded Goose, the Shot-out Eye.

But interspersed among them are shinier pubs with names like O'Neill's and O'Malley's. They seem incongruous here, and yet Irish pubs are far more widespread through the city than the other branches of Western capitalism which have taken root. I knew the Irish pub was popular across the world, but not to this extent. I can't find fault with the Czech pub so far, so I wonder why they need so many imported pubs. Is it just for the tourists? Is it part of the general craze young Czechs have for Western brands? Or does the Irish pub have some kind of magical allure that can entice people anywhere in the world?

I won't get a chance to find out today, because here we are walking into U Vejvodu, most definitely an indigenous Czech pub. This former brewery is now a large, echoing and very busy beer hall. The walls are covered in pictures of breweries and pubs from the past. The main bar crouches under a converted mash tun, gleaming copper. High above us, a glass ceiling shines blackly. Like many of the pubs we've seen today, there's the same strong art deco influence we saw at the brewery in Plzeň. When Czechoslovakia gained independence in 1918, the art deco movement was at its height. The style is preserved in pubs and breweries. Whether it was intentional or not, pubs themselves have become symbols of historic national pride.

The barman brings fistfuls of Pilsner Urquell mugs and stands expectantly by our table. Katerina quickly scatters seven beer mats, and finally the barman deposits a glass on each one. 'He won't put them down until you put the beer mats out,' explains Katerina. 'In some places you put out a number of beer mats, and that shows you are ready to order that many beers.'

I can't imagine that any other country reveres beer the way they do here; regards it as quite so precious. It makes me wonder again about the Irish pubs. Even here in U Vejvodu Guinness is on tap, a premium brand almost double the price of Pilsner Urquell. If I want an answer, I'm sitting with a group of drinkers who are probably more likely than most to be able to provide it. 'So why do you think there are so many Irish pubs here?' I ask.

They're quiet for a few seconds.

'Well, it's just this international standard, isn't it?' says Jeff.

'I think it's just that Guinness flogs Irish pub kits to anyone who wants them,' says Adrian.

'No, it's this idea of the *craic*. Everybody wants a piece of it, don't they?' says Tim.

'Right. I suppose so,' I reply. 'But what is the *craic* then? And why does everybody know about it?'

We're drinking at different speeds, and soon Adrian has drained his glass while Briony's is still almost full. She reaches across to pour some beer from her glass into Adrian's.

'No!' screams Katerina. 'Don't do that here.' She looks around anxiously, in case anyone has seen this serious breach of drinking etiquette, a massive insult to the beer.

We decide that we all know what the *craic* is, but none of us can find the right words to define this romanticized Irish pub experience that's supposedly more lively and real and fun than other pubs.

'How did it get like that though?' I ask no one in particular.

'Well, you'll have to go to Ireland to find out, won't you?'

'Well, I suppose I could . . .'

'Why not? It's St Patrick's Day in a couple of weeks. Go then.'

The crap traveller in my head says I can't just get up and go to Ireland on my own, but thinking about it more carefully, I realize I can't think of a reason not to. It might actually be fun. These beer trips are starting to become a habit; the randomness, the sense of reckless freedom, is intoxicating in itself. I know that after I return home from Prague, I'll be going to Dublin next.

But it turns out that I'm wrong. Because the following week something very unusual happens.

České Budějovice

I'm slightly disappointed not to be met at the airport by a bloke in shades holding up a sign with my name on it. Surely that's what high-class business travel is all about? We push and pull our luggage past clusters of drivers all waiting inscrutably for someone else, as they always are, then, right at the end of the line, there's a very tall man wearing a huge grin and a bright red sunhat with the Budweiser Budvar logo on the front.

This is Eddie. Eddie drives groups of beer people from Britain about once a month. After the first time, he brought his family along on the next trip to show them, because they didn't believe some of his stories about his passengers. Beaming, Eddie bundles us out to a minibus, loading our luggage into the back and opening a cooler full of Budvar at the front, and off we go. I suspect the hat might be setting the tone for our visit.

I'm back in the Czech Republic only a week after my last visit thanks to the rivalry between the country's two most prestigious beers. I've been having an occasional drink with John Harley, the CEO of Budweiser Budvar's UK operation, since he read *Man Walks into a Pub* and told the readers of *Marketing* magazine how much he enjoyed it. When I emailed him to let him know how much I had enjoyed my trip to Plzeň, he informed me I hadn't seen real Czech drinking until I'd been to Budvar's home town, and as he was taking a delegation of pub company executives to visit the brewery that week, he insisted I came along.

I haven't even dared tell Chris.

The drive from Prague Airport to České Budějovice takes about three hours. We speed south on empty motorways at alarming speeds, bottles clinking, the noise level rising, and I feel like I'm in the back of the bus at the end of *The Italian Job*; there's the same sense of ill-fated euphoria in the air. Roughly once an hour, Eddie pulls into a service station so we can empty our bladders and refill the Budvar cooler. Each stop further south, Budvar is about five koruna cheaper than it was at the last. By our final stop, forty-five minutes from České Budějovice, the premium beer that sells for three quid a bottle in London bars is twenty-five koruna (57p), about 30p cheaper than a can of Coke.

České Budějovice is a humdrum, indifferent town showing the usual signs of a giddy dash towards capitalism until we reach the centre and pull into a perfectly preserved medieval square, elegant facades facing across the cobbles onto a huge octagonal fountain in the middle. We check into the Budvar-owned Hotel Maly Pivovar (Small Brewery Hotel) and freshen up for dinner.

České Budějovice was defined by beer. It was founded at the end of the thirteenth century as a German merchants' colony, and everyone within the city walls was quickly granted royal permission to brew beer. Everyone, that is, apart from millers and barbers. Well, you know what they're like. And King Wenceslas was someone you didn't argue with.* The town brewed wheat beers and strong, dark ales. By the sixteenth century, kings and vice chancellors were having České Budějovice beers transported to their courts and 'borrowing' the brewers. A 'golden strip of Bohemian brewing' stretched from Plzeň to České Budějovice, and nearby towns were banned from brewing to allow it to flourish.

By the late nineteenth century, when Pilsner Urquell was celebrated across the Austro-Hungarian empire, the beer in České Budějovice was still of variable quality. This, coupled with Czech resentment against German economic control, inspired the natives of České Budějovice to build the Czech Joint Stock Brewery in 1895 as a symbol of national pride. It began brewing extraordinarily good beer. Despite the fact that the German-speaking establishment was publicly attacking it as undrinkable slop before the first batch had even been released, only two years later it was being exported to Prague, Vienna and Trieste. The rest of the beer-drinking world soon followed. As with Plzeň, the beer from České Budějovice became known after the German variant of the town's name as beer from Budweis, Budweiser beer.

---

* Obviously because he was the king, but even taking that into account he was a scary man. Historians have shown that, perhaps unsurprisingly, his exploits in the famous Christmas carol are almost certainly fictitious, and he was in reality something of a beer-loving psycho. For example, he forbade the exporting of Bohemia's Saaz hops under pain of death.

Even a variable Czech beer was likely to be better than the best efforts many other countries could muster, and Budweiser beer has had an international reputation for centuries. So much so that when Carl Conrad and Adolphus Busch, two German immigrants to the USA, spotted the lucrative market for beer among their compatriots, they chose Budweiser as the name for their brand. A few barrels of 'Imported Budweiser Beer' had already reach the United States by this time, but trademark law was unsophisticated, and as Adolphus Busch put it, 'their exports to America are very limited and do not amount to anything'.

Busch had no background or training as a brewer. He didn't even like beer: he preferred wine, and was heard describing his own product as 'dat schlop'. But he was a hell of a salesman, described by contemporaries as a man who 'sold the bad almost as facilely as he sold the good'. His father-in-law, Eberhard Anheuser, was a soap salesman who bought a bankrupt brewery in St Louis in 1860. Busch bought out Anheuser's partner, married his daughter, and Anheuser-Busch was born. The company acquired full rights to the Budweiser name when Busch's friend Conrad went bankrupt (mainly because he owed so much money to his good pal, Adolphus Busch).

Others had the same idea as Busch, and soon there were several North American Budweiser beers. In 1894 Busch argued before a commercial court that there was only room for one Budweiser in the USA. As everyone agreed the name derived from the town of Budweis, he contested that the rights to the name should be his, because he produced the product closest to the authentic article. 'The idea was simple,' he testified, 'to produce a beer of the same quality, colour and taste as the beer produced in Budějovice or Bohemia.' According to early labels, the beer was brewed using Saaz hops and Bohemian malt. Anheuser-Busch got their way, and American Budweiser beer became a trademarked brand that grew rapidly. By 1933 the label showed that the beer was made using rice, but claimed, somewhat bizarrely, that it still followed 'the original Budweiser process'.* However, it was obvious to anyone who picked it up that Budweiser was called Budweiser because it was an (increasingly poor) copy of a beer from Budweis.

After the end of Prohibition in 1933, Czech brewers resumed imports to the US, checking with Anheuser-Busch first and confirming that they were allowed to do so under agreements the two companies had signed in 1911. Five years later the Americans changed their minds, and began a campaign of aggressive legal action that has become the longest-running trademark dispute in the world.

Anheuser-Busch argued simply that they bagged the name first: they had trademarked the Budweiser name in North America in 1907. Why should anyone else be allowed to come in later than that and try to sell a beer with the same name? Well, because it might be a name, but it's also a designation of geographical origin that's been in use for centuries, replied the Czechs.

No, it isn't, said A-B.

---

* Rice is much cheaper than barley. A-B argue that American malt is stronger in flavour than European malt, so they have to use rice to dilute the flavour, and the huge cost saving is just a coincidence. Either way, there is absolutely nothing traditional about rice in either Czech or German beer production.

Yes, it is, said the Czechs. We agreed. There are legal documents saying so. Your founder said so in a court of law.

No, he didn't, replied A-B.

Yes, he did, said the Czechs. That's why he called it Budweiser, for Pete's sake.

No, it isn't, said the Americans.

He said so in a court of law!

Didn't.

He did!

Did not too.

Are you sure you're feeling OK? I'm worried about you.

I'm fine. But the name is a total coincidence.

A-B's argument, unconvincing to start with, was further undermined by frequent changes in their story. In 1921 they had argued that the name was Carl Conrad's idea, 'an inspiration ... a mental lightning flash through an electrified brain.' By 1953 they were saying it was Adolphus' idea. He had made up the name himself because he thought it 'would appeal to the American people'; it was nothing to do with Bohemia whatsoever.

The court accepted this and chose to overlook, or assumed it was mere linguistic coincidence, that as well as the beer they refer to today as 'The Genuine Article', Anheuser-Busch also brewed a beer called Michelob (which coincidentally sounds a bit like the Bohemian brewer Mecholupy), one called Liebot-schaner (which coincidentally sounds a bit like the Bohemian brewer Libocany) and had manufactured a 'near beer' malt drink during Prohibition called Bevo (which coincidentally sounds a bit like the Czech word for beer, *pivo*).

But the court in question was of course an American court, and Anheuser-Busch was and remains a very rich American brewer with very powerful American lawyers. Amid Czech claims of aggression and intimidation, in 1938 Budweiser Budvar lost all rights to sell beers in North America using the terms Bud, Budweis or Budweiser. Then, a few months later, the Nazis invaded Czechoslovakia; the country disappeared off the map and it didn't matter what they thought any more.

Fifty years later, Budweiser Budvar emerged from behind the ruins of the Iron Curtain to find that A-B's lawyers had been busy. All the earlier legal agreements to share the Budweiser name had been overturned. Now, not only was American Budweiser freely on sale across the world, including most of Europe, Anheuser-Busch were even claiming that the Czechs had no right to use the name the Americans had copied from them. The Czechs started winning a few court battles, and A-B decided that if it couldn't beat them, it would simply buy them. Budweiser Budvar was still state-owned, so a hostile stock takeover wasn't an option. Talks lasted for four years, but amid fierce pressure from groups like CAMRA and with allegedly derisory offers from the Americans, negotiations collapsed in 1994, and the litigation resumed. At the time of writing, the world's biggest brewer is employing the most powerful legal counsel its vast wealth can afford to attempt to deny the right of a beer from Budweis to call itself Budweiser in a hundred different lawsuits spanning forty different countries.

My favourite story comes from when the Americans decided that the Czechs should not be allowed to use the term Bud in the UK. Dave the landlord runs the Lord John Russell in Bloomsbury, a great pub that attracts an eclectic mix of people, including lawyers from the courts in nearby Holborn. He loves his beer, stocks an excellent range of English real ales and continental lagers, and has no time for brewery suits who try to rip him off. He's a big lad and speaks his mind in the plainest terms possible. One day a couple of weary-looking men came in and asked for pints of Budweiser Budvar. They stood at the bar talking, and Dave heard one of them say, 'If only we could find evidence that we used the term Bud before they brought this case.'

Dave asked what the problem was. They explained that they were representing Budweiser Budvar, and that Anheuser-Busch were about to obtain a ruling preventing them from using the term Bud, on the grounds that it was now to be a registered A-B trademark. As Budvar had never used 'Bud' in the UK, they had no defence. Dave thought about this, disappeared for a minute, and returned with his beer mat collection. He turned a page of the album, and showed them a beer mat. A Budweiser Budvar beer mat. One that had 'Bud. Budweis. Budweiser' printed across it.

'That's interesting,' said the suits.

'Let me know if it might come in handy,' said Dave. 'I'll keep it out.'

'Thanks,' said the suits.

A few hours later, two slightly more expensive suits came in, marched up to the bar and announced that they represented Anheuser-Busch, had heard that Dave was holding important evidence, and demanded he hand it over to them, implying, in Dave's understanding, that he might not remain in business unless he dealt with them. In extremely colourful language, illustrated by vivid gestures, Dave communicated how he felt about veiled threats, and showed them the door. He's still in business, and he still doesn't stock any Anheuser-Busch beers. Budweiser Budvar launched a new beer, simply called Bud, a few years later.

Budweiser Budvar's defence in the long-running dispute is that the town of Budweis has been brewing beer known internationally as Budweiser since before America was invented. Anheuser-Busch, according to president and CEO Steve Burrows, is 'strongly opposed to any geographic indication for beer, based on brewery location. Geographic location has no bearing on a beer's quality.' He goes on: 'We have invested hundreds of millions of dollars in the Budweiser and Bud names, making them among the most valuable brand names in the world.' In other words, it might be the name of your town, and you might have used the name first, but we have *so* much more money than you.

Curiously, Burrows shrugs off the fight, claiming that 'the dispute is not having a significant impact on our international development objectives', which begs the question: why are they spending so much time and money on it then? In 2005 they even took one case to the European Court of Human Rights which, when you look at the relative size and behaviour of the two parties, is a bit of a cheek.

Over dinner in the Maly Pivovar, John Harley tells me about one time he met two Anheuser-Busch executives. 'We were at an industry event,' he explains, 'and the seating plan was arranged alphabetically by brand name – God knows why. So I'm sitting there, and these two come up and sit down either side of me – I'm between two A-B people. Well, it was a great event; I didn't want to spoil it, so I just laughed and said something like, "Well this is nice, isn't it?" They looked over me at each other, got up and left without saying a word.'

At this point in our story, I'd just like to urge you to put this book down – just for a second – and visit www.anheuser-busch.com. Because if you don't there's no way you'll believe this next point: the company slogan, proudly emblazoned across their home page, reads, 'Welcome to the world of Anheuser-Busch, where making friends is our business!'

By the time dinner has finished, we've drunk a fair amount of foamy Budvar from the same dimpled mugs Yorkshire bitter used to be served in years ago. Budvar has a smooth, clean taste that is full and satisfying but somehow goes down much more easily than a 5 per cent lager has any right to do, and we're nicely stewed. We're getting a little overexcited, but this probably has as much to do with our being blokes away on a trip together as the quantity of beer we've drunk. We're on free passes. On tour. And we don't get to do this very often.

One of the many boasts the locals make is that Budvar, with its exceptional purity and cleanness, does not give you a hangover the following morning. This does however assume you stick to it all night. But we're a bunch of middle-aged Brits with nothing to lose, and not much time to lose it in. We are dangerous and wild. Well, we're a bit giddy.

One of the major rules of any big drinking culture, anywhere in the world, is that there is always a local spirit or liqueur with a special reputation. It's like a caged animal, sitting behind bars or in dusty drinks cabinets. Like a doner kebab, you only ever think it's a good idea once you're already quite drunk. It's probably a lurid green or yellow colour and, inevitably, tradition dictates it must always drunk as a shot, down in one. Chris and I met a perfect example in Hamburglar's bar in Madrid.

Playing this role in the Czech Republic is Becherovka. According to its website, this drink was invented after Josef Becher, a pharmacist, met the 'easily bored' Dr Frobig, an

English eccentric, who stayed with him at the House of the Three Skylarks, where the following conversation – or something very like it – occurred.

> Doctor Frobig: God, I'm bored.
> Josef Becher: Well, we can't have that. What do you enjoy doing?
> DF: Well, this may sound silly, but I have a passion for inventing blends of herbs, aromatic oils and alcohol.
> JB: *Shut up!* So do I! Wait there, my eccentric English friend, I'll go and get my gear. You and I have blending to do!

The two men 'soon became close friends'. Their issue is described by some who have experienced it – possibly euphemistically –as a 'deliciously herbal alcoholic elixir with legendary aphrodisiac qualities'.* Some people swear by it. Many more swear at it. Tourists invariably do the former on their first visit to the country, pick up a bottle in Prague airport duty free, and switch quickly to the latter the first time they try it at home. Among English casualties, the name inevitably mutates into Buggerovka. And now here comes a tray full of these things, and we're desperate not to appear impolite. Down it goes, in one. And here comes the next.

My last coherent thought of the evening is that at least the tickly cough that's been bothering me is now history.

*

---

* It's promoted with caps and condoms bearing phrases such as, 'Becher for your erection, condoms for your protection', which would have advertising authorities in most countries choking on their shandy. Perhaps more apt are the popular T-shirts reading, 'Becherovka: Not for Everybody'.

When Josef Tolar started working for the Budvar brewery in 1965 he was already something of a famous drinker. At university he would unscrew the large glass lampshade in his flat, fill it with coins scrounged from friends, the back of the sofa, wherever, take it to the nearby pub and ask them to take the money out and fill it with the appropriate amount of beer. Famously, a measure exists in Czech bars known as a *tolar*, which holds the same amount of liquid as the fabled lampshade. (Later, Mr Tolar's daughter, the beautiful Miss Tolarova, will tell us that the measure has always had this name; that her father's exploits had nothing to do with it. But the story still adds to his mythology.)

In 1968, when the Russian tanks rolled in to quell the Prague Spring, the Budvar brewery came under pressure to brew a little differently. Communist eastern Europe was essentially a large factory, different regions producing goods for the whole, according to their specialisms. Czechoslovakia was to be the bloc's brewery. This necessitated brewing cheaper beer in greater quantities. Mr Tolar said no. He liked making great beer, and could not be persuaded that the greater good of the Soviet bloc was a higher priority. This being Czechoslovakia, home of a kinder, friendlier face of communism, he wasn't disappeared or sent to a labour camp for his disobedience. Instead, the regime simply denied his family access to education. They also allowed him to stay in the job he loved so much, brewing the beer he loved, but on the same wages he started on. Years went by, and in 1985 he became head brewer, earning far less than the trainees he took on. When the Velvet Revolution happened in 1989 the most senior employee of the brewery was the lowest paid. But he was still there.

In the reception of the Budvar brewery we all stand as Josef

Tolar enters the room, immediately knowing it's him even though we've never seen him before. I feel nervous, like a child meeting Santa. Mr Tolar is a slight, unassuming man who looks like a junior school headmaster, his immaculate suit, waistcoat, shirt and tie all different shades of dun green. In fact, he reminds me of *my* junior school headmaster, Mr Hunter. At first I can't work out why. There's little physical resemblance – Mr Hunter was effectively a bald head with one of those novelty sunglass, big nose and moustache disguises you buy in joke shops at the seaside when you're eight years old, whereas Mr Tolar sports a full head of neatly trimmed jet-black hair that shows no sign of going anywhere fast as he approaches his mid-sixties, and a very tidy moustache. Whereas Mr Hunter was a little portly, Tolar has not a hint of a beer gut, despite the fact that he personally tastes and approves every single batch of beer that comes out of the brewery. But there's something. It's an alchemy of authority that few people have. If you met him you'd probably think he looked just like your junior school headmaster. Even behind his back, people refer to him as *Mister* Tolar.

He starts by showing us the brewery well. You might think that, when it comes to brewing, water is water. Don't let Mr Tolar catch you thinking that. 'The water here is extremely mild, very soft,' he tells us in slow, precise English. 'What is important, perhaps, is that this water is free from any adjuncts, or sterilizers, or chemistry. When the water is collected from the earth, really it is 9,000 years old. We are pumping water that has had no contact with civilization, no contact with chemistry, with agriculture, or with any other part of human activity.' See? I told you.

This is a man who personally inspects the fields where his

barley and hops are grown. He is alleged to have stood in barley fields all day, watching the sun pull the shadows across the hillsides, before rejecting crops that spend too much of the day in shade. He talks to us in some detail about the reasons behind the choice of 100 per cent Saaz hops, female hops that mature less easily. The essential oils and alpha acids that impart the flavour and deep, rich aroma of Czech pilsners are harder to get at, but he thinks it's worth it in the end. 'I say again. If hop acids are extracted by chemical process, it is not the same process. It is a bit old-fashioned perhaps, but we extract substances in the same way they were 200 years ago – nothing more.' You can see why the same regime that had East Germany knocking out Trabants – cars made from cardboard – must have adored him.

He shows us the brewing coppers, where the barley malt is mashed. Many modern breweries now use steel tanks, which do exactly the same job but look like any other piece of factory equipment. But traditional coppers are such a wonderful sight they are often still built in brand new breweries. They look fantastic even if you have no idea what they are for. But the Budvar coppers are magnificent. Huge and polished to the point where the metal seems to contain endless depths, they gleam so brightly that any copper you might have seen before seems like a mere dress rehearsal.

'These vessels are constructed from copper,' explains Mr Tolar somewhat needlessly. 'Nowadays more are constructed from stainless steel. More technical. Not so . . . nice.' Never have I heard such vague words carry so much suppressed passion.

We pause our tour between rows of long, underground lagering tanks. Mr Tolar goes into a detailed rationale of why these horizontal tanks are better than the outdoor vertical tanks you see in most breweries these days, which, echoing my experience in Plzeň, we can sum up succinctly for our purposes thus: they're better, all right?

Mr Tolar straightens up to make an announcement. A new Budvar beer has been brewed for the British market. It's still sitting in these tanks, and no one has tasted it yet – apart from Tolar himself, obviously. 'So it is necessary to make a test. You will have the opportunity to taste the beer just from the tank.' A groan of pleasure rises from the throng. 'And then you can guess how many days such a brew has been matured here.' The beer is a darker gold than normal Budvar. Its richer, sweeter taste betrays its strength: 7.6 per cent. The perfect pick-me-up for this point in the day. None of us guesses correctly about the maturation period. The answer is 200 days, longer than any other beer in the world. This makes it smoother than a beer of this strength has any right to be. We agree that a certain segment of British drinkers will love it, but probably not for the reasons Mr Tolar would prefer.

Everything down here is spotlessly clean. It feels neither modern and newfangled nor old-fashioned. It just feels optimal. The whole brewery is scrubbed to perfection. The floors are hosed down every twenty minutes to maintain the optimal level of humidity in the air. Later, when I listen back to my Dictaphone, I'm deeply embarrassed to hear myself saying, 'It smells like the sea. It's so pure. It makes you think that for all the crap beer does, it is we who corrupt it. Beer itself is pure and natural. It's only when it gets taken into our *bodies* and into our *minds* that it becomes a source of something bad.'

The tour is followed by dinner, and more Budvar. By the time we finish, it's after 11 p.m. The effects of a fourteen-hour drinking day are beginning to show. We're looking distinctly ragged around the edges, and the decorum that characterized our first meeting in Wetherspoon's at Heathrow airport two days ago has long vanished. An incredibly prim and formal man named Quentin – 'Call me Q' – is asserting that I'm a 'fucking northern bastard' while attempting to put me in a headlock, all the while explaining that this is a sign of the deep affection in which he now holds me. John Harley suggests we go to the pub.

The imaginatively named Budvar Bar is just across the main square from Maly Pivovar. It has been recently acquired by the brewery, possibly because it seemed inconceivable that a competitive brand could be stocked here, so close to their headquarters. It's a lovely pub, with wooden walls and brass bar tops and fonts that make the whole place glow like Christmas. The bar staff don't seem too pleased to see us. Apparently they're new. We ask for a round of beers, and the young bartender with his hand on the nearest beer pump says that there is no beer left, only schnapps, and the bar is closing soon anyway. This seems somewhat implausible in this town, and his claim isn't helped at all when his colleague comes up alongside him and cheerfully starts to splash beer into five big mugs. Our barman doesn't waver. He knows that if he breaks eye contact with us he will see the beer being poured next to him. Bravely – some might say foolishly – he continues to insist that there is no beer. My brain's black box – that little sober bit deep inside that's impervious to the damage being wreaked elsewhere and always keeps up a laconic, horribly fascinated commentary on my drunken actions – doesn't blame him. I wouldn't want to serve us either.

One of our hosts from the brewery leans across the bar

and says something in a low voice – I don't know what, but I'm guessing it's not an encouraging comment about how shiny they've managed to get all the brass. I smile greedily as the non-existent beer suddenly flows into thirteen big, fresh mugs.

We've got our beer; we're happy. And suddenly we're going upstairs, up to the top floor of the building. It's midnight. As we ascend, the sound of Black Sabbath becomes discernible. Then louder. Then very loud indeed. We go through a door at the top of the stairs and this is where everyone was hiding. The room is packed. This is our surprise party, with just one small technicality – we weren't actually invited. We're still surprised though. Outside the streets are empty. The other two floors of this, it turns out, vast drinking establishment are deserted. We've been here for an hour and seen no one go in or out. Maybe these guys just stay up here partying all the time. They stare at us as we take up positions at the corner of the bar.

The place is a hybrid of an Alpine ski lodge and ... something darker. A life-sized wooden voodoo doll bends over and leers down at us from the bar top, its face a grotesque screaming mask. Just in case this might be making me feel edgy, the decoration is thoughtfully enhanced by a two-foot-tall crucifix on the pillar in front of me, at face height.

With speech rendered impossible by the volume of the heavy metal, I look around and take stock. No matter where you go, no matter what your facility with the local language, in pubs and bars around the world you can tell the men's toilets from the women's as easily as you can in your local, thanks to the international sign language of male and female silhouettes. In bars like this it's even easier because the door to the men's is always propped open, so you can watch a line of mullets pissing away without even rising from your seat at the bar.

Black Sabbath switches into Rainbow's 'Since You've Been Gone'. Last time I heard this song I was thirteen years old, sitting in the cafe at Royston Baths, damp towel rolled under one arm, drinking a cup of Bovril for 5p out of the Klix machine and craning my neck to see if Lynne Brooks had left the pool yet. Then I realize the whole ambience of this place reminds me of Barnsley in 1981. It's not just the music; there's the mullets, the moustaches, the staring, the dimpled beer mugs. The huge fucking crucifix.

Despite the familiarity, I'm starting to get paranoid. It's the staring – some of these mullets look quite mean. We're singing along to the early 1980s heavy metal, and I become convinced that we're OK as long as we don't stop singing, as long as we carry on enjoying it. We can feel all these eyes boring into us, and I start wondering if it's going to kick off. Except it doesn't. It hasn't. This is the Czech Republic, remember. They don't fight over here when they're pissed. The chocolate boys I met in the first chapter said so. There is an atmosphere, no doubt about that – we are definitely intruding on something – but my black box realizes that in the UK it would have kicked off long before now. I start to relax.

Then John leans over and yells, 'Oh, I've just remembered why I got beaten up the last two times I was in here.'

There's a pause while I try to frame a decent response to this from the noise of six different simultaneous thoughts suddenly arriving in my mind. Eventually I croak, 'Oh, why was that then?'

'I was dancing like a twat.'

Prague

'I was out drinking with Bill Wyman the other day.'

John keeps starting conversations like this. We're back in the capital, a brief evening before flying back home to recover. We're standing on the Charles Bridge, beneath the statues that line it, looking at the view.

'You know Vaclav Havel appointed Frank Zappa as his culture minister?'

I didn't.

'It's what you get when you elect a poet as president, I suppose. He had him stay at his house and they drove around on specially made adult-sized tricycles, knocking into things.'

'I heard he had Lou Reed over for tea,' I chip in weakly.

'Yeah, and the Rolling Stones spend a lot of time over here as well. So Bill Wyman was telling me that they were over a few years ago, before he left the band, obviously, and they were talking to Havel and admiring Prague castle.'

'It is a lovely castle.'

'Yeah, well, that's what the Stones thought as well. But Wyman turns to Havel and says, 'You could do a lot more with that, you know. You know what it needs? Some decent lighting. How about we get our lighting technician to rig something up quickly for you just now, then when we've finished this tour he'll come back and do it properly.' And he did. So Prague castle is lit by the Rolling Stones' lighting man.'

The Czech Republic: a rock and roll country.

4

'A hundred thousand welcomes'

Dublin

I'm in hell.

In Dante's *Divine Comedy* hell has nine different circles, each one set aside for different types of sinner, with appropriate punishments. I've just found the tenth.

It's just before 6 a.m. I was counting on not waking up for another two hours. I drank quite a lot of Guinness last night. And outside my window somebody is carrying out an experiment to see how much noise you can make with an aluminium beer keg and a metal cellar hole cover. After a few goes, they figure out that if you bounce the keg from a decent height – the back of a lorry will do – onto the cellar hole cover *while it is in place over the hole*, you get a booming, hollow, bass drum effect that contrasts dramatically with the initial, piercing crash of the impact.

They want to make sure though, and an hour later they're still at it. By now I've realized they are making beer deliveries to Break for the Border, just across the alley from my hotel. What I can't work out is why they are doing it so early, or how they can be delivering so much beer to one place. I calculate they're doing about two kegs a minute. Over the course of an hour, that's 120 kegs. How? Why?

Then I remember Dante. I decide I must be in the circle of hell reserved for enthusiastic drinkers. An eternal hangover rendered physical, alive, with the sound of all the beer kegs we have emptied in our lifetimes being *bounced*, for all eternity. Surely, no punishment can be worse than this.

Oh yes it can. At 7.15, in the corridor on the opposite side of the room from the window, the *hammering* and *drilling* strike up a stereo of pure cacophony. It sounds like someone is trying to deliver breakfast through a solid brick wall, and refusing to concede defeat to the laws of physics.

I knew something was wrong when I checked in last night. Dining furniture was piled up to the ceiling just outside the door to my room. More worryingly, there was a large sign on the wall reading 'Danger! Keep away!' This is not what a crap traveller wants to see outside any room where they will be spending a night alone.

I check out of the hotel as quickly as I can. As I pack, the hammering, sawing and drilling has spread to three sides of my room. The pressure in my head makes me panicky. Downstairs, as the receptionist hands back my credit card, seemingly oblivious to the brain-splitting racket, a man appears with a circular saw and starts tearing into the pavement just outside the lobby. I can see the receptionist's mouth moving but I can't hear any sounds above the screaming saw. I grab the card and run away down the street, as fast as anyone can with a computer bag in one hand and a suitcase in the other, tears pricking my eyes.

I decided to come here for St Patrick's Day in the end, to try to understand what makes the Irish beer drinking experience so special. After centuries of occupation by the British, the Irish are almost exactly like us in many ways. And yet, as with several aspects of Irish culture, when it comes to drinking – what you drink, how you drink, where you drink – they're somehow *better*, more romantic, more universally appealing, more positive. Drinking is the single most popular pastime in Ireland, and beer is the stuff of miracles. Ireland's most important female saint, St Brigid, was a brewer. Her abbey included a leper colony, and one day it ran out of beer. She called for the lepers' bath water to be brought forward – why anyone was saving the lepers' bath water is unclear. She blessed it, and it transformed into delicious ale.

Neither Chris nor Liz could get off work to come with me, so I'm here on my own, and fairly nervous. I made contact with Cian Molloy, author of *The Story of the Irish Pub*, and last night we went on a pub crawl. The premise of Cian's book tells you a lot about the subject before you even start reading it: he profiles every pub in Ireland which has been in the same family for over a century. Over 100 qualify for inclusion, although only one remains in Dublin. Family is an important aspect of the Irish pub. In the seventeenth century pubs started to take English-style names like the Mitre and the Nag's Head, but in the late nineteenth century, at roughly the same time as people started to reassert their Irishness by reviving the 'o' before their surnames, pubs reverted to being named after the family name of the pub's owner or founder. Irish pubs still tend to be family owned and run, with very few belonging to the kind of chains that have colonized English town centres.

The economic boom known as the Celtic Tiger has transformed almost every aspect of Irish society, so that tourist-friendly Oirish clichés rub shoulders with one of the most dynamic and forward-looking cities in the EU. After centuries of famine, recession, depression and oppression that saw generations of young Irish abandon their homes and fan out across the world, people are now clamouring to get in.

This identity clash is manifest in the Dublin pub like nowhere else. Last night we popped into Davy Byrne's, famous for its role in James Joyce's *Ulysses*, and the meeting point for the people who celebrate Bloomsday every 16 June, the day the entire novel takes place. From the outside it looks little different than it did in Joyce's day. Inside it's now a continental cafe-bar, seemingly selling more Erdinger wheat beer than it does Guinness. But tourists still flock to Dublin in search of the 'authentic' Irish pub experience, and many of them still find a reasonable approximation of it.

At the start of the seventeenth century, Barnaby Rich, an English pamphleteer, made his view on Dublin and its pubs very clear: 'The whole profit of the towne stands upon ale houses and selling of ale. There are whole streets of taverns and it is a rare thing to finde a house in Dublin without a taverne, as to find a tavern without a strumpet.' He compared the ale he drank in Ireland to 'hogges-washe' and described it as 'unfit for any man's drinking but for common drunkards'. A century later, Sir William Petty estimated that a third of the city's buildings were ale houses. By the late eighteenth century, Dublin was home to 25,000 people, who shared between them 2,000 ale houses, 300 taverns and 1,200 brandy shops.

Nowhere was it more obvious that the origin of the word pub is 'public house'. Furnishing was usually domestic, with little distinction between public and private areas of the house. There are still parts of Ireland where it's common for drinkers to let themselves in with a key under the mat if the owner isn't around, help themselves to beer, stand on either side of the bar, and leave money on the counter when they've finished.

Dublin, however, has always had a little more grandeur. There are still over 700 pubs in the city centre, and while many of them have names indistinguishable from those of their rural counterparts, pubs like Mulligan's, Neary's and O'Neill's are ornately decorated with tiled floors, frosted glass, deeply polished wood and sumptuous fittings, much of which has changed little since they were built in the Victorian era.

As we made our way around these pubs, having a pint of Guinness in every one (Mulligan's serves arguably the best pint in Dublin), Cian and I were following in the footsteps of writers whom neither of us can ever hope to match in terms of either literary or drinking prowess. The poet Patrick Kavanagh would often start in McDaid's with the playwright and author Brendan Behan. Without fail they would be arseholed by lunchtime, at which point Behan would begin verbally and sometimes physically attacking Kavanagh, who would run round the corner into Neary's for some peace and quiet. I sat in the same spot at the bar where Kavanagh was once working on some poetry. A trainee barman once spilled a pint of Guinness over his papers. Kavanagh looked at the barman for a while and said, 'You may not be much of a barman, son, but you're a feckin' brilliant judge of poetry!' Other writers such as Flann O'Brien and W.B. Yeats were just as committed to keeping the city's pubs in business when they were on their home turf. And it used to be said that if a cub reporter on the *Irish Times* didn't file his copy with Guinness stains from the Palace Bar, he was in the wrong job.*

It became obvious as the evening went on that, wonderful though these pubs are in their own right, I wasn't going to find the full story in them. 'If you want to see the real, traditional side of the Irish pub, you need to get down into the country,' said Cian as we finished our last pints, 'Pubs represent a lot more people outside Dublin. You don't get a proper Irish drinking experience here.'

I nodded. 'I'm going to Celbridge tomorrow.'

Cian suddenly looked uncomfortable, staring at me as if I might be winding him up. 'As I say,' he continued slowly, 'you need to get down to the country.'

It didn't take me long to find out why he found this conversation a little strange.

Celbridge and Straffan

As an inexperienced traveller, I didn't think it was a stupid idea to call the Irish Tourist Board to ask their advice on my quest. Turns out I was wrong.

---

* The Palace continues to attract occasional notoriety. In December 2000 'J' out of the now-defunct boy band Five was arrested here for disorderly behaviour. Another drinker had recognized the band and started taking the piss, saying they weren't as good as Westlife, so 'J' punched him in the face. Charges of being drunk and disorderly were eventually dropped after a payment to charity and an agreement to keep the peace for two years. 'J' was as good as his word: the band stopped releasing records soon after.

'Tourism is not the Irish drinking experience,' the man on the phone said. 'Dublin is not the Irish drinking experience.' Then he suggested I go to Celbridge. Knowing no better, I booked a B & B there and followed his advice. It's not that there's anything *wrong* with Celbridge, exactly. It seems like a perfectly reasonable place to live if you work in Dublin and prefer a half-hour commute to the city's jaw-dropping property prices. But if by some remote chance the bloke who sent me to Celbridge ever asks me to recommend where he can see the heart of the English countryside, I'll send the bastard to Croydon and we'll be even.

I take the bus from the south bank of the River Liffey, and forty minutes later I'm knocking on the door of a spacious bungalow on the main road back into Dublin, about a mile or so outside Celbridge itself. 'So, are you here to work then?' asks the owner as he shows me to my room.

'I'm writing a book about pubs and beer.'

'Right . . .'

'And the man at the tourist information office told me to come here.'

'Right.' The landlord seems at a loss. 'Well, we do have pubs here, I suppose. Well. Right. I'll, er, let you get on with it then.'

Arthur Guinness grew up in Celbridge. His father was a rent collector for the rector of Celbridge, who was also Arthur's godfather. When the rector died, he left Arthur a hundred pounds, which the young man used to start a small brewery in nearby Leixlip. When he'd made a success of that, he left it in his brother's hands and bought the lease on a dilapidated brewery in St. James's Gate in Dublin. The canal network, on which Celbridge is a key point, was the secret weapon that allowed Guinness to conquer Ireland at a time when its beers were strictly confined to small regions. So the place has some historical significance in our story. Except, according to the PR people at the Guinness brewery, the Guinnesses actually lived in Straffan, five miles away.

Straffan was described to me as having 'a little more local colour' than Celbridge. The cab driver taking me there expresses interest, bordering on mild concern, when he realizes that I'm planning on walking into the pub there on my own.

The Straffan Inn has been called the last spit and sawdust pub in Ireland. The tatty banquette seats are shedding their stuffing. The low tables are surrounded by uncomfortable stools. There's the damp, yeasty smell I always thought came from beer-soaked carpets and bar towels, but the floor is tiled and there are no towels to be seen. Bottles of Bud and Coke sit sullenly on warm shelves. Guinness, Carlsberg, Bud and Bulmer's cider are on tap. The food extends to bars of chocolate sitting on a shelf under the spirit optics.

There are seven stools at the bar, and seven men sitting on them: a group of four older geezers, a space, then three younger blokes. All of them are watching the TV above the bar, talking about the Cheltenham Festival. They all stop talking and stare at me when I walk in, then, after a few seconds, pay me no attention whatsoever.

I buy my drink. There's no room to stand or sit at the bar, so I have to take one of the transcendentally painful stools. I couldn't be more conspicuous, the only person in the building not at the bar. Seven backs face me. After a minute or two, one of the backs leans closer to its neighbour, jerks its head in my direction and whispers loudly, 'Who's *that*?'

This is clearly not the place to find a traditional Irish

welcome. Eventually some women arrive to watch *Eastenders*. This makes the atmosphere a little less chilly, but also underscores that I am not part of it. No one invites me to their sister's wedding. No one tries to tell me their life story. In fact no one speaks a word to me. And, really, why should they? I've been reading too many whimsical accounts of journeys through Ireland. That way of life may or may not exist, but I'm not going to find it in a Dublin suburb.

I decide to finish my pint and head back to the B & B, but this takes longer than I planned. What I thought was a hangover this morning amid the beer kegs has grown steadily worse through the day. My stomach has set like concrete, the pain in my head has steadily intensified, and it takes me an hour to force down a pint of weak lager. I phone for a taxi and head outside into the driving rain. This trip is turning into a disaster, and I don't want to be here any more. The cab arrives. Twelve minutes later, I'm pulling the duvet up around my ears.

It's a dark and stormy night. Don't get me wrong, the weather's fine. The problem is here in the room – specifically in my skull. I've half-woken up, because the landlord of the B & B is trying to attack me. He's outside, sending thought waves through the wall. I don't know why, but here they come, penetrating my brain like scalpels. He's looking for something inside my head. Something he can use. I thrash around, trying to escape from the psychic bonds he's throwing around me.

The thrashing wakes me up properly, and I realize that all this is, of course, absolute rubbish. The landlord is not attacking me with mental probes. Why would he want to? He's a nice bloke. And, more to the point, how could he? I'm an idiot. No, it's not the landlord. It's a network of the world's scientists. They're trying to use my brain while I'm asleep. Except I'm not asleep. I can see my head as they do: neon boxes against a black background, each representing a different centre in my brain. Each time they open one I turn over and it snaps shut, but the action opens up another one. The struggle has me thrashing around again, and soon the sheets are soaking wet.

After eleven hours of this, I wake up. A bright, St Patrick's Day sun shines through the curtains and it's blissfully quiet – not a beer keg, hammer or circular saw for miles. The smell of fried breakfast wafts under the door, and doesn't cause my stomach to somersault. Peeling away the clammy sheets, I guess I was a tad feverish in the night. But I feel much better now.

After an enormous Irish breakfast of bacon, sausage, tomato, egg, black and white pudding, mushrooms and potato, I head out into the sunshine, back to Dublin for the big parade. There's a bus stop thirty yards up the road with a green symbol on it, and another one thirty yards after that with a yellow symbol. I check them both: neither has a timetable, nor any indication of which is the right one for Dublin. I pace between them, looking for clues. I'm back at the first one when a bus appears on the horizon – maroon rather than green or yellow, so no help there. It draws closer and I make out a number I don't recognize, and the destination Ath Cliath. No use to me; never heard of the place. I step back. As the bus hurtles towards me, the digital destination sign dissolves and changes to 'Dublin', and I remember that Ath Cliath is the capital's name in Gaelic. I stick my arm out and adopt a panicked expression, catching the driver's eye.

He nods, and the bus screeches to a halt on a muddy bank fifty yards down the road. I sprint gratefully towards it, bags sliding off my shoulders, straps tangling my knees as I slither through the mud. The packed crowds on the bus stare at me as I slide past them.

Dublin

As we reach the outskirts of the city, the driver makes an announcement over the tannoy: 'Attention please. This bus will not be mumble mumble mumble Dublin. In addition, we won't be mumble mumble station. Thank you.' Then he takes a sharp right and starts heading north, away from the city centre.

I have no idea where we're going, and I think I look stupid enough already without asking anyone what's happening. So here I am: on a double-decker bus in a country so close to home they rarely even ask to see your passport at the airport, a country where everyone speaks English and *Eastenders* is on television at half seven every night. And I'm hopelessly out of my depth. I knew I was a crap traveller, but not this crap.

I look around the bus. A few people look mildly annoyed, but no one is panicking or rushing to get off, and they all look like they're going to see the parade. (You can just tell.) I decide to stay on as long as they do. And when they all get off, we're somehow on the north bank of the Liffey, in the centre of the city.

People are lining the route ten deep, but not everyone wants to see the parade. As noon strikes I'm walking past Mulligan's, which is due to open any second. A crowd of ten people look at their watches impatiently, and before the clock chimes have ended, they're rapping coins on the windows, peering through, pacing around anxiously and muttering to each other in outraged exasperation.

For years, despite huge celebrations in cities like Chicago and New York, Paddy's Day in Ireland was a desultory affair, the parade consisting of a few marching bands and majorettes. It was a Catholic feast day and a holy day of obligation. People had the day off work, went to mass and had a family meal together. It was, literally, a very sober affair: the pubs remained closed all day. The only place in the whole of Dublin licensed to serve alcohol was the annual dog show, which was held every year on 17 March. While the rest of the world was remembering distant Irish cousins and great aunts, the population of Dublin was remembering how much it loved doggies, and every year the event was full to capacity.

Over the last decade St Patrick's Day has been massively improved – for one thing, the pubs are open. The parade now lasts about two hours, and is merely the centrepiece for almost a week of funfairs, firework displays and street entertainment.

Half a million people have come out to enjoy the day, which is unseasonably bright and warm. Japanese, Italians and Americans all press forward. The street vendor yelling 'Whistles! Come and gerrem! Blow yer whistles!' has, inevitably, a cockney accent. People are climbing on anything that offers a few inches more elevation, teetering on spiky fences, clinging to lamp posts. Several locals have brought stepladders from home. One enterprising family have two sets with a paint-spattered plank slung between them, so their five small children can balance on it precariously, five feet above the asphalt.

I find a place where I can see the backs of the heads of the Gardae lining the route, and decide this is good enough. We wait. The anticipation builds.

In our cynical world it's often said that to appreciate the magic of an event like this you should see it through the eyes of a child. It turns out I have no choice but to do so. When the first parade floats approach, a Mexican wave ripples through the crowd as parents hoist toddlers onto their shoulders, and my view becomes a tiny sliver between dangling Baby Gap shoes. I see most of the action through the eyes of one particular child: a talkative three-year-old with a perfect view, perched just behind me. To start with, he doesn't say much. I can tell the parade is upon us thanks to the sound of the first marching bands. They flit briefly across my restricted field of vision, followed by ranks of soldiers, shamrock in their hats, proudly carrying the flags of all the nations in the EU.

Then the three-year-old yells, 'A horsey! God bless ya, horsey!' A mounted policeman rides past, closely followed by two Canadian Mounties. A Native American, resplendent in extravagant feathers that echo the Irish tricolour, brings up the rear of the mounted group. This first wave prompts a thoughtful exchange between a group of Irish teenagers in front of me.

'Ah, look. It's YMCA!'

'Aye.'

'We've had the cowboy, the Indian, the policeman; now all we need is the . . . er . . .'

'The plumber.'

'Aye. The plumber.'

My three-year-old guide drowns out their laughter, shouting, 'Here's something! What is dat ting?'

'Dat ting' turns out to be the lord mayor's coach. It's an extravagant affair, fit for Cinderella, and as it sweeps past, I swear I can see Kerry McFadden leaning out of the window, waving at me. Initially I put this down to an aftershock of last night's feverish tremors. That seems the most likely explanation. Then one of the teenagers asks, 'Was that Kerry McFadden?'

His mates laugh. 'Nah, stupid,' one says, 'that was Miss World.' I assume he's making a sarcastic and unnecessarily cruel comment about Ms McFadden, but then I remember that Rosanna Davison, the current Miss World, is indeed Irish. It would make sense, I suppose. But now here comes the first float, and there on top of it, beaming fit to outshine the sun, is Chris de Burgh's daughter, the current Miss World. So if she's on the float, who the hell was that in the carriage? I suppose it could have been Kerry McFadden, but . . . *why*?*

The three-year-old has spotted something which, to him at least, is far more disturbing. 'Daddy, a vampire! A vampire, Daddy. Daddy? Daddy! *Daddy!* It's a *VAMPIRE!*' Clearly he can't understand why Daddy isn't killing the vampire, or at least making a run for it. He goes very still and quiet until the vampire is safely past. Then he pipes up again.

'He's a big fella isn'ee?' precedes a group of people wearing twenty-foot-high *papier mâché* bodies of cartoon barbarians and Roman charioteers. 'They can't see very well, those guys,' he adds thoughtfully as they stumble past. Next, a crowd of

---

* The following day's papers reveal that it was indeed the woman affectionately known in online celeb gossip circles as Chip Shop sitting in the mayoral carriage. They make no attempt, though, to explain how she got there, or what she thought she was doing in the coach.

blue sea demons, comedy Norsemen – the parade is starting to make sense as a sort of history of Ireland, until . . .

'There's crisps coming. They're not real crisps. They're coming though, Daddy.' Time stretches to eternity as I try to imagine what is about to enter my narrow field of vision. In the end, it's a bunch of people carrying large, identical placards of Walker's crisp packets. Cheese and onion colour. I can't help feeling disappointed.

Just as we're getting almost giddily surreal, the parade switches back to near-normality. Bands from Chicago and Italy march past, and then I hear bagpipes. This is Lume de Biqueria, a traditional folk group from Madrid, where terrorist bombs killed 200 only last week, and they're receiving strong, solemn and respectful applause along the entire parade route. No one shouts anything out. No one makes any obvious, melodramatic gestures. The Spaniards stare straight ahead, dignified, and suddenly I'm fighting back tears. I remember Cian Molloy saying to me, 'Ireland is a lot less cosmopolitan than the UK, but it's a lot more European. We really do consider ourselves to be part of Europe, and that's very much what Dublin is about these days.' And for the first and probably last time today, I fervently wish I was Irish.

'A *Dragon*!'

We're back to astounding floats, and the three-year-old is doing his job admirably.

'Look, a dinosaur that's supposed to go in the water! Why is there a ting behind it?'

It's starting to get a bit weird.

'What the hell's *That*?'

I turn around sharply, half-expecting the adorable little fella to have morphed into some diminutive mini-teenager.

No, he's still up there, looking angelic. But those words definitely came out of his mouth. He seems to be referring to a group of people gamely trying to create the illusion of a big monster via the use of some tie-dyed parasols. Or maybe he means the spiky demon on stilts.

'Oh, Jesus *Christ*!'

No. That was the spiky demon.

As the parade and its crowd of spectators start to thin out, I head off to explore central Dublin in the grip of St Patrick's Day. Grafton Street is teeming. The sheer weight of bodies should make it impassable, but somehow we all inch along, past traditional Irish musicians, past a group of lads performing a cappella hip hop, and of course a middle-aged couple with a ghetto blaster dancing a perfect tango, dressed immaculately in full costume. There are balloons and whistles for sale, green feather boas, furry snakes on sticks, inflatable hammers, and face painting. And there's stuff for the kids as well.

There's not a seat to be had in any of the very many pubs I visit. This is new Dublin, young Dublin, where over half the population is under twenty-five. Incomes have soared. People have cars and take foreign holidays, and resent the clichés of Oirishness perpetuated for the delight of tourists. In one bar I overhear a young man talking earnestly to his friends about the wall of debt, and the G4. Even today, on the biggest party of the year, young people are discussing the global economic situation. Then I tune into the accent, and realize they're talking about the G-force on the wall of death at the Paddy's Day funfair.

At around 3.30 I spot a schoolgirl throwing up in the

street. A couple of shirt-sleeved WPCs amble over to help her friends hold her up. The streets are starting to fill up with people looking increasingly the worse for wear. I wonder if they started drinking very early this morning, or if they have been drinking incredibly quickly, and decide it's both.

O'Neill's, a vast network of bars that bears no relation to its theme pub chain namesake, is unrecognizable from when I had a quiet drink the night before last. It's bursting with teenagers drinking pints of cider and flirting. Two girls who haven't seen each other since – well, it must have been afternoon break before double French yesterday – charge towards each other, embrace like lovers and scream like fire alarms for about five minutes.

I can't come to Dublin on St Patrick's Day and miss out Temple Bar, even if I would really like to. English stag and hen parties have helped transform the district into 'Ibiza in the rain'. Launched as a centre for arts and culture, it soon became a centre for alcopops and vomiting.

The crucial distinction in Irish pubs – traditional pubs have no amplified music while the newer ones blast out Kylie – has become irrelevant. The noise level is up to eleven wherever I go. There's simply no point trying to squeeze into most bars. I eventually find one place which is relatively empty – there are inches of space between some of the bodies. But even here a tall blonde girl laughing coquettishly and tossing back her hair causes a chain reaction of cracked heads across the room.

So this is twenty-first-century *craic*. It's like any city centre circuit I've ever experienced – Leeds, Plymouth, Glasgow, Newcastle – multiplied by a thousand. I had expected that I'd be able to contrast the traditional pubs, crowded with the old guys in their Sunday best, with the tourist traps in Temple Bar. But there's no distinction. For two days I've been drinking in pubs where I've been the youngest person by some distance. Now I'm the oldest, by the same margin. It's not that I'm not enjoying it – I am – but I'm not learning anything. I need to find out where all the old fellas spend Paddy's Day.

Ten minutes later I'm in a cab on my way to the Gravediggers. In my peripheral vision the streets look like a typical Hollywood B-movie depiction of post-apocalyptic dystopia, which always seems to consist of fires everywhere, no window left intact, gangs of youths wearing punkish fashions and running for no apparent reason, swigging luminous cocktails and overturning cars to the strains of bad techno. Of course, when I focus properly it's nowhere near this bad; there's no techno to be heard.

'The big increase in the country's wealth has caused a massive problem,' the cabbie is saying. 'Young people now have an expectation of making it big. If they do, they celebrate. If they don't, they feel aggrieved. It's an aggressive, competitive culture, and that's a very recent change.'

I hadn't realized before now, but the Irish are the world's second-largest beer drinkers behind the Czechs. Per capita consumption of alcohol increased by a whopping 46 per cent over the 1990s, when just about every other developed nation was seeing a gentle decline. An Irish friend of mine who has done lots of market research among Irish drinkers has reluctantly come to the conclusion that things are spiralling out of control. 'At its best, Irish drinking is brilliant. It's about shared communal rituals that go right back into our Celtic heritage,' she told me before I came here. 'For years we've had this image of the fun-loving, drunken Irish. But now we've literally reached saturation point in how much we drink. The old communities and traditions are breaking down, and it's such a fast transition to something new that alcohol is being used as a coping mechanism. Everyone says the problem is with younger drinkers and alcopops, but everyone's drinking too much, and no one wants to change their own behaviour.'

The cabbie illustrates this point perfectly. 'The Irish have always been big drinkers. It's the national pastime. Their parents drink, so what are they going to do? But now the kids of sixteen and seventeen are getting obese – drinking, smoking, no culture of exercise.' He pauses for a second. 'I mean, five pints of Guinness after work is nothing, but it's getting out of hand now.' He continues, 'But today is special. You have to understand, St Patrick's Day is a really big deal for the Irish people.' I nod. 'It's almost as important to them as, say –' he falls silent while he searches for a comparison large enough, '– as Cheltenham.'

The Gravediggers is ten minutes drive into the north of the city. Officially known as Kavanagh's, it acquired its nickname thanks to the ironic humour of the chartered accountants who drink there. All right, it didn't. It's called the Gravediggers because it's near Glasnevin cemetery. It's been here since 1833, and has been in the Kavanagh family all this time. It's on all the lists of famous Irish pubs, and has been recommended to me by everyone from Cian Molloy – it's the one pub in Dublin that qualifies for his book – to every cab driver I've spoken to. But the distance out of the city keeps it off many tourists' itineraries.

The pundits were right though: as soon as I'm through the door, without ever having been here before, I know it's the place I always wanted to spend Paddy's Night. Behind the bar the spirits are kept not on optics, but in antique wooden cabinets with glass doors, like a maiden aunt's drawing room, if maiden aunts, or drawing rooms for that matter, still existed outside fiction.* The central space is divided into a series of snugs by frosted glass partitions that finish just above head height; creating privacy while still allowing the ambient buzz to flow. Above the original tongue-and-groove panelling the walls are brown and yellow, as if cream paint stained by nicotine over countless years has been mixed with the tobacco-coloured paint you can now get that replicates this effect in a can. The ceiling is – let's be kind here – a rich, deep, golden caramel.

This is the 182nd Paddy's Day Kavanagh's has witnessed, and it shows. Whenever a barman is anywhere near a Guinness tap, no matter what order he is attending to, with his spare hand he pours two-thirds of a pint of Guinness and pops it on the bar. Rows of part-poured pints line the bar top, so whenever someone orders a pint, the famous 118-second pour is reduced to about twelve. This would never work in an English O'Neill's because the half-poured pints would sit there all afternoon. Here, they never rest more than a minute.

Something is troubling me. As a pub crowd, this isn't quite right. Then I realize what it is: there's a mix of all ages (over twelve), and they're all talking to each other. They're wearing the right amount of clothes in the right order, whether it's the younger guy in a T-shirt reading 'fcek you: the Irish Connection', or the flat-capped septuagenarian with whom he's deep in conversation. Signs around the walls read 'All children must be off the premises by 9 p.m.', and sure enough they are –

---

* And if the maiden aunt was a total lush.

they're all down in Temple Bar getting wankered on alcopops while their parents have a few beers here. They're a lovely bunch: they apologize if they bump into you, and no matter how busy the place is, they always stand back to let you through.

Pubs like this are as welcoming as you can get, because they have a mix of generations and are therefore not threatening to anyone. This poses a serious challenge to the whole idea of branded pub chains that streamline people according to their demographics and desires. Until now I've thought there was some sense in these chains, in that they create like-minded communities that are self-selecting rather than geographical. But after a few days in Ireland, I find myself thinking that it's obviously better this way. This is the Pub, the way people imagine it to be: noisy and boisterous, but just quiet enough to let you raise your glass or hear each other speak.

People here at Kavanagh's know the difference between merry and bollocksed, and are not looking for oblivion. And perhaps this is the missing ingredient when people try to define the *craic* – sure, it's the music and the laughter, but what makes it special is everyone being in this zone – under the influence, but steadfastly holding back from the point where they start to lose control, slur and become pains in the arse.

But the main reason I love it here is evident when I return to the bar for another Guinness. At home I have phenomenally crap bar presence – I struggle to get served when I'm right at the bar, in the barman's face. Here, even at a bar three deep, on the busiest night of the year, you simply cannot stand in the vague vicinity of the bar without someone leaning over and picking you out from the crowd, in the way I thought only headmasters could, and saying, 'Have you been served?'

But then, genuine hospitality, freely expressed, is a fundamental part of the Irish drinking experience. In England being a barman is something people do as a stopgap, but in Ireland it's the second most respected profession after teaching. In ancient times failure to provide food and drink for guests was an offence, particularly for those higher up in society. The *Crith Gablach*, an old law text dealing with status, states that a king who cannot ensure a supply of beer for his household every Sunday is not a proper ruler, and another text disparages a particular king because his guests did not leave his house 'with the smell of beer on their breath'.

A hospitaller, or *briugu*, was one of the most respected ranks in ancient Celtic society. According to legend, a brewer and a hospitaller were among the first people to land in Ireland after the biblical Great Flood. The rank of *briugu* was a great honour because it was also a great obligation. You had to ensure 'a never-dry cauldron, a dwelling on a public road and a welcome to every face'. Failure to provide food and drink for guests, whatever their means, could result in being stripped of the title. Some older publicans in Ireland still remember their parents and grandparents providing free meals and drink to anyone who turned up at their door asking for help. This attitude is obvious as soon as you arrive. Many countries have a national motto or creed, something ancient in Latin on a coat of arms that usually translates along the lines of 'God at my right' or 'Get off my land'. The Irish national motto, *Cead Mile Failte*, means 'A hundred thousand welcomes'.

*

The next morning I decide to head off any suspicion of a hangover with another huge breakfast followed by a mid-morning Guinness at Kehoe's, a 200-year-old warren of tiny snugs furnished in ancient wood. Supposedly the newest fixtures in here are the light switches, and they look antique. Nothing looks younger than seventy years old, including the punters. Behind the bar sit banks of small wooden drawers, where you'd expect the spirits optics to be. This dates back to when there were too many pubs in Ireland. Many places had to diversify to make ends meet, trading as general stores, drapers, hardware stores, butchers and shoe shops. Drawers like this would have contained tea, tobacco, spices and fla-vourings, until supermarkets and general ownership of cars made mixed trading in pubs obsolete.

I order my Guinness, knowing enough now to give a slight nod and head back to my seat as the barman says, 'I'll bring it down t'ye.'

The only sounds are the air conditioner and the occasional dink of a glass against a beer tap. The sun slants in through high windows, the shafts of light creating one of those perfect, idealized pub settings that only ever exist in staged photos.

As starter's orders at Cheltenham draws closer, Kehoe's gets busier. Until now a familiar hierarchy has been observed – locals at the bar, tourists at the snug tables – but as the bar stools run out, a group of regulars is forced to come and sit near me. There's a slightly less orange David Dickinson, a bloke with a thinning grey mullet, and the Man Who Laughs at Everything. He starts a conversation with the barman.

'John, how are ye?'

'Fine thanks, Sean.'

'A ha ha he he he he.'

'Pint of Guinness is it?'

'That's right, ha ha ha ha ha!'

'There you go.'

'Thanks. A *ha ha ha ha ha ha HAAAARGH*!'

As the hilarity subsides, they fall to talking odds, swapping betting tips, and being respectful to Sheila, the type of dark, brooding barmaid who Irish men go to war for and write songs about while they're on the battlefield, as she brings over the steady supply of Guinness.

I leave Kehoe's as the races start. With only a few hours left in Dublin, I still haven't seen the epicentre of the Irish brewing tradition, a place that for millions around the globe is nothing less than sacred ground.

The Guinness Storehouse opened in 2000 on the site of Arthur's original brewery at St James's Gate. The shell of the building is a century-old, imposing red-brick block designed to hold vast fermenting vessels. These are long gone, leaving cavernous spaces which have become a stunning cathedral to a brand and its creator, one of the most popular tourist attractions in Ireland, and possibly the best beer-related tourist exhibit anywhere in the world. In the centre, a vast 'pint glass' tower block has been erected, at the top of which sits the Gravity Bar. As you'd expect, the bar has emerged as a fierce rival to Mulligan's for the title of Best Guinness in Dublin, influenced in no way by the fact that the first one is included in the admission fee. The view has no challengers: in Gravity, the whole of Dublin and its surrounding hills lies spread out before you.

After his success in Leixlip, Arthur Guinness bought a two-acre site here in 1759. The existing facilities were so poor he managed to strike a deal that gave him the lease on the site for 9,000 years at an annual rent of £45 a year. At the time

Ireland was drinking bad ale and even worse whiskey. After twenty-five years of ale brewing, Arthur started experimenting with porter, London's most popular beer. Soon he was brewing the best porter in Ireland, and by the end of the century Guinness was better than the London porters that had inspired it. By 1799 the brewery had taken the decision to focus on the new drink to the exclusion of all else. Arthur's son, Arthur II, started to include some unmalted barley in the brew and roasted the rest of the malt more heavily, because malted barley was taxed while unmalted barley wasn't. The result was a porter that was darker, fuller-bodied and with a charred flavour. He called this 'extra stout porter', and eventually it became known simply as stout.

Rival brewers could see where Guinness was going, and stooped to increasingly desperate tactics to try to stop it. In 1815, the same year a wounded soldier at Waterloo famously claimed Guinness 'contributed more than anything else to my recovery', the brewers of Pimms Ale warned all decent Irish Catholics not to drink this 'Anti-popery porter'. Pamphlets explained how Guinness was mashing Protestant Bibles and Methodist hymn books into the brew, 'thus impregnating the volatile parts of the porter with the pure ethereal essence of heresy' which would brainwash anyone who drank it. After what can only have been an extraordinary piece of industrial espionage, one pamphlet stated categorically that Guinness had consumed 136,000 tons of Bibles and 501,000 cartloads of hymn books for this purpose.

But superstitious nonsense was no match for generations of inspired management, which used the canal network to spread across Ireland, and Dublin's position on the coast to quickly build up export markets and benefit from economies of scale, and those economies to ruthlessly undercut its rivals. There was also the fact that Guinness simply brewed better beer than anyone else. It was favoured by Robert Louis Stevenson, Charles Dickens and Benjamin Disraeli. By the end of the nineteenth century it was the biggest beer brand in Europe. In the First World War, English porter and stout were effectively wiped out as the government banned the use of dark, highly kilned malts to conserve energy, leaving the way open for the less industrialized Irish to clean up. By the end of the war, Guinness was the biggest beer in the world.

Of course, Arthur Guinness wouldn't recognize his business today. There isn't even a company called Guinness any more; it's now part of Diageo, the world's largest drinks supplier. Guinness itself is experiencing falling sales in Ireland and the UK as younger people drift away from beer and on to spirit mixers such as Smirnoff Ice – which also happens to be a Diageo brand. Around the world, it's a different story. As beer drinkers become more sophisticated, they are turning to the dark, mysterious brew as something special, an intriguing alternative to interchangeable lagers.

Guinness originally followed the British empire around the globe, brewing their Foreign Extra Stout high in alcohol and hops (a natural preservative) to survive long sea voyages. But the colonial tag was one the brewer was keen to shake off by the middle of the twentieth century. When the beer proved popular in newly independent Nigeria in the 1960s, Guinness built a brewery there. The underlying principle for expansion was, 'Guinness cannot expect to make money out of people if it does not allow them to make money out of Guinness.' It meant that within a few years of the brewery being set up, every aspect of the operation, right up to top management, was staffed and run by Nigerians, and the Irish withdrew from day-to-day affairs.

Guinness was originally sold in Nigeria as a tonic as much as an alcoholic drink. Part of its appeal is that its black depths imply virility. African men talk about it putting lead in your pencil, and the unofficial slogan is, 'There's a baby in every bottle.' If a Nigerian woman is feeling frisky, she'll leave a bottle out for when her husband comes home.

Even though a bottle costs half an average day's wages, one in every five beers sold in Nigeria is a Guinness. It is on sale everywhere from beach bars to suburban roadsides, where people sit with barbecue fires in oil drums, selling face-numbing pepper soup, euphemistically named 'bush meat' and bottles of beer to passing motorists.

So successful was Guinness's integration into Nigeria that if a passing Irish tourist was to mention that the beer was also popular in his country, the locals would express surprise and delight that he enjoyed African beer. Now that west Africans have taken over from the Irish as the world's mobile labour force, the 5,000 Nigerians currently living in Dublin are doing what any serious beer lover would: rejecting what they see as fake, Irish Guinness, and demanding the authentic Nigerian stuff. In corner shops across Britain and Ireland, in any area where there is a significant African population there will be the original Guinness from Ireland, Guinness Foreign Extra Stout, the 7.5 per cent brew imported from Africa, and another version of Foreign Extra Stout brewed here to compete with the imported stuff.

Today, the main vehicle driving Guinness around the word is of course the Irish pub, and here in the Storehouse I find a fairly comprehensive answer to the question that brought me to Ireland. Exhibits tell us that there are 1,800 Irish pubs in forty-six countries around the world, and that new ones are opening at the rate of one a day. And that's just the 'official' ones that Diageo/Guinness knows about through its subsidiary, the Irish Pub Company, and its rival the Irish Pub Design and Development Company. These businesses buy the old fixtures and fittings of pubs being renovated in Ireland, and sell them as kits around the world. You can even choose from different models, including the cottage pub, the old brewing house, the shop pub, the Gaelic pub, the Victorian pub and the contemporary pub. Guinness receives 2,000 enquiries a year from people wanting to open Irish pubs. One of the company's PR officers tells me they help to 'consider how they will have an authentic and legitimate Irish pub whether it's in Beijing or Madrid or Buenos Aries'.

According to the Storehouse, Irish pubs are 'a home from home' for the wandering Irish, and 'the home of the *craic*' for everyone else. And here on a tasteful glass screen someone has been brave enough to have a go at defining that elusive good time: 'Friends, people, good times, chat, laughs, dancing, music, food, drink, Guinness . . . an unmistakably Irish atmosphere.' It's obviously right, clearly the closest definition we're going to get in simple words. But despite using so many elements to describe a single idea, it still fails to pin it down: what is the 'unmistakably Irish atmosphere'? I mean that's what the *craic* is really, isn't it? The secret, magic ingredient, the bit that no one is willing or able to break down into words that reveal any more.

Guinness itself has a lot to do with the elusive nature of the *craic*, and is responsible for a large part of the Irish pub feel. As Cian Molloy told me, 'It's a slow pint. You get kids out in

Dublin now downing three vodkas in a matter of minutes and running down the street to the next bar. Three pints of Guinness and you're not running anywhere.' The famous two-part pour takes just under two minutes. The whole thing is about slowing down, taking time out. It's not hard to see how this has an increasing appeal as the world speeds up.

Around the world, people buy a little bit of Irishness when they need to lighten up. Cian Molloy thinks that because the Irish are famous drinkers, the rest of us feel we can misbehave a little if we drink in an Irish pub. 'If you live in a country that's maybe more uptight than we are, you go into an Irish pub and you have an excuse for being drunk. It makes it acceptable.'

There's just enough time left to visit Dublin's oldest pub. Ten minutes down the road from the Storehouse is the Brazen Head, more medieval rooms connected by tiny corridors. The walls and fireplace seemingly date back several centuries and, more tellingly, the red linoleum floor looks like it has seen at least thirty years' service. But when I get into the bar, there isn't an Irish accent to be heard. Half the drinkers are carrying souvenir bags from the Storehouse. There's – *gasp!* – amplified music, seemingly some kind of *Best Celtic Hits in the World Ever!* CD on eternal repeat. A laminated menu explains that 'there are no strangers here, only friends who have never met', and offers Irish stew and soda bread alongside a range of ciabatta sandwiches and panini specials, climaxing with steamed mussels marinara 'alive-alive-oh!'

I feel let down, betrayed, that Dublin's oldest pub is also its most touristy. But what did I expect? That they would keep it deliberately austere, barring entry to all the Italians and Canadians who found it in the same tourist guide as I did, so that I alone could experience the authentic ambience of Irish drinking from days gone by? Well, if I'm honest, yes, that's exactly what I was expecting.

In hindsight, with all the maps and guides and posters of famous Irish pubs, I was always going to get an experience that catered for tourists rather than locals. The one exception of Kavanagh's has merely whetted my appetite for the authentic Irish drinking experience. I need to get beyond Dublin, beyond even Celbridge. If I'm really going to find the legendary *craic*, I need to look further west. I need to go and see Billy and Declan.

Galway

The only direct flight to Galway from London is a twin-propeller plane from Luton Airport. Passenger planes often seem too big to fly until you see one like this, which is obviously too small. The flight is fine, apart from the final two minutes. As we approach Galway, our landing is severely hampered by the fact that the Atlantic Ocean seems to have been relocated into the sky. It's clearly as confused by this as I am, and is having trouble finding its way back. Most of it is falling onto the airport. 'You're very welcome to Galway,' says the stewardess as we aquaplane across the runway. I know it's just the local idiom, but phrasing it this way makes it sound as if she's saying, 'Go on, take it. We don't want it any more.' When the plane finally stops skidding and comes to a juddering merciful halt, those of us in the first ten rows have to stay seated until everyone in the back is off. So we don't tip up.

Declan meets me at the airport. His greying hair makes

him look older than his thirty-six years, and gives him an air of gravitas and serenity that, I imagine, allows him to get away with the kind of behaviour you really don't associate with archaeologists.

'Couple of lap dancers on the plane,' he says as we wade through the airborne sea towards his car.

'Lap dancers? I didn't see anyone who looked like a lap dancer.'

'I recognized them. One of them was a tall girl, dark hair. Billy and I have been known to visit the lap-dancing club. At one point they knew us by our first names.' He pauses as we clear the car park barrier. 'One of them wanted to come and work for us.'

'Work for you?'

'Sure, she was a diver.'

'A lap dancer who was a diver?' I seem to be stuck repeating everything Declan says.

'Yeah, we have an underwater archaeology unit.'

'Oh. Right.'

We meet up with Billy and start the evening in Neachtain's, in the heart of Galway's revitalized city centre. The main streets are pedestrianized, brightly lit with coloured bulbs and full of life. Every other doorway seems to be a pub. This is Ireland's party city. There's the jazz festival in February, the international poetry festival in April, the Film Fleadh, arts festival and Galway races at the end of July, and the international oyster festival in late September. Galway has long been a magnet for musicians, artists, actors and intellectuals, and the streets are always full of buskers and performance artists, many of whom would be worth stopping to look at if the many excellent pubs weren't calling to you.

Billy went to school here with Declan, but he looks much younger. He's very tall, has tight curly hair and the garrulous enthusiasm of a Labrador pup. They're an odd pair you wouldn't naturally expect to see together – temperamentally they seem so different – but every minute I spend in their company over the next day or so is so entertaining I'd pay an admission fee for it if I had to.

Neachtain's is an ancient place, wonky shelves groaning with bottles of whiskey, the wood almost black with age. It still features two of the original snugs, 'for girls from the country', says Declan without elaborating.

The famous politician Richard Martin used this place as his town house in the late eighteenth and early nineteenth centuries. He campaigned passionately for human and animal rights, earning the nickname 'Humanity Dick' for his efforts. While he was away campaigning, he hired Theobald Wolfe Tone as a tutor to his children. Wolfe Tone, later a revered fighter against English occupation, thanked his employer by allegedly shagging Martin's wife Elizabeth, producing more children and ensuring more tutoring work would be there if he needed it. Luckily for him, Martin – who also earned the nickname 'Trigger Dick' thanks to his fondness for duelling – didn't suspect. Otherwise Wolfe Tone may never have lived long enough to mastermind his disastrous attempts at an invasion of Ireland from France at the head of a revolutionary army.

After elaborating on Wolfe Tone's exploits ('He was banging Martin's wife right above our heads!' emphasizes Billy somewhat unnecessarily) Billy and Dec start talking about the recent smoking ban in pubs which has been introduced as part of a total ban on smoking in enclosed workplaces. Some pubs have reported plummeting trade, but those in Galway town centre certainly seem busy enough, and in the main bars at least, everyone is complying with the regulations.

The ban is spawning new drinking customs. Declan points to a pint sitting on an empty table, a beer mat placed on top of the glass. 'That's the smoking signal,' he says. 'It means, I've gone outside for a fag. I haven't finished my drink, don't take it away.' In pubs where many are anxiously eyeing the tables for any sign of a vacant seat, no one moves in to the absent smoker's spot.

The ban has also accelerated the famous Irish pub crawl. Guinness is no longer quite the slow drink it once was. People are anxious to move on so they can smoke between pubs, Billy and Dec in particular. Ten minutes after we arrive, they're bundling me out of Neachtain's and lighting up.

'Obviously it's all right in the summer; it's great to stand or sit outside,' says Declan, 'but then you get the smokers complaining when non-smokers sit at the outdoor tables. You wanted your smoke-free pub, get back in there.'

'Half the time the non-smokers are pissed off with the ban themselves,' says Billy. 'They're feeling left out. All the smokers go outside and have a great time.'

It's harder in winter of course, but it didn't take long for the Irish to come up with some ingenious solutions. Only days after the ban came into force, the BBC reported that a pub owner near Dublin had bought a double-decker bus, parked it beside the pub and declared it a 'smoking bus'. After taking legal advice, he reasoned that if he voluntarily cleaned the bus himself and didn't allow his staff in, he wasn't breaking the new law because the bus wouldn't officially be a place of work. Another Dublin bar removed a windowpane and put in old-fashioned stocks, so desperate customers can stick their heads out through the hole for a smoke. I ask Declan and Billy if they've seen anything like this. They smile and suggest we move on to our next pub.

In the Dew Drop Inn we get our pints and move through the pub to the yard outside. In a narrow passageway on the way to the toilets, among the stored empty beer kegs, the smokers stand chatting and drinking. A few bench seats add to the comfort. But the feature we're really interested in is above us: a roof that keeps out the freezing downpour without officially making this an enclosed space. Wooden poles and hard plastic sheeting stretch halfway across the open passage. 'The law is all about enclosed spaces,' says Declan. 'There was so much debate about it when the ban came in, and they decided that an enclosed space was defined as anything that was 50 per cent or more covered by a roof.' He gestures upwards. 'This is how they got round it.' Above the half-roof, about three feet further up the wall, is an identical half-roof coming the other way. Depending on your point of view, the passage is either 100 per cent enclosed or 100 per cent open. It's a small work of genius.

In every pub we visit the atmosphere feels more like a house party than a town centre bar. Everyone seems to know each other. People mingle. Almost everyone is drinking Guinness, most of them in big rounds. We think we take round-buying quite seriously in England, but it's a point of national pride in Ireland. A real man sticks to his round, and the round is drunk at the fastest man's pace. Everyone has to buy their round, so if you're out in a large group, you'll drink seven or fourteen pints, depending on how big the night is.

It's not uncommon to see new pints being put down in front of people who have fallen asleep or passed out.

We end up in the Crane Bar, one of the most famous pubs in Galway for traditional Irish music sessions. We go upstairs and find bodhran, fiddle and guitar playing gently while people chat away. We talk about tourism, and Billy and Declan, overlapping, tell me about the dolphin that lets women swim with it – only women. Even though the spot where the dolphin hangs out was tricky to find, the farmer who owned the land along the shore soon became frustrated with the number of tourists stopping there. He solved this by painting his own double yellow lines on the offending stretch of road. The plan backfired only because of his short-sightedness. As he only bothered to paint the short stretch on which he didn't want tourists stopping, he succeeded in clearly marking what had until then been a difficult-to-find spot. Now tourist offices simply tell people to look for the yellow lines, and they've found their dolphin.

We're on our fifth or sixth pints now and the stories are coming fast and furious. I've no idea if any of them are true, but it hardly matters.

'Galway's a great place to go out drinking,' starts Dec; 'the only danger is bumping into the animal lover with no arms,'

'Pardon?'

'He's an alcoholic fella who goes in the pubs around Galway. Sure, there was a travelling circus, and he snuck his way in past security to get a look at the tigers and lions, because he liked them so much,' says Billy.

'He decided to pet them—' says Declan.

'And the only way to get into the cage was through the

hatch they use for feeding 'em,' interrupts Billy. 'Now the tigers know the only thing that comes through there is food.'

'So when he puts his arm through to pet them, they rip it clean off. The fella thinks for a bit, decides to try and save his arm . . .'

'He reaches through with the other one to try and grab it. So they take that one off too. So he's got no arms.'

'He passes out, but they find him and take him to hospital and save him.'

'He's got prosthetic arms now, but he won't wear them.'

'So look out for him. You don't want to be drinking in the same pub as him.'

'He'll be there in the toilets, an' if you go in he'll be like, "Err, can ye help me out here?" '

'If you're next to him at the bar he'll ask you to help him out by getting the money out of his trousers—'

'But he'll have pissed himself because he's been waiting in the toilets for so long and no one's gone in because they know he's there—'

'So look out for the animal lover. You'll recognize him—'

'He stinks of piss and he's got no arms.'

Implausibly, there are people shushing. Then I realize this is because someone is about to sing. The music so far has been entirely instrumental. Conversely, it seems the singing will be unaccompanied. A middle-aged man in a red silk shirt and a black fisherman's cap sings 'Sammy's Bar', a typical Irish ballad incorporating love, loss, booze, death and glitzy American cars. The beautiful refrain – 'The last boat's a-leavin'' – has nothing whatsoever to do with the narrative thread of the song, but beds in the requisite air of uniquely Irish bruised romance. It's the crowd's favourite bit, and those who are good enough join in and harmonize. In the pauses between stanzas the entire building is silent apart from the eternal soft hiss of the Guinness taps.

The Guinness is definitely better in Ireland, smoother and silkier. It's been said, perhaps less than seriously, that the reason the Irish are so maudlin abroad and so welcoming at home is down to the quality of the Guinness. It is a pint that intimidates people. But if you think you don't like it, that can only be because you've never drunk it in Ireland.

There's talk now of going out to The Cottage, where they do a lock-in, so we can continue in the flow. But Declan points out that it's Mary's party tomorrow night, so we should probably take it easy just now and conserve our energy. We all accept that this is a good idea, and leave the session in full swing. It's 1.30 a.m.

And that is the most concise, succinct definition of the *craic* that I can offer.

Connemara

'I was staying with nuns in Nairobi—'

'Ah! Tell him about Sean and David Hasselhof and that English girl!'

'Declan came over to spend all my money—'

'And the time we stumbled across that midnight mass in the bush and had to knock up the people in the mud hut to ask where we lived!'

We're together again, in Declan's car, heading out into Connemara on a Saturday afternoon that has already managed to pack in three springs, a brief summer, two crisp autumns and several long dark winters. Declan is driving the outbound leg, and Billy has agreed to stay off the pints until this evening and take over as designated driver. 'My mate Pete was going to drive, but he had to go and measure a child,' says Billy.*

The purpose of this trip is to show me a few traditional pubs outside the city. This is where the John Wayne film *The Quiet Man* was shot, and it has come to define a vision of brooding, desolate Irish beauty ever since. We skirt around Lough Corrib, the largest lake in the Republic of Ireland, through fecund peat bogs and below massive balding granite mountains that look more solid than anything else in the whole world.

Where the road crosses the Bealanabrack River at the Maam Bridge stands Keane's pub. A funeral party is just getting going. The deceased grew up locally, lived in London for most of his life and requested that his ashes be scattered here. 'Help yourselves to sandwiches now,' insists one of the mourners. As we take our seats in the front bay window of the spartan public bar, looking back out over the valley we've driven through, shafts of bright wintry sun break through the

---

*   Billy's friend Pete really does have a job measuring children. People apply for their kids to be used as team mascots at sporting events, and it's important that they are below a certain height, otherwise they obscure the all-important sponsorship signage on TV and in photographs. Pete has to measure prospective candidates to make sure they really are the height the parents are claiming.

(After this chapter was written, Pete the Child Measurer got a new job. There's this bloke he knows who has a luxury yacht moored down in the Mediterranean. Every few weeks Pete has to fly down there and turn the engine over, take her out for a bit of a spin, generally make sure that everything is all right. He is also more successful with girls than any other man in Galway.)

clouds above the biggest mountains. I'd like to stay in this pub – in this particular seat – for the rest of my life.

But Ireland play Scotland in the Six Nations rugby in half an hour and there's no TV here. So we move on along the north side of the lough, past the ruined monastery on a small island, and into the village of Cong, which seems to sit on the water itself. I resolve to come back here with my ten-year-old son for a father–son bonding fishing trip at the earliest opportunity. I don't have a ten-year-old son – or any children at all, yet. And I don't enjoy fishing. But that's the effect the place has on you. And possibly because we're in such perfect surroundings, Ireland thrash Scotland.

The sun is setting as we head back towards Galway, and it's dark when Billy decides we should stop off at his local, about twenty minutes outside the city. But Campbell's Tavern is locked and unlit. Undeterred, Billy leads us to the back door and into a maze of bars. We meet Orla, the barmaid, who confirms that the place doesn't open for another hour and a half. Thirty seconds of Billy charm later, she says, 'Are you boys absolutely *gasping* for a drink?' We all nod, she gives in and starts pouring the Guinness, specs askew on her nose, swearing constantly but pleasantly. Billy says, 'Pete here's writing a book on beer and pubs around the world; that's why he's here. You might be in it, Orla!' The trouble with Billy saying this is that even I don't believe him, and clearly Orla doesn't. Nevertheless, she gives us our pints.

But Billy is right. I hadn't actually pieced the thought together before now, but I realize that I am in fact going to write a book on beer and pubs around the world. These visits to Spain, the Czech Republic and Ireland are the start of something much bigger. What began as idle curiosity about how the pints-and-curry British night out compares with continental drinking – a simple reaction to being goaded by some Czech chocolate marketers – is becoming a dangerous obsession.

I've embarked on a global tour of beer drinking culture by mistake.

Even if the underlying principles of drinking are similar around the world, and even as beers such as Budweiser and Heineken try to dominate globally, it strikes me now that some of the most important aspects of drinking remain belligerently diverse. While there are strong similarities in beer culture across continents thousands of miles apart, there are glaring differences in drinking behaviour across national borders. Here and in the UK beer is drunk in pints and half-pints, and if you value your manhood it'll be a pint every time. Spanish men – and women – have a far more macho culture but are quite happy to drink from 200-millilitre glasses. Bavarians drink by the litre. In northern Europe beer is seen as old-fashioned and uncool; in southern Europe it's new and trendy. In the UK lager has become the only beer to be seen drinking in the most fashionable bars, whereas in the New York equivalent you really should be holding an ale or stout, derided as hopelessly naff in most London watering holes. Table or bar service? Bottled or draught? Foreign or home-grown? Pubs or bars – and what exactly is the difference there anyway?

Every place I go raises more questions, and the idea of going somewhere else in search of answers is the only way forward. Reading about a traditional Irish music session is no substitute for hearing it first-hand like I did last night. Seeing people go misty-eyed when they recall oompah music – yes, oompah music – at Oktoberfest, watching them start to swing air-steins in time to a trombone only they can hear, I know I have to get inside those giant tents for myself. I want to feel the bite of a painfully cold lager cut through the dust of the Australian outback, wash down *moules et frites* with lemony Belgian wheat beers and have beer with sushi in neon-lit karaoke bars with red-faced Japanese salarymen. So far I've noticed similarities and differences in beer drinking culture across Europe. Are the similarities superficial or profound? Are the differences fundamental or transitory? Is there such a thing as a global beer drinking culture, or is it all determined by national characteristics? My legs go weak when I realize the enormity of what I've begun.

But the Irish part is almost over. I have a plane to catch, the first of many more. We say goodbye to Orla, and leave the pub just as it opens.

I have managed to answer some questions on this visit. I've discovered why Irish pubs are the best in the world: they take the basic elements of the pub and present them in a purer, simpler form, free from brewery ties and the concerns of big business. They don't try too hard to keep up with the times; they can just relax and be themselves. Irish pubs are the dreams English pubs have when they're closed.

And I know that I've experienced the *craic*. I know what it is now. I may be no closer to being able to describe it, but I think this is part of the point – you're always chasing it. If you want to know it for yourself, I can recommend the perfect place. Just watch out for the animal lover with no arms.

5

'The smell of freshly poured beer is the smell of my country'

London

Liz takes the news of my newly defined quest remarkably well.

'That's great! You'll enjoy doing that,' she says.

'What, so you don't mind me going off around the world drinking beer?'

No, I think you'll find it really interesting. And you need a break from all the work you've been doing. I bet it would make a really nice book.'

'But I'll be away from you for long periods of time.'

'I'll catch up with people like Joy and Debs and have some girlie nights in. In fact Debs knows some people in Belgium and Australia she could put you in touch with.'

'It'll cost me a lot of money.'

'It's your money, lovely. You've earned it; it's up to you how you spend it. Where will you go then?'

'Well, Oktoberfest in Germany is a must. It's a few months away, so I'll spend the summer going everywhere else. I'll have to go to America, and, oh God, if I'm going to do this properly I'll have to go to Australia, and to China because that's the world's biggest beer country by volume now. That could be quite dangerous.'

'No, it won't. Loads of people go travelling to China.'

'So you're not going to try and talk me out of it then? You don't think it's a really stupid idea?'

'You're nervous about travelling, aren't you?'

'No . . .'

'You are! Well don't use me as an excuse not to do it. I think you definitely should.'

I should have known. Liz has always been the spontaneous, adventurous one in our relationship. No one believes she's a few years older than me because she has the garrulous enthusiasm for life of someone twenty years younger. She's one of those people who energizes a room when she walks in. It was naive of me to think she might give me an excuse to drop my idea of a global quest to find the meaning of beer. In fact, this whole idea is more like something she might do.

'Where are we going first then?'

'We?'

'Well, if there are interesting places I'll come with you. You can go with Chris or your other friends to places like Oktoberfest because I bet it will be horrid. But I'd love to go to China. I'm coming to Australia with you. We can see my cousins Tom and Alec. And you'll need a female perspective. We drink beer as well, you know.'

'Right. Well, I was thinking, I've seen some varied styles of drinking across Europe. And I was wondering what would happen if you mixed them all together. And then I thought, there's a place where that's actually happened. Somebody ages ago was telling me about the EU quarter in Brussels, where people from all across Europe go out drinking together. So I thought I'd go to Belgium.'

'Isn't Belgium really boring?'

'No.'

'Hmm. I'll just join you at the weekend then.'

'Oh. OK. I'll start, um, organizing things.'

A few weeks later, I'm boarding a plane to Brussels. My seat is in the first row behind the curtain that separates us from business class, from where you can hear the champagne corks and laughter and smell the gourmet meals. I'm in the window seat, which means I have to ask the smartly grey-suited young man in the aisle seat to move. He doesn't look at all pleased by this.

'*Don't* tread on the briefcase,' he snaps, clambering out of his seat.

'Well, *don't* leave "the" briefcase in the middle of the floor where I have to stride over it, you pompous cock,' I retort telepathically, glaring at him as he sits back down and reopens his *Daily Mail* with an impatient flourish, like he's seen people do on adverts for business travel.

I dearly want to get out my laptop to show that my penis is at least as big as his, but the flight is only forty minutes long, and the laptop takes almost that long to boot up these days. I've barely had time to take a bite of my 'sandwich' and hand the remains back to the stewardess in silent horror before we're coming in to land.

For a proper foreign country, Belgium is unfeasibly close to the UK. Brussels is the same distance from London as Barnsley is in the opposite direction. We descend over a patchwork of fields similar to the UK, but neater and lusher. Angular canals, lined by immaculate rows of poplar trees, slice decisively through the fields. As we near the ground I'm struck by the fact that churches are easily the tallest buildings in the dotted villages, as if the Belgians are frightened of building upwards and spoiling the flatness. As we touch down, even the airport control tower peeks apologetically just over the trees.

Grey Suit has finished his *Daily Mail* and is now reading an article in *Business Traveller*. He doesn't look up once as we come in to land. This is an important touch; if you're pretending to be an important business traveller, it's vital that you give the appearance that the whole process of shooting through the air at 500 miles an hour before arriving in a country where everything is familiar but different, like the world in a bad-cheese dream, is the dreariest experience imaginable. I wish I had trodden on 'the' bloody briefcase.

Thinking this, I realize I'm excited and very happy to be here. I'm glad Liz refused to talk me out of doing this. It's going to be an adventure. And if you think excitement is a strange reaction to arriving in Belgium, that can only be because you have no idea how wonderfully bizarre this much-derided country can be.

Brussels

In its history, Belgium has been the property of France, the Netherlands, Austria and Spain. After Waterloo, the Congress of Vienna redrew the map of Europe, creating the United Kingdom of the Netherlands out of the north Netherlands –

which had been independent since 1648 and corresponds to the modern-day Netherlands – and a territory variously known as the Spanish and the Austrian Netherlands – modern-day Belgium.

Everyone agreed that this new kingdom would be a handy buffer state between France and Prussia. Everyone, that is, apart from the inhabitants of the former Spanish/Austrian Netherlands, mostly Catholic, who didn't take too kindly to being ruled by the Protestant Dutch. In 1830 a performance of a banned opera about the Naples rebellion of 1647 convinced the inhabitants of Brussels that they would prefer independence, and they started the Belgian revolution. In 1831 the great powers met in London. Britain suggested the creation of an independent Belgian state. France and Germany agreed, even though years later De Gaulle described Belgium bitterly as 'a country invented by the English to annoy the French'.

Modern Belgium consists of two parts: Flanders to the north, where people speak accented Dutch, and Wallonia to the south, speaking accented French. Oh, and a couple of cantons of German speakers. Brussels exists in the middle, a compromise capital that doesn't belong to either half, and speaks Dutch, French, English and German. Belgians invented pigeon racing, chips and the saxophone. We can forgive them that last one because when they brought hops to Britain, they invented modern beer too. Moreover, the Great Gilles Carnival in the town of Binche involves a parade of people wearing huge headdresses made of ostrich feathers pelting spectators with oranges to the beat of frenzied drumming, and gave us the word binge.

'The smell of freshly poured beer is the smell of my country'

And, bizarrely, the British still labour under the misapprehension that this is a boring country.

Belgium seems always to have been in the wrong place at the wrong time. The French historian Jules Michelet described the country as 'the meeting place of wars' where 'the blood does not have time to dry'. Waterloo was fought here, as was most of the First World War. After so long as Europe's battleground, it makes some kind of sense that Belgium is now the home of Europe's government.

I look out of the window of the cab at the glass and metal walls of Brussels' EU quarter. A city that had brief flashes of Paris back around my hotel suddenly resembles Manhattan.

'There is a lot of new building here,' says the driver.

'You wonder why they need any more buildings, with so many already,' I say.

'It is the same as with world wars.' He shrugs. 'Never-ending.'

Thursday is the big night in the EU quarter because everyone goes home for the weekend on Friday. Every bar is rammed with grey suits, all of them a bit excitable after taking off their ties and loosening their top buttons for the evening. And they all seem to be drinking pints of Stella Artois. I suppose I shouldn't be too surprised – Stella is a Belgian beer after all – but blokes in suits standing around clusters of briefcases, pints in hand, feels like something I should have left behind when I boarded the plane at Heathrow. They may be speaking French to each other but the behaviour, the atmosphere around drinking, is definitely English.

I move on, deeper into the zone, closer to the massive glass

edifices around Place Schuman, home of the European Com-
mission and the Council of Ministers. I stop at a stall, pass on
a deep-fried snack advertised as 'cheese crack', and order some
frites. There are twenty different sauces to choose from, and
I feel cruelly cheated when I realize that every single one of
them is mayonnaise with something else mixed in.

After finishing the *frites* I need a beer to counter the mayo.
I follow a group of Irish, Spanish and Italian eurocrats – all
speaking English with the occasional lapse into French –
through the door of the Hairy Canary, an Irish theme pub
that advertises its opening hours as noon till 3 a.m. The
eurocrats all order glasses of *kriek*, a cherry beer, while I opt
for Brugs wheat beer, which the Irish barman serves in a
Kilkenny pint glass. The walls are covered in old photos of the
Beatles, Rod Stewart, the Mallard steam engine and ancient
advertisements for English walnuts. I manage to grab a seat
next to a German and an Italian having a furious argument in
English about a piece of paper. An Irishman and a Spaniard
greet each other with kisses on both cheeks.

From the Hairy Canary I follow the increasingly visible
packs of multinational pub crawlers to O'Dwyers, and then to
James Joyce's. When you mix all the colours of the rainbow
together, you get brown. Mix all the drinking cultures of
Europe together, and you get an Irish pub – or rather an Irish
theme pub, which is essentially an English pub with a bit of
Gaelic tat on the walls.

So I have another question answered, and I can't help
feeling disappointed by it. Maybe it's just that I'm looking
for an experience different from the one I get back home,
but I can't help thinking that faux Anglo-Irish pubs simply
represent drinking at its lowest common denominator. It's

not something anyone sane would travel specially to take part in. Just as well then that outside the EU quarter Belgium is arguably the most mind-expanding country on the planet if you're thinking about beer. I decide I need to explore the rest of it.

It should be no surprise that on the international beer scene Belgium plays the role of eccentric uncle. George Simenon said, 'The smell of freshly poured beer is the smell of my country,' and people have said that what France is to wine, Belgium is to beer. This is true as far as it goes, but imagine if the French suddenly started mixing different vintages and *crus* together to see what happened, or left wine open to the elements, or started bunging cherries, raspberries, strawberries, dried orange peel, ginger, figs, aniseed or honey into it, and you start to get a better picture of the Belgian beer scene. For serious beer lovers, Belgium is a playground where you leave your preconceptions and preferences at the airport or Eurostar terminal. From pilsners, red and brown ales to wild, spontaneously fermenting *lambics*, fruit beers, white beers, spiced beers, beers produced by Trappist monks and beers of up to 12 per cent alcohol, it's a never-ending journey of discovery.

Even non-aficionados are starting to catch on that there's something different here, thanks in part to the dramatic recent growth of Interbrew, Belgium's biggest brewer, now known as Inbev.* Unlike many other products, when it comes to beer,

---

* When I started writing this book, Interbrew was the third biggest brewer in the world. By the time I finished it, Inbev was runaway leader, having merged with the South American giant Ambev. By the time you read this it will probably have changed its name again and could well have formed the first global government.

people around the world are still pretty loyal to their local tipple. Among the huge global brewers, Inbev are the ones who sort of accept this. They're as doggedly determined as Heineken, SABMiller, Coors and Anheuser-Busch that their global brands will be the biggest and most loved on the planet, but Inbev also promote a range of 'speciality beers'. Consequently, drinkers around the world are slowly developing a taste for unusual Belgian brews like Hoegaarden and Leffe. On any bar, the former in particular is going to look a little strange: served in a glass bucket, pale and naturally cloudy, it messes with your ideas of what beer should look and taste like.

But if you think Inbev's speciality brands are strange and interesting, you've seen nothing until you pick up a beer list in a typical Belgian bar. There are around 120 breweries in this small country producing around 500 different beers in ten or twelve major styles, which divide into around fifty or sixty sub-categories. Leffe and Hoegaarden are the alternative rock groups who have signed to a major label and provoked cries of 'Sell-out!' from purist fans.

I decide to ease myself in by speaking to Inbev, who I know from work I did with them on Stella Artois.

Leuven

It's with some wariness that I board the train to Leuven. The train timetables are unsettling. Instead of finding your destination then looking up what time the next train leaves, you have to refer to the time first and see what trains leave at that point. It's difficult to work out if you're thinking, I need to get to Leuven; what time can I get there? but perfect if your need is, I've got to get out of here now; where can I go in the next ten minutes?

That aside though, Belgian trains are punctual, tickets are cheap, platforms are clearly signposted, and the staff don't treat me like a criminal (I'm definitely not in London any more). On the train a polite ticket inspector asks, *'S'il vous plaît?'* for my ticket, says, 'Thank you,' in English when I give it to her, and says something in Dutch as she hands it back to me.

You can't help noticing that Leuven is much more Dutch than Brussels, a mere twenty kilometres away. We are in Flanders, the Dutch-speaking part of Belgium, but Leuven is almost aggressively Dutch, if that's not too ridiculous a thing to say. But more than that, the first thing you notice about Leuven is Inbev. Admittedly the train is slowing down, but it takes us almost two minutes to pass the Artois brewery. Storage tanks stand sixty feet high. Mountains of crates await refilling on one side, collection on the other. Squadrons of lorries lumber about. Giant Stella Artois logos, old and new, dominate various buildings and towers across the complex.

This is, in part, a pilgrimage. My professional interest in beer began when I was working on Stella's UK advertising, and during three years on that job I never once managed to blag a visit to this, the brand's home. Our relationship has been a little strained of late. I've been flirting with all these new, eclectic, exciting beers, and have grudgingly accepted that, for all the great times we've had together, Stella is not the most interesting beer in the world. Stella for her part has been putting it about a bit, steadily stealing the sensibilities of young lads on Friday nights in every town and city across the UK. But your first love never dies. I have some time to kill, so

I stop at the Piazza Brasserie on the Martelplein, a curiously synthetic-looking square facing the train station, and order a sandwich and a beer.

I feel a little nervous, like meeting up with a former lover I haven't seen for some time. The beer arrives in a curvaceous, tulip-shaped goblet. It has the most beautiful golden colour, served with a full inch of foamy head. It looks perfect. There's a light aroma suggestive of summer fields, and the taste is perfectly balanced – satisfyingly malty and wonderfully bitter. So it's not challenging. So it's not a riot of different flavours. So what? It's a warm summer afternoon, and there can be no better beer for the moment.

It's hard to reconcile the beer in front of me with the 'wifebeater' of English urban legend. At 5.2 per cent, Stella is a little stronger than most other premium lagers, but there are far stronger beers drunk widely in Belgium. The difference is that here people don't drink pints. At home it doesn't matter what the beer is, how potent it is; it has to be drunk by the pint or you're a bit of a girl. People have often asked me why Stella gets them so utterly trashed compared to other beers. Now I know: it's because they're drinking it wrong.

Frederic de Radigues agrees. Half an hour after I've finished my beer I'm sitting in his corner office in the Artois brewery. The Inbev marketer talks passionately, constantly drawing diagrams to help illustrate his points. 'If I go for a beer with you now,' he says, 'we'd just have a Jupiler or a Stella Artois, because sadly we would only have five minutes to talk. But if we go to drink tonight, we would probably have a Leffe because we have more time, an hour or two.'

'So you're saying you choose a beer depending on how long you have to drink it?'

'Yes. How else would you do it?'

'In England we would drink a pint of strong beer in the same time as a pint of weaker beer. So you order a stronger beer if you want to get more drunk.'

Frederic looks aghast. I'm sure this is not the first time he's heard about British drinking habits, but sitting here the contrast does seem to be particularly marked.

'Beer has a social role,' he continues. 'A beer like Leffe, with more body – it would be a waste of money and a waste of pleasure to drink it very quickly. In Belgium we have a certain respect for what is in the glass.'

While the surprising truth is that most Belgians like to drink straightforward lagers just like everyone else, the demand for Inbev's speciality beers is reassuringly strong and dynamic. '*Gueuze* was the biggest back in 1970,' says Frederic. 'In the mid-seventies it was British beer and amber beers. In the mid-eighties it was wheat beers, then Abbey beer. Now fruit beer is growing very quickly. The consumer is always searching for different taste experiences.'

I ask him if Belgians are proud of their contribution to the world of beer. 'Belgium is not a proud population,' he replies. 'We have done some fantastic stuff, yes, but we do not go on about it. If you want to discover us you can, but we won't tell you how great we are. Because we are not that convinced we are great.'

It strikes me that this is like the country itself. Brussels doesn't put out like other capital cities. Take a quick look, and it's grey and bland. But take the time to get to know it and it reveals beautiful and interesting depths. Belgians are happy with what they have, and seem almost to prefer it if the rest of us don't notice how great it is here.

My time is nearly up. 'Can you recommend any good bars I should visit?' I ask.

'I have prepared a small list . . .'

Next, I meet Sabine Sagaert, another Inbev marketer. She's a little more forceful about Belgian pride, as she is about most things, but we're still a long way from flag-waving territory. 'Beer for Belgians is the same as wine for French people. It is the roots, the history of the country. All the ingredients of beer are in your back garden here. In general there is pride about beer culture among Belgians. They do recognize how special their beer is around the world. Visit the supermarket and it immediately gives you an impression of what beer means to Belgians. You see the lagers – common, everyday stuff – then you see the speciality beers. They are good for almost nothing in terms of volume, but retailers find it very important to sell it. People expect a very large choice of speciality beers. In fact, you should visit some supermarkets and beer shops as well as some bars. I have prepared a small list . . .'

An hour later I'm sitting in the cafe at Leuven train station. If this was a British train station, I'd be sitting in a tiny, cramped Lemon Tree caff, if I was lucky enough to find one that was open and had seats in it. If I was really desperate for a beer, I might have been able to buy a can of Stella for a couple of quid, and if it was one of the classier branches of the chain, I might have got a plastic beaker to drink it out of. Here, on the platform of Leuven station, I'm in an elegant, airy space where tall windows stretch to a thirty-foot-high ceiling. A waiter brings me a glass of Stella in its correct, branded tulip glass. He places a branded drip mat on the marble-topped table and gently sets the glass down, its painted logo directly facing me.

On the next table are three men in their late forties: one has a Leffe Brune, one a Leffe Blonde, the third a Duvel. I know this because, again, each one is in its unique, branded glass. The smart woman in her late thirties sitting alone across the room has an Orval. The elderly couple in the corner are each nursing a Hoegaarden.

Checking the lists of bars and shops prepared for me, I realize five days is nowhere near long enough to do justice to Belgium. The consolation is that there doesn't seem to be a crappy bar in the whole country.

Brussels

It's a dull, rainy afternoon. I walk through unlovely streets as mundane and grey as home. Mundane, that is, until I reach the Grand Place. Even the leaden skies and freezing mid-July rain cannot dampen this magnificent square. The broad, cobbled, traffic-free space is filled during the day with market stalls selling flowers. The fifteenth-century Hôtel de Ville (which has never been a hotel) takes up almost the whole of one side, its facade covered with scores of carved figures, chivalric flags hanging above them. The Maison du Roi (which has never been a royal palace) stands opposite, and the Hôtel Saint-Michel (which, amazingly, is a hotel) dominates the eastern end of the square with yet another imposing but delicate facade. Between these three buildings are the tall, narrow guild houses, each one ornately decorated.

The smell of waffles and an infinite number of other products cooked or baked with an awful lot of butter becomes inescapable. It's said here that, 'While the French love food, Belgians love to eat,' and, 'If France is the gastronomic heart of Europe, then Belgium is the continent's stomach.' Brussels has 1,500 restaurants and more Michelin stars per head than France, but they seem as partial to artery-clogging fare from street stalls as they do to fine cuisine.

I leave the square and head north up rue de Montagne – 'mountain street' of course – a name which possibly reveals a biting sense of humour hitherto unsuspected among Belgians, given that the street gains maybe ten feet of height over its length, in what is otherwise a very flat city.

At the top, in surprisingly good shape after my climb, I find Mort Subite. As far as I know, this is the only bar to have inspired a ballet, written by one of its more famous patrons, Maurice Béjart. The nicotine-yellow walls are scuffed and chipped, the ceiling blotchy. The ten-foot-high mirrors are mottled, their gilt surrounds stained brown. With its antique coat hooks, stained-glass windows and long strips of tables, I could be drinking here at any point in the last century. It's just after 5 p.m. and the place is buzzing. Over half the bar's patrons are women, and every one of them is drinking beer from small, bulb-shaped glasses: bright red beer, muddy brown beer and the odd black beer thrown in here and there. I've never seen a bar quite like it. It feels like coming home.

Like every decent Belgian bar, there's a long menu of beers to choose from. But amid all this choice there's something I have to face. I decide to get it over with, jump in at the weird end, and order a *gueuze*. Whatever expectations you might have of a beer, a *lambic* or *gueuze* (pronounced *gerzer*) will confound them. *Gueuze* beers are unique to Belgium, and are brewed with wild, natural, airborne yeasts rather than the carefully cultivated laboratory-kept yeasts used in every other beer in the world. The result is a character that's complex, unpredictable and not to everyone's taste.

Mort Subite *gueuze* is about the same colour as a rosé wine, but cloudy with a tight, foamy head. It has an aroma of apples and very ripe fruit. And the first sip makes my tongue explode. It's definitely sour, a fact that has alarmed various parts of my mouth and sent it into spasms that cause me to pout and wince at a couple sitting across the bar. No, it's sweet and sour. By the third sip it tastes like cider – yes, definitely Woodpecker. After that, I start to like it. The flavours of fruit, beer and – it's definitely there – cheap cider enjoy a Tarantinoesque Mexican stand-off on my tongue. Even though it's not particularly strong in alcohol, it takes me an hour to drink my 330-millilitre glass.

This gives me time to worry about the bilingual bar snack menu, which has an altogether darker feel to it than the menus Chris and I chuckled over in Madrid. It starts innocently and predictably enough: *croque-monsieur* is translated simply as 'gentleman's toast', while *croque-madame* is 'women's toast'. Nice of them to take the trouble and all that, but hardly worth the bother really, was it? Further down though, the menu gets odd. I know what steak tartare is, but its friendly local nickname is *cannibale*. And what's this? *Tête pressé*. Oh God, I know what that means. It means pressed head. A pressed head sandwich. And yet the English translation, trying to put on an innocent front, is 'Brussels meat'. I don't know which is more disturbing: what the sandwich is in French, or the way they've tried to cover it up in the translation. And while we're at it, isn't it odd that Mort Subite, the name of both the bar and the beer I'm drinking, means Sudden Death?* I'm not sure whether they're trying to mess with my brain, or persuade me to eat someone else's.

I try a few more bars, and sample beers that only seem normal because I just had a *gueuze*. Westmalle Dubbel is chocolate brown, 7 per cent ABV and coats the tongue with a spicy, burnt bitterness. Westmalle Trippel is a whopping 9.5 per cent, which while tasting strong (not all beers at this level do) is a pleasant, complex, balanced drink with hints of orange and banana rather than a brutish alcoholic hit. By eight thirty I'm feeling pleasantly mellow, but despite the potency of the beers I'm not remotely drunk. Their complex characters prevent anyone without a serious drinking problem from downing them too quickly, which makes them extraordinarily enjoyable.

Later in Chez Leon, one of the many restaurants just off the Grand Place, I go for a complimentary glass of Maes with the inevitable *moules et frites* – mussels and chips, the Belgian national dish. I've gone off mussels a little since I realized how much they resemble the head of the creature from the *Alien* films if you get them out of the shell intact, but these are excellent – like you would expect them to be, only better.

Maes is a straightforward pilsner lager, and the second-biggest-selling beer in the country. For all Belgium's wonderful beery weirdness, pilsners account for 80 per cent of all the beer drunk here. I'd be the first to admit that Maes doesn't have a shred of the character of the other beers I've tried so

---

* They claim it's the name of a popular card game which used to be played here. But they would say that, wouldn't they?

far, but it's clean and crisp, a nice refresher after the heavy beers I've been drinking.

The restaurant is busy with happy families and couples, tourists and locals. It's a pleasant spot, until I ruin things by snorting beer down my nose. I can't help it. Above my table there is a certificate, proudly proclaiming Chez Leon to be an ambassador of tourism in several languages. That's *ambassadeur de tourisme* in French. *Ambassadeur van het toerisme* in Dutch. Or *Tourismus Botschafter* in German.

I think I'm like most British men in that as I get older, I obviously become more mature. But it doesn't matter how rounded and worldly I become, my inner schoolboy is always there, watching and waiting for moments like this. As soon as he sees the word *Botschafter*, he's gleefully texting all my adult friends with the news while I order another beer.

I wait to see if anyone texts back, but no one seems as excited by the word *Botschafter* as I am. And then an eight-year-old boy runs past my table and shouts at his parents in the voice of a fully grown man. I haven't made a mistake: he's definitely a child rather than a very small adult. And that man's voice definitely just came out of his mouth. He vanishes abruptly before saying anything else. Now that's not right.

And then fragments from the day that I've blocked out until now begin to fall into place: the man pacing slowly up and down rue de Charbon in a karate suit, talking to himself and punching the air. The coach full of identical Japanese nuns. The two paraplegics racing their electric wheelchairs down a cobbled street, one of them (the winner) with a dwarf hanging off the back. And I remember: Belgium is the home of surrealism. I think of the pressed head sandwich. It's in the air. It's institutionalized. This is not just a case of, 'You want to watch Jacques, he's the office joker. *Completely* mad at the last Christmas party.' I mean, chips and mayonnaise, for God's sake.

When we were in sixth form at school, whenever we did something Mad! it was always surreal as well.* But surrealism is more than just Mad! or wacky; it's about releasing the language and imagery of dreams into everyday life, as demonstrated by famous Belgians – yes, famous Belgians – such as René Magritte, Paul Delvaux and James Ensor. It's also demonstrated by a country that has a beer called Kwak and is responsible for *lambic* and *gueuze*, and whose national symbol is a small urinating boy who stands just outside my next destination.

The Café Poechenellekelder stands just across the road from the most famous Belgian statue in the world: an eighteen-inch-high figure of a little chap having a piss. The statue is smaller than you expect, nestling in an alcove six feet up on a street corner, and would be easy to miss were it possible to approach this tiny landmark from any direction without fighting your way through Manneken Pis souvenir shops, Manneken Pis themed cafes, signs telling you how close you are to the Manneken Pis, and banners simply celebrating the existence of the Manneken Pis.

So you reach it . . . and it's a tiny statue of a boy having a piss. Admittedly he's really enjoying his piss, way more than he has any right to, leaning back and firing it out at a showy angle. Perhaps there's some artistic merit in that – it really

---

* Mad! always has an exclamation mark when you're between about fourteen and nineteen years old, even when it's sitting in the middle of a sentence.

captures the glee that small boys feel when they're pissing anywhere other than in a toilet – but it still doesn't explain why the statue is so famous, why it is to Belgium what Big Ben is to England, or the Statue of Liberty is to the USA. Perhaps it's the different outfits he is occasionally mysteriously dressed in, always with flies down to allow him to continue pissing uninterrupted. Perhaps it's his range of jaunty hats. I don't know, and I don't care. Thinking back to De Gaulle, you have to start wondering whether this whole country isn't an elaborate Monty Python sketch.

I'm not the only person to have been profoundly irritated by the Manneken Pis. He was stolen by the British in 1745, then again by the French in 1777. In 1817 a French ex-convict smashed him to bits, and was jailed for life. They managed to glue the statue back together, and he's been mildly disappointing tourists ever since.

I'm baffled until I spot a yellowed, framed press cutting on the wall of Café Poechenellekelder. It dates from the Second World War, and shows a cartoon Mannekin Pis, wearing a Belgian cap, pissing on a bunch of panic-stricken Nazis under the headline *'Pourquois Pas?'*, with the slogan *'Delivrance!'* in block letters across the bottom. Suddenly I understand: he's the embodiment of the Belgian national character. Belgium could never have an Eiffel Tower or a Statue of Liberty – that would be far too obvious, too gauche. Belgium is a plucky, anarchic nation that lives for eating, drinking and taking the piss. The whole existence of the country – the story of its creation, the two different, mismatched halves with their different languages, each borrowed from neighbours they hate – really is the world's most elaborate practical joke. Throughout history they have pissed people off just because they find it funny. Even resistance to the jackboot had to have irreverent and mildly distasteful humour leavened into it. And the biggest joke of all is that it's now the capital of Europe. EU bureaucracy horror and bizarre regulatory decisions now make perfect sense as more Belgian gags at everyone else's expense. Belgium presents a boring image to the rest of the world, and hides behind it, sniggering. What else could such a bunch of people possibly have for an icon?

The next morning I head over to the Brasserie Cantillon et Musée Bruxellois de la Gueuze, an unassuming building in a gloomy, nondescript street in Anderlecht that houses one of the wonders of the brewing world. At Cantillon, they make *lambic* and *gueuze*. Here in Anderlecht there's something magical in the air.

Like any beer writer, I can, and probably will, wax lyrical about all the ingredients that make up beer. But the catalyst that transmutes these base substances into liquid gold (or brown or red or black) is yeast. We've only really understood the behaviour of yeast – really known what it is – for the last 130 years. Before that we knew there was something, but it was seen as so miraculous it was sometimes referred to as godisgoode (we can all turn water into wine, given a bit of fermentation time). The earliest brewers simply left their bowls and jars of wet barley out in the open air, and natural airborne yeasts would descend, froth away, and leave an alcoholic beverage in their wake. There are countless different strains of yeast, each imparting its own flavour. Depending on the luck of the draw, some yeasts would produce a beverage that tasted great, others would not. Over time, brewers could identify particular areas where the invisible airborne inhabitants produced the best beer. In the west of Brussels the beer was so good they carried on making it like that even after everyone else started using scientifically isolated and cultivated yeasts. Beers fermented naturally in this way are known as *lambics*.

With a young *lambic* there's still a large degree of pot luck as to what it will taste like. These beers tend to be sour and acidic, but subtleties of taste beyond that are anyone's guess. The beer is then aged in oak barrels, often for years, and as *lambics* mature they mellow and grow more complex. The brewer selects different, contrasting *lambics*, old and young, and mixes them to produce *gueuze*. There's no scientific method to this – producing a beer that people will enjoy is entirely down to the brewer's intuition, skill and judgement. As you have probably guessed, Belgium is the only country in the world that still makes beer this way.

A century ago there were eighty *lambic* breweries in Brussels; now there's just Cantillon. Their beers sell all over the world and are as revered by people with better palates than mine as much as the rarest malt whisky or vintage wine. The brewery has been in the same family since it was founded in 1900, and I'm greeted at reception by the great-granddaughter of the original founder, Madame Claude Van Roy. Her husband Jean-Pierre now manages the brewery. He looks up briefly and nods, while his wife gives a quick rundown of the place and the brewing process.

'The brewery is very quiet just now. We are brewing the bitter *lambic* beers only from October,' she explains. 'But we are now making the fruit beers. The first delivery of raspberries arrived yesterday. We receive the first cherries soon.'

Ah yes, the fruit beers.

As if *lambic* and *gueuze* were not strange enough already, many have raspberries or cherries added to the barrels to produce sweet, fruity beers. Cherry beers are known as *kriek*, raspberry as *framboise*. If this sounds like the basis for beer-based alcopops, it couldn't be further from the truth. The best ones have a wonderful balance of sweet and sour, and are closer to crisp, refreshing rosé wines than anything else. *Kriek* and *framboise* are made by several breweries around Belgium, but Cantillon goes further and makes Vigneronne, with the addition of white grapes, and Fou'foune with apricots.

After this introduction I'm free, along with the Bulgarian wine-shop manager from Hampstead who is the only other visitor, to wander the brewery unaccompanied. We stroll through the various stages of the production process, followed curiously by the brewery cat. The brewery spiders keep an eye on us too, from their webs across the skylights, between the rafters and in the spaces kept between the racks of oak barrels to prevent the gradual seeping of flavours from one vintage to another. It's terribly bad luck to clear spiders out of a *lambic* brewery, and not just on superstitious grounds; they keep flies away from the fruit fermenting away in the barrels.

We're both so engrossed in taking pictures of this beautiful old barn of a building and its ancient but still busy equipment that we fail to read our tour guides properly and end up back at reception having missed out half the tour. Jean-Pierre barks angrily at us and shoos us back upstairs. Finally we finish the tour and are allowed to taste the *gueuze*. Nothing prepares you for it. The first sip tastes like cider, but not Woodpecker this time – I only think cider because it's the closest thing within my frame of reference. A few sips later and I learn to appreciate that it has a unique and wonderful taste all of its own.

I buy some to take home. The beers are bottled in champagne bottles, which are specially strengthened because champagne also undergoes a secondary fermentation (hence the fizz). 'You must wait three days before opening. Serve cool, but not cold. If it is a hot day, you can put them in the fridge for three hours – no more. Otherwise, keep them in the cellar.'

With this advice – or should I say instruction – Madame Van Roy says goodbye, seemingly quite keen to see us leave. But I haven't quite got everything I need. 'I'm actually writing a book about beer around the world,' I say. Her smile freezes in place, her eyes wide and glassy. I ask a few questions about who buys and drinks Cantillon beers, and if she has any ideas about the origins of the tradition of *gueuze* brewing and why it has survived. She mumbles a few things about Belgian tradition and pushes a free set of beer mats and a poster at me, looking pleadingly at me as she does so, begging me to leave. So I do, wondering if something sinister is about to happen after the door closes behind us, or if it's just that, when he left Barnsley, Michael Parkinson took the town's entire ration of interpersonal skills with him.

Antwerp

Antwerp, as everyone knows, is the centre of Belgian beer drinking. Apart from maybe Bruges. And possibly Brussels. And Ghent or Mechelen, and maybe Namur.

I think we've established beyond all doubt now that

Belgium is not a boring country. So I try to remain blasé when I discover that Antwerp is also the second-largest port in Europe, despite not being on the coast. I yawn at the revelation that it is the world capital of the diamond industry and increasingly one of the leading centres of high fashion.

But I'm here for the beer. Summer seems to have arrived early, and after a sweltering walk along the quayside of the majestic River Scheldt, I have built a healthy appetite for my first glass.

Hangar 26 is a massive converted boat shed that houses, among other things, an ad agency staffed by friends of friends, who have agreed to meet me for a drink. We go to the Kaii Café, several floors up in Hangar 26 with a long, wooden terrace facing out onto the river. The sun dips into the water, causing the various power-boaters, water-skiers and jet-skiers to shimmer in the golden light, as Werner de Smet, a Belgian advertising executive who gets to enjoy this view every single working day of his goddamned life, orders the beers.

Beer preference in Belgium, as you might expect, is quite regional. Here in Antwerp the ubiquitous drink of choice is de Konninck, a brown ale served in a globular glass known as a *bolleke*. This is not one of those amusing translations that becomes an unintended but fitting pun – *bolleke* is Dutch for small ball, and everyone here knows exactly why the English find it so funny. Somehow this makes it even funnier; when you are ordering de Konninck it is customary simply to ask for a *bolleke*, and to do so remains amusing for all concerned for several rounds.

'If you think that's funny, you should try asking for a *fluijte*,' says Werner, cryptically.

Slowly, Werner's colleagues finish work and join us, until

we're a big table of twelve, enjoying the sun and the beer. I'm distracted from the seething jealousy I feel for these people by Jef Raeman, who urgently needs to give me his take on beer in Belgium. Between the ages of twelve and seventeen, Jef attended a boarding school neighbouring the Westmalle Abbey. The masters knew it was pointless to tell the boys they were not allowed to drink beer, so they attempted a compromise, barring only Westmalle Trippel, the 9 per cent beer, hoping this would temper things. I don't know how successful this policy was, but Jef emerged as a man who looks incomplete without a glass in his hand.

'The problem is that beer is not aspirational in Belgium,' he says. 'You can buy beer cheaper than you can buy water.' He thinks for a second. 'You know, water is pretty aspirational.'

Werner places much of the blame for this at the feet of Inbev. He would; he does some work for their arch-rival, Belgium's second-biggest brewer, Alken-Maes. He feels that the Belgian giant has commoditized beer in its native country. 'Beer is still shown far too traditionally. The tone and the humour in ads has not evolved.'

This develops quickly into a proud defence of local beer and a fierce criticism of everyone else's. I'm taken aback by the venom they have for Inbev's beers, but this is nothing compared to how they feel about Heineken.

'It's *piss!*'

'My father, if he catches me drinking Heineken, he says, "You are not my son."'

'But it's one of the most famous and successful beers in the world!' I argue.

'Maybe. But it is not as good as our village beer.'

The Flemish hate the Walloons. You could be forgiven for

thinking this would mean they had an affinity with the Dutch, whose language they share. But no. The only thing the Flemings and Walloons agree on is how much they all hate the Dutch. Harry Pearson, in his book *A Tall Man in a Low Land*, recounts a speech given to him by a Flemish man that has strong parallels with the one I'm hearing now:

> 'The difference between the Flemish and the Dutch can be seen in cheese. Here in Flanders we make many different kinds of cheese. Hard cheese, soft cheese, goats' cheese, sheep's cheese. We make orange, white and blue cheeses. Cheese with herbs and with rinds soaked in beer. Hundreds of cheeses. Great cheeses. But nobody outside Belgium has heard of them. The Dutch make one kind of very tasteless cheese and the whole world knows about it. That is the difference between us and the Dutch.'

Jef leans halfway across the wide table to make his next point: 'We Belgians taught the *world* how to drink beer.'

'And eat chocolate,' adds someone.

'Chocolate I don't care about,' continues Jef, without breaking eye contact with me, 'but beer – we *rule*.'

'So why don't you have any time for Inbev then? If you're proud of Belgian beer, well, Inbev are making it famous around the world.'

'Inbev are the only Belgian company with a worldwide profile, and we love them for that,' explains Werner. 'We're so proud of them and the fact that they are Belgian, now they have become the biggest brewer in the world and overtaken the Americans, Anheuser-Busch. But inside Belgium they rule everything. They buy up all the bars and then prevent small brewers' beers from being sold there. They want to put everyone else out of business. And so we hate them.' He pauses. 'Not as much as we hate Heineken, obviously. But we don't like them.'

'But you can't deny that they make some good beers. What about Leffe and Hoegaarden?'

'*Paf!* Sugared water!' says Jef. (Yes, he really does say *paf*.)

'We are just proud of Belgian beer.' Werner shrugs. 'We're proud of Antwerp beer. People in Bruges are proud of Bruges beer.'

'And we're proud of Antwerp music!' shouts Jef.

Werner looks a little uncomfortable. 'Er . . . yeah . . .'

'But beer. Beer, we taught the world how to drink.'

'Well, we will,' corrects Werner.

'Yeah, we will.'

'Excuse me . . .'

'No!'

Not the response you expect from a waiter, but he does seem to be having a hard day. He screams an extended volley of abuse at a couple sitting a few tables away from me, then disappears.

Fortunately I'm not in a hurry. The cloudless Saturday morning sky and beautiful light on the buildings of the Grote Markt make the situation very bearable indeed. Every European flag imaginable flutters from the massive, imposing town hall. In the centre of the square stands a statue of Brabo, made duke of Brabant for killing a giant who used to chop off sailors' hands on the Scheldt. He's surrounded by fountains that spray outwards, not into pools or anything conventional like that, but onto the bare cobbles, which for some reason seems supremely decadent.

I'm starting to realize how conducive a town square is to creating the perfect beer moment. Open spaces force you to relax. People slow down when they emerge into them from crowded streets. Cafes can spread outside properly, without getting in anyone's way, and you can sit for hours watching the world stroll past.

The De Valk Brouwerhuis, for that is where I'm sitting, has a mere thirty beers on its menu. I decide that if I do succeed in ordering anything, I'll have a Tongerlo Dubbel Blond 6°, 'a light, fruity beer with a soft and frank taste'. After the frankness shown by the waiting staff, I don't see how I could order anything else. Eventually a new waiter appears. He returns to the couple the last bloke screamed at, shouts at them again, then takes orders from the entire terrace, me included. Forty minutes after I first sat down, my beer arrives, served with minimal ceremony and maximum frankness.

Having recovered from the *bolleke*s and even the *Botschafter*, I need to look elsewhere for juvenile giggles. There's one beer I've been keeping an eye out for since I arrived, and here it is on the menu. I've been dying to do this. I want a Kwak.

Justly described as a 'unique Belgian speciality', this beer has been brewed by the, er . . . Kwak family since 1791, when Pauvel Kwak invented it. Kwak takes the tradition for unique, branded glassware one step further than its peers. It's served in a stirrup cup: a glass with a round, bulbous base that doesn't stand up on its own, and therefore comes equipped with a wooden stand. The glasses are stolen so often that many bars ask you to leave one of your shoes as a deposit until you return your glass.

Just as I'm ready to order, Liz joins me, after arriving last night while I was with Werner and Jef and subsequently inspecting every antiques shop in Antwerp. She beats me to it: 'Two Kwaks, please.' She smiles at the waiter, and he's a man transformed. He beams back and waddles off, saying, 'Two Kwaks. Kwak, Kwak!' She has this effect on people.

The beer is deep amber, 8 per cent and very rich, tasting of caramel, butter and malt. 'It's horrid,' says Liz. Well, she's entitled to her opinion. And I'm entitled to her beer.

We eat lunch just behind the Grote Markt, in the shadow of the cathedral – literally. The restaurant is called In der Schaduw Van de Kathedraal, a name that lends further support to my theory that Dutch is a language made up on the spot just to mess with the heads of stoned Brits. Written Dutch looks exactly like what one would type after two or three Kwaks, full of English words only with too many 'I's, 'J's and 'W's. And the Dutch all speak excellent English, right? That's because secretly English is their first language. You can imagine the conversations signwriters have in Dutch public spaces.

'What shall we put for "Entrance"?'

'*Ingang.*'

'Yeah, good one. What about "Exit"?'

'Easy, *Outgang.* No, hang on, that's taking the piss. Let's make it *Uitgang.*'

'Good one. Fancy a pint?'

'Yeah, I'll have a Jan Smit's, cheers.'

Bruges

When William Wordsworth visited Bruges in the nineteenth century he found grass growing in the streets of a forgotten town. Until the sixteenth century this was the most prosperous city in Europe, thanks to the River Zwin. Then the river silted up, and Bruges became a backwater. Its obscurity saved it from the rabid modernizing tendencies of the Belgians and the ravages of the Industrial Revolution, and it remains a perfectly preserved medieval town. In the nineteenth century the British started visiting, staying, opening tea rooms and attracting more Brits. Today Bruges gets two million tourists a year, most of them British, coming to buy armfuls of lace and chocolate. The guidebooks that tell you this often forget to mention that Bruges is yet another beer mecca.

There are two places in particular that make Bruges an essential stop on my quest. The first is Erasmus, a restaurant that boasts a list of 150 beers and a menu that uses as many of them as it can in its recipes.

When I start talking about beer as the perfect accompaniment to food, my friends usually get a look on their faces that means, OK, that was interesting what you were saying about beer until now, but you just crossed the line into sad, obsessive fanboy geekdom, and I'm not sure I trust you around sharp objects any more. Beer writers and brewers around the world are getting terribly excited by it, but outside this closed circle no one seems to want to know. Beer is all right for a drink, and maybe a pint will go quite nicely with a steak and ale pie or even bangers and mash, but it's just not sophisticated. It's stodgy. It's not delicate. And most importantly of all *it's not what people do.*

All this might be true if your idea of beer stretches only as far as a pint of Foster's or a can of Carling, though there are dishes that even the shittiest supermarket own-label lager can enhance. But there are things that beer can do and places it can go that are still surprising to people who have been taking it too seriously for decades. And we're in *Belgium*. If there's anywhere on the planet to show what beer is capable of, this is the place.

There are three basic principles to matching drink and food: comparing flavours, contrasting flavours and cutting through. Wine is fruity and acidic. There are, obviously, lots of foods that it compares and contrasts with. But beer can be malty, caramelly, earthy, tart, bitter, sour, creamy, tangy, chocolatey, even fruity. It compares and contrasts with at least as many foods as wine, arguably even more. And the carbonation in beer means it cleanses and refreshes the palate, resetting your taste buds. When you have a decent selection to play with, you can match beer across a range of food that leaves traditional pub fare as a distant memory, and perform feats of gastronomic titillation that would make wine blush. And for the first time I my life I'm in a restaurant that understands this. In fact, for me to say Erasmus understands beer and food matching is like a twelve-year-old physics student telling Stephen Hawking he shows a bit of promise.

Liz starts with cheese croquettes, and I have scampi which turn out to be prawns. I choose beers for us both which I hope will send a very clear signal to the waiter: I know what I'm doing here. He rumbles me in an instant, smiles a smile that says, Oh, you want to play at matching the perfect beer with each dish do you? Well, I see what you're trying to do, but your first choice reveals that beyond some very basic principles you have the knowledge of a new-born child. All that in a brief smile. Incredible. He dismisses my selection and brings us a suitably light (as in only 6.5 per cent) unfiltered beer called Saison Dupont, a hoppy, fruity, dry beer that cuts through the greasiness of both our dishes, brings out the flavour of the prawns – sorry, scampi – and I daresay does the same to the cheese.

For the main course I have cod cooked in Chimay, a spicy Trappist ale. Liz has beef casserole cooked in a brown beer and served with an apple sauce. I reach for the beer list again and the waiter slaps it away. 'Can I suggest a Moinette Blonde for you, sir, and for Madame, I think, a Westmalle Dubbel?'

'Can I have a glass of wine?' asks Liz.

I stare at my wife balefully – not angry, just disappointed.

'A Westmalle Dubbel sounds great,' she says.

For dessert we share a very sweet chocolate mousse. I jump in and order a *kriek*, because I bloody well *know* that *kriek* goes with sweet chocolate dessert. The waiter spits in my face, laughs, and brings a Bush Ambrée instead; a 25-centilitre bottle poured into two tiny bulb glasses. It's 12 per cent, the strongest beer in Belgium, and has aniseed flavours. And it's a match so perfect that dessert wines around the world lie awake in their cellars worrying about it.

The other noteworthy thing about Bush beer is that it bears no resemblance whatsoever to a bland, mainstream American lager. But this didn't stop Anheuser-Busch (remember them?) obtaining a ruling in the International Court of Arbitration recently to prevent Dubuisson, the company that brews Bush beers, from selling anything under the Bush name anywhere in the world apart from in Belgium, France, the Netherlands, Luxembourg, Italy, Switzerland and Portugal. Apparently, the world's second-biggest brewer (93,000,000 barrels a year) felt that Dubuisson (12,000 barrels a year) might pose a threat to its business. You could be forgiven for wondering where this confusion arises, given that A-B's brand is called Budweiser.

But A-B also make a beer called Busch, a budget brand that sells in the US, Canada and ... Taiwan. Bush had already decided voluntarily to call its beer Scaldis in North America to avoid any confusion, so that just leaves Taiwan where there might be any danger of conflict, and Dubuisson are far too small to worry about selling their beers there. Remember how their case against Budvar rested on the fact that Anheuser-Busch trademarked the name first, and that was all that mattered? This time around, it mattered little to them or their lawyers that Dubuisson had been selling Bush since the 1930s, whereas A-B's Busch was only launched in 1955.*

The perfect end to the evening would be a final drink at Bruges's other beery landmark, the place CAMRA describe as 'one of maybe a dozen beer bars in the world that you have to visit before you die'. Brugs Beertje has a list of 250 beers, and some specials off-list for the really serious beerspotter who knows what to ask for. The bar is hidden away in a narrow, cobbled backstreet, and hardcore beer fans come from across the globe to drink here. By the time we find it, the anticipation is unbearable. But of course they've chosen this weekend, the height of the tourist season, to go on holiday themselves. The place is closed.

This is a quiet part of town – it looks mainly residential. The only tourists here are those with maps and guidebooks, looking for the street signs they think will lead them to beer heaven. As we stand outside the shop translating the 'Gone on holiday' sign for the fifth time, sure we must have misunderstood, three more groups of people approach and forlornly try

---

* Remember how it goes? Yeah, that's right! 'Welcome to Anheuser-Busch, where making friends is our business!'

the door, as if the drawn blinds and the beer writer weeping and wailing and pounding the cobbles like a child who has been told to go to bed because he's overtired don't give a clear enough indication. You can taste the grief.

There's a bar next door that does a brave job of trying not to look like the slightly less attractive friend of the girl everyone wants to get off with at a party. It doesn't even bother trying to compete on the beer front, with a mere fifteen choices on its menu. Instead, it attempts to complement its illustrious neighbour by offering over fifty different gins, including apple, grapefruit, banana, chocolate, lemon and 'jonge special cockney' varieties. This seems to be of interest to Liz for some reason. I'm too disconsolate to resist.

The next day, I persuade my stoic wife that a visit to the nearby malting museum would be a good idea. We stroll through Bruges on a quiet morning. It's like a more rural Amsterdam, or a more picturesque Cambridge. Moss and grass grow up between the cobbles, suggesting that the absence of cars is the norm. Small pleasure boats ferry people up and down the gently curving canals, under slightly humped bridges. And then you turn a corner and you're in yet another square full of medieval guild buildings and churches with gold-plated statues perching on gables, the flags of Europe flying from windows and stand-alone flagpoles, and tourist-trap cafes with terraces on the cobbles that would be irresistible were it not for the constant threat of English-style rain.

The Brouwerij en Mouterijmuseum 't Hamerken is an old yellow-brick building nestled down a narrow backstreet a hundred yards from the canal. With its tall chimney, ten-foot-high wooden doors and high windows, it's a cynical bastard yuppie property redeveloper's wet dream.

Malting is a fascinating part of the brewing process. No, don't skip ahead, it really is. There are many different varieties of malt, and choosing the right one has an enormous influence on the character of the finished beer. What I find so interesting is that these varieties are created not by the cultivation of different types of grain – broadly speaking, barley is barley – but from what the maltster does to it. For the starches inside the barley to convert into fermentable sugars, the grain has to start germinating and sprout. The skill of the maltster is in stopping the germination at exactly the right moment, by roasting the barley. If you roast it lightly you get a pale malt, which is used in lagers and pale ales. Go heavy, and you get something for a dark beer or stout. There's a whole range in between, and some complex beers mix several varieties. Maltsters are adept at roasting grain to precisely the right degree for the required character of the beer, and it's amazing how many different flavours can be teased from grain by the application of their skill.

The museum has a collection of old malting and bottling equipment, including a barrel-cleaning machine which looks like it belongs at Hogwarts, and a range of beer mats which offers a whole afternoon of sniggering at unintentionally amusing names of beers past and present. There's a reconstructed bar from 1900, many aspects of which are just becoming fashionable again now. And like all the best brewery tours, there's beer at the end included in the €2.50 admission. At the top of the building, the bar has hop bines running around the walls and a collection of 200 pewter tankards hang from the beams. Four beers are brewed here: Brugs Blond, a light, pale ale; Steenbrugge Dubbel and Steenbrugge

Trippel, both abbey beers; and Brugse Trippel, a fantastic, full-flavoured blond.

The barman is short and stocky with a serious, mournful expression. Like Madame Van Roy at Cantillon, he seems slightly freaked out when I start asking him questions.

'How many breweries are there in Bruges?'

'Two. This one and another one. But next year this brewery closes down.'

This pulls me up short. 'What? Why?'

'It has been bought by Palm.'

Breweries close. It's a fact of life in a world where we are gradually drinking less beer and where for centuries the laws of economics have rewarded fewer, bigger companies. But after spending an hour looking around this place, after seeing the stained-glass coat of arms commemorating a hundred years from 1872 to 1972, and after drinking this damn fine beer, this is nothing less than a crying shame. I say as much to the barman.

'Well, there are too many beers in Belgium.' He shrugs philosophically. 'These beers that we make, they are not drunk by the people of Bruges. They do not drink speciality beers. Maybe every now and again at home they will have a Trippel, but ... mostly we sell to tourists. French and American, mainly.'

'Do your beers sell abroad?'

'I don't know. A little in Italy, perhaps, someone once told me. Palm sell their beers in Europe, in America, but here, they buy everything.'

Belgian speciality beers don't have the infrastructure to compete in the modern world. They need to sell their beers abroad to make their business viable, and only the biggest can really do this. The big brewers buy the brands that look interesting, but to them a beer is only really a recipe and a branded glass, so they close down small, inefficient, traditional breweries with centuries of history and brew the beers in modern, efficient plants that benefit from economies of scale.

But there's a huge temptation to say, 'To hell with economic reality, what about the fucking *romance*?' Beer is about tradition, craftsmanship, authenticity, artisanship and magic. If the Belgian beer market does lose its character, it would imply these things are meaningless, and that would make the world a much less pleasant place to live in.

Maybe the majority of beers will survive. The whole thing about each beer having its unique branded glass, for example, is really more of a clever marketing gimmick than anything to do with allowing the aroma of the beer to circulate beneath your nose. The shape of the glass is carefully designed to make the liquid look as appetizing as possible – narrow bodies enhance the golden glow of pale beers; squat, bulbous shapes add to the complexity and mystery of dark beers. Branding the glasses and presenting them with their own drip mats creates a sense of theatre that the biggest brands on earth are only just starting to catch on to. The internet allows us to find out about these beers, rate them for others, and even buy them and have them delivered to our doors.* I try to remain hopeful.

'Maybe Palm will keep the museum open,' says the barman.

*

---

* Some selected websites are listed at the back of the book. If you still can't be bothered to come to Belgium to experience its beery cornucopia for yourself, I urge you to order a mixed case from one of them. I promise you will be delighted.

As we head back towards Bruges's main square the rain attacks viciously, and we're forced to duck into an American theme bar for shelter. We have a couple of Leffes, and while we're drying off we decide to try our luck on the bingo machine. These are an institution in Belgium. They look like pinball machines, but are much less fun to play, yet ten times more addictive. Instead of a big picture of a haunted house or a space battle on the back panel, there are six bingo cards. You fire balls up under the glass the same as pinball, but there are no flippers to control them – just holes with different numbers written on them, surrounded by springy buffers. There are three buttons on the top of the machine labelled X, Y and Z, and another button on the front.

I fire a ball. It goes into a hole. The words 'Game Over' appear on a screen. This has to be the most rubbish game I have ever played in my life. There's no point to it, no skill whatsoever. I fire another ball, and sure enough it goes into a hole again. This time I've won three euros. Maybe it's not so bad. I would like to take the money and run, but I can't work out how to make the machine pay out. I become aware of a couple of teenagers standing behind me, snickering. I press a few more buttons at random, and now there are three balls in play simultaneously. Lights are flashing all over the place. The snickering grows louder.

'Perhaps you should let these boys show you how it's done,' says Liz. This is a skill unique to women: to say something that seems inarguably reasonable on the surface, but in fact emasculates the target of the comment as surely as a pair of razor-blade underpants. I step back, leaving ninety-five cents credit on the machine just to emphasize my impotence. One of the youths pushes past me, grunting under his hoodie. You'll forgive me, under the circumstances, for thinking uncharitably about him: the stunted, hooded, grunting little form resembles nothing so much as a Jawa from *Star Wars*.

He hands his 25-centilitre glass of Jupiler to his friend and begins pumping coins – probably stolen – into the machine, grunting as he does so. I resist an overwhelming urge to cuff him around the ear.

'What do you have to do? You show us how it's done,' says Liz, as welcome as a fart.

The Jawa makes some noises in his grunting language, gesturing at his friend. In the imaginary film of my journey, subtitles appear on screen at this point. If I was writing them the words would be, 'We sell droids for scrap,' but the mundane reality is that they're probably something like, 'Do not talk to me while I am in the zone. Fool, you speak a little English. Explain to these idiots what I, the master of the bingo machine, am doing.'

'You have to get the ball into the holes that are lit up,' explains his handler in English.

Suddenly it's clear to anyone with any sense that different holes are lit each game. You can mess around with the odds by increasing or decreasing your stake, lighting more or less holes. You're allowed to nudge the table slightly, but it tilts if you get too aggressive. If you miss all the holes and the ball reaches the bottom, you get another go. Simple.

'Fockeeng sheet!' yells the Jawa as he fails to do this. Then, 'Hey, Milo,' as he increases his stake to six euros, fires off another ball and gets it into a lit hole. He's just won eighteen euros. He does a little Jawa dance and high-fives Milo.

He fires off another ball, and shortly thereafter spits, 'Motha*focker*!'

'You know all the wrong English words.' Liz laughs a little nervously.

'Fockeeng BEECH!' he screams at the next ball, rather than my wife.

'He watches a lot of rap videos.' Milo shrugs.

I'd dearly love to stay and watch him lose all his eighteen euros with agonizing predictability, and then his original stake, then any other money he has to his name, before walking out of the pub a broken Jawa, inconsolable and crushed. But we have a train to catch, and it's stopped raining.

As we head back to Brussels and, ultimately, London, I realize my trip here was far too short. It's a typical Belgian paradox that outside the bland drinking of the EU quarter lies possibly the most interesting and varied beer culture in the world. There are enough different beer styles and wonderful cafes in the country to keep you entertained for months. And it's only the same size as Wales. No one I spoke to seemed to be able to explain precisely why Belgium pursued such a different path to its wine-drinking neighbour to the west and south and the lager swillers to the north and east. But an educated guess would be that it's a delightful mix of reverence for tradition and an enduring philosophy of brewing that can be summed up as, 'I wonder what'll happen if we do this?' Rather than being a boring country, you can't help thinking the world would be a much more colourful place if everyone was a bit more Belgian.

6

'Beervana'

London

When I was about eleven, our teacher asked each of my class in turn what we wanted to be when we grew up. I said, 'Author.' The abuse that followed this stupid reply wasn't as bad as it could have been, because the class wags decided 'author' was far funnier and more abusive than any of the massive and inventive range of other nicknames in their verbal arsenal.

Having my first book published meant that I finally gained the satisfaction of shouting drunkenly, 'Ha! I showed 'em, the eleven-year-old *bastards*! I wrote a *book*!' But Liz keeps suggesting that I let all that go. Another perk is that I occasionally get to meet some of the more talented and successful authors I share a publisher with. In my view, there is no one alive who puts words on paper better than American novelist Don DeLillo. And because I've mentioned this to every single person at my publisher at every available opportunity, his publicist took pity on me and invited me to the great man's latest book launch.

I was star-struck, happy enough just to gawp at him, standing there in his cords and Birkenstocks, drinking a beer, being human and real. But the nice publicist insisted on introducing me to him.

'Don?' she said. 'Can I introduce you to Pete? He's a big fan, and a fellow writer.'

Fellow writer? I was a fat, wheezy Sunday league football player meeting Pele in his prime. Don could see I was just going to stand there saying 'gmphhh' and 'hurrrrrrrr' unless he led the conversation. He's probably used to it.

'So, what have you written?' asked the man who has defined what it is to be human at the dawn of the third millennium.

My heart ached to be able to say that, like him, I've articulated the thoughts we all carry around in our heads in a way that's almost telepathic, hypnotic, on the street and yet, at the same time, in the clouds.

'I've written a book about beer,' I said.

Something extraordinary happened: the eyes of the world's greatest living novelist lit up. 'Beer!' he said. 'I gotta sit down with you and talk about this!' I gaped, astonished, as he pulled me away from the cluster of people he'd just been discussing great literature with.

It turns out that when Mr DeLillo is at home in Brooklyn, articulating the hidden song of his nation, taking the invisible music and arraying it on the page in bright daubs and subtle shades, he likes nothing better than a bottle of Bass Ale by his side. That's Bass Ale from Burton-on-Trent, England. Brooklyn brews some fine beers of its own, but none as fine, in the Great Man's opinion, as a foaming bottle of Bass. 'So what I wanna know is this,' said Don, leaning forward. 'Here I am in the country that makes the greatest beers in the world. And I'm staying at the Savoy, which is one of its finest hotels. And the only beer they've got is Budweiser. Why is that?'

As is his wont, in that deceptively simple question, the poet of our postmodern reality nailed a phenomenon of extraordinary complexity: in this case, the Great American Beer Paradox.

The United States drinks more beer than any other country in the world, although China is overtaking it. It's dominated by a handful of giant brands, with Anheuser-Busch sitting on an incredible 50 per cent market share. Bud is the second-biggest beer brand on the planet. The biggest? Bud Light. Anheuser-Busch, Miller and Coors together account for 80 per cent of all American domestic beer consumption – and any normal drinker would be hard-pressed to discern any difference between their main beers.

But Don (he wouldn't mind me calling him Don – that's the kind of guy he is – and we're mates now, me and Don) is not alone in his appreciation of English ale. Bass is the third-biggest-selling bottled beer in the whole of New York. Don can't be drinking all of it. Bass isn't even close to being the biggest imported brand in the country as a whole. And, imports aside, America's small craft brewers are reviving extinct beer styles or creating new styles entirely, pushing beer beyond the limits of what we thought it could be. It's been estimated that, counting imports, there are an incredible 3,400 different beers on sale in the United States. The fact that

95 per cent of America's $75 billion market* consists of delicately flavoured imitation Pilsners makes it all the more remarkable that there are more different styles of beer available there than anywhere else on the planet. America, one of the blandest, most corporate, homogenized beer markets in the world, is also, in the words of legendary beer writer Michael Jackson, 'the most interesting beer scene in the world'. Where do you even start trying to unpick that?

Most American beer writers (of which there are a surprisingly large number) start in 1620 on board the *Mayflower*, or rather at Plymouth Rock, where the Pilgrim Fathers were put ashore 400 miles short of Virginia, their intended destination. 'We could not now take time for further search or consideration, our victuals being much spent, especially our beere,' mourns the log. This isn't the start of America's beer story though. Over a century earlier, on his fourth voyage to the Americas, Columbus found the indigenous people drinking beer made from maize, the taste of which reminded him of English ale. In South America *chicha*, made from maize or whatever else grows well, has been an important part of life as far back as records go.

But whatever the locals were making, it wasn't deemed good enough by the colonists. In 1623 the Virginia Assembly urged immigrants to bring malted brewing barley with them. In 1629 John Winthrop, the first governor of Massachusetts, no doubt helped himself into that position by turning up at the colony with 10,000 gallons of beer. Brewing was a vital part of life in the early days of Harvard University. The first

---

* Beer is worth more than music, movies or mobile phones.

president of the college, Nathanial Easton, was dismissed in 1639 for failing to provide enough beer for the students. At a time when students were required to pay part of their fees in brewing malt, you can understand how this must have rankled.

George Washington, Thomas Jefferson and Benjamin Franklin were all keen home brewers who were often asked for their recipes. Washington's recipe for 'small beer' is still displayed in the New York Public Library. The Declaration of Independence was signed over pints of ale in Philadelphia's Indian Queen Tavern. And in 1814, after a few beers at the Fountain Inn in Baltimore, Francis Scott Key set some new words to 'To Anacreon in Heaven', an old English beer-drinking song. He called it 'The Star-Spangled Banner'. It turned out to be quite a hit.

So I have to go to America, a country built on beer. I have to understand the beer paradox here if I am to truly understand beer at all. And there's only one place to start. The first long-haul flight of my global quest takes me to Chicago, to connect with a short hop north to America's self-proclaimed brewing capital.

Milwaukee, Wisconsin

It takes a long time to clear American customs. It's late by the time we land, and unless I want to miss my connection and spend most of the night in the airport I need to take drastic steps to get to the front of the queue. So I barge past old ladies, trip up pregnant women and hurl people on crutches against the wall in my headlong dash to passport control. Of course, I could have just followed the example of the French family I sprinted past two minutes ago, who saunter past me to the first available booth, ignoring the queue of a hundred English people harrumphing so loudly we're almost in danger of being heard.

Several hours later, I'm happier than I have ever been in my life to see a Holiday Inn. I've never been happy at all to see a Holiday Inn before now, come to think of it, but this is different. Apart from the fact that I'm so exhausted I'd sleep in a ditch, the hotel doesn't make me feel like I've been robbed at knifepoint, like British business hotels do. 'Basic' here is different from 'basic' at home, and I feel neither delighted nor ripped off, just satisfied that I get exactly what I deserve for the money I've paid. It's an unusual feeling, and quite nice. I check in and change my clothes, then do that bizarre thing which I always do when jet-lagged and tired beyond sleepiness – I go down to the bar.

'Sam Adams, please.' Samuel Adams is the largest craft beer in the States, a wonderfully malty, aromatic Bavarian-style lager.

'I'm sorry?'

'A Sam Adams.'

'Couldyourepeatthatplease.'

'A – bottle – of – Samuel – Adams – lager – please.'

'Oh, a Sam Adams. Coming right up.'

'Thank you.'

'Sure.'

I've already noticed that people here say 'Sure' instead of 'You're welcome'. It makes them sound wounded and sarcastic, as if they don't believe you're really thanking them. I sit and worry about the fact that I seem to be running into language difficulties in an English-speaking country, drinking my beer, waiting on principle until I've been awake for twenty-four hours before retiring, satisfied, to my lovely, vast, cool bed.

Milwaukee is a small city by US standards, overshadowed by Chicago to the point of being a mere satellite. Parts of it may be beautiful – I've no idea; I can't see anything through an unseasonable downpour that seems to be following me across continents. All I knew about it until recently was that it was home to *Happy Days* and *Laverne and Shirley*. Laudable though this is, my admiration of the Fonz doesn't really justify a visit. But Milwaukee was also the centre of American brewing's golden age.

Until the mid-nineteenth century, America favoured English-style ales and porters. But between 1840 and 1860 political upheaval in Europe sent 1,350,000 Germans to the US. In 1850 there were 431 breweries in the country; ten years later that figure had risen to 1,269, and most of them brewed lager. German brewers brought carefully preserved samples of lager yeasts with them, and on the shores of Lake Michigan they found abundant supplies of clear, fresh water, edged with fertile plains for barley and hops. In winter the lake provided enough ice to keep lagering caves cool all year round. By the 1880s German immigrants accounted for a third of Milwaukee's population.

The taste for German-style lager soon spread across the country, and in 1871 a cow in Chicago paved the way for Milwaukee's brewers to achieve national dominance. Allegedly, the beast started a fire in a barn on the property of Mr and Mrs Patrick O'Leary which took out most of Chicago – including its brewers – in a blaze that lasted almost two days. Milwaukee charitably stepped in with emergency beer, and

Chicago got accustomed to the taste. Soon Milwaukee's Schlitz was proclaiming itself 'the beer that made Milwaukee famous', a claim that it really had to share with Pabst, Blatz and Miller. Word spread, and Milwaukee was soon supplying more than half the nation's beer. The infamous Prohibition campaigner Carrie Nation once said, 'If there is any place that is hell on earth, it is Milwaukee.'

Ah, Carrie Nation.

Even though she stands as the absolute antithesis of every principle I hold dear, I can't help but have a sneaking affection for the woman who, more than any other individual, became a figurehead for America's Prohibition movement. As if one beery paradox isn't enough, the beer-loving US has always had a deeply ambivalent relationship with drinking. Prohibition between 1920 and 1933 is one of the most infamous periods in American history, the culmination of decades of activism that saw the nation's mighty brewing firms, some of the most powerful, well-connected businesses in the country, get utterly trounced . . . by a bunch of women.

Carrie Nation spent a difficult childhood with a mother who often mistook herself for Queen Victoria. In adulthood she was a striking figure, dressed from head to toe in black after her first husband drank himself to death two years into their marriage.* Despite remarrying, she described men – all men – as 'nicotine-soaked, beer-besmirched, whiskey-greased, red-eyed devils'. The more waggish reader may imagine responding to Ms Nation with a quip like, 'So I suppose a

---

* When I showed photographs of Carrie to some people, they said, 'Well, you would, wouldn't you?' and, 'She's got a face like John Prescott licking piss off a nettle.'

snog's out of the question then?' But you wouldn't have done. In any hall of fame for scary, domineering women, Carrie Nation would make Margaret Thatcher, Boadicea and my old maths teacher Miss Johnson look like Shirley Temple, any girl called Maisie and Joe Pasquale respectively. Because Carrie Nation was six feet tall, and went around with an axe.

Many of the Wild West's 'devils' had wives and families who went neglected and hungry while they drank. Along with the rest of the Women's Christian Temperance Union and groups such as the Anti-Saloon League, Carrie Nation mounted an increasingly successful campaign to persuade individual states to go dry. By 1890 one such state was Kansas, but the law was not being enforced. With a group of her sisters, Nation prayed and read the Bible outside a saloon in the town of Medicine Lodge, hoping God would force it to close. Eventually she grew bored waiting for the Almighty, strode into the saloon with her axe and smashed the entire place to matchwood, while patrons fled and staff stood agape. Between 1900 and 1910 she was arrested thirty times for being sober in charge of an axe in what had until very recently been a saloon. She paid her fines from lecture tours and sales of souvenir axes. In her own words, she was 'a bulldog running along at the feet of Jesus, barking at what he doesn't like'.

Early silent movie footage survives of one of her attacks. It's astonishing: the controlled, focused violence that erupts from this prim woman with her round spectacles and black bonnet is mesmerizing. If Carrie Nation had told me drinking was terminally bad for my health, I daresay I would have believed her.

But the Prohibitionists probably would have succeeded without her. They had another even more powerful weapon:

the brewing industry itself. Aggressive sales practices among brewers were common. Many went into saloons and bought drinks for people, or offered free lunches to persuade drinkers to linger instead of going home to their families. Even friends of the brewing industry found such practices indefensible, but the industry wouldn't listen. As the storm clouds of Prohibition gathered, brewers refused to believe such a law would ever be passed. When spirits manufacturers suggested a joint campaign, they huffed, 'The beer business has nothing in common with the whiskey business. Quite the contrary. Their interests are apart and, under present conditions, antagonistic.' As late as 1916, a brewing trade publication declared, 'All people hate drunkards and whiskey makes them. Men drinking beer exclusively may become "funny" but never drunk.'

As the brewers sat and watched, the Prohibitionists added anti-German sentiments and crop shortages from the First World War to their armoury. More and more states voted to go dry. Way before it became illegal, being seen to drink simply became socially unacceptable.

In 1920 the Volstead Act outlawed the manufacture, sale and transportation of any drink stronger than 0.5 per cent alcohol. President Woodrow Wilson vetoed the act, raging, 'These miserable hypocrites in the House and Senate . . . many with their cellars stocked with liquors and not believing in prohibition at all – jumping at the whip of the lobbyists . . . The country would be better off with light wines and beers.' His veto was immediately overturned. Nevertheless, from the start it was clear to anyone sane that Prohibition was never going to work. Fermentation is a natural process. Apart from the point raised by Bill Hicks in relation to marijuana ('If you outlaw something that occurs naturally, isn't that kind of accusing God of making a mistake?') how could anyone stop people brewing at home?

The trials of Anheuser-Busch illustrate perfectly the folly of Prohibition. Anticipating the law change, they launched Bevo, a 0.5 per cent 'near-beer'. A young Gussie Busch (grandson of founder Adolphus) boasted that it was 'such a perfect imitation of our Budweiser beer that our experts could not determine, from taste, which was the [non-alcoholic] beverage and which was the beer'.* Originally it did very well, but once Prohibition was actually introduced, sales nosedived. A public that previously had found drinking unacceptable decided it was fashionable as soon as it was illegal – it had an allure. They quickly acquired a taste for illegal hard liquor such as bathtub gin, which was more freely available than ever before, and had no need for a non-alcoholic beer.

Despite Bevo's troubles, Anheuser-Busch survived thanks to the determination of President August A. Busch, Adolphus' son and Gussie's father, who ruined his health keeping the company afloat by sheer determination. Oh, and then there was the small fortune Anheuser-Busch made through a deal on brewing materials with murderous gangster Al Capone – whose illegal beer was by all accounts not too bad. Anheuser-Busch also diversified into other products, including Smack. Given the company's fondness for litigation, I should probably clarify that this was the name of a chocolate-covered ice-cream bar, not, as it is now, a nickname for heroin. Most of the country's brewers were not so fortunate.

---

* By which I think he meant that the non-alcoholic beer tasted as good as a real beer, rather than the opposite. But it is tempting to misinterpret him.

Bizarrely, the people voted for 'dry' politicians whenever they could, because what you said and what you did were entirely different. Will Rogers commented bitterly that people would 'vote dry as long as they can stagger to the polls'. Finally, in 1932, Roosevelt stood for the presidency on a repeal platform. He won one of the biggest landslides in electoral history, and Prohibition was repealed at midnight on 7 April 1933. At 12.01 a.m., the brewers of Milwaukee and St Louis opened their gates and shipped fifteen million bottles of beer. The first consignment from Anheuser-Busch went to the airport, from where it was flown across the country and then delivered to the White House and to pro-repeal lobbyists in New York by the company's new Clydesdale horses. Of the 1,392 brewers in operation before prohibition, only 164 remained. But for a short while these survivors simply couldn't brew quick enough for a thirsty populace.

Seventy-odd years after Prohibition, America still has an odd relationship with beer. Some on the extreme religious right compare it to heroin and crack. Most authorities agree that access to it and consumption of it must be controlled, but they don't seem to be able to agree on how. According to Dwight Heath,

> Some [states] require that the interior [of pubs] be visible from the street, whereas others specifically forbid that; some require that food be available wherever drinks are served, and others insist that it not be ... There are states in which all drinkers must stand at a bar while drinking, and others that insist they be seated ... until recently, some required that women use a separate entrance from men and that they (together with couples) occupy a separate room.

Perhaps all this explains why, on my walk around America's former brewing capital, I'm having trouble finding a bar. As I reach Milwaukee's lake front the storm thins out a little, and I begin to realize why no one writes much about the town in tourist guides. Liz would be the first to attest that design is not my forte, but I've played a lot of SimCity and if I was building a town on the shore of a lake this size, I'd probably put a parade of bars and restaurants looking out over the water. There'd be a harbour for pleasure craft and yachts, surrounded by fish and seafood restaurants. Possibly, reluctantly, I'd give in to a few souvenir and novelty shops. Milwaukee went for a huge car park, a convention centre and Highway 794.

I walk for an hour through the streets, and even though the rain has cleared up I count five other people out here with me. Milwaukee supposedly has over 5,000 bars, the highest number per capita in the country; why there don't seem to be any in the downtown core is therefore a little mystifying. There are no shops either. To coin a phrase, there's no 'there' there.

If you think I'm being unduly harsh, come with me to the Grand Avenue Mall (I find it eventually, hidden behind a nondescript facade with little outward evidence of the shops within). In the souvenir shop one of the most popular T-shirt designs reads, 'Welcome to Milwaukee. Don't worry, beer makes it better.' Unless it's a cruel prank to wind up tourists, which it probably is, the highlight of local cuisine seems to be Just for Joy cheddar beer soup ('The name says it all!'). Even my tourist guide, written by a local, describes the population as 'beer and bowling knuckleheads'. The best endorsement it can give is, 'Hang out here long enough and you'll appreciate it.'

Jet lag kicks in towards the end of the afternoon, and I decide I really need to take a seat and order a beer. I choose Mo's Irish Pub across the road from the mall, partly because it promises me, 'The first time a guest, the second time a regular,' and partly because it's only the second pub or bar I've spotted all afternoon. I order a Miller Lite, not because I want to, but because I promised myself I would drink the local beer wherever I go. I don't know why I feel the need to make an excuse, and I hope I'm not turning into a beer snob – though after Belgium this is a vague possibility – but the truth is, I've never been keen on mainstream American beers. Even by the standards of the blandest European lager, they're thin and don't *taste* of beer. It's telling that most people drink them straight from the bottle, because poured into a glass they're not even the colour you'd expect beer to be. Prohibition has much to answer for.

After the initial rush following the repeal of Prohibition, young people who had grown up with only soft drinks were telling the brewers that their beers were too bitter, not sweet enough. Many brewers changed their formulations immediately although, intriguingly, Anheuser-Busch steadfastly opposed any change to the Budweiser recipe. Even their most vociferous critic – and I would happily devote the rest of my life, warrior-monk-like, to attaining that title most coveted among beer writers – cannot deny that A-B thinks it has a genuine commitment to beer quality. They use whole hops instead of pellets, a claim few English real ale producers can make; they lager their beer longer than many of their competitors; and throughout their history there are repeated examples of their refusal to compromise on the brewing process to make faster profits. And yet their beer, along with every mainstream

American brand, is significantly lighter, thinner and less tasty than the European beers they supposedly resemble. Despite the argument often deployed by beer enthusiasts that rice is substantially cheaper than malted barley, I honestly think that cost is not the issue here. They do this *deliberately*. They think this is how beer is *supposed* to (not) taste.

Miller thinks and acts in a similar fashion, and Miller pretty much owns Milwaukee; every street shows evidence of their presence. Lite is their best-selling beer. It does have a wonderful pale golden colour that manages to stay the right side of the line between 'delicate' and 'watery'. There's no aroma whatsoever, but that could just be me. There's a slight malty taste that disappears astonishingly quickly, and then, when I swallow, it leaves behind an aftertaste that's distinctly papery – something I haven't tasted since we chewed up tickets on the school bus and spat them at each other – and lasts long after anything else in the beer has vanished. Now that just isn't fair. Without the aftertaste it would hardly be the world's best beer, but it would at least be refreshing. With it, it's the worst of all possible worlds: no enjoyable taste when it's there, and a nasty present when it's gone.

The next day breaks with a clear blue sky and a brighter attitude. I bound down to breakfast and am wondering what to order when I see four spherical objects squeezed tight into a corner booth: Dad Sphere, Mom Sphere, Junior Sphere and Sis Sphere. And they're all eating a similar buffet selection to the one I had yesterday. Panicked, I order the fruit platter, along with an English muffin onto which they try, and fail, to sneak extra butter, and a glass of Tropicana orange juice.

'I'msorrycouldyourepeatthatplease?'

'A glass of Tropicana.'

'A Trooper *Connor*?'

The waitress goes away to consult. In her situation I might perhaps look at the menu to see if I could make a connection with anything that sounds remotely like 'Trooper Connor' and comes in a glass. But she has less nervousness about causing deep feelings of inadequacy and embarrassment than I do.

Today I need to interview some people. First I phone the splendidly named Randy Mosher, a graphic designer, beer writer and one of the leading lights of the American home brew movement. He lives in Chicago. Home brewing was only legalized in 1979, by Jimmy Carter. Since then an estimated two million Americans have declared themselves happy to be described as home brew enthusiasts.

If there's a beery stereotype in the UK even more negative than the bearded, sandals-with-knee-length-black-socks real ale fundamentalist, it's the home brewer in his shed foisting something green and potent on you, whining nasally that it only cost three pence a pint to make, one taste filling you with the urge to scream, 'Three pence? For this? You've been ripped off, mate.'

Randy seems aware that I might harbour this image of home brewers, and he's quick to head me off. 'Home brewing is not just a way of getting cheap beer and beating taxes. People are into it for flavour and variety, not to get drunk. They try to make interesting recipes, or brew as close as they can to established beer recipes. It's all about getting better as a brewer, and the aim is winning awards.' Later, I read about the thriving industry in tracking down the correct malts and yeasts to brew facsimiles of famous beers. But what kind of person does this?

'They tend to be people who've settled down and got their own place. Certainly no younger than late twenties,' says Randy, 'but more people are coming into it now. Lots of women, which is really exciting. They're more along the lines of wine drinkers – highly educated, making pretty good salaries. People out of microbiology. Artists. Crafts people. Also the slow food movement people. Home brewing beer and craft beer is an extension of trying to beat back corporate hegemony.'

It almost makes me want to try home brewing when I get home. *Almost.*

Next I go to the other extreme and phone the Miller Brewing Company. I've been given the name of someone who might help me by an incredibly friendly and helpful man at SABMiller in the UK.

'Hi, can I speak to Molly Reilly, please?'

'Molly Reilly is no longer with us, sir.'

'Well could I speak to someone else in the PR department?'

'Not unless you can give me a name or extension number.'

'I just gave you Molly Reilly's name. Can I speak to her replacement?'

'Not without their name or number, sir.'

'Look, I'm a writer trying to write something positive about your company. Isn't this a strange way of handling your PR?'

'Well, to keep down the excessive solicitation we get, we limit it to people who already know the name and number.'

'Wow. I've never been called an excessive solicitation before. Thank you.'

This will turn out to be the only snotty treatment I receive from any brewer I approach in any country in the world.* But I don't know that yet, so this brush-off in no way influences my attitude to Milwaukee's number-one tourist attraction: the Miller Brewery Tour.

The billboards on the way out to the brewery build the anticipation: '42nd and State. Since he never asks for directions,' and, 'Our tour only lasts an hour. We know. It's hard.' This folksiness belies the reality when you finally arrive: Miller Valley really does occupy an entire valley. The cab drops me in front of the giant visitors' centre, where I wait with around eighty other people for the tour to start. It's not just for beer nerds: there are lots of families, around fifteen kids under ten. There's a Jesuit priest in full costume. There's only one guy in the room on his own, and he's taking photos of odd things, scrutinizing everyone else and writing incessantly in a small notebook.

I browse the shop, which contains everything onto which you can possibly stamp a Miller logo, and a small history and corporate exhibition of the brewery. The latter tells us that SABMiller makes 'America's favorite beers', which would probably come as a shock to Bud and Bud Light.

Keith and Justin, two healthy, clean-cut students on

---

* Apart from Anheuser-Busch, obviously. While writing the Belgium chapter, I contacted them posing as an ordinary punter to find out about where Busch Beer was sold, and received a prompt reply. When I contacted them again on the same email address (none of their many websites give phone numbers or any other contact details for press enquiries) telling them why I wanted this information and asking if they would like to give their side on the various stories about them in this book, they didn't even acknowledge receipt, let alone reply, despite several follow-up emails. 'Welcome to Anheuser-Busch, where making friends is our business!'

summer break, are going to be our tour guides today and they outline what the morning has in store. We're going to start off with a short film, see the brewery, then drink some free beer at the end. The eight-year-olds cheer loudly at this, until Keith or Justin quickly points out that for them this means root beer. The film cuts between helicopter shots swooping over Miller Valley and close-ups of fields of barley and clear, flowing streams. The hiss and glug of a bottle being opened and poured, thundering repeatedly through the speakers, has the desired effect. It's Miller Time!

We start the tour at the packaging facility, which in my experience of brewery tours normally comes towards the end. The facility consists of three canning lines and two bottling lines, and can package a quarter of a million cases of beer in twenty-four hours.

'This is South Packaging,' says Keith or Justin. 'Anyone guess what the name of the building across the street is? 'Correct. West Packaging. Between both buildings we do half a million cases of beer every single day, or the capacity of 16,500 Olympic-sized swimming pools.'

The labelling machine, we are told, does 800 labels per minute.

Next we walk to the shipping warehouse. 'We truck and train 4,000 cases of beer a day out of here. Drinking a six-pack a day, it would take you forty-three years to empty a train. We fill 400 trucks a day. We have five other breweries around the nation.'

Even as a beer writer, I'm getting bored by this blizzard of statistics. Can this really be Milwaukee's biggest tourist attraction? I think back to yesterday afternoon. Yeah, it probably is.

Next, we're shown the cellars where Frederick Miller originally stored his beer, which are now empty.

And that's it.

At no point do we actually see the brewery, and it seems we're not going to. I ask Justin/Keith about this. 'Well, the process of brewing was covered in the video at the start,' he says, 'and anyway it's pretty boring.'

Now hang on. If the magical process by which beer is created is boring, whereas the logistics of how it is put into cans and 'trucked and trained' and how many bloody swimming pools they could fill is fascinating, then I really don't like it here any more and I'd like to be taken home now.

But there's still the free beer to come. Throughout the 'tour' I've been at the front of the group, near Justin and/or Keith. People have been doing that shy thing where no one wants to be picked on for being teacher's pet. But as Justin/Keith announces that we're off to the Miller Inn for our free samples, the shyness wears off and my English politeness sees me pushed firmly towards the back.

We take our seats in a beautiful old bar. Immediately the sound of a locust swarm fills the room, or maybe it's eighty people ripping through 150 packets of complimentary pretzels in less than thirty seconds. Glasses of Miller High Life appear. Fortunately (given we're in the brewery), it's a vast improvement on the Miller Lite I had yesterday. It's very cold, very pale and again has hardly any aroma to it. It has a thin taste, but when I swallow instead of the papery aftertaste there's a lovely full peachiness that hovers over my tongue for just a second, then disappears. It's a pleasant surprise.

After this first drink we're moved across the road to the 'beer garden' and given tokens for two more samples. The beer garden turns out to be a concrete forecourt on the edge of the main road through Miller Valley, decorated with a few window boxes to offset the constant roar of the trucks flashing past. By now, all pretence of decorum has vanished from the throng. Bollocksed on twenty-five millilitres of lager, there's an unseemly scrum at the bar for more. I order Leinekugel's, Miller's answer to the craft beer movement. It tastes identical to High Life. We sit at tables to write our free Miller Time postcards. I write as many as I can, to as many addresses around the world as I can think of. It's a gorgeous day, and I'd like nothing better than to sit somewhere pleasant and let the afternoon drift. But I'm in Milwaukee. I say goodbye to Miller and head back to the other end of Milwaukee's brewing spectrum.

Randy Sprecher has an old-fashioned air about him. In his fifties, sporting a magnificent salt-and-pepper moustache, his formal courtesy and modesty seems to belong to a bygone age. He describes himself as a surf bum who did his national service in Germany, returned home and discovered he couldn't bear to drink American beer any more. He set up the Midwest's first microbrewery in a suburban street along the lake shore. That was twenty years ago, and the Sprecher Brewery now enjoys a growing reputation.

Randy speaks very quickly. Most people in Milwaukee do, but I think that Randy is just always in a rush. He's busy with the nationwide launch of a range of non-alcoholic sodas, but takes time to give me a whirlwind tour of his brewery. From the outside it's just another industrial unit. Inside, it's the smallest brewery I've ever seen, jerry-built into the space available. After a brief glimpse of everything we head into his indoor beer tent for a tasting.

I manage to call my own bluff almost immediately.

Randy introduces me to a range of around ten beers. He's very proud of his IPA, bigging it up: 'It's 8 per cent, packed full of hops.' He asks me what I'd like to try. It seems impolite to ignore his obvious hint, so I say the IPA sounds great.

He looks at me oddly. 'Ooo-kaaaay ... going straight in with the heavy ones, huh? Well, if that's what you want.'

At this point I remember one of the most elementary rules of beer tasting, or any tasting come to that. You start light, and you gradually work heavier. That way, your palate can fully appreciate delicate flavours before being swamped by big ones. By asking for his strongest-tasting beer first, I've effectively said to him, 'Quite clearly I don't know the first thing about beer, despite blagging my way in here and taking up your valuable time on the flaky premise that I'm a beer writer.'

He hands me the IPA in silence.

'I, er ... don't have the most orthodox approach to beer tasting,' I stammer. 'You see, I mainly write about the social and cultural aspects of beer and the people who drink it.'

'Oh. OK.' He doesn't sound convinced.

'Look, here's my first book,' I plead, handing him a copy.

Just then, we're joined by Don 'Wambo' Wambach (that's what it says on his business card), the brewery's marketing director.

'Hey Don,' Randy says. 'Come and meet ... Sorry, what's your name again?'

'Pete.'

'Pete. Pete. Don, Pete here's a beer writer from England but he doesn't actually know much about beer. He says he writes about the ... you know, culture surrounding it. And all that.' He turns to me. 'Do you have a business card, Paul? Might help me remember your name.'

We taste the Hefe Weiss German-style wheat beer, the English-style Pub Ale, the Black Bavarian lager. When I've tasted North American craft beers in the past, you could see what they were trying to do, but they were always colder and fizzier than the European styles that inspired them. They were like a competent covers band playing a pub gig: you could recognize the songs – they weren't played badly – but they had none of the magic of the original. Randy Sprecher's beers taste exactly like the styles they are meant to be. The wall above the bar is laden with evidence of prizes they have won in international beer competitions.

'This is a very welcome antidote to the Miller Tour,' I offer.

'Ah, the old numbers game,' Don and Randy both say at once. 'Numbers. That's all those guys talk about. Nothing about the quality of the beer, only the quantity of it.' Randy shakes his head sadly. 'The thing is, a lot of people want to drink those beers. People buy beer the way they buy milk. Is it in date? Great! Away we go.'

We talk a little more about the strange shape of American beer drinking, and then it's time to go. Randy escorts me out front and shouts to the receptionist, 'Hey, could you get a cab for Phil?' We say goodbye. He disappears back into his office.

Five minutes later, just as the cab is pulling up outside, he rushes back out, clutching the copy of *Man Walks into a Pub* I just gave him. I'm sure he's about to say, 'Here, you forgot this.' Instead he says, 'I've been looking through it. You have some very interesting chapter titles here.' The change in his manner is obvious; he's finally bought my story. 'It was great to meet you. It's a good thing you're doing. Come back soon. Bring some friends.'

I like Randy. I like his beers and his sodas. I'm glad that, despite my incompetence, I've managed to convince him that he hasn't just wasted an afternoon.

On the way back into town we drive past the abandoned Schlitz brewery, a once-magnificent building that now has a condemned, almost embarrassed air about it, as if it senses that it would have been levelled long ago if only Milwaukee had the heart to do so. I'd like to think there's some symbolism here: the behemoth abandoned in the middle of the city while the nimble, passionate Randies pop up in the suburbs.

In the 1940s Schlitz was the biggest beer brand in the world, comfortably ahead of Budweiser. There had been nationally famous brands since the railroads first joined up the nation and refrigeration made it practical for brewers to sell beer outside their own state. Inevitably, those breweries which were ambitious and far-sighted enough were soon putting the slower, smaller ones out of business. After the big cull of Prohibition, the Second World War saw another change. Beer cans had been introduced in 1935, and brands like Pabst, Bud, Schlitz and Miller, who adopted the new technology early, were able to selflessly donate 15 per cent of their output to the armed forces. Come 1945, hundreds of thousands of demobbed servicemen returned home with a taste for the big, national beers.

Gussie Busch, now in charge of A–B, wanted to be number one. After Prohibition, a three-tier system of beer distribution had been introduced. To prevent the unsavoury practices in saloons from re-emerging, breweries had to sell to independent wholesalers, who in turn supplied bars and off-licences.

And yet, in 1934, 1942, 1969 and 1977, Anheuser-Busch was charged with several thousand instances of 'trade practice violations' – cajoling, bribing and threatening distributors – for which it was fined hundreds of thousands of dollars. Gussie's defence was that everyone else was doing it. I'm sure they were, but Gussie must have done it better; Budweiser overtook Schlitz in 1957 and has been number one ever since. Anyway, the Busches often act in a manner that suggests they consider themselves above the law.*

It was Gussie who claimed credit for our favourite phrase,

---

* Gussie's son Peter, by his third marriage, shot his best friend in the face and killed him, and escaped without a custodial sentence. His nephew Billy bit off a man's ear in a bar fight, and got away with it. Nine months later Billy, arrested after another fight, reportedly said, 'I'll buy my way out of this,' and was acquitted. Years later, he allegedly delayed a TWA flight in Chicago so that Domino's could deliver his pizza. He also had some advice for one of the flight attendants: 'If anyone drinks other than Anheuser-Busch products, ask them to leave the plane.' But first prize in the 'I fought the law and you know what? *I* goddam won' competition goes to Augustus Busch IV. In 1983 Gussie's grandson, the man almost certain to take over as the next chairman of the company when his dad, August III, gives up the reins, was driving a car at high speed which crashed, killing his female passenger. Witnesses reported him drinking 'six or seven' vodka cocktails before getting into the car and driving away so quickly that friends who were supposed to be following him to a party could not keep up. Urine tests which could have convicted him of driving under the influence mysteriously disappeared from the St Louis hospital where they were being kept, before police could examine them. Blood tests were put through a centrifuge, rendering them useless. No one could explain how either incident happened. Investigators seeking a prosecution claimed they felt intimidated. No charges were brought against him. Two years later he was chased by police at high speeds through St Louis, refusing to stop. When the police finally pulled him over, he sped off again, almost hitting them. He escaped with one month's probation.

'Making friends is our business,' even though it was coined by someone else.* It seems that his interpretation was, 'Making friends *in the right places* is our business.' As St Louis police gathered every night in a tunnel beneath the brewery after their shifts to drink as much free beer as they wanted, and the Busches made friends with union leaders, state governors, congressmen and presidents, Budweiser went from strength to strength, and soon all the Milwaukee brewers could do little more than react to the conditions the Busches set. Schlitz and Pabst entered steady but ultimately terminal declines.

I spend my last night in Milwaukee making a concerted effort to get out around some bars. This is harder than it sounds when you're on your own in a remote city where the bars appear to be camouflaged, but I'm determined.

Stretching along the front of the Milwaukee River that splits the town, Water Street is the meeting place of the students from Marquette University and the downtown businessmen who go there to ogle them bitterly. I eat a burger and watch the baseball in the Water St Brewery, a brewpub with a good range of craft beers. The game is a veritable beer grudge

---

* The unofficial (and among the family deeply unpopular) biographers of the Busch family, Peter Hernon and Terry Ganey, recount the following story of a day aboard the *A&E Eagle*, the company yacht that Gussie used to entertain friends. According to Harry Chesley, an ad executive, another boat was blocking the *Eagle*'s way. A crew member, Rawlins, 'shouted out, asking the boat to move, but nothing happened. Gussie said to try again, and Rawlins cries out, but nothing is done. The other boat is still blocking us. Finally Gussie says to poor Rawlins, "Tell those sons of bitches to get their goddam boat out of the way." Whereupon Rawlins says, with a slight stutter now, "But, Mr Busch, aren't you forgetting that making friends is our business?" Gussie did a double-take, smiled and said, "Fuck you, Rawlins, you're fired."'

match: St Louis Cardinals (from Bud's home town, owned by Anheuser-Busch) versus the Milwaukee Brewers (sponsored by Miller). I watch for quite a long time, and despite an awful lot of throwing, hitting, catching and running, the score doesn't change. It's 3–0 to the Cardinals in the bottom of the fifth with two out. Then someone hits the ball into the stands, does a home run, the two that are out come in, and the score remains the same. I've never felt compelled to defend cricket before, but if I ever hear an American complaining about the impenetrable nature of our game again, I won't be responsible for my actions.

Fortified but confused, I drift from brightly lit brewpub to murky bar to big, British city-centre-style drinking shed, encountering students, karaoke, Billy Idol records, a national pub quiz, lots of neon, projector screens and retro video games. The baseball game plays continually, everywhere I go.

Overall, I'm struck by how similar Water Street is to a typical English town centre. Half the same brands are here, and the style of drinking is definitely the same. In the end I have a good time and I'm glad I came to Milwaukee, but I'm no nearer figuring out America's relationship with beer.

The Cardinals eventually win 4–0. Don't ask me why.

New York, New York

'The United States isn't really one country,' says Philip Van Munching, over lunch. 'There are huge differences across the States. People get at Americans for only speaking one language, but it's all right for you guys: you get on a plane in Europe and you're forty minutes away from someone else's country.

It reminds me of an old Bill Cosby skit – I speak southern; I speak Maine; I speak Manhattan. If someone tells me his fadda hadda hat attack I know he wasn't attacked by a hat.'

Philip is the man who unwittingly inspired me to write about beer, so I felt I had to stop over in New York to meet him. Philip's grandfather was the first man to import Heineken into the United States, kicking off the whole premium imported-beer craze here. Philip worked for the family firm in the 1980s, helping to maintain Heineken as the biggest imported brand until Heineken decided they wanted to run things themselves, bought out the Van Munchings, and promptly lost leadership of the import segment to Corona. Philip's experience left him with a jaded view of the American beer industry, and he wrote an absorbing and hilarious account of the follies of the big American brewers called *Beer Blast: The inside story of the brewing industry's bizarre battles for your money.*

I read *Beer Blast* about a year after I started working on Stella and Heineken ads, and thought, you know, someone should write a book like this about beer in Britain. Hey, hang on . . . My book turned out to be quite different from his, but when I started it, *Beer Blast* was my inspiration.

When I tell Philip this is the reason I wanted to have lunch with him, he takes it pretty well. It strikes us both, rather awkwardly, that I may be his biggest fan, and that's a situation that always has the potential to get a bit weird.

'How does the difference in the States show itself in beer?' I ask.

'Well, craft beers and imports are very urban – the coasts plus Chicago and Detroit. And there are big differences in the amount people drink. New Yorkers are big beer drinkers. But there are similarities as well. The thing about Americans is we're always looking for ways to define ourselves. And beer just *has* to be packaged. In a bar most guys will choose a bottle, so everyone can see the label and how cool they are. But mostly we drink at home now. We spend time in the suburban sprawl, drive to each other's houses to socialize. Beer gets drunk at the barbecue or in the basement. The cliché of the guys getting a big slab of beer and going over to watch the ball game, that's true of the lower middle class more than anyone else, but everybody likes their bottle of Bud with dinner.'

Beer Blast tells how in the 1970s the American beer market went haywire. Budweiser wasn't growing fast enough for Gussie's son, August III, 'Three Sticks' to his friends.* August III was and still is a workaholic, a man who, according to one very senior former executive, was 'power drunk. He can't remember the distinction between respect and fear. He instils fear and thinks that's respect.' In 1975 August III executed a coup to remove Gussie, his own father, from the running of the company.

With the old man out of the way, he set about building Anheuser-Busch's market share with a ferocity like no one had ever seen. Marketing spend was so colossal that no other brewer could compete. Within a decade of August III taking over, Budweiser held sponsorship rights to all 24 US-based major league baseball teams, 20 out of 28 NFL teams, 23 out of 24 basketball teams, 13 out of 14 National Hockey League teams, 9 of 11 Major Indoor Soccer League teams, over 300

---

* Or to paraphrase a character in *Withnail and I*, 'Three Sticks to everybody. He didn't have any friends.'

colleges and about a thousand alternative sports. The Beer Wars had begun in earnest. One beer importer said of Anheuser-Busch: 'They're tough, tough, tough, really ruthless. They seem to have the absolute intention of running everyone else out of the business.'

Schlitz attempted to counter by cutting the brewing time of their beer. In what a former boss of mine came to call 'The *Ker Plunk!* strategy', they removed something that kept their brand afloat (rather than a sharp plastic stick, as in the game, in their case it was lagering time) and no one noticed any difference. So they did it again. Still no difference. So they did it again. Suddenly the marbles fell: beer started hitting the shelves with snot-like strands of matter in the bottle, because proteins hadn't been properly filtered from it. The 'snot' was harmless to everyone except Schlitz themselves. The brand died within a few short years.

Miller survived because in 1969 the family sold the business. Having made a fortune selling Marlboro cigarettes, Philip Morris had both the money and the know-how to compete in the Beer Wars. As *Beer Blast* puts it, they 'brought marketers' skills to what had always been essentially a street salesman's industry'. In 1975, the same year as August III's coup against Gussie, Miller introduced Lite, a low-calorie beer. They launched it with the genius tagline, 'Everything you want in a beer . . . and less', and quickly moved on to the even better, 'Tastes great. Less filling.' Turning a low-cal proposition into a subtle suggestion that, rather than being a bit of a girl, this meant you could drink more of it. Miller's sales rocketed from seven million barrels in 1975 to 31 million in 1978.

Anheuser-Busch and Miller went head to head. A-B staff

had T-shirts and caps printed with the slogan, 'Miller Killers'. Miller cheekily applied for the rights to launch 'Gussie beer'. Each launched lawsuit after lawsuit against the other, until the Bureau of Alcohol, Tobacco and Firearms* stepped in and told everyone to calm down. The two companies had sworn to destroy each other, yet when the smoke cleared, they were both in rude health, better than they had ever been. But the floor was littered with the corpses of Schlitz, Pabst, Blatz, Rheingold and scores of other regional and smaller national brands. The only other survivor was Coors, a culty brand from the Rockies that snuck up while no one was looking. Despite boycotts over their treatment of blacks, gays, women and Democrats, despite allegedly lying about using Rocky Mountain spring water in their beer, claiming to be concerned about the environment while being one of the biggest polluters in Colorado, and forcing staff to take lie detector tests about their political allegiances, Coors emerged in third place. And that's how America wound up with three brewers controlling 80 per cent of the market.

Philip now writes joke books and books for kids. He's a nice guy who has been badly burned by the beer business, and I can tell that, given the choice, he'd rather not talk too much more about it. We trade war stories about our respective dealings with Heineken and finish our magnificent steaks. He signs the copy of *Beer Blast* I brought with me, writing, 'To Pete, the only person who will admit to reading this more than once!'

After saying goodbye to Philip I head south down Broadway

---

* What other country on the face of the planet would see any logic in putting these three things together?

and through Greenwich Village. My personal summer clouds have found me again. It's not just gravity pulling this water earthward, it has jet propulsion behind it. The concrete canyons of Manhattan's streets make the rainfall more depressingly dramatic; you can only really *see* rain against something other than clouds, and because the buildings are taller, you can watch the rain falling from much higher up, which makes it seem to fall even further and even harder.

I dodge into bars when the rain becomes particularly vicious. I love the barfly routine you can get into here if you're on your own. I sit on a stool at the counter. If I have my head down in a book or I'm writing, I'm left completely undisturbed apart from when the level of beer in my glass falls to an inch, and then someone immediately appears to ask if I'd like another. If I look up to take in my surroundings, the bar staff smile pleasantly. If I give any signal that I'd be interested in a conversation, they're right there chatting about the beers, the never-ending ball game, the rain. After nearly a week in the States, a dollar tip for each pint feels entirely reasonable in exchange for this level of service.

Late in the afternoon I spot a bar painted all black outside, with red curtains pulled closed across the windows. Through the door all I can see is a dull red glow. The smell of a university gig venue wafts out. A stag's head perches above the bar, almost hidden under a collection of lacy red, black and pink bras draped from its antlers. A sign taped on the mirror behind the bar reads, 'Do not touch the bartenders.'

I order a Sam Adams. The guy leaning on the bar next to me, bulging T-shirt and wispy ponytail, snorts with derision when I speak. All the guys perched at the bar are drinking bottles of Bud, apart from one nursing a Pabst Blue Ribbon. I didn't think they even made this stuff any more.*

Damp and bedraggled, as evening falls I find the Blind Tiger, New York's premier ale house. It has over twenty beers, and just to show willing, also boasts 'the finest range of potato chips in the city'. I'm here to meet Garrett Oliver, brewmaster of the Brooklyn Brewery. His Brooklyn Lager is often described as 'pre-Prohibition lager', in that it has colour, taste and no rice.† He is also author of *The Brewmaster's Table*, and possibly the world's most charismatic beer-with-food evangelist. Garrett asks me where I've been so far, and laughs when I tell him how few places I'll be visiting.

'Shoulda gone to San Diego,' he says. 'That's where a lot of interesting things are happening just now. They're getting really hoppy.'

'Ooh, I like hoppy beers,' I say.

He raises his eyebrows. 'These beers are getting *really* hoppy. They're experimenting to see just how many hops you can get in. I mean, I like to pack lots in of different varieties, but they're just *cramming* them in, over a hundred IBUs.‡ I

---

* I find out later that there is a growing market for 'relic beers', the brands that disappeared in the Beer Wars. Now brewed under licence as budget brands, they sell for nostalgic reasons, but also benefit from the protest against globalization and saturation marketing. In Portland, Oregon's (and possibly the country's) only anarchist bar, Pabst outsells Miller Lite. But something tells me that my friend here is not drinking it to demonstrate solidarity with the anti-capitalists.

† Brooklyn is increasingly available by mail order in the UK, and is even creeping into a few bars. Check out the details at the back of the book.

‡ IBUs are International Units of Bitterness. In the UK, no one outside brewing and beer nerd circles knows what this means, nor should they be expected to, but it's a term you regularly see in beer reviews, one of those

thought they were doing it just to see how far they could go. But you go out there, and people are actually *drinking* this stuff. It's really selling.'

We find one behind the bar and get a sample of it. It is served in a whiskey-tasting glass, which is entirely appropriate. I take a taste and wince. 'It's basically just hop juice,' I say.

'Yes, it is,' says Garrett.

This is extreme beer, beer making pushed to its limits. Many of the keenest craft brewers are not content with recreating classic styles, they want to push beer as far as it can go. Samuel Adams brews Utopias, a 25 per cent ABV beer, far stronger than anyone thought biochemically possible, which sells to collectors for upwards of $200 a bottle. The Dog Fish Head Brewery (motto: 'Off-centered beer for off-centered people') worked with the archaeologist we met in Spain, Patrick McGovern, to recreate the beer found in Midas's tomb. Midas Touch Golden Elixir is made with white Muscat grapes, honey and saffron. But the most popular pursuit at the moment is discovering what concentration of hops we can drink without our faces imploding.

Garrett talks with immense passion about all areas of food and drink, but he really takes off on the subject of beer with

---

aspects of beer writing that alienates everyone apart from the hardcore. For years, IBUs signified to me the closed-shop elitism of beer appreciation. But in the United States I find out what it means, and like many of these things it's quite simple if someone takes the trouble to explain it in simple terms. So let me have a go. The bitterness in beer comes from the alpha acids in hops. One unit of bitterness is equivalent to one part per million of these acids in the liquid. It's a revelation of how sensitive human taste buds are that most of us can detect these acids' presence at levels as low as five parts per million. Most beers are between ten and thirty IBUs. Many American IPAs are around fifty. Over a hundred is just silly.

food. 'Food is where the rubber hits the road.' He explains that wine cannot do everything with food, that beer has caramelization and roast flavours that wine can never have, and that these flavours are the ones we like best in food. 'I believe it's race memory – the flavour of fire is among our favourite flavours,' he says.

Then there are spices. They distort wine flavours, turning white wines hot and red wines bitter. Even according to wine experts, there are many foods that are simply no good with wine. 'Wine enthusiasts talk about "tricky ingredients". Know what these ingredients are? Eggs, cheeses, chillies, smoked meats, smoked fish, tomatoes, ginger, curry, chocolate, avocados, garlic, vinaigrette dressings, spinach, artichokes, asparagus, cumin . . . Beer goes with them all. Wheat beers are light, spritzy and wonderful with eggs. Spicy Belgian ales work wonders with chillies, cumin, ginger and curries. Rich imperial stouts are full of coffee and chocolate flavours and match chocolate desserts perfectly.'

Garrett duels with sommeliers in front of audiences of food and drink writers. Typically there will be seven dishes, with seven wines and seven beers to match. Each tells the writers why the match has been chosen, and the audience votes for which goes best – the beer or the wine. 'The first time we did it, it goes right to the wire, three all. And the sommelier pulls out this match that I would never have guessed, and it shouldn't go but it does, fantastically. Four–three to the sommelier. But as I was leaving all these guys were coming up to me and saying, "Well, in terms of what you wanted to prove, you won. Because going in here tonight, every single one of us would have said there's no competition between beer and wine, and you almost won the whole thing. You proved us wrong."'

I'm ravenous after all this, and Garrett suggests we go to the Grammercy Tavern. Hardly a tavern, it's actually one of the finest restaurants in New York. It's not the kind of place just anyone can turn up at and expect to get a table, but Garrett isn't just anyone – he created their extensive beer list. The restaurant is packed, but the *maître d'* recognizes Garrett, and we have a seat within ten minutes.

'A great restaurant teaches you something,' Garrett says. 'If it doesn't, it might be a good meal but it's not a *great* meal. Beer is an opportunity to teach, to reveal and inspire.'

I learn a lot over the course of this meal. I have a fantastic grilled squid starter with a Brooklyn Scorcher, a light, summery beer. 'It's a seasonal beer. These guys have the last few casks of it. It's hard to find.' Then we both have a fatty cut of pork, with a Belgian abbey beer onomatopoeically named Corsendonk.

After that, there's a cheese menu. I've never seen one of these before. You choose three, five or ten cheeses from a list of about twenty. I get two very big, hard goats' cheeses, and a surprisingly lovely gouda. They also go fantastically well with the Corsendonk.

Cheese is the battleground on which Garrett seems most comfortable. 'Wine has a handicap here,' he explains. 'Beer and cheese have a lot in common – both come from a farm. They're both flavours that come out of a field. Cheese is mouth-coating, and wine bounces off. Also, cheese can blunt the characters of a wine and soften it. Beer, which is carbonated, has a scraping action that cuts through the cheese, breaking it up and cleansing your palette. Think ploughman's lunch – it makes sense.'

I go back to my hotel with a very full stomach and a head that's spinning not from the alcohol, but from the potency of the ideas I've been exposed to tonight. Beer is a subject we find so dull in the UK there is not a single regular column about it in any national newspaper or magazine. In New York it seems like the most exciting thing to hit food and drink in years. I feel like we're in a new age of discovery and experimentation. And the attitude around it is one of celebration, friendship and inclusiveness. Garrett is compelling, but I can't just take his word for it; I need to venture deeper into the heart of American beer. I need to face something that, by UK standards, would be the very heart of closed-shop beer nerdiness. I'm going to a craft beer festival.

Portland, Oregon

I spend the day flying over giant cornfields and the Rocky Mountains, crossing thousands of miles of America uninterrupted by cloud, with little evidence of human habitation. It's a shame they've ruined the word awesome here through overuse, because there is no better term to describe the sight of the country rolling beneath me.

This is the part of the trip I've been looking forward to the most. Oregon is the spiritual home of the American craft brewing movement. It's not where craft brewing first began – that would be San Francisco, where Fritz Maytag, heir to the household appliances company, bought the ailing Anchor Brewery in 1965 and reintroduced America to beers other than thin imitation-Pilsners for the first time since Prohibition. Nor is it home to the biggest craft brewery – that's Sierra Nevada down in California again, if you're not counting Samuel Adams, which many don't because it has grown so big and now has its beers brewed under contract. But Portland boasts more breweries than any other city, and hosts the Oregon Brewfest. The event is tiny compared to the Great American Beer Festival, which happens every year in Denver, but seventy-two brewers and 80,000 drinkers from across the nation will be here.

'It's *never* this hot here,' says Chris Crabb, one of the organizers of the event along with her husband, helpfully also called Chris Crabb. The female Chris takes time out from running the information tent to brief me, give me a press pass and an unlimited supply of beer tokens. I like her already.

'It was a hundred and three out here today. It's usually around eighty, tops. We were worried it might ruin the event.'

Did I hear this correctly? Why would this weather ruin an outdoor beer event?

'Well, when it's this hot you want to stay inside, where it's air conditioned. And you want to drink water, not beer.'

It's a point of view, I suppose, but not one shared by the crowd. The place is jumping. There are the requisite number of beards and bellies, but there are also fratboys in backward baseball caps, ageing Deadheads (the Grateful Dead spent a lot of time here), guys in their sixties with crisp white socks pulled up to their knees, creases ironed into their shorts and those special flip-down shade attachments on their spectacles, and girls. In fact, there are more girls than boys: girls with their boyfriends, girls in mixed-sex groups, and girls in large groups of girls. Every minute or so spontaneous cheers rise from one or other of the tents, sustained for thirty seconds or more for no other reason than that people are here, they are happy, and they can.

The spirit of the event is evident from the fact that there is no judging – it's not a competition to find the best beer; it's a celebration of beer's diversity. The half-pint beer glass emphasizes that this is about tasting and discovery. 'It's two tokens for a taster; four fills the glass,' says Chris. It seems churlish to ask why we don't just have one for a taster and two to fill the glass so everyone can carry half as many tokens, so I don't.

The programme features a beginner's guide to beer appreciation, a guide to different beer styles with a summary of what beers are available in each style, and a beer-o-meter, which rates every beer by its colour and bitterness in graphic form. Detailed tasting notes describe the beers effectively in a way any novice could understand.

'We call Oregon Beervana,' Brian from the Oregon Brewers' Guild tells me proudly. 'We have the highest concentration of craft beers and brewpubs in the US.'

'Why Oregon, do you think?'

'I guess it's because we're more indoorsy – it's colder up here. Well, apart from today. We have the highest concentration of bookshops as well. We have the best-educated drinking population in America. We're more into music . . .' On cue, a wandering oompah band starts up nearby. Their instruments are painted in psychedelic patterns, and they're playing Miles Davis covers.

Brian takes my programme and marks ten or so beers I need to try. Widmer's Muscat Love is a 'sweet, fruity aroma with grape, lemon and tangerine notes, backed with subtle, herbaceous hop tones and a faint pulsing malt'. Dog Fish Head's IPA 'presents a complex aroma of citrus, apricot and brandy' through to a finish that is 'smooth with lingering fruitcake notes'. And, if you're feeling brave, Lagunitas IPA is 'a pusillanimous fusillade of malt, hops, more hops, yeast, and just enough water to make it runny . . . capable of removing the enamel from teeth and restoring a high gloss finish to fine wood furniture'. It's all a far cry from the Great British Beer Festival, where you can be made to feel deliberately excluded if you don't already know exactly what beer you want.

Even as a fan of beer, I never knew it could open up such a banquet of flavours as this. And I never would have dreamed that a beer scene could be so welcoming and relaxed. But Portland is an extremely laid-back kinda place.

There's a polite rivalry in the Pacific north-west between Portland and Seattle, the kind you see when middle class English couples visit each other's houses for dinner and spend their whole time as guests cooing over the decor, the food, the impeccable taste in music or art, the pets and children, before spending the whole journey home bitching about the decor, the food, the cloying cuteness of the pets and children, the trying-too-hard taste in music or art. Both cities are liberal, relaxed, set in beautiful surroundings, but in the 1970s, when each had the opportunity to spend a lot of money improving itself, their paths diverged. Seattle decided it wanted to be on the map of great American cities, and invested in sports teams and a giant phallic needle to show that under its cultured, sensitive exterior, it was one of the guys after all. Portland planted lots of trees and invested millions in free, air-conditioned, regular, punctual public transport. For those readers currently living or working in Britain's cities, I'll say that again: free, air-conditioned, regular, punctual public transport.

I spend the next morning roaming around this strange and wonderful town. Chuck Palahniuk, the author of *Fight Club*, lives here. He has written an alternative travel guide to Portland which maps its mental space as much as the physical. He begins by talking to another Portland-based writer, Katherine Dunn. Dunn's theory is that everyone looking to make a new life migrates west. Their ancestors came to America; the ones who still hadn't found what they were looking for made their way across the continent until they reached the Pacific and there was nowhere left to go. As a result, the USA's left coast is the home of its visionaries and dreamers: from Bill Gates in Seattle to the movie industry in Hollywood. But, says Dunn, once you arrive at the Pacific seaboard, the cheapest place to live is Portland. This is the city the 'most cracked of the crackpots', the 'misfits among the misfits', make their home. As Dunn says, 'We just accumulate more and more strange people. All we are is the fugitives and refugees.'

After lunch I board the *Portland Spirit*, a pleasure cruiser on the Willamette River. This year is the twentieth birthday of the Bridgeport Brewing Company, Oregon's oldest craft brewery, and they've invited their friends and everyone who's anyone in the local beer scene on a cruise to help them celebrate. Three vaguely menacing guys with beards, bellies and backward baseball caps stand at the front of the boat, glaring at everyone. One of them picks up a mandolin, the next an acoustic bass, and the third starts hammering a xylophone. 'Let us know back there if we wake anyone up,' sneers the mandolin player after a muted reaction to *Summertime*, their opening number, 'and we'll stop.'

Oregon has over seventy microbreweries and brewpubs, twenty-odd within the Portland city limits. In terms of breweries and brewpubs per capita, the city leaves even Munich standing, and can claim to be not only the brewing capital of America, but also the world. Across the US as a whole, craft beer accounts for one in every hundred beers people drink. In

Oregon, that figure is somewhere between one in six and one in four.

Over frenzied xylophone solos and mandolin licks, I talk to various people from Bridgeport. Karl Ockert, the brewmaster, came up here after graduating from a brewing and malting sciences course in California where most of his classmates went to brew for Anheuser-Busch. In the early 1980s Portland had a strong pub (as opposed to bar) culture. These pubs were full of ex-servicemen who had done tours of duty in what was then West Germany, and returned home to find American beer lacking. Likewise, the city's restaurants were patronized by well-travelled, curious diners. Karl's flavourful, European-inspired beers found a welcome home in both.

Since then, the commitment to interesting beer has remained constant, even as different styles have waxed and waned. In the mid-noughties Bridgeport, like many craft breweries, is finding that it simply cannot brew enough IPA. India Pale Ale is an old British style that, as the name suggests, was brewed for export to India at the height of the empire. In order to survive the journey in drinkable condition it had to be strong in alcohol and highly hopped, creating a potent but very refreshing bitter, sparkling ale. There are IPAs in Britain today which are perfectly fine beers in their own way but whose only relationship to the original IPA is that they are wet and contain alcohol. The Americans are taking the original hoppy concept and pushing it in the opposite direction.

Bridgeport IPA has a massive, unmissable aroma of piney forests and citrus fruit. The intensity of it reminds me of the hit you get when you stick your nose into a glass of rich, dark, mature red wine more than a beer. It has a floral taste that hovers, followed by a dry, fruity bitterness that makes my tongue jump and quiver. The contrast between this and British beer is exactly the same as that between Old and New World wines. The same flavour components are there, but they come in much bigger blocks, are much more obvious and accessible and, to me, much more satisfying. Unlikely as it may seem if 'America' just makes you think 'Budweiser', beers like Bridgeport, Sierra Nevada in California, Goose Island in Chicago, and Brooklyn in New York are quickly gaining a reputation as some of the best in the world.

'I think we have a different attitude to brewing,' says Karl. 'In the UK you had a real ale tradition that was almost wiped out. CAMRA rescued it, but because they were trying to preserve something, their whole focus is still on tradition and looking back. Here, the tradition of making decent beer was completely wiped out. Destroyed. There was nothing to preserve. So craft brewers started with an attitude of experimentation. We don't worry about whether something is traditional or not, just if it's great beer.'

Jason Noble Lee is the Bridgeport brewpub's head chef. Like everyone else here, this is a man who clearly loves his work. He speaks the same evangelical culinary language as Garrett Oliver, only with a more manic, extreme accent. 'When you were in Milwaukee did you hear of Beer Butt Chicken? No? It's a local delicacy, man! It's real trailer park. You take a can of Pabst, drink half of it, and shove the can up the chicken's butt, into the cavity. The beer cooks in the bottom of the can and infuses the chicken.' He goes on to tell me about his experiments with porter and stout chocolate cakes, and how he's trying to make a hop-flavoured crème brûlée by packing

Tupperware boxes full of eggs and fresh hops for six days, so the eggs absorb the hop flavour. For the first time I wonder if you can take this beer gastronomy thing too far.

While Jason gets into an argument with someone about hops, I eavesdrop on groups of people sitting at nearby tables having serious discussions about the merits of various IPAs, or arguing about the best cheese to go with beer. And that's just the women.

We're joined by Kevin from Oxfordshire, who came here because he 'had to get away from England' and settled in Portland 'because in all the US it's the place that's most like England – not just the beer, but in every way'. A debate ensues as to how long we all think Budweiser has sucked for. Kevin asks me if I knew that until the Second World War Bud was as good as anything from Europe. Jason disagrees, saying they started using rice and corn instead of malt during the Great Depression, and he reckons it's sucked since then.

People start telling stories about Anheuser-Busch that, if true, add a whole new level of meanness to their story. If the company was not so litigious, I'd share some of them here. 'They actually seem to enjoy being the bad guys,' someone says, wonderingly.* It's the only negative conversation I hear anyone have about any other brewer, big or small, the whole time I'm in Portland.

The Bridgeport brewery and pub occupies a century-old ivy-covered red-brick building in the middle of Portland's old industrial district. Long-abandoned tram tracks run down the

---

* 'Welcome to the world of Anheuser-Busch, where making friends is our business!'

middle of the street before turning abruptly into disused warehouse delivery bays opposite. On a very sunny Sunday lunchtime there's a constant dull roar from the traffic climbing concrete ramps to the Fremont Bridge, arcing sixty feet above the Willamette River, but apart from that there's only birdsong. I'm on the deck outside the pub, enjoying the sun. Young couples sample beer from tasting trays, talking about walking holidays in Patagonia. The tasting trays are a hit. For five dollars you get a four-ounce sample of each of eight beers, arranged on a circular mat with tasting notes. You start with the light, crisp, Blue Heron pale ale, move through copper ale, amber ale, bitter and IPA, to stout and barley wine.

Walking from the brewpub back into town, I only get a couple of hundred yards before I spot a Rogue brewpub. Rogue ales are big in every sense of the word – served in 750-millilitre bottles, they have massive flavours and tend to pack a powerful alcoholic kick. I've had them before from specialist beer shops in the UK, and I'm torn between a desire to try Rogue on its own turf and a bizarre new sense of loyalty to Bridgeport. I needn't have worried; the first brand I see on the bar is Bridgeport's Ropewalk, amid a range of sixteen other ales on tap – half Rogue's own, half their competitors'.

Rogue's stated goal is, 'To provide the finest naturally brewed varietal beer for those who enjoy quality, pleasure, a touch of mischief and, most importantly, good taste.' This attitude is perfectly represented by fantastic beers that gently take the piss out of themselves. Dead Guy Ale, for example, is 'in the style of a German *Maibock*, using our ale yeast "Pac-man",' so called because it eats all the fermentable sugars. Yellow Snow Ale is 'a pale ale, saffron in colour with a smooth malt balance and a floral hop aroma with a spicy dry finish'.

Each comes with a long list of the international brewing awards it has won. Once again, the tasting notes are written to make your mouth water, conjuring up visions of a farmhouse kitchen table, memories of Christmas, images of pine forests, a palette of autumnal earthy tones. I don't see how anyone could read these and not want to plunge in and start experimenting.

I get chatting at the bar with a self-confessed Californian hophead, here to explore the outer limits of beer bitterness, and once again find myself in a place where I feel I could spend the rest of the afternoon. But research demands I move on. I ask the barman if he can tell me how I get to the Horse Brass Pub – a place many people have told me I *really* can't leave town without seeing. ('It's a traditional English pub – you know, full of smoke and everything.') The barman smiles and says, 'I'll take ya. This is the end of my shift and I'm on the way down there myself.'

Mike the barman is heading to the Horse Brass for the big party. Last year a popular Portland brewer was crushed to death while working on his car. This is the first Brewfest weekend since the tragedy, and his friends, fans and fellow brewers are gathering at the Horse Brass to commemorate him by finishing off the last of his beers. As we walk through the sunny late afternoon, whole streets dappled by trees, my heart aches for Portland. I complain to Mike that I have to leave in the morning. But I'll be back, hell, I'll be back, and I'll be bringing half of Britain with me: the gentle, friendly, smiling, kind, warm, big-hearted half. They'll love it here.

Mike interrupts my reverie, saying, 'Let's just pop in here for one on the way,' pushing open an unmarked door. I follow him in, and am stopped in my tracks by a very shapely, very naked woman. 'This is Mary's Club.' Mike smiles. 'It's Portland's oldest titty bar.' Even the sleazy side of Portland comes with a warm, nostalgic glow – and an excellent selection of craft beers.

The Horse Brass is a monster in the heart of a leafy suburban street. At least twice the size of any English pub I've ever been in, it has a long, central bar crowded with row upon row of beer taps. It's not a brewpub – it brews no beer of its own – but it stocks seemingly every craft beer in the state, as well as Stella, Heineken, Boddington's, London Pride and Young's Bitter. It's busy, relaxed, good-natured and energetic all at the same time and, Jesus Christ, there's a Sasquatch sitting in the corner.

Bravely, Mike walks straight up to it and starts talking. 'Don! Can I introduce you to Pete Brown! He's a beer writer from England. Pete, this is Don Younger. This is his pub.'

Well, if he says it is, I doubt anyone is going to argue with him.

Don Younger sits under a shock of silvery-grey hair that sticks out at all angles. A bushy, white beard obscures the bits of his face the hair doesn't. The only features you can be sure of are startling blue eyes, bugging out from his face like golf balls, and lips as red as the eyes are blue, pursed either in concentration or disapproval.

With surprising dexterity, Don leaps off his stool and shakes my hand. A deep, rasping noise, the sound of rocks being ground together, of tectonic plates shifting deep underground, emerges from under his beard. 'Great to have you here. You know Michael Jackson? He was here once. You should have been here earlier. I know all those guys. Damn.'

He shuffles away, and beckons for me to follow him. We go into his office, where he raises an arm in the direction of a stacked bookshelf. 'Look. Books. I got everything.' He edges slowly towards an annexe at the back of the room, again beckoning me to follow. Inside there are more packed book-cases. The arm rises again. 'Books,' he repeats. He turns around, gestures back into the office. 'Books. Books. I know all these guys. I know everyone. I got 'em all.' And it seems that he does. Shelf upon shelf of beer books, from arcane texts on brewing science to histories of regional English breweries to the more ubiquitous world beer guides. With the pub's array of beers and this shrine to beer lore, it's clear to me that I'm in the presence of possibly the biggest beer fan in the world. Fan is exactly the right word. He's not a brewer. He's a retailer of beer only by default. He simply loves it – not just the liquid, but the whole life surrounding it. Even in the most welcoming city on the planet, I feel privileged to have been allowed inside his inner world only seconds after meeting him. I feel obliged to ask some respectful questions.

'How long have you been doing this?' I whisper.

'Ah, that's complicated. Damn. You shoulda been here *earlier*.' He's walking back to the bar now, so I follow.

'What made you decide to start running the pub?'

'Too complicated. Damn. I could have told you everything you want to know. Why didn't you get here earlier?' He wanders off to talk to someone else in the bar.

It turns out that Don is a Portland legend, synonymous with the local brewing scene. He used to work for Lever Brothers, and hated it. Then, in 1976, he spent an evening drinking with friends and woke up the next morning clutching a slip of paper bearing his signature, confirming the purchase of the Horse Brass, a traditional English pub. He had no idea what a traditional English pub was like, but he has always followed a strict code: 'Whatever you say or do when you're drunk, you have to follow through with the next day or give up drinking.' Since that point, Don has run the Horse Brass with remarkable good grace. But he has also stuck to his philosophy that he will never talk business after lunch for fear that he won't remember the conversation. This explains a lot.

When he bought the pub Don drank mainstream American lager, but every night his bar manager would hassle him to try a bottle of Bass Ale. Eventually he gave in, and switched there and then. The Horse Brass began stocking imported beers, and was one of the first places to give bar space to the embryonic craft beers that started coming up the coast from California. The Horse Brass now has over fifty American, British and Belgian beers on tap. In every respect other than this vast range, it strives to be as authentically English as possible, with bangers and mash, steak and kidney pie and, er . . . Scotch eggs on the menu.

Next, Mike introduces me to Lisa Morrison and her husband Mark. Lisa is Portland's 'Beer Goddess', a beer writer who runs a group called Beer Bitches, encouraging women's appreciation of . . . well, it's in the title. She has a Beer 101 class which delves into the history of women's association with beer, from the ancient Sumerian goddess Ninkasi to medieval brewsters and beyond.

'Women just have better palates than men,' she asserts flatly. 'Guys are too hung up on making everything technical and scientific; it's all about degrees plato and units of bitterness. Women taste beer, they know what they like. I find that if someone likes Chardonnay, they'll enjoy a wheat beer. If you like strong coffee, dark chocolate or Merlot, then a stout or a porter may be more up your alley. It's simple really.'

As time passes our conversation starts to deteriorate and involve a fair amount of giggling. Mark points to a mocked-up milk carton sitting behind the bar. In the space where pictures of missing children are often displayed, there's a picture of an empty pair of jeans, somehow standing up on their own. Above the picture is the line: 'Missing: Don Younger's Butt.' Mark then points to Don, who is now standing with his back to us. Sure enough, he has no butt. There's his torso. There's his seemingly empty jeans. There are his feet at the bottom.

It's been a long drinking day. I go to the toilet and realize I'm very drunk indeed. I know I'm in the Horse Brass Pub, but I have absolutely no idea where I am in relation to my hotel or anywhere else in Portland, or how to get back. It's time to make my excuses and leave.

'S'been great, guys', I slur back in the bar, 'but I've got a flight home in the morning.'

'OK, we were just getting ready to go. We'll drive you back,' says Mark. He hasn't drunk as much as the rest of us. I don't *think* he joined in the malt whisky slammers we had half an hour ago. Either way, I have to go.

Just as we're about to leave, I feel a sharp poke in my ribs. There it is again. I turn round, and Don Younger is standing there, poking me. He presses something into my hand and shuffles back to his stool. I look down and see that I'm holding a commemorative horse brass like you would see in a traditional English pub. It was cast in 2001 to celebrate twenty-five years of the Horse Brass Pub being around. I'm touched and, as Lisa and Mark's reaction attests, I'm honoured.

In the ten-minute drive back to my hotel, we swap business

cards and Lisa and Mark demand that I return to Portland as soon as I can, bringing Liz with me. They insist we stay with them. As I stumble out of the car, they're planning itineraries for the visit.

I have never in my life encountered hospitality like Portland has offered this weekend. In the back of my notebook are the names of countless pubs I really, really had to visit while I was here, scrawled in maybe five or six different hands. I can't remember who the writers were. I arrived knowing no one. I'm a writer, and people wanted me to write nice things about them and their hometown, but there's more to it than that. Somehow, this corner of America has evolved into a model beer society. If beer is all about sociability, this is what happens when love of great beer and the great times that go with it are given full, pure expression, when beer appreciation and beer enjoyment become one. It really is Beervana.

The country may be dominated by the huge corporations that churn out Bud, Miller and Coors, but what comes across from the smaller brewers I've met is a reverence for British beer and pubs, tempered by a feeling that the British beer establishment is elitist and out of touch. People like Garrett Oliver and Karl Ockert are almost as critical of CAMRA as they are of the big brewers. They just want to make the best best-tasting beers they can. And if that's achieved by a combination of tradition and innovation, then what, precisely, is the problem?

The two ends of the American brewing spectrum represent the main traits that, for me now, characterize the American mentality: the craft brewers with their eternal questing, exploring spirit, pushing back the wild frontier; the big corporations embodying the seemingly insatiable desire for scale and dominance. Whether we're seduced by the marketing and bullying sales tactics of the latter, or the character, body and passion of the former, it seems likely that one day soon we'll all be drinking American beer.

7

'Mate, are you right?'

Sydney

As any traveller knows, passport control is uniformly stern the world over.

Australia is different.

In front of Liz and me in the queue, a young attractive Japanese woman presents her passport.

'Hmm . . . I'm afraid we're going to have to pull you in for an interview,' says the officer, trying not to smile.

The woman says nothing, staring straight ahead.

'I've got a new pair of handcuffs I haven't tried out yet,' says the officer.

Still, she says nothing.

'I'm sensing that you're not tempted by that. OK, have a nice day,' he says, handing back her documents. Then it's my turn. Unsure of what to expect, I'm only a little let down by a cheery, 'Hello, mate, how's it going?'

Australia is a country whose most popular prime minister

was called Bob. In the UK, 'Bob' would confine your political career to trade unionism – you'd have to become 'Robert' if you wanted to stand any chance of getting a 'Right Honourable' in front of it. But Bob Hawke won four consecutive elections for the Labor Party and gained the highest popularity rating of any prime minister since the introduction of public opinion polls. He ended strife between the unions and their employers, introduced Medicare, oversaw Australia's bicentennial celebrations, and made huge leaps forward in equal rights for women and for Aborigines. This is more than enough to explain his popularity, but his ratings peaked *before* most of these achievements. Australians loved Bob because for many years, he held the world record for speed-drinking or 'skulling' beer.*

Like Bill Clinton, in his youth Bob was a Rhodes scholar at Oxford University in the 1960s. He tells the story in his memoirs:

> A system operated at dinner in the Great Hall under which if an offence was committed – in my case coming to dinner without a gown (some bastard had borrowed mine) – one was 'sconced'. This meant having to drink two and a half pints of ale out of an antique pewter pot in less than twenty-five seconds. Failure to do so involved

---

* The record was broken by a man called Leo Williams, a law student from Queensland. In Australia Leo hasn't yet been prime minster, but he went on to play rugby union for Queensland, have a successful legal career (appearing before the high court of Australia eleven times), become a consul for Western Samoa and an honorary ambassador for Queensland. He is also the head of the rugby world cup organization, and has been personally thanked by Nelson Mandela for bringing rugby back to South Africa.

paying for the first drink, plus another two and a half pints . . . I was too broke for the fine and necessity became the mother of ingestion. I downed the contents of the pot in eleven seconds, left the Sconcemaster floundering, and entered the *Guinness Book of Records* with the fastest time ever recorded. This feat was to endear me to some of my fellow Australians more than anything else I ever achieved.

Two and a half pints in eleven seconds. Even if the *Guinness Book of Records* hadn't bowed to neo-puritanical pressure and stopped accepting drinking records, I can't see Tony Blair beating that one in a hurry.

According to famously misanthropic travel writer Bruce Chatwin, there was quite a bit not to like about Australia, but even he was taken by Australia's beer culture, writing, 'One of the few moments of happiness a man knows in Australia is that moment of meeting the eyes of another man over the tops of two beer glasses.'

I've been looking forward to Sydney. Apart from its stunning beauty, fantastic weather and great food, Australia is a crucial stop on my quest to figure out the whys of beer drinking. Some pundits claim that part of Britain's drinking problem is simply genetic or cultural: Anglo-Saxons are just predisposed to getting bollocksed in a way our Latin cousins are not. Others argue that climate is a fundamental factor, that we drink because it's cold, dark and rainy all the time. So Australia forms a fascinating control for our international experiment; the population is largely from the same genetic pool as back home, but the climate is much more pleasant. So what happens?

Liz's cousin Tom moved out here a few years ago with his wife Kirsten. He meets us at the airport, and leads us out into a gorgeous Sydney spring day, the sun climbing into the north-west of a clear blue sky.

The old 'joke' about Australia is that it is upside down. It's not, of course. But it *is* back to front. Tell anyone you're going south of the equator, and they will inevitably urge you to watch for the water going the wrong way down the plughole. This is true, and mildly interesting in its own way, but it does suggest an unhealthy obsession with the trivial. My point is this: call me melodramatic if you like, but *hasn't anyone noticed that the sun is going the wrong way around the sky? Jesus Christ, it's in the north! That's just not right!*

Tom and Kirsten live on the north shore of Sydney Harbour, a stone's throw from a slim crescent between two cliffs called Freshwater Beach. In the time it takes me to walk from my house to the White Hart, my local, Tom and Kirsten can be jumping the waves on the beach where surfing was invented. There's a pub between their house and this beach, with that other great Aussie institution, the drive-through bottle shop, right next door. While I won't hear a word against Tom's hometown of Newcastle, I can understand why he's living here instead.

Having said our hellos, showered and changed, Liz and I go for a bracing walk to try to stave off the jet lag. Over the headland from the bay, we're soon overlooking Manly Beach, a shallow golden strip that curves around gently for a mile or so.

Manly is an affluent suburb built on an area named by Captain Arthur Phillip, the first governor of New South Wales, who looked at the shore from his ship, saw the Aboriginal people of the Kay-ye-my clan and declared how confident and manly they looked. With his odd and somehow depressing literalness, Phillip ensured that this lovely suburb will remain the butt of juvenile jokes for ever more. We walk past the Manly Boathouse, the Manly Italian Restaurant and Manly Seaside Kebabs, each of which conjures up its own somehow camp image. The Beach Pit, Manly, and Ivanhoe of Manly are the only places that avoid the obvious invitation to snigger by constructing the name in a different way. But Ivanhoe of Manly is still funny anyway, because it's called Ivanhoe of Manly. Ivanhoe of Manly is a pub. I have to confess that I'm quite nervous about ordering my first beer – it's not as easy as you might think.

The key to understanding this vast country is to recognize that until 1901 it was a collection of separate colonies that just happened to be on the same huge land mass. Make no mistake, everyone here is bloody proud to be Australian, but in many ways – and certainly with regard to beer – it's your state or territory that counts. Until the last few years your state's beer was 'the best beer in the world, mate'. Beer from every other state was undrinkable piss, so bad that 'a thirsty horse wouldn't drink it', even though non-Australians, who of course by definition are simply not as good at drinking beer, might struggle to discern any difference between them. Eventually an Australian might concede that anything was fine if you were thirsty enough, and more importantly, that any-thing was better than Pommy beer, which they swore was served 'at blood heat'.

Equally important is the nomenclature surrounding what you actually call your beer, and how you order it. The website www.australianbeers.com provides an essential guide to getting it right. A Queenslander in his local would typically enjoy the following exchange:

Barman:	Mate, are you right?
Queenslander:	Pot o' Fourex, thanks, mate.
Barman (after getting money):	Thanks, mate.
Queenslander (after getting beer):	Thanks, mate.

However, this same ritual observed in New South Wales would result in a very dry evening.

Barman:	Mate, are you right?
Queenslander:	Pot o' Fourex, thanks, mate.
Barman (looking confused):	Sorry?
Queenslander (thinking very hard and speaking slowly):	Sorry, a schooner o' New, thanks.
Barman:	You from Queensland, are you?
Barman (after receipt of money):	Cheers.
Queenslander (after receipt of beer, trying to fit in linguistically):	Cheers.

Venture into the Northern Territory, and none of this will wash. Instead, the correct exchange would be more along the lines of:

Barman:	Mate, are you right?
NTer:	Green can, thanks, bloke.
Barman (after receipt of money):	Thanks, bloke.
NTer:	Thanks, bloke.

To crack the code, you need to know that beer is served by the tin, and different brands have different-coloured tins: a blue can is Foster's, Green is Victoria Bitter, yellow is Fourex, and so on.

If you think this sounds complicated, let's go back to the first two examples. Part of the confusion was over Fourex versus New. You just need to know that these are informal names for Castlemaine XXXX and Toohey's New, and you're OK. But there was also that need to switch from 'pot' to 'schooner'. The most important characteristic of beer in Australia is that it must be very cold, so it is served in small measures. But the climate varies across the continent, and so, therefore, does the preferred quantity of beer. In Sydney you default to a schooner (425 millilitres). In Queensland, where it's hotter, it's a pot (285 millilitres). In South Australia you might order a pint (425 millilitres), but you shouldn't confuse this with a New South Wales pint, which is 568 millilitres. You could perhaps play it safe and stick to a schooner, but you'd be thrown by the fact that in South Australia this would get you 285 millilitres, instead of the 425 millilitres everywhere else, which in Victoria and Queensland would mean you'd actually be drinking a pot rather than a schooner, even though in New South Wales and Western Australia this measure is a middy. In the case of the latter you have to call it this, because a 575-millilitre measure is already called a pot. Once you've mastered these technicalities, you might want to try ordering a pony, a bobbie, a ten, eight or six, a handle, a seven, a butcher, or simply a glass – or perhaps a small glass.

I'm shaking as I approach the bar in Ivanhoe of Manly.

I know what the right bar call is in theory, but I'm still too nervous to make it. Eventually I manage a passable imitation of someone for whom English is a second language, pointing weakly at the bar and mumbling, 'Umm . . . two Hahn?'

The barman doesn't ask me what size, and gives me two schooners. I've let myself down, confirming my status as a wanky tourist, and I sense the barman is disappointed in me as well. There's a certain *froideur* to his manner. The beer is of course very, very cold. It's refreshing like ice cream, too cold to taste of anything really, but still manages a crisp, lagery bite.

Towards the back of the pub a neon sign announces the Aquarium Lounge, the pokie room. Pokies – poker machines – are a universal feature of Australian pub life, because Australians are obsessed with gambling. Casinos were legalized in the 1970s, and in 1984 an act was passed allowing pubs to have gambling machines. Australia now has 180,000 poker machines, 21 per cent of all the gambling machines in the world.

Ivanhoe of Manly reminds me of a northern English working men's club from the early 1980s. We sit at tiny tables on high stools in a large, open, high-ceilinged room, decorated with wood panelling and mud-brown furnishings. It's about 3 p.m., and the bar is filling up with people in ones and twos, coming in for a schooner or three at the end of their shifts. Mainly they sit in silence staring at the big screens on the walls. Fox 2 is showing the US Open, Fox 1 is, of course, showing last Saturday's English Premiership football. Night Life, a local version of MTV, completes the mix and provides the soundtrack. I suppose this is Rupert Murdoch's native land, but it still feels like he's invading.

And what bar food does this down-at-heel, slightly depressing pub offer? I pick up a menu. Of course. Burgers and pies and chips and ... market fish (today's is pan-fried ocean trout) with sauté potatoes, spinach, roast tomato and orange and seeded mustard dressing. Celeriac soup with garlic oil. Rare beef salad with roast sweet potato and blue cheese dressing.

Like Britain, Australia has recently experienced something of a personality transplant where food and drink are concerned. Until the 1970s Aussie cuisine was based on the standard, no-nonsense British meat and two veg template. Pies were the highest form of culinary excellence,* with the pièce de résistance being the pie floater – doesn't the name just make your stomach growl? A South Australian speciality, this is an upside-down pie in a bowl of watery mushy peas and tomato sauce.† If you were feeling less hungry, Aussies would boast of bush tucker like fat, pasty witchetty grubs, or Vegemite sandwiches. Vegemite is a spread made of yeast extract seasoned with heady national pride.

Then, Australia relaxed its (at best morally dubious) immigration policy and allowed in people from non-Anglo Saxon countries. Italians and Greeks had been there since the Second World War, and in the 1970s Asians were admitted. Australia realized it was sitting among a vast cornucopia of fresh, tasty ingredients, a gastronome's dream. Aussie wine makers learned how to create some of the world's best. Australians have slipped from being the third-biggest beer drinkers in the world on a per capita basis to ninth. Today, even a 'rough as guts'

---

* To be honest, they still are, and rightly so.

† This also happens to be a Barnsley speciality. Liz still tells the story of how I treated her to this meal the first time I took her to Barnsley, and plays it for laughs. But if it's a good pie, I honestly don't see what the problem is.

pub will have fine wine and fresh seafood rubbing shoulders with icy beer and basic stodgy tucker.

Manly Wharf sits at one end of the Best Commute in the World. Ferries leave every thirty minutes for the journey to downtown Sydney. The Manly Wharf Hotel overlooks the bay, so you can grab a schooner and watch the ferries approaching, timing your drinking near-perfectly to catch the next one. I mean, obviously, I'd rather go for a fresh juice, but the juice bar doesn't offer the same vantage point as the hotel. Best to be safe.

I order a schooner o' VB, and still can't shake the feeling that I'm a fraud even as an Aussie bloke behind me orders exactly the same thing. Then I spot something I hadn't expected: a beer called Four Seasons, which as far as I can make out, changes four times a year. Just now it's a 'spicy winter warmer', dark and rich. I decide Liz can have the VB and I order one of these.

'Have you tried the spring ale?' asks the barmaid, 'It's gorgeous.'

'No, I wish I could, but I'm only in town for five days.'

'Well, it'll be spring by then!'

Of course, the winter warmer is served just above freezing, but I'm surprised to see craft beer here.

Like every Pommy who comments on how cold Aussie beer is, I had previously linked it to the climate. But while today is sunny, it's not warm enough to play outside without a coat on. Yet glasses come from a freezer cabinet kept especially for storage and go under pumps encrusted with ice. Cold beer is no longer just a practical consideration, it's a religion. I carry the beers out to our table on the deck overlooking the harbour, and when I put them down the glasses tear the top layer of skin from my hands. OK, they don't. But my fingers do go numb and it takes five minutes to rub the feeling back into them.

The ferry is liveried in cream and dark green like some 1940s steam train coming to take us on a grand tour. It feels impossibly touristy and perfect for what is, for most people, the standard workday commute. We finish our drinks as it pulls into the dock, and board as the gate opens.

The rocky, wooded headland that forms the western side of North Harbour juts out into the main harbour for maybe half a mile or so. As it starts to fade out into the water and the swell hits us from the seaward side, it teases us with a succession of views. First the tops of the skyscrapers of the Central Business District (CBD) appear, then their torsos. Then finally you clear a rocky promontory and ... there's another outcrop a few hundred yards further on, tapering to another point, hiding one of the most iconic and beautiful cityscapes in the world for a few minutes more. This happens again, and then again, and the desire to see the full view flares into an obsession. I keep willing the boat to clear the next headland, and it keeps taunting me with another rocky point, always just a bit lower than the last one, but not low enough. Come on! We've seen the skyscrapers! You know what we want! Show us your curves! Get your bridge and opera house out! And finally, after stretching the moment of revelation past all credulity, the last rocky headland falls into the water and That View of Sydney is revealed, framed by a luxury yacht in the foreground, airliners dipping between the struts of the harbour bridge behind.

There's a majesty about how downtown Sydney fits

together that's not immediately apparent from all those post-card shots. From here, the skyscrapers of the CBD seem rooted in nothing but parks and gardens. It looks like a comic-book vision of the utopian city of the future. In fact, you don't really see it even in science fiction any more – we're too pessimistic with our projections now to imagine anything like this.

After about half an hour, the ferry pulls into Circular Quay in downtown Sydney. We head off up to our right, out along a spit of land that ends with the south side of the bridge, known as The Rocks. In one sense it's the kind of place most cities have, the formerly seedy industrial district which has been revamped and is now the centre of stylish eating and drinking. But this is the spot where the First Fleet – the first party of British convicts and their guards – landed in 1788. In doing so, they founded the first of the colonies that would eventually become Australia.

The early colony, dependent as it was on the navy, was founded on rum and the lash, and the first governors encouraged the establishment of a brewing industry to wean people off the grog. It was difficult to brew in the heat, without proper equipment or materials, and for most of the nineteenth century beer was known by a variety of colourful nicknames such as squirt, sheep wash, stringy-bark, shypoo and shearer's joy.

Originally this was an open-air prison, but gradually huts and streets emerged. The early settlers soon realized they had discovered excellent harbour facilities, and once transportation of prisoners ended in the 1840s The Rocks became the colony's primary trading port. It remained a place, according to Commissioner J.T. Bigge, 'distinguished . . . for the practice of every debauchery and villainy ... inhabited by the most profligate and depraved part of the population'. Reluctant sailors were shanghaied from the pubs, some of which still stand. The whole area was quarantined in the early 1900s thanks to an outbreak of bubonic plague. And in the 1970s the place was almost flattened to make way for new skyscraper developments, until the unionized workforce flatly refused to bulldoze their country's heritage and forced a compromise that preserved much of the area.

In the heart of The Rocks stands the Fortune of War, which claims to be Sydney's oldest pub. It's not the only pub that makes this claim, but it was built in 1828, only forty years after the First Fleet landed. The walls are covered in clippings and historic documents.

Three people come and stand next to us at the bar.

'Fourex Gold, please, mate,' says the first one, with a hint of a suppressed smirk.

'You're gonna struggle, mate,' replies the barman, deadpan.

'You blokes don't know what real beer is,' replies the customer.

From the way they are talking, I assume barman and customer are old friends, and this is a routine that happens every day. Then the customer asks what there is to do around here. The barman tells him there's live music at the Three Wise Monkeys, and, 'King's Cross is the red light district, but there's a lot of travellers there.'* This is obviously the first time they have been here. I can't imagine this exchange taking place in this way anywhere else in the world.

The draught beer fonts in the Fortune of War are not just

---

* Some things are the same whichever side of the world you're on.

cold; they're encased in solid ice. It grows on the outside of the brass, thanks to an inert gas being pumped around just below the surface of the metal. It looks great, so great I have to take a photo of it. This prompts some sniggering from the Queenslanders. A minute later they ask me to take their picture, almost certainly taking the piss, and we introduce ourselves. Because piss-taking doesn't always have to be malicious.

Big Ben, Jamie and Shazza are from Brisbane. 'You're from England? Jeez, mate, you'd hardly notice,' says Big Ben. (It's not malicious, remember.) 'So, mate,' he continues, 'if you're from England, do you know Tony from London?' I laugh politely, and all three of them roar with delight. 'You got it! You got it! Fair play, mate. The last time I said that to an English guy he blew up at me.' Big Ben adopts a contorted stiff-upper-lip accent, 'Have you any *fucking* idea how big London is? How the *fuck* should I know Tony?'

I might take photographs of beer fonts, but I'm all right. I've demonstrated that I'm not a Whingeing Pom, and we're now best mates. I ask about the Fourex ordering. Brisbane is the capital of Queensland, the state known as XXXX Country. Why are they here in Sydney if the beer is so much worse?

'Oh, mate, we're just down to go out and have a good time. Brizzie is coming up. It's a big city now. But it still feels like a country town compared to Sydney and Melbourne. It could never compete on the nightlife. Couldn't live down here though. Too hectic. The people are too stuck-up.'

As Liz and I leave the pub the early spring sun is sinking over the harbour, and the air over The Rocks is heavy with the smell of seafood frying in butter. We meet up with Fred

Madderom, who runs an ad agency here, and over a few beers he talks about how Australians share the British enthusiasm for drinking to get hoonered. Cricket is a focal point, with a new custom of hiring 'beer wenches': scantily clad women who fetch beer on a more or less continual basis so you and your mates don't miss a second of the game. 'Except most guys know they aren't going to see the end of the game,' says Fred.

Fred's mate Russell is eager to tell me about the beer diet he has invented: 'It's real simple: you drink as much beer as you want, and you work out like a bastard every day of the week.'

More of Fred's mates join us as dusk falls, and every single one of them asks me if I've heard of the Darwin stubbie. A stubbie is a squat bottle that contains 375 millilitres of beer. A Darwin stubbie is the same shape, but six times bigger. If Australia was still considered as a series of separate states, the Northern Territory, of which Darwin is the capital, would be way out in front in the world drinking stakes, with an average per capita consumption of around 200 litres a year.

Towards the end of the evening, a professional acquaintance of Fred's staggers in. He's been drinking since lunchtime, and when he hears I'm visiting from Britain he decides to give me a formal welcome. This consists of calling me a Pommy cunt, and grabbing me in a tight headlock so he can be sure of my full attention while he explains to me precisely how much better the Australians are than the British, citing the medals tally from the recent Athens Olympics with a level of mathematical detail that belies his drunken state. He gives me the overall totals and then the precise calculations of bronze, silver and gold medals per capita of total population of the two countries. Then he stands up, insists on buying drinks for us all, and sways to the bar, where he is gently and diplomatically refused service. Citing jet lag, Liz and I decide it's time for bed.

The next morning, we're wide awake at 4 a.m. The parrot squawking outside the window doesn't help. We wait for it to stop, but instead it's gradually joined by a range of Australia's famously individualistic fauna in an infernal pre-dawn chorus. First there's the dog-being-kicked bird. This is joined by the randy-tomcat bird, then the old-man-whistling-the-first-line-of-his-favourite-song-over-and-over-again bird. It starts to rain and they all shut up, apart from the dog-being-kicked bird, which seems to like it. Then the cruellest bastard of them all comes along: the electronic-alarm-clock bird, the one that goes *be-be-be-bip, be-be-be-bip, be-be-be-bip* very quickly and highly pitched. They must have designed those clocks to sound just like this bird – it's identical. The only thing that could be more irritating is the Nokia-ringtone bird, which I'm expecting any second when our real alarm clock finally joins in.

Today I'm meeting David Downie, the mastermind behind australianbeers.com. Dave is a twenty-nine-year-old lawyer who loves not only beer, but also the culture that surrounds it and what that culture says about being Australian. When I found his website I knew immediately that this was someone who thought about beer in exactly the same way I did. I asked if he would like to meet up when I was in Sydney, and he said he would love to. Then he mentioned the 1,000 kilometre flight he would have to take from Brisbane. But he didn't seem to mind.

We start off in what Dave refers to as a 'wanker bar', a

smart new establishment on the harbour front overlooking The Rocks and Circular Quay. We sit at a strangely high and bizarrely uncomfortable table as a white-coated waiter fetches our beers. I tell Dave about Big Ben, Jamie and Shazza, and how I was struck by the incredibly matey rapport they instantly had with the barman.

'Yeah, that's fairly typical,' Dave replies, 'and Sydney is the worst place in the country for that. It's the coldest city in Australia. I used to live down here but it's not friendly enough for me. The people are rude and ignore you compared to everyone else. It goes with being the biggest and having all this big business here.'

We look around at the suited clientele and at the Asian fusion menu before us. By my standards the service is still friendly, but Dave is clearly not happy in this kind of environment. It's not that he's intimidated by it – he's a lawyer who used to work here – it's just that this is, to him, a far cry from what Australian drinking culture is all about.

We move on through a range of Sydney's pubs, and we compare notes about beer culture. Is there a nerdy aspect to what Dave does?

He shakes his head. 'We don't have any equivalent to CAMRA here. It's not that kind of thing. I mean, everybody drinks beer. We don't have this whole class thing. We're one of the few countries probably that talks about something being in the national spirit. We say if something is un-Australian, and it's un-Australian to not drink beer.'

After a quick lunch we take a cab into the suburb of Camperdown to meet Chuck Hahn at his Malt Shovel Brewery. Although he denies it during our conversation, American-born Chuck is probably Australia's highest-profile brewer. He used to work for Coors in Colorado before heading for Australia and New Zealand, where he helped run a couple of the southern hemisphere's biggest breweries and develop various new brews. In the late 1980s he set up his own venture and created Hahn Premium and Hahn Light. When the business merged with New Zealand's Lion Nathan, revamped versions of these beers became some of Australia's favourites. In 1998 Chuck decided to get back to doing what he loved most: creating craft beers with flavour and character. He opened the Malt Shovel Brewery, and began producing porters, IPAs and amber ales, selling them under the brand name James Squire after the man who arrived a convict, built Australia's first commercial brewery, and died a rich and free man.

Chuck is in his late fifties, tall, slim and in better shape than anyone his age has any right to be, let alone someone who works around beer. His casual dress and easy-going manner suggest a guy on a weekend fishing trip in the mountains rather than one of the most well known brewers in the world. I tell Chuck that it's great to find beers like his in Australia, where I thought people only swigged freezing-cold lager.

'We talk a lot about beer R & R,' says Chuck in a warm, mellifluous accent halfway between Colorado and Sydney: 'beer *relevance* and beer *reverence*. Castlemaine XXXX is a beautiful, refreshing beer. Now there's nothing wrong with refreshment, but there's a place for something else as well. Premium and speciality beer is now 10 per cent of the whole Australian market, and it's growing. People are drinking less, but better.'

'Do people drink your beers as cold as they do everything else?'

Chuck tries to be diplomatic, but it's easy to see where his sympathies lie. 'Australians like their beer cold.' He smiles. 'It's usually served between two and five degrees. As I said, it's about refreshment. But with a meal, say, beer should be served at a warmer temperature.'

Chuck admits that he's fighting a losing battle, trying to persuade people to drink warmer beer. But even if they're drinking them at the wrong temperature, people like his beers. He's opened the James Squire Brewhouse, a big pub in Sydney, and recently another in Melbourne. 'Beers are matched with food, and served in nicer glassware,' says Chuck. 'We don't market our beers: we just brew beer we like to drink ourselves, and it spreads by word of mouth.'

Dave is in awe after meeting Chuck. 'Isn't this great? My country's highest-profile brewer, and I'm sitting here spinning shit with him just because I put together this crappy website. It's a good life.'

'That's beer for you,' I agree. We hurry through the fine drizzle.

'Shame about the weather,' says Dave.

'Was it nice until a couple of days ago?' I ask.

'Yeah, it was.'

'Yeah. People say that wherever I go now.'

Dave's a big lad, and I'm starting to struggle to keep up with him. Schooners are somewhat smaller than pints, but they go down very quickly, and I have no idea how much I've had. By the time we meet one of Dave's mates and head back to The Rocks, I'm afraid I'm rather drunk.

We visit the Hero of Waterloo, which, like the Fortune of War, also claims to be Australia's oldest pub. Below us are cellars and tunnels from where sailors were carried out to ships once they had drunk to the point of collapse. There are signs everywhere of the past. There's also a sign saying, 'Monday night is pie night! $5 from 6 p.m.' Sadly it's Thursday today, so it's just schooner night.

We talk about the roots of Australian drinking culture. Much of it has its origins in the shearers, who would work a whole season in the wool sheds before heading back to the city to spend their earnings – although many of them would never make it that far. Towns like Gundagai on the Sydney–Melbourne road in New South Wales were lined with 'hotels'. Many Australian pubs are still called hotels, though they stopped offering accommodation – and in many cases even food – when they realized they could make money far more easily from these hard-drinking men. Often shearers were 'lambed down'. The pay cheque would go behind the bar, and the shearer would stay in there drunk until it ran out – or until the barman claimed it had. Pick up any book on Australian beer folklore – and there are a distressingly large number – and it will be full of stories and songs from places like this.

Some time later, I'm helped into a cab, which I manage to navigate back to Freshwater Beach. When I get back to Tom and Kirsten's, Liz is in full flow, telling them about the evening last week when I returned home to find her and a couple of friends in front of the TV, the bottles of IPA I had lugged back from the States lying empty around them. 'We've decided this is our favourite beer,' Liz had said. 'I don't even like beer, but this is lovely,' Joan had said. 'Can you get us some more?' Liz had said. 'No, it's not on sale anywhere this side of the Atlantic. That was all I could carry back with me,' I had said. And they refused to even *look* guilty.

I tell Tom, Liz and Kirsten that we will enjoy together the special millennium beer Chuck gave me, that he said it went really well with cheese so we have to go out now and find the best cheddar in Sydney, and I'll brook no argument. 'I'm not drunk. Chuck-Chuck-Chuckie Hahn,' I add for emphasis.

'Yes, lovely, we did that joke already,' says Liz, an iron fist of a telling-off inside a velvet smile.

'Chuckie Hahn, Chuckie Hahn,' I reply.

'Yes, we know.'

'Chuckie Hahn, let me rock you, let me rock you, Chuckie Hahn, let me rock you, that's all I wanna do.'

'I think it's time for bed,' says Kirsten.

I wake up after a full uninterrupted night's sleep to find a glorious clear blue sky ready for my trip to Bondi Beach. I spell that out because it's one of those moments when I finally agree with everyone from random people in the street to my mum: I'm a lucky bastard.

I meet Dave at Icebergs, a Returning Servicemen's League club on the cliffs at the southern tip of Bondi Beach. RSLs are similar to British Legion and UK working men's clubs, but whereas these have largely disappeared as everyone except old men in flat caps opts for smarter, (s)wankier bars, Australia's classlessness means they are still popular with anyone who fancies paying a little less for a beer in return for a nominal membership fee. I had thought that, by definition, they would be a little tacky. Until now. It's just as well that my quest is not for the best bar in the world. If it was, this would be the final page. Because *nothing* can beat this.

Bondi is smaller and more urban than I expected, more like a ridiculously beautiful English seaside town than the wild expanse of gleaming sand and palm trees I had imagined. But as far as pub locations go, it'll do. The beach may be short, but it's deep. And anyway, the point is, it's not about the land here but the sea, and that's magnificent. Beneath a nippy sapphire sky, the blue-green water is almost entirely foam for the last thirty yards as it attacks the shore. Directly below us are a couple of swimming pools built into the rocks. Huge waves crash and fizz into them as a few mad souls swim grim lengths. After an uncertain late morning the sun is back out, and the surfers are venturing forth into it.

Dave is waiting for me on a deck that runs along the outside of the bar, about sixty feet above the surf. 'It's perfect weather for surfing,' I say. 'Somehow it seems a bit perverse to be spending the whole day in a pub.'

Dave looks at me and shakes his head. 'Mate, this is what it's all about. You sit in a bar on the beach. You've got an ice-cold beer, the beach, the sea, the surfers, the ladies, all laid out in front of you. Life doesn't get any better.'

We sit in silence for a few moments, looking out, until Dave earns my undying gratitude by saying, 'Mate, I was in a world of pain this morning. I woke up and thought, Jeez, I've only been on this guy's quest for one day. How must he feel?'

We talk about beer, celebrity, pubs, ambition, beer, being a writer. Every time I make a point which I think is interesting, Dave looks at me sympathetically and says, 'Mate, you told me this last night.'

Then he asks me about Pommy beer. 'Is it true you guys like to drink it warm?'

'No, that's a total myth!' I say. 'Lager might be served around freezing here, but it's cold in the UK as well. It's never more than three or four degrees. And while bitter is warmer, you can hardly call it *warm*. If warm is room temperature –

which is what red wine is served at – that's around eighteen or nineteen degrees Celsius. A pint of real ale or Guinness is best served lightly chilled, say at around seven or eight degrees. If you've been outdoors in temperatures of seven or eight degrees, you know that's pretty chilly.'

Dave's eyes widen, and his voice drops to little more than a whisper. 'Seven or eight degrees? So it's *true* then. You *do* drink it warm!'

As afternoon heads for evening, Dave rounds up a few friends to come out and join us for a Friday-night pub crawl in downtown Sydney. We start off at Darling Harbour, a new development of bars, clubs and shops. As we get there, I count the seconds. I know what's coming. Ah, here it is: 'This is a wanker strip. Full of wanker bars.' I feel I know Dave well enough now to point out that this is an expression he uses a great deal. He has a low wanker threshold. This in itself tells you a great deal about Australian drinking life.

I like the harbour front, and even Dave can't complain about the James Squire Brewhouse, a new, trendy-looking place committed to serving Chuck's Hahn's fantastic beers, along with a food menu to complement them, at non-extortionate prices. Here, in lager-swilling Oz, in one of the smartest bars in one of the hippest districts, the smartest people are all drinking pale ales, amber ales and porters. Sure, they're still served just above freezing, killing off most of their character, but even so they're a lot more flavourful than lager. And the bigger point is: people are drinking these beers because it is cool to do so. I really am on the other side of the world.

Tom joins us, delighted at having an excuse to come out for a few beers, along with a couple of his mates. We're quite a big group now and when it's time to move on we need several cabs to take us to Woolloomooloo, the Sydney district with the most Australian-sounding name in the world, the place where all the country's surplus Os come to die.

We end up in an RSL, which looks like a bookie's with a pub in it. Late at night, this strikes me in some ways as a great idea: just get rid of the wall between two establishments often adjacent to each other and usually with the same clientele. But it does change the atmosphere of the pub, and you can't really relax when there are signs everywhere asking, 'Is gambling a problem for you?'

People start to drift away in ones and twos, and without my really noticing, it's soon midnight. The contrast with eleven o' clock closing in the UK could not be greater. It's a very similar crowd, in very similar pubs doing pretty much the same thing. But because there's no artificially early end to the evening, the whole atmosphere is far more relaxed. A lot of people leave before eleven because there is no pressure to stay out till the end. Those that want to stay later drift away when they feel like it.

At about half past midnight we leave the pub to go to Harry's, a Sydney institution. Even Russell Crowe has been known to come here and allegedly hurl racist abuse at the staff when he's in town. Harry's Café de Wheels is an old-fashioned trailer that sits on the street, decked in Union Jacks and yellowing photographs and press cuttings. I have a curried chicken pie floater, and it tastes like heaven. The atmosphere around Harry's is chilled and good-humoured. This is not just down to the quality of the pies, nor the fact that Russell Crowe is out of town. People are drunk, but happy and relaxed. If there is anything genetic about our predilection for drinking to excess, this demonstrates that it still does not need to be unpleasant. It's difficult to believe that this is the same country which had the early closing nightmare of the 'six o'clock swill' until a generation ago.

The six o' clock swill was the name given to the carnage that Australia endured through the middle of the twentieth century thanks to a policy that proved beyond any doubt that limiting access to alcohol has an effect that is quite the opposite of what is intended. Pubs and bars closed at 6 p.m. People got out of work at 5 p.m. That meant an entire evening's drinking was condensed into an hour, with the result that drinking was only ever unpleasant and desperate. Pubs were simple watering holes, and after they had closed the streets were full of disaffected drunks. Australia endured this from the First World War until the 1960s.

Now they open as long as they want. RSLs charge a nominal membership and stay open almost twenty-four hours a day – they simply have to nominate any two-hour period when they close for cleaning. But at the same time there are very clear campaigns and guidelines on what you are drinking and what the effects are, stiff penalties for any bar that serves someone who is obviously drunk, and ever-tightening drink-driving laws. The enthusiastic but benign Friday night drinking that results gives a clear indication that, more than climate or genetics or anything else, drinking behaviour is governed by culture. And that culture is created by the laws that govern it.

Penrith

I'd been told that if I wanted to see true Australian drinking, I had to get out into West Sydney. Inland from the city, a big, flat plain stretches thirty-odd miles to the foot of the Blue Mountains, so called because of the haze that rises from the eucalyptus trees on their slopes. This area has become a suburban sprawl where tourists fear to tread, populated by people who work shifts and go to the pub as soon as they're off. And on a Friday and Saturday night, many of them head to the Penrith Panthers RSL, the largest club in the southern hemisphere, where they queue up for a chance to play one of the 2,000 pokies. The Panthers is not mentioned in any tourist guide I've seen, and I feel I can't leave town without a visit.

It's almost a disaster. Arriving after a long, slow train journey, I find a map outside the big mall in Penrith which has Penrith RSL clearly labelled on it. That sounds like my destination. Ten minutes later I'm standing outside a building the size of a cinema multiplex. It's big, but smaller than I had expected. There's a security guard inside at the bottom of a bank of escalators.

'Is this the really big club, the main one in town?' I ask him.

'Yes, it is.'

'Ah, good, right. Thanks.' I head for the escalators.

'Excuse me, sir, I need to see some ID.'

Shit. I didn't bring my passport with me. Technically, RSLs are private clubs for members and their guests, but rules are pretty relaxed. They let you buy a day membership, but officially this requires ID. This is the first time that anyone has insisted on it though. I decide to play dumb. 'Um, why?'

'Club rules. No ID, no entry. No exceptions.'

'Ah. Right. You see, the thing is, I've come all the way from England to write a story about your club. I didn't realize I needed ID. I mean, it's not an age thing, is it? I'm clearly old enough. How does me being who I say I am make any difference? And why would I try to be anyone else?'

'I can't let you in.'

'It's my last day here,' I plead. 'It just took me nearly two hours to get here from Sydney. I haven't got time to go back and get my passport.'

'No ID, no entry.'

'But I've just travelled 13,000 miles to write about the biggest club in the southern hemisphere!'

'Oh, right, you should have said.' I adopt a bright expression, full of gratitude at what I anticipate is a change of heart. Then he says, 'You don't want here, you want the Penrith Panthers RSL.'

'This isn't the Panthers?'

'No.'

'But I just asked you if this was the big one and you said it was!'

'They won't let you in either.'

There's nothing to be gained by asking him if he he was bullied or had a smothering mother, or if he has ever kissed a girl. I bid him a curt good day and follow his shaky directions towards the Panthers RSL.

I know immediately when I finally find it that it's the right place. The Penrith Panthers World of Entertainment is too big to be described as a big club. It's the size of a shopping mall, sitting in the middle of a mall-sized car park with fast food outlets orbiting the fringes, just in case the journey from your car to the club's interior is too long to make without a sustaining burger and fries.

My new friend with the tiny penis clearly hasn't yet phoned to warn them not to let me in, because after hardly any pleading at all the lovely girl on the door gives me a scolding for forgetting my passport and ushers me quickly inside.

The mall comparison was no exaggeration. Inside, although there are some separate restaurant concessions, the bulk of it is one vast space, cleverly broken up by split levels and mezzanines into a rambling warren of pleasure palaces. It's an amalgam of every legal form of low-to-middlebrow entertainment imaginable. I wander around for about fifteen minutes without once retracing my steps, past the theatre where Foster and Allen are playing next week, past the hotel, the function rooms, the brasserie and the Italian restaurant, through a huge central pit full of pokies – each with one button to call for assistance, a second button to order an at-pokie drinks service – flanked on all sides by bars, underneath that pit through the massive Burger King, which is called Hungry Jack's here, a video game arcade and a room full of pinball machines, and finally into a large bar area full of pool tables. Aussie Rules Football plays on a ten-by-fifteen-foot screen, and a dozen other large TV screens dotted around the room show different channels, all of them sports. Additional screens show keno, the bingo-cum-lottery game that reduces people to gawping zombies more efficiently than all other forms of screen-based entertainment put together. There's a bookie's at the far end of the room: yet more screens, showing race results and odds. Even the vending machine selling crisps has a sign illuminated by flashing lights, reading, 'JACKPOT VEND – WIN FREE PRODUCT'.

I'm surprised to find myself thinking that this is a great place to spend a wintry Saturday afternoon. There may be 2,000 pokies, and there are many people here to play them with serious intent, but more people are here simply to hang and chill out, have one or two beers, watch the game, have a chat. The drinking and the gambling are broken up by each other and by everything else on offer. I could happily stay here all day.

But it's a long way back to central Sydney. It's our final night in town, and as a very rainy dusk falls I realize that after only an hour here I need to make my way back for dinner with Liz, Tom and Kirsten. I leave with a genuinely heavy heart made all the more poignant by the fact that, even if I return to this beautiful city someday, when I do I won't be researching a book on beer, so there is no way I will ever come back to Penrith.

Melbourne

I step out of Flinders Street Station into central Melbourne on what feels like the first day of spring. I'm on a busy road junction next to the Yarra, an Antipodean Seine. Across the road is the huge, gothic St Paul's Cathedral. Opposite the cathedral is Federation Square, full of buildings with curious angular walls that look like a haphazard collection of child's building blocks. We're definitely in what the *Rough Guide* describes as the most arty city in Australia.

The beautiful, golden-coloured station has stood here since

1910. The domed tower above me features a bank of old clocks which still show the times of the next trains on each of the lines. Meeting 'under the clocks' is a Melbourne tradition and, sure enough, at precisely 3 p.m. a car pulls to a halt beside me and the passenger door swings open. I get in, and we speed off. 'Good to meet you, mate,' says the driver, a trim, laid-back man in his fifties with a grey beard and sandy hair.

It's inevitable that, in pursuit of my quest, I will meet fellow lucky sods. Dermot O'Donnell works for Carlton United Breweries, Australia's biggest brewer, owner of Foster's and VB, among others. He's a 'beverage ambassador', which means he gets paid on a regular full-time basis to go out and tell people how great beer is, and show them how nice pubs are. That's what he's doing with me this afternoon. 'I'll take you round and show you why Melbourne has the best pubs in Australia – and I did live in Sydney for a few years,' he told me on the phone a few days ago, three hours after I emailed CUB's website asking if anyone could speak to me about Australian beer drinking while I was in town.

Melbourne and Sydney are both world-class cities, and naturally compete with each other. While Melbourne has a little more European flair and intelligence, Sydney is the glamorous one. Sydneysiders insist there is no rivalry because there is clearly no competition. Melburnians – and Dermot is one – beg to differ.

We tour the southern suburbs, with Dermot driving and drinking light beer, and suggesting a range of other beers for me to try. Over here, 'light' doesn't necessarily mean low in calories; it means low in alcohol. As Dave Downie said, not to drink beer is un-Australian, so this seems to be the only traditional beer drinking country that has gone for low-alcohol beers in a big way rather than switching to soft drinks. They tend to be around 2 per cent alcohol, because tests show that at this level the body metabolizes alcohol as fast as you can drink it, and yet there's just enough there to give it a passable beer character.

My first impression of the city is that it is in a different country from Sydney. The suburbs are laid out in a grid system that, with its harbour and hills, Sydney never could have. Wide main streets with big corner hotels suggest a modern interpretation of the Wild West cowboy town, with the odd palm tree thrown in.

We hit a place in Brighton that's a cross between a trendy north London eatery and a fashionable Soho bar. It catches people wandering up from the beach with tables out on the pavement, 'which is something they just couldn't do in Sydney'. The smell of a coal fire wafts through from the back, powerfully homely. We check out Khyat's Hotel, an English–Aussie hybrid more English than anything else I've seen out here. It's like a 1930s Surrey roadhouse, with a big public bar and a lounge or 'Ladies' Bar'. 'The original idea for Melbourne pubs was based on the UK tavern,' says Dermot. 'Right up until the 1980s, they had to have stables and a place to lay out a corpse. Back in the 1880s there were no morgues, so you needed somewhere.' We finish off in the Sandy – the Sandringham Hotel – another big pub with a drive-in bottle shop on the side. It consists of a big bistro room which fills with diners at the weekend, a pokie room and a public bar with the now familiar bookie's wall at one end.

I tell Dermot that Australian drinking seems more grown-up than it is in Britain. He agrees, but says, 'It wasn't always like this. Remember the six o'clock swill.' And Dermot does: he was working as a barman at the time. I'm thrilled; this is something I've read about in books as a historical event, and now here's a beverage ambassador giving me his eyewitness account.

'Blue-collar guys would be in from 4 p.m., office workers at five. We'd go along the bar with a beer gun attached to a hose. You didn't even look up. If there was money on the bar next to the glasses you'd fill them with one hand and take the cash with the other. If there was no money on the bar you missed that one and went on to the next. They'd work in shouts of eight guys. All of them would buy a round, so you'd have sixty-four beers on the bar.'

'They'd have eight beers between five and six? That's a fair amount.'

'No. They'd all order eight beers at five *to* six, after they'd been in there drinking for an hour already. The bar stopped serving at six but they had till quarter past to drink up, so at five to, no matter how much they'd been drinking until then, they'd order sixty-four beers between them and try to drink them in twenty minutes before the police came in to drag them out at quarter past.'

Dermot drops me off back in McKinnon, the south Melbourne suburb where Liz and I are staying with Tom's brother Alec, his wife Gill and their family. Dermot leaves me with a big armful of books, an appointment to tour the brewery, a list of more pubs I should try – more than I'll ever be able to fit in without a chauffeur, like I've had this afternoon – and an invitation to lunch on Friday. I try to thank him. 'Shit, don't thank me,' he protests. 'Bloody Carlton United are picking up the bill.' I decide I'd like to be a beer ambassador when I grow up.

The McKinnon Hotel is just around the corner from Alec and Gill's house. After dinner, Liz and I take seats at the bar, an elongated oval. One other customer sits at the far end, about forty feet away. On the other side, glasses sit in a long refrigerated trough. We ponder what must have happened to prompt the notices displayed all over the bar reading:

> Due to recent events, all minors must be
> off the premises by 8.30 p.m.
> NO EXCEPTIONS

One TV screen shows the Australian *Who Wants to Be a Millionaire*, a big screen shows greyhound racing, three carry teletext betting forms, and there's an Easybet machine. The pub has its own tips on a blackboard by the door. Everywhere you look, if there isn't a way of gambling money, there's a celebration of gambling culture.

A question that niggled me in various places in Sydney finally takes shape and demands an answer: is this a pub with betting in it, or a bookie's with a bar in it? Hundreds of discarded betting slips carpet the floor beneath our stools. The place is illuminated by harsh fluorescent strip lighting. Security cameras watch us from above the doors. There's no doubt in my mind that it's the latter, and this fills me with incredible sadness. I don't mind the mix, but it's quite clear that there is no balance – that it's tipped way too far the other way.

If you've grown up in a place where a pub's character reflects that of its neighbourhood, you might conclude that McKinnon is a fairly rundown part of town. Not so: this is a suburb where the houses are so beautiful that when one comes up for sale the neighbours pretend to be prospective buyers just so they can go and snoop around. But more of Australia's pubs are heading this way, the combination of drinking and gambling marginalizing pub life, making it something unsavoury even in the heart of pleasant, friendly communities.

Just as I'm thinking this, draining my glass ready to leave, the barmaid asks if we'd like another. She's so friendly, charming and engaging that I feel bad about being so negative about her pub. She almost manages to reverse my conclusions and make me stay for another. But not quite.

The Carlton Brewhouse is a fifteen-minute tram ride out of the CBD in the busy suburb of Abbotsford. Carlton United celebrates its centenary this year, a century during which 'Australia's own brewery' has grown to dominate the country. It now brews over three million barrels a year.

My companions on the brewery tour include a pair of young studenty couples, a Chinese family and four oddlooking and excitable older guys. By the time we get on the minibus to take us around the site, these four are shouting and cheering. They've been on the tour before, and enjoyed it so much they're back. Our guide is in her late forties, a charismatic mix of warm, bossy and down to earth, a young Dame Edna Everage. She's been tipped off about my visit. It doesn't take her long to figure out which one I am, and she asks me what my itinerary is. It's a pleasant variation on a now-familiar conversation.

'How long are you in Australia for?

'Ten days.'

'That's not long enough.'

'I know.'

'That's two pubs.'

'Yes.'

'You're going to Queensland though, yeah?'

'No, just here and Sydney.'

'Well, you say that, but obviously you mean here, Sydney and Tassie.'

'Just here and Sydney.'

'And New Zealand. Obviously.'

'Just here and Sydney.'

'Not even *Darwin*?'

After the tour,* the highlight of the afternoon is that I get to see the VB ads, running on a continuous loop on a big screen in the visitors' centre. VB is the brand that finally shattered Australia's habit of only drinking your own state's beer. It now accounts for 60 per cent of CUB's output, and a quarter of all beer sold in the country. It's the most popular brand not only in Victoria, but also New South Wales, Northern Territory and the Australian Capital Territory around Canberra. Even in Queensland, self-proclaimed XXXX country, the native brand sits alongside this welcome guest from Victoria.

Dave Downie reckons the crisp, easy-drinking character of the beer and its low price have contributed to this success. But without doubt the driving factor is the advertising. In the 1960s Victoria Bitter (actually a lager) launched a campaign featuring real, tough, Australian men hard at work – manual stuff such as digging ditches and sawing wood – working up a sweat and a big thirst. Over swelling orchestral music, the

---

* You didn't really want to hear about more lagering vessels and fermentation time, did you?

actor John Meillon (Paul Hogan's grizzled mate in *Crocodile Dundee*) tells us how you can get thirsty, in lines that have been recited verbatim to me by every Australian man with whom I've discussed beer since I got off the plane.

> You can get it in a hole
> You can get it up a pole
> You can get it any old how
> Matter of fact, I've got it now

He then tells us, 'A hard-earned thirst needs a big cold beer, and the best cold beer is Vic.'

These ads penetrate directly into the cerebral cortex of the Australian male. Even after Meillon died of liver disease in 1989, the Aussie bloke would not countenance the campaign being changed. New ads were made, the voiceover constructed by cutting and pasting words from previous Meillon ads. You could tell what had been done – it sounded wrong – but nobody cared. It added to the charm, as did the facial hair in some of the footage as it became increasingly anachronistic outside places like Penrith.

The point was that this was the kind of bloke Australian men wanted to be. The more they took on white-collar jobs in offices, the more necessary it was to prove that as soon as they got out of the office, they weren't afraid of a bit of bloody hard yakka. It's part of the culture that unites Australia: a culture based on unpretentiousness, no one getting above their station, and the ability to simultaneously take the piss out of this attitude. The more naff the ads became, the more popular they were. By stumbling across this, VB became the first beer to conquer the country.

The ads have now been changed because, according to

Peter Sinclair, general manager of beer for CUB, the balance has shifted – just slightly – with the advent of metrosexual man. 'Australian men no longer need to physically sweat to show they're working hard. They're more urban than rural, more no collar than blue collar,' he told the Australian media in November 2004. But the basic principles didn't change. 'We're not afraid to take the piss out of ourselves. Let's remember we're selling beer, not frozen peas. It should be fun.'

During the post-tour tasting session I get talking to the studenty couples. One of them, a winter-dressed surf dude, explains, 'It's my girlfriend's birthday so we thought we'd all come here for a treat.' He gestures to the long-suffering girlfriend, who looks up, smiles weakly, nursing her pony of VB. I give her a laugh of commiseration. Surfer Dude doesn't seem to get the irony.

CUB also brews Foster's. But no one in Australia talks about it. The beer that defines the Australian no-worries attitude abroad is seen at home as some kind of fake, an unloved child who has left home pretending to be something it is not. Despite huge marketing spends around events like the 2000 Sydney Olympics and the rugby world cup, the kindest reaction shown by the average Australian drinker is a pretence that it doesn't exist.

In the souvenir shop I buy some VB beer mats and stubbie coolers, the foam tubes Australians slip around their bottles to keep them cool. Before now, I've seen people bring these back to the UK and thought, how sad. Whatever possessed them to think that these would be in any way cool? Whatever it was, it's now possessed me as well. Now I'm here, I realize that not only do I need enough of them to hand out at the next party we have, they will also make a perfect gift for Chris and a few of my other mates.

One result of Australia being so far from anywhere else is that the people have become self-absorbed, and write endless books on every aspect of 'Australiania'. There was a big surge in books about Australian pubs and beer culture from the late 1960s to mid-'70s, when Australian beer drinking peaked in per capita volume terms. In second-hand bookshops, I find volumes of photographic celebrations of Australian pubs. Classic Australian pubs have a very definite look, quite similar to New Orleans-style architecture, with verandas and balconies featuring ornately carved balustrades running the whole length of the buildings. Inside – or on the verandas – there are invariably crowds of hard-looking blokes covered in dirt or plaster, for some reason either barefoot or in heavy working boots, sporting elaborate sideburns and moustaches on deep-lined faces. Queensland pubs of the '60s and '70s feature middle-aged men wearing short-sleeved shirts, shorts, nylon socks pulled up to their knees and shiny black brogues. Somewhat implausibly, one picture caption describes this as 'typical Queensland dress'. I know it's extremely hot there, but there are limits.

I've been dying to see some of these places, and perhaps I would have succeeded in doing so had I not committed the gravest error of my short travel-writing career by neglecting to research thoroughly before I sorted my itinerary. I booked our flights a couple of months ago, and subsequently decided that while we were here I would visit the outback and see some proper rough-as-guts places, the kind of pubs people fly small planes to get to and have empty cans piled thirty feet high out the back, the only discernible feature amid miles of flat dust. I wanted to visit somewhere like Marble Bar on the edge of the Great Sandy Desert after reading accounts like this one, in a book called *Folklore of the Australian Pub*:

Marble Bar used to have more records than any other town in Australia – or the world for that matter . . . They say it held at 112 degrees for thirty-two days one time. It's got the record for the longest drought, the biggest white ants – the ants ate up the first pub so they built another one out of galvanised iron, and called it 'The Ironclad'. The ants ate that up too – or so they reckon. One thing I do know, they sold the hottest beer in Australia there. Once, in the excitement of a game of marbles, a bloke asked the barman for a saucer. The barman asked, 'What for?' 'So's I kin pour me beer out an' blow on it, says the bloke, 'It's too bloody hot to drink otherwise.'

I figured I would just turn up at Sydney or Melbourne airport and get a flight to one of these places, stay overnight and come back. But it turns out that the Great Sandy Desert is half a very large continent away and would take at least half a day to reach. But there is one possibility of getting out of the city and seeing something a little wilder. In Victoria and New South Wales the mountainous interior saw a nineteenth-century gold rush rivalling that in the United States, and it was fuelled by beer. I should go to one of the old mining towns. That's where I'd see some of these pubs, and meet some of these rugged, hardened drinkers.

Bendigo

It comes down to a choice between Bendigo and Ballarat. Neither clinches it on having the funniest-sounding name, not when we've got Geelong and Wangaratta and Warrnambool and Yarrawonga and Wodonga and Tangambalanga to choose from. Both were big gold rush towns. But the Gold Mines Hotel in Bendigo is the first pub you see when you open a copy of *Australian Pub Crawl*. It looks magnificent, like an American Wild West saloon trying to disguise itself as a wedding cake. Liz and I pack an overnight case and head for Bendigo.

It's not what we expected.

I'd imagined gold rush towns to be hard-bitten, dusty Wild West-type places. This probably makes me as stupid as any American tourist who comes to London expecting everyone to be wearing Victorian dress in gas-lit, foggy streets. Life *was* hard here – 120 years ago. But the reason people rush for gold is that it brings great wealth. Once gold was discovered, places like Bendigo and Ballarat grew with astonishing speed into fine, elegant towns. The fact that prospecting has been replaced by tourism means Bendigo is immaculately kept, bustling and full of gift shops, gardens and wine lodges. It's not exactly the wild frontier.

Bendigo tourist information centre is run by Marj – yes, Marj, it says so on her badge – and Ray. 'Ray was a ten-pound Pom,' Marj tells us. 'He came here in 1950.* When he came

---

*   Brits who took a one-way passage down under for £10 in the decades

over he was engaged, but his fiancée wrote to him and told him her mother was very ill and she couldn't come, and she married an American instead, so I got Ray!'

The Gold Mines Hotel, our reason for coming here, is now just a restaurant and bar, so we can't stay there. 'The guy who built the Gold Mines was very clever – he owned the mine and owned the hotel as well,' says Marj. 'He paid the miners not at the mine but at the hotel, to make sure they just handed all their wages back to him over the bar.'

My next choice is the Shamrock, right in the centre of town. During the gold rush the temptation to celebrate your win was enormous, so wherever the miners went, grog shops were not far behind. But they didn't stay grog shops for long. 'The Shamrock was rebuilt three times over the years,' says Marj. 'As the money just kept coming into Bendigo they got all these Italian architects into the town and built grander and more ornate buildings. You'd start off with a tent, and a few years later you'd have a palace made out of marble. The miners would all go into the Shamrock wearing their muddy boots. After closing up, the staff would sweep up the dirt from their boots and sift it for gold themselves.' This was a town so rich, even the dirt was valuable.

The Shamrock, it turns out, is fully booked. Some business convention. Finally, we get a room at Marlbrough House, another beautiful, balconied, ornately decorated B & B, but with no pub or bar. 'Come back any time; we're not going anywhere,' Marj and Ray shout after us.

Apart from an obsession with temperature, the most

---

after the Second World War, lured by the promise of a better life, after Australia realized it needed to 'populate or die'.

defining aspect of Australian drinking is the life-or-death importance of getting in your shout. We may be proud of our tradition of buying rounds in the UK, but in Australia it verges on a religious rite. It was out here in the goldfields that buying drinks for each other became an unwritten law. Any man who struck lucky was expected to go out into the road and shout for everyone else to come and have a drink with him, so 'shouting' became synonymous with standing a round, and stayed in the language after the gold dried up. Anyone who goes into a traditional Australian pub and drinks alone is said to be 'drinking with the flies'. If there are people at the bar you may choose to buy your way into the group by shouting early. You need to be aware though that it will then prove impossible to leave the pub until everyone in the group has returned the shout.

The Gold Mines Hotel is a five-minute cab ride from central Bendigo, and turns out to be the most un-pub-like pub I've ever been in – a cursory bar area with no beers on tap. The barman tells us what he knows about its history, but it's not much. Back outside in the torrential rain, we call another cab back into town.

We chat to the driver and I complain about the weather, expecting the usual 'It was fine until [whichever day I arrived in town]' response. But we've gone up a level. 'We've had the worst drought for as long as I can remember, and I've lived here all me life. Water reserves are down to 20 per cent. The local reservoir that feeds the farmland is down to 2 per cent. So we're sure glad of this rain.' Yep, the rain. It's followed me into an area that is officially defined as desert, a place that doesn't even know what real rain is.

Next on the list of traditional drinking places is the

aforementioned Shamrock, a hotel which, with its balconies and verandas, has to be the last word in gold rush architecture. Apparently, the balcony is very popular for late-afternoon drinking. It sounds perfect.

We draw close, and just looking at the place makes me feel as if I've been dropped in New Orleans. Immaculately preserved, it gives a strong flavour of what the town must have been like 130 years ago. And then we see that the Shamrock has new owners, people who think the best thing they can do to improve this stunning building is to drape a ten-foot-high banner down one side of the balcony with the Comfort Inns logo on it.

Oh shit.

When it comes to inappropriate – some might say wilfully misleading, to the point of taking the piss – names, Comfort Inns is the one to beat. The only brand name I've encountered less descriptive of the reality is Quality Hotels and, guess what? They're part of the same group.

The Comfort Inns/Quality Hotels I've stayed in before have without exception caused me to give serious thought to suicide. Every time, they have been grand old buildings that look magnificent from the outside, like this one. They are buildings that stir your soul, that take you back to a grand age of travel and touring, when people didn't drive; the few that had cars 'motored'. They took trains and went on grand tours. They arrived at buildings like this with large trunks in tow and had to fight their way out of capes, hats and gloves before they could check in.

When the Comfort Inns/Quality Hotels group get hold of these buildings, they seem to leach out every drop of charm, grace, glamour or vitality, ripping out their interiors and installing a standard of accommodation that, to me, makes a Travelodge look like the latest Ian Schrager New York concept.

I hadn't realized they'd got this far. We steel ourselves and go in.

We ask if there's a bar. No one knows anything about being able to drink on the balcony, but there is Lil's, just on the other side of reception. This turns out to be the home of Bendigo's largest collection of pokies, games like Tabaret and keno and sad, empty, middle-aged people mindlessly feeding the machines with money they don't have. There's an ATM in the hotel lobby where these people can withdraw the last of their savings, but at least it provides a surface on which to plonk the half-hearted signs warning against the dangers of gambling: 'You can win every time on gambling machines.' Hang on, I'll read that again: 'Can you win every time on gambling machines.' Perhaps if there was a question mark at the end of this emphatic warning against the dangers of gambling addiction, it wouldn't be quite so easy to misread. Anyone would think they were tacitly trying to encourage people to gamble more.

Next to the ATM sits a glass case displaying the prizes which can be won in a regular raffle: a badly knitted Bob the Builder doll, a hamper, a bottle of cheap fizzy wine – all the more pathetic in a town that sits in the centre of an array of fantastic vineyards where world-class wines can be bought for next to nothing. All in all, a great excuse for an early night.

The next morning we find a couple of valuable additions to our exotic Australian bird collection. We're woken in the morning by the R2-D2 bird, then almost killed by the pedestrian-crossing-signal bird. Australia is famous for the sheer variety of life-threatening animals which call it home –

eight out of ten of the world's most poisonous animals are found here – but as far as I'm aware this one has so far gone unreported. This may be because so few of its victims live to tell the tale. It sits in trees above pedestrian crossings and does a perfect imitation of the crossing signal, but only when a big truck is approaching. We're very lucky.

The unrelenting, driving rain, unseen here for at least a generation, means that most bars are sparsely populated. But I don't think I'm far enough out into the wilderness to get a real sense of what Australian drinking is like anyway. Bendigo may not be Sydney or Melbourne, but it could be Leamington Spa. There's no sense that we're intruding into an established and individualistic beer culture. There's none of that left here, though Bendigo is a pleasant town, and well worth a visit if you just want to chill out among disarmingly friendly people. And if you're a pyromaniac, there's a great hotel in the centre of town that I can heartily recommend.

Melbourne

The Great Britain is a curious pub in the suburb of Richmond. It doesn't look like the most welcoming place: painted in black emulsion on the outside, the colour scheme continues on the inside walls and detailing is provided by the gaffer tape that holds together what must once have been a piece of carpet.

All my instincts are telling me that I should feel an acute sense of danger, but I like this place. The carpet, the smell and the ramshackle furniture all suggest a very dodgy London pub, but it's actually quite endearing. One wall features an aquarium built inside an old TV set. There are stained-glass windows that look like they date back to the 1920s. The lounge bar, ever-so-slightly more salubrious than the public bar in which I'm sitting, is decorated in a succession of strips of differently patterned flock wallpaper, never repeating, like an Indian restaurant on acid. The shelves behind the bar are home to a collection of bedraggled stuffed animals. There's a boar's head wearing a baseball cap and chewing a couple of cuddly koalas. A sort of bison. A prairie dog trying to disguise itself as a kangaroo, wearing woolly gloves on its raised front paws. An elk or gazelle with only one horn.

There are ten draught beers on the bar, and a price list on the wall features thirty different bottled beers, enough to qualify this for inclusion in CAMRA's list of proper beer bars if we were in Belgium, although I can't see the people who compile that guide ever coming in here. All in all, this is not what I expected from the home of Piss, Australia's frankest beer brand. Piss also has a light variant called Piss Weak. Both beers are heavily flagged as '100% natural', which in any other context would make them sound more appetizing.

I had expected Piss to be a simple marketing wheeze to gain attention, like Death cigarettes in the UK, with little or no integrity or regard for serious beer connoisseurship. But if the long list of craft beers in the Great Britain wasn't a big enough hint, a few minutes chatting to Chris Hodges, the owner of the Great Britain and the man behind Piss, proves how wrong this assumption was.

Chris is in his thirties, dressed in black with a trim goatee. He's one of the most laid-back people I've met here, which is saying something. ('I appointed a manager, took a few years off, came back,' is his summary of his recent career.) But beneath the surface he reveals that this is not so much a job as a calling. He describes the Great Britain as 'more than just a service provider' for the 'young student lefties' who drink and catch up with their friends here, make it their local for two or three years and then move on. He launched Piss to head them off from the big lager brands before their loyalties were fully formed, and it quickly becomes evident that he's more interested in the craft beers he has on the bar than in the mainstream lager market he's taking the Piss out of.*

By stocking Piss on the bar next to quality beers like Coopers Sparkling Ale and Little Creatures, and not stocking any of the big mainstream lagers, Chris is saying, 'If you don't want to drink Piss, drink craft beer.' And the happy surprise is that Piss itself is a very decent lager, well balanced and malty with a nice fruity aroma. The joke is on Tooheys and Carlton United, who can only pretend that this cheeky little brand doesn't exist.

The next morning, Liz and I meet Dermot O'Donnell at Bell's Hotel in South Melbourne. He introduces us to Billy Bell, the proprietor. We recognize Billy from the photograph of him sitting naked in a big copper brewing vessel in a press cutting on the wall. Billy is in his sixties, bald, bespectacled and moustachioed, and utterly charming. While we taste one of the beers – a German brown lager brewed with American hops – he gives us his edited, well-rehearsed life story. 'I went to a conference of licensees a few weeks ago and I was laying down the law. Some of 'em were getting a bit narked with what I was saying, and this woman stood up and asked what right I had to be lecturing them like this. I said, "Love, I was

---

* Or should that be Pissing into?

conceived in a pub, born in a pub and raised in a pub. I'd sacked the cook and knocked up the barmaid by the time I was fourteen." She didn't give me any trouble after that.'

The reason Billy was lecturing the licensees in the first place is that he's one of the architects of a quality control scheme called Pubs, Pots and Profits. Standing out against the tide of pokies and bookie-pubs, he advises licensees on their cellars, lines and bar equipment, so they can make money from beer rather than gambling. 'I go into a place and I think, I can get thirty dollars more out of a keg than this bloke. You go in and the glasses are dirty, the lines are ratshit, the cellar is all over the place. You improve that and you're not forced to pour beer away, and people come back to drink it.' The scheme now operates in over 1,000 pubs. I'd love to stay and drink with Billy all afternoon, but I have a date with Chloe.

Chloe is Australia's most notorious pub resident, and the country's most famous painting. She was created in Paris in 1875 by Chevalier Jules Lefebvre, and brought to the Great Melbourne Exhibition in 1880, where she caused a huge ruckus. The reason for this is not just her rare beauty, but the fact that she is stark naked. Two years after the painting was finished, the model organized a huge party at which she killed herself by drinking 'a decoction of match-heads'.

Chloe was acquired by Young and Jackson, Melbourne's most famous pub, in 1908, and instantly entered pub folklore: repressed Victorian sensibilities, loads of drink, a life-sized picture of a naked woman – you can imagine the stir, not to mention the stirrings, she caused. Her most famous encounter was captured in verse. 'Snowy' White had lived a sheltered life until he came into Young and Jackson for a drink. He spotted Chloe, whereupon:

His face and neck at once turned blazing red;
It seemed to burn him with a fiery heat;
He threw away his glass, and turned and fled
Out through the door, and into Flinders Street

He proceeded to cause chaos with the traffic, because his face was glowing so brightly everyone thought all the lights were red.

Chloe is now kept upstairs in the restaurant named in her honour, to save such embarrassment from ever occurring again.

Dermot has brought us here for a stunning lunch, and he has the waitress running up and down the stairs to get us the best beers in town. After lunch, we head round yet more historic pubs, and all too soon we have to go. In a few hours we're due back at the airport for the next long haul.

Australia is a vast country, and for the first time on my quest I feel tempted to come back and do the proper traveller thing, backpacking around the whole place, staying in hostels, shouting rounds in flyblown shacks. I'd like to write a whole book about Australian drinking, but so many people already have.

This in itself is interesting. That famous drinker Winston Churchill said, 'History is written by the victors.' This is not entirely correct, but British history was mostly written by people sympathetic to the temperance cause, and the historical role of beer and brewing is given short shrift. So it's revealing that in Australian history beer is crucially important whereas temperance campaigners are usually referred to as 'wowsers'. This is such a brilliant word. Without knowing what it means, you can only assume it's a derogatory term that probably has something to do with inflated self-importance. It's a word that inspires people to rich and satisfying attempts at definition. H.L. Mencken said a wowser was, 'A drab souled Philistine haunted by the mockery of others' happiness.' In 1910 the Australian *Daily Telegraph* reported the deputy leader of the Labor Party defining a wowser as, 'A man who, being entirely destitute of the greater virtues, makes up for their lack by a continuous denunciation of little vices. The word carries with it the implication of certain shortcomings in manly fibre.' The word's very existence tells you that Australia has no time for this kind of behaviour. The fact that it is a word still in mainstream use, as well as in serious tomes, tells you all you need to know about a country where beer drinking is a national institution, an article of faith.

8

'Toriaezu birru'

Tokyo

As we close in on Narita airport after a long overnight flight, the cabin crew chivvy us back into thin, brittle wakefulness. Unnaturally bright voices urge us to bring our seats to the upright position and stow our tray tables, then carry on with the special bit where they ask passengers travelling in First or Club World today to please put away their personal footrests and screens. Deep in World Traveller class, this makes me imagine that the instructions then continue on a closed channel, in that sing-song voice they use with the emphasis on all the wrong words, to say, 'and could you please make sure you *are* fully dressed, courtesans are returned to *their* rightful seats, and take a moment to look around you to make sure you have cleared *away* any spare cocaine wraps that *may* still be lying around your private suite'.

We sink lower over stunted hills covered in dense green foliage sprouting up in petrified fountains, layer over layer of bamboo and thick, heavy leaves. Between these outcrops, small fields lie in orderly patterns, meticulously kept. And then I'm in Japan.

In cultural terms this is far as away from home as I'm likely to get on my quest. Where do you even start to try to get to grips with a country that lived in self-imposed exile from the rest of the world until the 1850s? A country where, outside the main cities, European faces are still rare enough to provoke fits of giggles? And a country that had never heard of beer until a century and a half ago but now drinks more of it than anything else? Up to now I've seen some interesting differences between countries, but Japan demands a total readjustment. Everywhere else, people have had different clothes and a slightly different flavour of Western liberal democracy. Here, the organizing principles by which society runs are different. Even though the Asian economic bubble burst in the early 1990s, Japan still makes you feel like you're stepping ten years into the future. It's in everything, right down to the most mundane consumer goods. In advertising, whenever anyone wants to do a really impressive presentation about future trends, they just get some packaging from Japan and say, look, this is how far-out things are going to get. Not even reports of huge typhoons heading for Tokyo can dim my eagerness. As we taxi in, I'm twitching with excitement and sick with fear.

As soon as we're off the plane, gratuitous use of advanced technology is everywhere we look: digital video signs above the baggage carousels; an interactive guide to the airport in the arrivals hall; and out by the exit the pièce de résistance – an overview of Tokyo's road traffic situation, lights flashing where congestion is severe, all the better for being a bit old-fashioned, electronic but not screen-based, like something from one of the Roger Moore-period James Bond movies. And our flight number here from Heathrow? BA007.

I figured I should do some proper background reading before embarking on this particular trip, and I'm very glad I did. Most Japanese beer drinking happens in *izakaya*, tiny bars which sell food and beer to salarymen on their way home. But there are three additional very significant types of venue. Firstly, there are what we might politely call hostess bars, where business entertaining is done – and there's a lot of business entertaining to do. Secondly, karaoke bars, which we know all about. And thirdly, roof gardens on top of high-rise department stores which are heavily sponsored by brewers and usually charge a fixed fee of around 3,000 yen (£15) for all you can drink.

Now be honest: you weren't expecting that last one, were you? It's so counter-intuitive, I'm wondering if it was perhaps the result of some kind of drunken parlour game played by Japanese cultural arbiters, where the aim was to take three random unrelated concepts – in this case beer, department store rooftops and gardens – and fuse them into a convincing whole. If I had been undecided about including Japan on my itinerary before (I wasn't) this would have made my mind up.

My developing skills as a traveller mean that I also learn in advance that a taxi into town from Narita costs around £150. We take the Airport Limousine, which only costs £15. They call it a limousine, but really it's a crowded bus. As we pull out onto the motorway I notice we're driving on the left. Even though this is the same as Britain, it somehow feels perverse. We're in a foreign country, and people in foreign countries are supposed to drive on the right. This humdrum, perverse familiarity is more unsettling than the strangest differences Japan has offered so far.

The journey into central Tokyo takes nearly two hours, time enough for me to study katakana, the Japanese alphabet. The book I'm consulting says it is relatively easy. Relative to what, it doesn't say. I'm obviously not expecting to learn a complex language in five days, but I'm hoping to pick up a few basic principles and to be able to write 'beer' in Japanese. But not only do the basic rules or principles elude me, individual characters remain stubbornly difficult to memorize. The only thing that sticks is that the Japanese word for 'doing' is 'shite'.*

Beer was inadvertently introduced to Japan by Matthew Perry. No, not that Matthew Perry – Commodore Matthew Perry of the US Navy. Its arrival in the country was announced by cannon fire. The feudal shoguns had pursued a strict isolationist policy for 250 years when, in 1853, the USA made them an offer they couldn't refuse. As was the fashion at the time (Britain following a similar policy with China) the Americans decided the best way to persuade the Japanese to trade with them was to take a squadron of 'black ships of evil mien',† under Commodore Perry's command into what is now Tokyo Bay, delivering a letter from the president using the ship's cannon for punctuation. Not exactly subtle, but just as it does for all gangsters, it worked a treat.

---

* Obviously, this is hilarious, but it's also a bit scary. When I was very small and I had to do a – well, a shite – my mum and dad would euphemistically refer to it as my 'doings'. Mere coincidence? Not when you're suffering from jet lag.
† The Japanese described Perry's fleet as korobune, black ships. The word is still used today to describe unwelcome foreign pressure.

The Japanese concluded that the only way to repel the 'barbarians' would be to embrace their technology and grow stronger. A voracious appetite for Western things grew instantly, sparking a policy of 'Japanese spirit, Western things.' Ever since, Japan has taken Western ideas, adapted them, and sold them in brain-numbing quantities back to the people who introduced them.

One of the first such Western things was beer. When the Japanese delegation was invited aboard Perry's flagship, beer was served. It went down well, and one of the delegates, Dr Koumin Kawamoto, later found a Dutch book on brewing and taught himself the essentials. In 1869, as the newly restored emperor urged Westernization and industrialization, Japan's first brewery was opened. Initially, the locals had to be bribed to drink beer. But soon, as they did with many Western things, the Japanese took beer and made it their own.

As soon as Liz and I have checked into our hotel I leave again to get across town for my first appointment. With a population of twenty-eight million, Greater Tokyo is the largest metropolitan area in the world. The city centre consists of twenty-three wards or *ku*, and covers 238 square miles. Our hotel is in Shinjuku-ku, a district in the west of the city full of government and banking buildings, all mirrored skyscrapers and elegant boulevards. I need to get to Asakusa, a more historic district to the north-east. I have an hour to get there, so a cab would be useless through the narrow, traffic-choked streets. I need to summon every shred of my fledgling traveller's experience and brave Tokyo's railway system.

There are two entirely different systems: the subway and the surface lines. The over-ground trains subdivide into Japan

Railways (JR) lines and a whole bunch of 'private railways'. You might expect one to be central and the other suburban – this is roughly the relationship between London's Underground and over-ground trains – but that would be too simple: here, the two systems overlap entirely. Some of the underground trains are on the surface, and some of the over-ground trains dip underground. On some maps all the lines of both systems are in black. On others some lines are colour-coded. The JR map shows most but not all subway lines and the subway map shows some of the JR lines, but in an entirely different graphic style from the JR map. There's a big central loop on both maps, which may be the same line, but it's an oval that lies on its side on one map and stands on its end on the other.

And yet, somehow, millions of people get to work every day. I stare hard at the maps in my guidebook, flicking between the small-scale JR map, which incorporates the suburbs and private lines, and the large-scale subway map, which doesn't, looking for anything that suggests they represent the same city – a station name, the shape of a line. The experience is like one of those Magic Eye pictures that were popular for half an hour in 1993.* You stare at a random pattern for ages, unable to see anything coherent, until your eyes blur and shapes start to appear, and gradually it makes sense.

Even this is a lot easier than it used to be. Japan has traditionally discouraged tourism, but has mellowed since it

---

* It was from half past two till three o'clock on a Sunday afternoon in August, since you ask. I was at the Reading Festival at the time and they were on sale there. By the time I got home, they'd become a sad cliché. As had many of the acts on the festival bill, come to think of it.

hosted the 2002 World Cup: the names of the stations are now displayed in our familiar alphabet as well as kanji. I've just about figured out where I need to go and how to get there when an elderly Japanese man approaches me to offer his help. He speaks no English and obviously I don't speak a word of Japanese, but he insists on making sure I've got it right. He points out the right platform, then takes me to the ticket machine and shows me where to insert my money and what buttons to press.

In Tokyo even travelling by tube is fascinating. Ads not only cover the carriage walls, but also hang on banners from the ceiling. The beautiful women in them are paler than I am, while the men have dark tans. Where couples are together, the contrast is so striking they could be of different races. Notices everywhere prohibit the use of mobile phones. The parallel with no-smoking areas at home is unavoidable: the signs are similar, and people behave in a familiar way, clutching their handsets anxiously, waiting for their stop and the next fix. Denied the use of technology, most people simply fall asleep – more than half the occupants of this busy carriage are dozing. My first thought is that they must be exhausted from the effort involved in decoding the maps, but working hours here are long, life is lived at a frenetic pace, and people get their rest wherever they can.

Tokyo reminds me of *Thunderbirds* – the original TV series, not the rubbish 2004 live-action film. It shares the same optimistic 1960s view of what the future will look like: smooth, moulded concrete and sleek, sexy technology. As I exit Asakusa station, on the banks of the Sumida River, I spot a cruiser whose design I'm almost certain was lifted straight from 'Danger at Ocean Deep', the episode where

International Rescue had to save *Ocean Pioneer II* without using their radios.

On the theme of needing to get out more, the other big influence in Asakusa is the designer Philippe Starck. What this man has done to the Asahi headquarters – my destination this afternoon, just across the river – eclipses the most overblown imaginings of any sci-fi writer hoping for a shred of credibility. My limited interaction with Starck's work before now has given me a disturbing image of the designer as a hyperactive child, the sort you can play and have fun with for a while, and everyone's laughing, until the child starts getting hysterical and you have to say, 'OK, Philippe, time to tidy up now and get ready for dinner/bed/your medication.' Because children need to be set limits. If not, it will inevitably end in tears.

When Philippe came to Tokyo I'm afraid the polite-to-a-fault Japanese failed to draw a line and say, 'Now that's *enough*, Philippe,' or, leaving our analogy behind a second, 'Now hang on, are you taking the piss, or what?' or any of the other phrases that run through my mind as I struggle to find words for the things on the far bank.

The Asahi building is supposed to look like a giant glass of beer. You can sort of see this if someone suggests it to you, as they did to me, but without any clues you'd never guess. It looks like what would happen if you tried to build a pint of beer out of Lego bricks. For a start, it's rectangular rather than cylindrical, so I'm lost right there. The main body of the building is clad in gold-tinted glass, to represent the liquid. The top three or four storeys are white, jutting out at irregular angles, just like the foam on the top of a pint doesn't.

This is bad enough – misguided, but just about forgivable. But sitting right next to the Asahi building is the Flamme

D'Or, a giant obsidian box with curved sides and a flat top onto which some giant has seemingly coiled out a thirty-foot-long, golden turd. Officially the turd is a flame, hence the name. But to get back to our analogy, it's the kind of flame which would prompt a visiting aunt to say, 'Oh, hello, Philippe. What's this you've drawn for me? Oh, I say, that's, er ... lovely. What is it? A *flame*, you say? Aren't you clever?' before turning to the child's mother and asking in a quiet voice, 'How old is he now? What do his teachers say about his progress?' Even if we were to allow that it is a flame, what is it doing on top of the giant box? The box has portholes in it, and the curving sides faintly suggest the prow of a ship, but why on earth would you design a building to look like a ship that's on fire? Alternatively, perhaps it's an altar. But why would an altar have portholes? Shit, why on earth would you design a building to look like an altar in the first place?

Given that Starck designed both buildings, simultaneously, there's a strong whiff of absinthe around the decision to site them side by side. There's no relationship between them whatsoever, no sense of comparable scale. The overall effect is of a pile of toys that haven't been tidied up.

Asahi Super Dry is one of my favourite lagers, but this hasn't been sufficient to prevent one of the recurring themes of my many 'spawny bastard' conversations being exactly how I expect anyone to swallow the idea that a trip to Japan is a valid part of a book about global beer culture. Don't the Japanese just drink sake? Well, even leaving aside the pedantic point that sake is better described as a rice beer than a rice wine (rice being a grain, beer being fermented grain and all that), the truth is that the Japanese drink more beer than they do anything else. Japan is the sixth-biggest beer producer on the planet, brewing forty-three million barrels, and Asahi Super Dry, as well as being Japan's favourite beer, is the world's seventh-biggest-selling beer. It didn't get there on its healthy but modest sales in Soho sushi bars.

'Dry' beers paid a brief visit to Western drinking culture in the early 1990s. No one really explained what they were, so they quickly went the way of every other designer beer fad of the time. But the principle really is quite simple. Beer is created when yeast ferments sugars present in grain, but grain possesses both simple and complex sugars. Normally, the yeast can't do much with the complex ones, and they remain in the beer, adding body and flavour. In the 1980s Asahi perfected a process for breaking down these complex sugars into simple sugars. More fermentation takes place, so the beer is stronger but has less flavour. Doesn't sound great if you're a serious beer fan, but dry is very different from the usual flavour-free mainstream imitation Pilsners. Dry beers are delicate, but retain a crisp, refreshing bite and leave no aftertaste.* Dry beer had instant appeal in Japan, where most beer is drunk with food. As well as being a perfect complement to sushi, it cuts through greasy, fatty dishes, of which Japanese cuisine has a surprisingly large number.

In Asahi's reception, near the top of the pint, I meet Takeshi Kato.† A little over a week ago I emailed Asahi's UK office, asking if anyone in Japan might be able to spare half an

---

* I'm told by some fans that Asahi Super Dry is the only beer you can drink at lunch time and go back to work with no trace of beer breath. I wouldn't know about that of course, but it sounds believable.

† Before we all start with the poor Inspector Clouseau impressions, it's actually pronounced *katt-oh*, not *cay-toe*.

hour or so of their time to talk to me about Japanese drinking culture. Most brewers have obliged requests like this so far; some have not. Mr Kato, Asahi's manager for Europe and America and possibly the most senior representative I've met of any brewery so far, has arranged the following. First, I'm getting a two-hour presentation on the size and shape of the Japanese beer market by Mr Takaaki Watanabe, manager of lifestyle and culture research institute strategy planning head-quarters and head of getting as many words on a business card as possible. Then we're going to spend the evening together out in Tokyo. And tomorrow Mr Kato is spending his entire morning taking me up to the nearest brewery, an hour outside Tokyo. This itinerary has already been restructured once thanks to me screwing up my arrival time in Japan. Over the next day or so my reaction to my hosts will evolve from, 'Got this sorted,' through, 'Blimey, these guys really have pushed the boat out here. What have I done to deserve this?' to, 'I am forever in Mr Kato's debt. I'm embarrassed. There must be something I can do. But there just isn't.' If you've spent any time in Japan, you might recognize this as a typical progression.

We start off with the presentation on the Japanese beer market. Sorry, in fact we start off with a presentation of gifts – beautifully produced books on the history of Asahi – then we get to the market data. Of course, the data is in Japanese, so it proves slow going. The charts show the results of various questions put to a panel of beer drinkers on a rolling, weekly basis. Mr Kato and Mr Watanabe work hard to translate. Of course, I don't know a single word of Japanese. Or so I thought. We get to a section on what food goes best with beer. Mr Kato tries to tell me about steamed salted beans as a snack and skewers of grilled chicken. My addiction to Japanese restaurants at home means I'm soon shouting 'Edamame!' and 'Yakitori!' delighted with myself, while they smile and nod politely.

I come completely unstuck on the section about the main occasions when people drink beer. The obvious ones are all in there: out with friends, with a meal, and so on. But at the top of the list, with 24.6 per cent of the vote, the most popular beer drinking occasion is . . . after a bath or shower.

'When do Japanese people normally, ah . . . take a bath or shower?' I ask.

A whispered consultation, and then: 'Most often, I would say, when they finish work. As soon as they arrive home.'

You *see*? It's not bizarre at all. It's humid here. Those crowded trains – it makes perfect sense. I realize that everything in Japan obeys a perfectly logical system. You just need to turn your brain around by ninety degrees before you can see it. I also learn that 18.5 per cent of Japanese people prefer to drink out of a clay mug rather than a glass. Thick foam is considered an essential property of a decent beer, with ads for all brands showing a creamy head sliding over the top of the glass. It's believed that the slight irregularities in a ceramic mug help keep the head tighter and creamier. Another question asks which kanji you would use for beer, given that it is not Japanese.* 'Foam' comes top, with 25.7 per cent.

---

* As if Japan wasn't interesting or complex enough, it has not one but three alphabets. The oldest is kanji, of which there are over 8,000 characters. Kanji is used to represent abstract concepts as well as names and everyday words. An average adult Japanese speaker must know at least 2,000 off by heart. Then there are katakana and hiragana. These are each alphabets of forty-six characters, each of which represents a sound. You

The big shock is the rate at which beer's position in Japanese society is declining. For a long time Japanese brewers were taxed on the malt they used, but not the finished product. So they learned how to make a beer-like liquid using a fraction of the malt, called *happoshu*, which looks and tastes like watered-down beer. It took a huge chunk of the market in a few years in the late 1990s, until the tax loophole on malt was closed. Now, Japanese people tend to drink *happoshu* at home on their own, serving proper beer to guests and drinking it in bars and *izakaya*. But beer is also being hit by the growth of *sho chu*, a distilled spirit made from sweet potato, rice or barley, often mixed with fruit juice (most commonly soda and lemon or grapefruit) to make *chu hai*. All the big brewers are bowing to the inevitable, launching their own versions of these drinks and redefining themselves as 'beverage providers'.

After the presentation, we head up to one of the bars on the top floor of the building for a quick glass of Asahi. Like my first beer in every country so far, it tastes like the best beer in the world.

The best (let's make that only) compliment I can pay the Asahi building is that being inside looking out is as dramatic as standing outside looking in, only for the opposite reasons.

---

might think you would only need one of these alphabets, given that they do exactly the same job, but, you see, they don't: katakana is used to represent foreign concepts while hiragana is used to represent the same sounds in native Japanese words (apart from when it is placed above or below kanji, in which case hiragana used to explain how to pronounce the kanji, and isn't called hiragana any more, but furigana). Simple. So, given that beer is a foreign concept, it only has a phonetic katakana, which represents the word *birru*, or beer. Asking people what kanji they would use for beer therefore gives a real insight into how they perceive it.

From the inside of the cubist foamy head, Tokyo lies strewn before us, neon flickering into life, incongruous against the humdrum buildings still visible in the misty grey twilight. There are no discernible landmarks as such; it's the sheer *quantity* of view that makes me catch my breath, mile after mile of buildings that I want to recognize but which remain elusive. As the grey deepens, the neon flares up on all sides, and I realize that this is a city meant to be seen at night.

After this preview, we head downstairs to get the tube to Shinbashi, central Tokyo. We walk through Chuo-dori, a street full of Western-style shops so expensive they seem to stock only one cardigan each, displayed on plinths in the middle of acres of space, to a set of stairs leading down to a bar so tastefully designed I expect antibodies to emerge from the walls and assimilate or destroy me – whatever they have to do to prevent me from spoiling the perfect lines with my lumpen presence. Shorn, stumpy silver birch trunks stand encased in columns of thick engraved glass. To our left, broad cedar tables provide communal seating for large groups. To our right, lacquered bamboo screens stop short of the ceiling, creating dining rooms that are private while still allowing in the general hubbub of the restaurant. We turn right.

We sit on low benches surrounded by immaculate elegance, natural materials feng-shuied to within an inch of their existence. My hosts watch me closely. I watch them back, locked in an etiquette stand-off, determined not to cause offence. A moment of truth arrives with the hot towels. It's one of those decisions that has been plaguing London for a few years now: do you daintily dab your hands, or do you go for the full steamy-face thing while it's still almost too hot to bear? As a huge fan of the latter approach, I'm grateful when Mr Kato and Mr Watanabe bury their faces. I follow their lead, finally screwing up the spent, cold, damp towel on the table as they neatly fold theirs into little pads and place them to their left. I unravel mine and copy while they pretend not to notice.

We share shiyaki, pork skewers in crispy golden bread crumbs. 'It's typical to share one dish among everyone,' says Mr Kato. 'Even though you are not family,' he adds, without the meaningful pause I just implied. We share a variety of tofu tastes; some of them recognizable as tofu, others leaping up like Glenn Close at the end of *Fatal Attraction* to scare you with associations you thought you'd left behind: solid blocks of matter like the skin from condensed milk, dips that take you back to early school dinners and institutional coffee that grew a skin as it cooled.

Then there's Aberdeen Angus beef with spring onions, water chestnuts, chilli sauce and cucumber. The idea is to wrap the whole thing in lettuce leaves and somehow retain your dignity while eating it. While I fail to do this, Mr Kato and Mr Watanabe point out somewhat apologetically that this is more Korean than Japanese.

Mr Kato and Mr Watanabe appear keen to hear my opinions on the drinks range, so I ask to see the menu. It has more varieties of *sho chu* than sake – as you'd expect, given it has supplanted Japan's national drink as second-favourite to beer. I interrupt my perusal of the list with as many interested comments as I can make, things like, 'Oh, that's interesting'; 'What is this drink like?' 'Is this one popular?' When I lower the menu, a large glass of every drink I've made a comment about is on the table in front of me. Just me – my hosts are still happy with their beers, happy to watch what I do with a sweet potato vodka, a malt vodka and several varieties of *chu hai*.

I'm trying to write all this down. I have to. It's why I'm here, and I never thought it would be this ... well, *this*. Mr Kato and Mr Watanabe watch me intently, muttering to each other as I write. I apologize profusely as I keep scribbling, but I have no choice. I've only had three hours sleep in the last two days, and no food since breakfast on the plane twelve hours ago. If I don't write down the details of this feast now, I'll have no recollection of them by the morning. That would be a crime against the restaurant and an insult to my hosts, these two lovely, smiling men opposite, who have given up their afternoon and evening to be with me. I try to think of a way of thanking them as profusely and eloquently as I can.

'I don't want to go home!' I wail.

They grin back at me, amused, infinitely tolerant. Mr Kato orders a cocktail, finally, to keep me company. I need to hang on. I can and will get through this with my dignity intact.

I pick up a piece of karage – grilled, marinated chicken, one of my favourite dishes. Just as I'm trying to take the meat between my teeth, my chopsticks slip and splay and knot themselves into a wide X between my knuckles. My fingers are fenced in across my chest, and I have a lump of deep-fried meat dangling from my mouth by a sinew, swinging across my chin. My first instinct is to grab it again with chopsticks, but I only succeed in knocking it, making it swing more violently. Mr Kato is talking to me, pretending not to notice. I nod enthusiastically to show I'm listening, causing the lump of meat to lurch crazily around my face leaving greasy trails across my cheeks, my chopsticks clacking emptily in mid-air.

But this is one of the best meals I've ever eaten. Apart from the food and the ambience, the habit of sharing an orgy of different dishes makes it a communal experience which sits perfectly with beer. I don't want the meal to end, but I'm stuffed. And if we stay here, they're going to expect me to finish the long line of drinks in front of me.

Reluctantly I say goodbye to the restaurant, making small mewling noises which I can only hope will be interpreted as expressions of infinite gratitude. We say goodbye to Mr Watanabe, and Mr Kato walks me to the station from where I can most easily get back to my hotel. On the way, I realize the alcohol has had more of an effect on Mr Kato than it had on me. He's weaving slightly, nudging into me. But then I decide that it's me who's drunk, and he's acting to make me feel more comfortable, sparing my blushes. He's my new best mate.

Then he starts saying things I don't understand.

We're walking down a neon-bathed shopping street, and he says, 'Look! No shaving foam!' He grins and gestures expansively. For a while I struggle with this. True enough, I can't see a can of Gillette anywhere. 'The English, they don't care. But here . . .' I concentrate. What does shaving foam come in? Aerosols. What else comes in aerosol cans that might affect the appearance of a street? Spray paint. See? You just have to work it out. He's talking about graffiti.

He must be.

I get back to our hotel room just as Liz's food arrives. She has been shopping while I've been with Asahi and had been back in the room for an hour or so, itching to swap stories of our experiences. Bizarrely, I've woken up now. We agree that she's allowed to eat, then we must head up to the top floor of our hotel and visit the Rhapsody Bar.

How can this city just keep getting better? There's one spare table by the window. We're torn between the view outside and the spectacle in the bar. The view makes me want to write poetry or propose marriage to someone, so it's just as well I'm with my wife. Inside the bar there's an office party in full swing. A live band plays cover versions of Western disco hits, and the crowd is going for it in a big way. To the strains of Donna Summer's 'Hot Stay' [*sic*] and a cha-cha-cha version of Kool & the Gang's 'Celebration', everybody is on the floor. One woman starts off shifting from foot to foot, then starts to add a few flourishes. Soon she's in full flight, throwing the most bizarre shapes, all jutting elbows and knees, losing herself in the music. One of her colleagues gets up close behind her and starts to copy her moves, mimicking each jut and tic, and the thing is, he's not taking the piss.

The band goes into, 'I'm your Venus/ I'm your pyre/ Auto-fire.' The lead singer draws an invisible lasso around her head and shoots it into the crowd with each chorus. I've always admired Japanese food and aesthetics. Now I'm here, I'm falling for the whole package. Japan is starting to make sense.

The next morning, I meet Mr Kato successfully at Ueno train station, thanks to the time he took when we parted last night to draw me a map and write a meticulous set of directions with several phone numbers just in case. We have an early start at the brewery because the Tibetan prime minister is also visiting today. They did ask if he would mind me tagging along, and the cheeky bastard replied that, actually, he would. So they're squeezing me in beforehand.

A half-hour train ride among more dozing commuters, followed by a half-hour taxi ride through the immaculately ordered countryside, and we're pulling in through the gates of the Ibaraki brewery. This is Asahi's flagship: relatively new among their nine breweries, the most modern, the most impressive and the closest to Tokyo. Three tall flagpoles stand in the driveway. One flies the Japanese flag, the next Asahi's logo, and the final one the Union Jack. I assume they must be expecting some important Brits, but when we get into reception I am the only visitor.

A smiling tour guide is waiting for us, dressed in a neat uniform which reminds me of an early 1960s air hostess. She leads us into a 250-seat auditorium, gestures for Mr Kato and me to sit in the middle, about ten rows back, and stands at a podium at the front, about fifty yards away from us. She begins a presentation, which Mr Kato translates. I couldn't feel more self-conscious if I were sitting here naked.

This short welcome is followed by a film on a vast cinema screen. It's the same kind of thing I've seen at other big modern breweries: shots of barley and clear flowing streams, sweeping helicopter views of the brewery, forcing you to appreciate just how damn wonderful beer is all over again. But this being Japan, the message is a little more thoughtful than the normal corporate guff. Asahi is about the pursuit of great taste. Because great taste leads to increased vitality. So great beer doesn't just taste good – it makes you more alive.

The film ends, and a low hum fills the auditorium. I look to the sides, expecting to see curtains sweeping in to cover the screen. But there are none. Instead, I realize the noise is caused oby the screen sinking into the floor to reveal a massive aquarium behind. The strains of 'The Blue Danube' fill the theatre and a huge shark swims by. Mr Kato picks a grape from a banquet which has just appeared, and in an appalling eastern European accent says, 'The behaviour of the aquatic predator is a constant fascination to me. Is it not to you ... *Mister* Brown?' just as the torso of the last sarcastic beer writer floats past.

Sorry, let me do that bit again. The film ends, and a low hum fills the auditorium. I look to the sides, expecting to see curtains sweeping in to cover the screen. Instead, I realize the noise is caused by the screen sinking into the floor, to reveal a glass-fronted brewhouse a few yards away, a vast structure with curved walls, huge copper brewing kettles shining within. Between here and the brewhouse is an ornamental lake, teeming with fat koi carp. And no sharks. I'm not ruling out piranhas entirely though. Not just yet.

We start our tour at a viewing gallery above the brewhouse, looking down on employees manning a vast bank of computer screens. They are dressed in identical powder-blue uniforms with shiny white hard hats, such as a megalomaniac's private army might wear in a climactic battle with escaped British seamen. Away from the window, Mr Kato calls me over to a large metal pillar. There's a dramatic hum, and it starts to open up, sliding down from the ceiling to reveal a glowing core within. No, I'm serious this time. The glowing core turns out to be a film showing the action of yeast. It lasts about ten seconds, then the cylinder heads back to the ceiling. The whole opening and closing sequence takes three times longer than the film itself. So ask yourself: why would they design it like that if they weren't *trying* to make it like a Bond villain's lair?

We walk over to the outside window to admire the view of the ranked giant storage tanks outside. These tall cylinders, like grain silos, were pioneered by Asahi but are now common throughout the world and are the tanks that upset everyone when Pilsner Urquell adopted them. After fermentation, Asahi store the beer for two months to mature, just at freezing point. The immense volume of liquid gives a more consistent quality. Mr Kato asks me how long I think it would take to empty one tank if I drank a bottle a day. I guess twelve years. The correct answer is 2,100 years. And there are 254 of these tanks. Should I ever fall into a coma and wake up to find myself the last surviving human in a dystopian futuristic nightmare, I know where to head.

Asahi (which means rising sun) had been brewers for just under a century when, in 1987, they introduced Super Dry. By early 1990 it was their biggest seller. Over the next few years it took Asahi's share of the Japanese market from 10 per cent to nearly half. I can't help thinking that it might be doing even better if the company resurrected an eighty-year-old ad featured in the display telling me all this, which has the lovely slogan, 'Best doshy beer'.

I love the attention to detail here. We watch the bottling lines, which is always therapeutic, and I learn that the man who invented *kaiten* sushi – the restaurant format where dishes come around to you on a conveyor belt – had the idea after visiting an Asahi bottling line. I also learn that the crown bottle top which we take for granted always has twenty-one dints in it – this gives it a triangular load-bearing capability, which maximizes stability. OK, not the most earth-shattering revelation ever, but how many brewers do you think even *know* that?

The tour ends in the bar on the top floor, a long way up this high-rise building stuck in the middle of miles of flat farmland. Tokyo is hinted at by a distant brown haze to the south. Electricity pylons and long, straight roads suggest what the American Midwest might look like if it sat in a greenhouse climate. A hostess shows us into a private dining room, to a table where a Japanese flag and a Union Jack form an X over a basket of smoked cheeses and small bags of rice sticks. She serves us a range of beers, including Asahi Black, a sweet, caramelly black lager. She backs out of the room, bowing, after delivering each one.

Finally, we head back to the station. But before we board the train, Mr Kato invites me to lunch. This man has given up almost a day of his time now to educate me on the Japanese beer market. Having been in the country for twenty-four hours, I feel like I could write this entire chapter on what I've already learned. I can't imagine how I can even begin to thank him for his hospitality. So instead, just before we part, I gravely offend him by offering to pay for lunch.

Joe Maekawa and Norio Nishizuka have jobs at the Tokyo office of McCann Erikson, a global advertising agency and occasionally work on beer. They also drink a lot of it. Joe is plump and laughs loud, heartily and often. Norio is slim and handsome. He tells me that he doesn't drink as much as he used to since he got married. He says his wife has divorce papers ready for the next time he comes home drunk. I consider trying to tell him that Liz has a similar arrangement for next time I do my impression of Papa Lazarou from *The League of Gentlemen*, but decide it won't translate.

The first thing I want to ask about is the salaryman drinking culture. A salaryman is any middle-ranking white-collar worker, and everyone I know who has visited Japan has told me that they go out en masse straight from work, three or four nights a week, and get riotously drunk, often ending up sleeping on train platforms, briefcases behind their heads, or in a micro-hotel, before going back into work the following morning. This is what we saw in our hotel bar last night, and it's from this behaviour that we get the stereotypical image of the red-faced Japanese unable to take their drink, up on tables with their shirts off, bellowing karaoke. I want to find out how much of it is true.

Joe and Norio are quick to confirm the importance of the big group. 'At 5 p.m., we would typically go with our colleagues to an *izakaya* and talk. You always start off with a beer. In a traditional Japanese company, if the supervisor of a section drinks beer, everyone else has to drink beer. You pour beer for each other – traditional Japanese behaviour is very communal. There's a saying – *Toriaezu birru* – which means, 'Let's just start off with a beer for now.' It always leads to more, but we always say it. After beer you'll move on to something else. When the engine starts running, then you tend to drink more *sho chu* and so on. After we've eaten, there's what we call *nijikai* – the second party. You're a bit drunk; you move to another place. Quiet people come out of their shells.'

'Why do you always start off with beer?'

'Beer deepens communication. We value communication very much. It marks a change from on to off. With beer, you can express your true self. If we had a beer now, we would talk about management. Our Australian boss comes out drinking with us, and he wants to talk about sport and women. But the work stuff is what we really want to say. We don't feel able to say this stuff most of the time.'

This confirms what I've read about drinking marking the end of work-time rules. After only one drink, it's common for Japanese workers to tell their bosses exactly how useless they are and how much better they would be at their job. The next morning the hierarchy is back in place, and no one mentions what was said or done the night before.

One book on Japanese business etiquette describes drinking as 'social intermission'. During the day, individual needs must be suppressed to maintain social harmony and the well-being of the group. But Japanese business is based on mutual trust and rapport, and this is built up more easily and quickly outside business hours. Drunkenness is encouraged as a means of social bonding. As a person's 'soul' is revealed when he drinks, if someone refuses to join in, he has something to hide. Chris Francis, a market researcher, told me he has seen similar behaviour in Taiwan and Korea, where if anything it is more raucous. Chris talks about 'common transgressions' creating powerful bonds. Or as he put it, 'Once you've had your knob out and you've been knocking golf balls around the room with it, you've shared something.'

This all starts to make sense of the drunken stereotype. It's not just a case of alcohol loosening the tongue; there's a symbolic change of status. I think back to Mr Kato last night, and his exaggerated drunkenness now makes sense: anything he said to me was off-limits, outside work, because we had been drinking. In such a formalized culture, it's a vital release valve.

I get an acute sense from Joe and Norio that, important though this style of drinking is, it has had its day. 'Today, people do not go out as much. When the supervisor asks if people are coming for a beer, the younger ones will say, "Sorry, I'm going to the gym."'

The Japanese economy enjoyed decades of seemingly perpetual growth, but then the bubble years ended. It hasn't been growing for a while now. The idea of a job for life has gone. When it was there, everyone being happy together was fine. Now, people are losing their jobs, and there's more individualism. 'Drinking friends are becoming rivals,' says Norio. 'Japanese people never really had forceful competition, and we had two big societies: family and work. Now, young people have friends and hobbies outside these circles. The two old societies are perceived as uncool. The development of cell-phones means you can be in touch with your friends immediately. The big status symbol is how many addresses you have in your phone memory. A quarter of people under twenty-five work in dead-end jobs and pursue artistic careers. This may be common in the West, but it's a very new thing in Japan.'

Apart from what this tells me about Japan, it confirms a lot more of what I've been thinking about beer in a broader sense. If I'd simply walked in here as a stranger and asked these people to tell me about the inner workings of Japanese society, about the changes and insecurities they face, I would probably have got some polite flannel or at best some vague generalizations. Ask about beer, and it's a lens that opens everything else up.

Next I meet Dave McCaughan, Joe's 'Australian boss', a man who they say 'drinks like a colander'.

'Beer is a fundamental part of the culture in China, Japan, South-east Asia. We just don't realize how important it is,' says Dave. 'You should see it in the first hot season. The beer gardens spring up; they're the most amazing places. There are building sites all over, and in the middle of summer they stop construction for two months and just bring out these huge beer gardens. The cranes are covered up with beer signs, just out of nowhere.'

As an outsider (even though he has lived here for ten years, he's definitely still an outsider) Dave has an interesting take on beer's role as a switch between on and off modes. 'Even if they're not going out, guys will drink a beer every afternoon on the way home. They'll sit and drink that one beer, and won't have another one. It's the thing they do at the end of the day to unwind. There's one guy here who gets up at five-thirty in the morning, drinks a litre of beer, practises piano for three hours and then comes into work. He doesn't drink it any other time.'

Dave believes the problem with beer for younger Japanese is that Dry was the ultimate bubble product. 'Drink this, and the silver bullet of success will be yours.' For many who grew up during the recession, beer is their dad's drink, so they drink *sho chu* instead. 'Because no country has new stuff like this place,' says Dave. 'Even in the depths of recession, if you're a young guy there's a new product every day. The time frame for new stuff is three weeks. If it's not a success it's off the shelf.'

On top of that, there's the greater disillusion from the collapse of the economy. 'When I first got here, you'd be out on one of those sessions three or four nights a week. Now you go to the younger guys and ask them if they're coming out for a drink, and they say, "Why? Did something happen?" All the big brewers have German-style beer halls, and they never even used to have to advertise. There's one in the basement here, and now we're constantly getting stuff on our desks saying come down this week and we'll give you all the sausages you can eat for an hour, all that shit.' He pauses and thinks, before continuing, 'You know, it always worries me how young Japanese just go, "give me sausages!"'

Dave still loves the culture. 'When the Japanese are drunk they laugh a lot, and sing a lot, and they don't fight. They do the karaoke thing, then go out and piss into the road, facing the traffic. There's a lot of traffic? Stand six inches back.' They find it offensive when we blow our noses, so I suppose it evens out.

Dusk is falling by the time I leave the building where Joe, Norio and Dave all work, the same deep charcoal grey I saw from the top of the Asahi building last night, the kind we only see in England just before a savage thunderstorm. Instead, in the darkening Ginza streets, I meet Liz in a fine drizzle that pushes us along the pavement amid a damp rush of quickening commuters. I'm looking for a place Mr Kato gave me a glimpse of last night, just before we parted. In the heart of the Ginza district, trains rumble through the city on red-brick viaducts. Under the arches, where an English citydweller might expect to find litter and the stink of piss, is the best place in the world. Instead of a cardboard city, there are rows of tiny, densely packed *izakaya* built into the sides of each arch, catering for people on their way home, stopping for just the one – all right, make it three – before heading out into the suburbs. This is known as drinking 'under the guardrail' –

below the train tracks – and it's the heart of everyday Tokyo beer drinking.

Each bar consists of a barbecue grill, a fridge, a cash till, seating space for about twenty people who don't have intimacy issues, and plenty of bunting and neon signs. And although it's another cliché, I'm afraid this is where we must introduce *Bladerunner*. With its neon signs and dense barbecue smoke, it couldn't be more obvious if the only exception to Mr Kato's observation about graffiti was 'Ridley Scott woz 'ere' written on the viaduct in three-foot-high shaving-foam letters. He must have taken one look at this and seen an entire career roll out like a red carpet before him.

We choose Ton Ton Yakitori for our first drink, our *toriaezu*. We're drawn in by the sweet smoke from the teriyaki sauce on the grill, and by the proprietor, loud Hawaiian shirt just about covering his generous stomach, shouting orders back to the bar while he pulls us to a table. We're tightly packed, two rows of stools crammed into the three feet allowed between the shared tables. Trains rumble over our heads every two minutes, rattling the tiled floor. Paper lanterns line the front of the bar, marking the boundary from the path down the middle of the archway.

Most *izakaya* carry just one beer brand. Mr Kato and Mr Watanabe explained that each brand spends a great deal of money to lure a bar into its fold. The Ton Ton is a Kirin place. We're drinking Kirin from Kirin-branded glasses, under Kirin paper lanterns, with Kirin posters covering the curved walls. The Asahi place is just across the passage. The staff there are all clad in Asahi T-shirts and aprons, serving Asahi beer in chilled Asahi glasses taken from an Asahi-branded fridge, illuminated by an Asahi neon sign.

One person tends the grill, one the till, another washes and dries plates and three work the tables. The contrast between the furious pace of the workers and the relaxed atmosphere they create for their customers is remarkable. Our bar is full now, but every time two spaces become free, the jolly man in the Hawaiian shirt is back out front, working the passing crowd. It never takes him more than thirty seconds to get the seats occupied again.

It's striking how similar all this feels to Spanish tapas culture. People stay on average for about half an hour, having a couple of drinks and a few snacks, before moving on. It's inconceivable to think of having beer without food, or vice versa. It's also very similar to the set-up in Singapore, according to a mate of mine, Jacob, who works there. He told me about hawker centres, where twenty-four-hour food and drink stalls crowd together and people sit in the middle of them drinking iced Tsing-Tao beer. Singaporeans call it talk-cock-sing-song, because they sit talking rubbish and are prone to breaking out into song at any point. If you get hungry mid-session you just wave at a stall owner and they bring you a plate of something delicious. 'I often snack on barbecued squid or fried noodles with clams at 4 a.m.,' says Jacob.

Under the guardrail, you order food by the skewer, and Liz does so with gusto. Soon we have yakitori (roast chicken – we know that one); *junagino* (chicken gizzard), *tan* (its heart), *leba* (tongue) and *nankotu* (cartilage) arrayed before us. Intoxicated by the atmosphere rather than the beer, my wife is feeling adventurous. She polishes off the heart first. She's feeling confident, and she goes for the gizzard. She pops a piece into her mouth and chews, once. Her face falls. Her eyes go glassy, staring through me. I take the skewer from her unresisting hand and eat a piece. It's unusual.

'It's crunchy,' whispers Liz, finally.

I nod. 'If it weren't crunchy I suppose it would just be ordinary chicken.'

'I just wanted to be able to say I'd eaten gizzard,' she says tearfully, finally swallowing. She pushes the plate across the table. 'You've got to eat the rest of it.'

'I don't want to. You ordered it. We can just leave it.'

'No. That would be insulting.' Her voice falls to a whisper. 'You must finish it.'

And in that one, short conversation we see how marriage works. By the last piece of gizzard, I'm almost enjoying it. The gizzard, I mean.

Over several more skewers, a few bowls, some *sho chu* cocktails and a few beers, we decide we could stay and drink here all night, and possibly every night for the rest of our lives. But while I think I have found the heart of Japanese beer drinking, the essence of it, there's a lot more we need to see.

It's dark by the time we leave the arches under the guardrail. Back out on the Ginza streets, we're stopped in our tracks, and spend the next half-hour taking pictures of neon. Signs and screens are piled on top of each other, storeys high, in every direction. Every traffic intersection makes Piccadilly Circus look like a country village during a power cut. Even Times Square is a distant runner-up. We spend so long walking the streets and taking photographs, the bars are closing by the time we try to get another drink.

The next morning, we decide to have breakfast in our hotel's traditional Japanese restaurant rather than at the main buffet.

This turns out to be a bad idea. Minus our dignity, we head for Ebisu Garden Palace, an ultra-modern complex of malls, cinemas, offices, restaurants and trees. This is where the Nippon Beer Brewery, later Sapporo, started brewing in 1887. At the time this area was called Mita Village, and later became Yebisu, or Ebisu. Sapporo, now Japan's third-biggest brewery and the owner of the museum, still brews beers with that name. At the heart of the complex lies the Ebisu Beer Hall and Museum, where I'm hoping to learn about the history and culture of Japanese beer drinking, as well as trying a few different beers.

We enter via a broad, curving staircase into the main hall, where a classical piano recital is taking place. Nothing should surprise me about Japan any more, and yet this does. A crowd of around a hundred people sit quietly, watching the pianist perform in front of giant, gleaming brewing coppers.

We slip into the museum, a broad arc of rooms curving behind the auditorium that turns out to be little more than a collection of large display boards charting the history of brewing in Japan and the Sapporo brewery. This is still fine for my needs, or would be were it not for the randomness of Japanese translation. Every display board has a title in English, such as 'Japan's encounter with beer', or 'Beer brand explosion'. Underneath, all the text is in Japanese only. The accompanying photos are still intriguing. One features a beer hall from a hundred years ago, with Japanese men in formal kimonos, their hair in tight top-knots, playing pool. Towards the end there's a quiz to test what we've learned. 'Let's see how you do!' reads the title in English, before displaying all the questions in Japanese only.

The final exhibit is the Magic Vision Theatre, a bizarre mix of holograms and model-making about fifteen feet across. Figures appear in different parts of the display, 3-D images that I had until now believed were confined to science fiction. According to a leaflet, it tells the story 'of the mysteries of the good taste of beer in an interesting manner'. So we get the tale of how Gambrinus, the king of beer, engages in a desperate contest of wits with 'The Evil One' of the forest. The winner gets the heart of the beautiful Beer Fairy. Apparently it's an allegory.

It becomes clear that the real point of the museum is the euphemistically named Tasting Lounge. All black-lacquered wood and gleaming floors with a long bar curving along one wall, the place is packed. I was the only person looking at the museum exhibits. Everyone else who can't be bothered with the piano recital – and that's a lot of people – came straight here.

You buy tokens from a vending machine, then exchange these at the bar for a choice of different Sapporo beers. Not for the first time, I notice a huge German influence. Yesterday Dave told us that a crude generalization of Western influence in Japan would be: the British built their ships, the Dutch built their cannons, and the Germans came out and showed them how to use it all. There's still a widespread belief that anything decent in beer must originate from Germany. So Yebisu beer is a Dortmunder-style lager, Yebisu dark is a Bavarian black lager, Edelpils a German Pilsner. These are accompanied by 'beer crackers' – that's what it says on the packets. The atmosphere is humid, and we soon make full use of the cloth provided to mop up the condensation that trickles constantly down our glasses and puddles on the lacquered table.

'Toriaezu birru'

It seems that whole families come here to drink through their Saturday afternoons. At the next table sit five middle-aged people. The oldest bloke has fallen fast asleep. He's swaying slightly, but has that sack-of-spuds thing going on: there's no tension whatsoever in his upper body, so his centre of gravity keeps him upright.

Many people are working through trays consisting of four small sample glasses, complete with tasting notes. That's what I need. I stand up and get some money out, and an ancient Japanese man appears beside me, powder-blue blazer and white sun hat, gently pushing my money back towards me, then hobbling over to the bar and returning with two fresh beers and two packets of beer crackers. We thank him profusely, and he's bowing back. Five minutes later he returns with small brown cylinders of smoked cheese.

When our glasses are half-empty, the old man buys us another beer. I look uncomprehendingly at Liz. 'I caught his eye,' she admits. 'There was a really cute little toddler walking past. I was smiling at the toddler and I looked up, and he was smiling at the toddler as well and we both sort of acknowledged each other.' I should have known.

We're trapped. Most people seem to be settling down for the day, the old man and his family included, and he obviously thinks we're along for the ride. This would be fine, apart from the fact that we're due to meet Miyoko, a colleague of Joe and Norio who set up yesterday's meetings for me, and her husband Nick. And it looks like I'm not going to get my tasting tray.

We need to devise a plan. The old man is watching the level of beer in our glasses, trying to look casual about it, casting sidelong glances and pretending he was just looking to toast us when we spot him doing it. We'll have to use stealth and deception. Liz decides we need to end it by reciprocating with some token of gratitude. Pretending to go to the toilet, she sneaks up to the gift shop by the exit, buys a bottle opener shaped like a glass of beer, and has the staff wrap it, which they do beautifully. When she gets back to the table I spring out of my seat, we neck our beers and dart over to the old man's table before he can react. Liz presents the gift with both hands, bowing. The poor old bugger looks absolutely horrified, but his friends and family are whooping with delight, roaring with laughter and slapping each other on the back. We back away, leaving him holding the gift, and head up the stairs. As we near the top, a powder-blue blur shoots past us. By the time we get to the door, our new best friend is standing there, bowing low, holding a beautifully wrapped package that's far too large to be a beer-glass-shaped bottle opener. It turns out to be a box of beer jellies, a local delicacy we spotted earlier on the shelves alongside beer biscuits, beer soap and the aforementioned beer crackers. The old man's honour has been restored – for now. I pull Liz away before the situation has a chance to escalate into an exchange of title deeds on our respective houses.

Miyoko and Nick have given up their Saturday afternoon and evening to show us any parts of Tokyo we wish to see, driving us between them in Nick's SUV. My residual English sensibilities scream that we're taking advantage of their hospitality, but it becomes evident in our conversation that we would be grossly insulting them if we refused. Having both spent time in the West, they do compromise by reluctantly allowing us to pay for the odd drink through the course of the evening, but it doesn't seem to sit comfortably with them.

We start off by looking at a traditional Japanese beer garden. I've been wanting to see one since I read a description given by an American writer in the late nineteenth century:

> . . . gems of art and delicate comfort. Graceful arbors covered with clematis, paths of neat matting, colored lanterns and bright-clad and bright-eyed Japanese maidens are the elements of the composition which lift the visitor from the prosaic German or American beer garden to the poetry of enjoyment.

This is followed by the caveat that all this beauty was undermined by the minor grammatical errors in the English-language sign at the gate, but I decide that even if this travesty hasn't been amended over the intervening century, I can probably tolerate it.

We're not seeing it at its best today. The driving rain has scared the punters away from the acres of tables and driven the hardiest hardcore of revellers into one heated tent, where they keep the staff busy fetching trays of beer and fried food. Kirin and Budweiser banners snap angrily in the chill wind, flicking rain at us as we walk past. Back home it's August bank holiday weekend, and for the first time since the airport, there's something about the city that feels familiar.

We then take a steady crawl around various *izakaya*, eating teriyaki and edamame, octopus and tofu and raw chicken, drinking beer and sake, talking about the cultural differences we have all seen between East and West. Our final stop is a tiny restaurant near Nick and Miyoko's home. We have hot, salty ginkgo nuts, smoked dried fish, peanut tofu and fruit, all tiny portions of exquisite tastes. I read that a visiting dignitary to Japan was given a feast of eighty-five courses. I can believe it now. After six hours of steady eating, drinking and talking we must have had fifteen or twenty dishes, and we are neither full nor drunk nor bored.

Next comes the egg of a striped mullet. 'It's rare,' says Miyoko, looking up briefly from a tube map, a sheaf of printed web pages and our *Time Out* guide in which she is carefully marking all the pubs and bars she thinks we may find interesting tomorrow, 'like truffles.' I scarfed mine down straight away; I thought it was some kind of beef jerky. I pretend there's some left in my bowl and I'm still eating it, but Miyoko doesn't notice – she's busy trying to think of the right frame of reference. 'Or maybe it's more like caviar or foie gras. Anyway, it's very precious.' I start to wonder what kind of restaurant this is.

Our waitress asks if we like the bowls we are drinking from. I hadn't given mine much thought, but you have to say yes, don't you? Then she tells us they are over a hundred years old. I put mine down abruptly while the waitress goes to fetch a book on antique ceramics and shows us photographs of the 150-year-old spoon and 250-year-old saucer sitting before us.

Towards the end of the meal there's a full, proper Japanese tea ceremony. Belatedly, it emerges in a very modest, round-about way that the chef is one of Japan's best. After some coaxing, the waitress fetches us a selection of the books he has written. I decide that an appropriate level of gratitude would begin with me learning all three Japanese alphabets as soon as I can so I can read them. It can't be that hard. My second decision is that I can never again kid myself that I know anything about preparing beautiful food. Finally, after accepting a couple of the valuable antique bowls as gifts, we are allowed to leave. Of course, Nick and Miyoko refuse to allow us to pay for anything.

I think everyone understands that we must go to Roppongi. It seems an insult to even suggest it after this evening, but having seen the very best that Japanese eating and drinking has to offer, I am also duty-bound to see the worst. Roppongi is the area where the gaijin drink. 'If you have to see it, you really need to go tonight,' says Miyoko. 'It's like 42nd Street in New York. Friday and Saturday, they keep going all night. You can see karaoke and multinational dining. There is a Mexican darts bar and supermarket.'

It's a testament to how unappetizing this sounds that it finally finds the limits of Nick and Miyoko's hospitality. They will only drive us the twenty-minute journey to Roppongi, give us some tips on where to go and their umbrella. 'We're not coming in there with you,' says Miyoko in forthright tones. We wave a bleary goodbye, and we're on our own.

It's eleven thirty, and Roppongi is just getting going. Ever since American servicemen partied here in the 1950s, this is the place Japanese mothers vainly warn their teenage daughters to steer clear of. The atmosphere in Paddy Foley's, 'Tokyo's Original Irish Pub', is different to anything we've experienced since landing at Narita. Chelsea play Southampton live on big screens. Draught Guinness, Boddington's and Heineken are 1,300 yen (£6.60) a pint. A plastic bucket sits on the bar next to a sign reading 'Tips welcome'.

The streets are busier than the bars. People try to hustle us into clubs by assuring us that we won't have to pay them for the privilege of entry. Drunken Japanese girls are carried around by their mates, and big American guys swagger aggressively. Bars sit one on top of another, storeys high. Their neon signs are similarly stacked in vertical strips, listing what's at 1F, 2F and so on. So while the signs for places like Ronin, Club Zeus, Mad Max Darts Bar and Tokyo Jail S & M Fetish Show Pub look tempting, we can't get a feel of what they are really like without going in.

We manage to keep going until around 4 a.m. We spend half an hour in a deserted karaoke booth trying to make the equipment work or find someone to help us. We find one English pub that's better than most pubs in England. Finally, we end up in a hot dog restaurant at 4.30 a.m., upstairs among tables full of Japanese teenagers fast asleep until the trains start again in a couple of hours.

All too soon, it's time to leave Tokyo. Like so many places on this journey, four or five days is a laughably short time to spend here. It may be an industrialized city on Planet Earth built and populated by human beings, but it's about as different from everywhere else as you can get within that definition. And yet the underlying principles of beer drinking are the same. It's still about sociability, still about mates. Beer provides the vital release such a formalized society needs to remain functional.

But we've seen that even Japan is no exception to the inevitability that, wherever you go now in the world, people want to look like Westerners, dress like Westerners and drink like Westerners. The conversations we've had with people suggest the traditions of Japanese drinking may be eroding. Roppongi's Irish pubs are part of the same trend that sees the big international imitation Pilsner brands creeping in to replace bowls of home brew in African shebeens and Mexican villages. Whatever different and interesting drinking culture I might find, I worry that I might be recording its passing. But Japan has always taken Western ideas and made them its own. This is one place we will definitely come back to, and whatever does change, I'm pretty sure Japan will still be endlessly surprising and deeply seductive.

Shanghai

Our hotel issues us with business cards featuring a map with the location and directions in Chinese, so we can give them to cab drivers to get us home. People here really don't speak very much English at all, so this is a necessary and thoughtful touch. Our guidebook tries to give us a few pointers on communication but really doesn't make things any better. It spells out a few key words and phrases, explains how crucial it is that we get the accents on the various symbols exactly right, otherwise we'll be saying something entirely different, then fails to give any indication whatsoever what this correct pronunciation might be. We're just going to have to improvise.

The hotel is in the middle of the French Concession, amid elegant streets of colonial houses. Shanghai opened up to the West after the end of the opium wars, and from 1842 to 1949 the city was a playground carved up between the French, English and Americans. Depending on your attitude to colonialism, it was either the Paris of the East or the Whore of the Orient. Instability across the region sent the peasant Chinese flocking to the relative safety of the city, where they provided a cheap workforce hardly distinguishable from slaves, living in workhouses and making the Westerners rich. In 1934 life expectancy was twenty-seven. In 1937 municipal refuse workers picked up 20,000 corpses off the street. At the same time, there were more cars here than in the whole of the rest of China put together. It was in Shanghai – described at the time as 'a city of 48-storey skyscrapers built upon 14 layers of hell' – that the Chinese Communist Party was founded. Mao Zedong was at the first meeting. As the West frets increasingly about China's burgeoning power or gasps in horror at its human rights abuses, it's galling to realize that everything we fear or dislike about the modern country is a direct result of our own colonial excesses.

I wanted to stop off in Shanghai, just for a night or two, because China is now the largest beer market in the world. The Chinese have always been very enthusiastic drinkers, even though beer as we know it is a recent arrival. This is almost certainly the birthplace of distilled spirits, and in remote parts of the interior fermented horse's milk is still the beverage of choice. Drinking is a vital part of religious and cultural festivals, and Confucius even expounded a theory of 'moral drinking', believing alcohol could 'harmonize the blood' and improve one's health, cheer the spirits, dispel melancholy and bring happiness. It's still a common belief in China that drinking is the wellspring of creativity. Li Bai, a Tang Dynasty (AD 618–907) poet, wrote:

> How many great men are forgotten through the ages?
> Great drinkers are better known than sober sages . . .
> I only want to drink and never wake up.

Appropriately enough he died when, after getting stociously pissed, he started a conversation with the moon's reflection in a pond, fell in and drowned. This was seen not as the tragic end of a drunken idiot, but the ultimate sacrifice in pursuit of art. Moderate drinking remains not just acceptable, but a moral imperative. There is even a constellation of stars called the Alcohol Stars Flag associated with good fortune and happiness.

Germans built the first brewery in the country in the port of Qingdao in 1903. The beer, known by Qingdao's previous spelling, Tsing Tao, is easily China's most well known export of any product. But for most of the twentieth century beer remained niche. China is divided into twenty-one autonomous provinces, each favouring home produce and regarding other provinces as foreign. When the economy opened up in the 1980s everyone had to have a brewery. Beer was expensive, so as well as providing employment and hinting subtly that the water was pure, this also said there was enough money around for small luxuries. By the early 1990s there were over 800 breweries in the country, producing brands with names like King Benefit, Cloudy Lake, Dragon-and-Elephant and Double Happiness Guangzhou. Average per capita consumption is still relatively low, but has nearly quadrupled over the last seventeen years.

All of which makes it slightly surreal that we can't find a bar in Shanghai. We spend the afternoon exploring the French quarter on foot, initially just wanting to soak up the sights. We see many wonderful things: street markets selling antique Maoist propaganda and 1930s drinks posters; a whole street full of stalls selling nothing but fried prawns; and a bird, dog and insect market where the air is filled with a shrill, staccato chattering noise which we eventually trace to lines of people hunkered down among row upon row of earthenware jars.

Inside each jar is a cricket. People keep these and make the crickets 'sing' by poking them with straw. There are hundreds of jars, all different sizes with crickets selected accordingly to fit snugly within them.

After an hour or so we decide that, while we're still enjoying the sights, when we see a bar we'll stop for a drink and a sit-down. Two hours later we decide to forget the sights and devote all our energies to finding somewhere that will sell us a beer. My radar is down. After visiting so many cities, I can look at a street or area and I just *know* where the bars should be, but in Shanghai they aren't there. On every street corner where there should be an Irish pub, every alley where there should be a tiny bar, there are none. Banner ads strung across narrow streets taunt us with images of ice-cold Tsing Tao and Tiger beer but give no clue as to where there might be a bar that sells it.

China's beer consumption is concentrated mainly in the prosperous coastal cities, in particular Beijing and Shanghai, where the average income is double that elsewhere. So we're in the best place to get a drink in the country that drinks more beer than any other, but we manage to walk through the centre of the city for hours without finding anywhere to get a drink. For the first time, I get a real sense of how big China must be.

Finally we come out onto the Bund, a former towpath for pulling rice barges along the broad Huangpu River which developed into the focal point of colonial Shanghai. Elegant facades of beautiful early-twentieth-century Western-style buildings line the river, causing mixed feelings. You can't help but love the Bund's broad architectural sweep, but it couldn't look less Chinese, and is a constant reminder of who built this part of the city, and how. Perhaps this is one reason why the view from the windows of the Bund's hotels and offices is changing so dramatically.

Only ten years ago the Bund looked across at swampland and pig farms; now, it's one half of a Mexican stand-off between old and new Shanghai. This is Asia's fastest-growing city, home to nearly fifteen million people and the most rapidly evolving metropolis on the planet. The Bund may reflect Shanghai's glorious and decadent past, but the city's future is in Pudong, across the river. In this vast area, eight times the size of Canary Wharf, the architect Richard Rogers is building a new city. The sun flares back at us from mirror-fronted skyscrapers that self-consciously rival Manhattan's best shot, but the scene is dominated by the Jinmao tower. A structure of pink and silver-blue globes held together by concrete struts, this eighty-eight-floor building (eight is China's lucky number) is the fourth-largest structure in the world. When you see this skyline, you are struck with a calm and absolute certainty that our new century will be dominated by China, and it will be run from here. It's as simple as that, and there's nothing anyone can do about it.

We decide that a drink in a hotel bar is our only option. The Peace Hotel is the most famous hotel in the whole of China. In the 1930s Victor Sassoon, Charlie Chaplin, Noël Coward and George Bernard Shaw enjoyed cocktails while admiring the stunning views from the rooftop bar. The sun is setting. This will be the perfect moment.

We sweep through the hotel's stunning art deco reception to the elevators, and step out of them minutes later into a bridal receiving line. The happy couple are standing under an arch of flowers in the space between the lifts and the bar. We turn round to attempt a quick exit via the elevator, but it's been called down to the ground. They all have. And they're not moving from there, no matter how desperately we press the buttons. We back into a corner, but it's too late: a spotlight hits us. We look up and find ourselves staring down the lens of the camera filming the event. We smile sheepishly and look back at the bank of elevators. They're still not moving, and neither is the camera. It stays trained on us, ignoring the bride and her guests. It takes five minutes for the lift to return. Five minutes of someone's big day during which we are the centre of attention, not her. I only hope there's such a thing as *China's Funniest Home Videos*, and that the happy couple have that kind of sense of humour.

Back out in the thickening dusk I'm getting desperate. We stumble away from the Bund along Nanjing Donglu, the main shopping street, as the neon flares into life. There's a Pizza Hut, a McDonald's and what looks like a KFC until you look closely at the colonel and realize he's actually an ancient Chinaman in the same pose. But there's no pub or bar. Finally, about half a mile down from the Bund, we spot a first-floor bar inside the Sofitel Hyland Hotel, and stagger in. Le Pub turns out to be not just a bar, but a brewpub, brewing several of its own beers on site. Five hours after we left our hotel, we taste this weekend's Best Beer in the World.

Fortified by three of these and some deep-fried Western bar snacks, we head back out into the neon-bathed streets. We're in the heart of the commercial district, and it takes a long time to get past some of the shops. Every one is laid out like an exclusive department store, products displayed beneath glass-topped counters, whether antique calligraphy equipment or cans of Reeb, China's budget beer brand. Smartly uniformed staff line up to help if we want a closer look at something. Liz is entranced.

And then we walk past a German-style beer garden. I know that's what it is because it says 'German beer' in English and Chinese on the awning at the front. Eager to try German beer Chinese-style, we head in and find a table. The beer list consists of three different sizes of draught Budweiser, bottled Bud, Bud Ice, Tsing Tao (in which Anheuser-Busch has a 30 per cent stake) and Heineken. This menu is held in a Budweiser-branded plastic stand. The bottles are kept in a Budweiser-branded fridge. The authentic-looking Bavarian-style ceramic draught beer font has a Bud logo on it. There's a curiously small stage, where a one-man band might be able to rock out cautiously, and that's Bud-liveried as well. The backdrop to the stage is a poster we've seen all over Shanghai this afternoon featuring the recovering alcoholic Elton John holding up a bottle of Bud and grinning for the camera, his autograph almost as big as the Bud logo. I'm pleased to see he's so comfortable around beer these days, and wonder why he hasn't extended his endorsement of the world's biggest beer brand to the West, where both he and it are much more well known. As I can't have a German beer, I order a Tsing Tao. It tastes suspiciously like Bud.

I've grown accustomed to this in the West, but here it's just depressing. It seems that Anheuser-Busch won't be happy until they've bought everything, as though they resent the very existence of any beer brands they don't own. And their dominance seems consistently to be based on money rather than the character of the beer. It strikes me that Budweiser is the King of Beers in the same way that Michael Jackson (not the beer writer this time) was once the King of Pop:

self-appointed, with little basis in fact and with a knee-jerk response to legal action should anyone dare question their undeserved appropriation of the title. Think the comparison is facetious? How about the fact that Grant's Farm, the Busch family home (a house which they owned, rented to the brewery, then *charged expenses to the brewery for living in)*, was a fairyland with a menagerie of animals, a fake mountain populated by goats modelled on one near Gussie Busch's Swiss wife's home, and coal buckets made of solid gold. Now who does that remind you of?

We retreat to our hotel, in a quiet part of the French Concession, to discover that the peaceful street that runs along the back of the gardens a few yards away is where most of Shanghai's bars have been hiding.

Maoming Lanlu is one of Shanghai's main night-time destinations. A small gate leads directly out to it from the hotel grounds. The street is filled with neon signs and loud music. Attractive women sit on stools outside every doorway in a manner that screams dodgy strip joint. But this is different. The girls show us to vacant seats at the bar. I expect to get hit with a cover charge, but it doesn't come. Although the clothes confirm this is the city's playground for the rich, there's no side; the people are simply being welcoming – to those who can afford to drink here.

Most people at tables seem to be clutching Aussie-style stubbie coolers, but when I look more closely, I realize these are dice shakers. In the midst of Saturday-night drinking, dancing and flirting, everyone with a seat at a table in every one of the bars on the strip is playing mah-jong, shaking and slamming dice on tables, faces expressionless.

Bar after bar reveals a fascinating mix of East and West.

It's already obvious that China will be the dominant economic power of the new century; the more interesting question is what will happen culturally. On the surface it looks as if Western culture will conquer all. Everywhere I look, there are baseball caps, designer jeans and 'I ♥ New York' T-shirts. Everyone is drinking Heineken, Tiger, Bud or Coors Lite. The clothes are Western, the music is Western, but the people are Chinese; the only other foreigners seem to be spouses of the locals. Rocking, tight bands play phonetically translated cover versions of Pink and Christina Aguilera hits, talking to the crowd in a mixture of Chinese and English between songs. But just like in Japan, in both the clothes and the music there's a sense that the Chinese are converting Western things into a style all their own.

We patrol the strip from end to end and have a fantastic time. I decide that one of the main problems with Britain is that we don't have enough neon. We should cheer up a bit. Like fireworks, neon is uncomplicated, colourful and exciting. It makes you feel happy.

Back in the hotel grounds we visit the Face Bar, tables spilling out onto the manicured lawns and gravelled pathways. We sit and listen to the crickets and the drunken laughter, gazing up into the night sky. A monumental skyscraper, wedged close enough to the hotel to feel physically intimidating, stares back at us. It seems insane, but this is the first time I've noticed it. I wouldn't be surprised if they built it just now while we were out.

The next morning I wake up with a hangover, jet lag, a stinking cold and aching legs from all the walking yesterday. It's quite a combination, and I feel lower than at any point on the trip so far. I cheer up when, after a morning of museums and flower markets, we stumble across the Paulaner Brauhaus, where we sit in a high-ceilinged glass conservatory, listening to a band play Western pop on traditional Chinese instruments, drinking German beer served by Chinese women in Bavarian dress. It's the kind of place that would make purists blanch, but that's the purists' problem.

We're in the heart of the French Concession now. We walk past what looks like an American suburban house and notice a sign reading 'The Blarney Stone'. We head in.

The authentic Irish barman brings over our drinks, and asks us where we're from. 'This is kind of an oasis for Western people,' he tells us. 'The Chinese are sociable enough, but they come in here, see this and walk out again. You get the tourist groups that come to Shanghai, go to Beijing and to Shaanxi to see the clay warriors; they go home and say it was great, but ten days in China was enough. But if you duck into a place like this, that stays completely isolated from Chinese culture, you can recharge yourself, go back out and do another ten days of China. That's how a lot of expats survive. We love it, obviously, but you do need a break after a while.'

'So do Chinese and Westerners not really mix at all then?'

'No, they do, but, God, you have to be careful. The Chinese don't have the custom of going out for a drink like we do, but they socialize at meals, big groups at round tables that spin round so you can share the food. At big banquets they do drink, and they go insane. There's this white spirit; it's face-numbing. They drink it to oblivion. They have this custom called *kenpai*, down in one. And if you're a Western guest, they insist on toasting you individually. So they each have one, and you have about forty. That's a favourite trick.'

He also challenges my view on how smooth China's path to world dominance might be. 'People think you can come to Shanghai and make loads of money, but it's not that simple. If you're a Westerner, you need a Chinese partner otherwise you'll get screwed. And there's a good chance your Chinese partner will screw you anyway. The thing you've got to know is there's still lots of propaganda. Like, they're building all these apartment blocks. The ones on the way in from the airport?'

I remember them and nod.

'Yeah, well look at them at night. There's no lights on. They're all empty. Just for show. There's a massive property bubble here, and the stock market is overvalued.'

The world's big brewers learned all this to their cost in the 1990s. Brands such as Foster's, Becks and Carlsberg invested and lost millions here before pulling out. A week before we flew in, someone gave me a chapter from a book called *Mr China*. It's the true story of the author's involvement in a programme of Western financial investment in China that steadily trickled down the drain. The story of their purchase of China's Five Star brewery is both tragedy and comedy, a brilliant evocation of the pitfalls involved as China tries to attract foreign investment but still do things its own way.

Breweries are still run by hierarchy and committee. Central to Chinese business and society is the concept of not losing face, so business discussions often start far more aggressively than you'd expect. The author has to deal with Madame Wu Hongbo, chief engineer of the First Light Industry Bureau of the People's Municipal Government of Beijing, a 'Chinese

Boadicea' who accuses him of 'talking in dog farts' and describes the ever-worsening situation at the brewery as 'a right stir-fry of pubic hairs and garlic'.

Most of the money the Westerners invest in the brewery simply evaporates over one weekend, paying previously undisclosed 'creditors'. No one does any work. No one can be fired or promoted because the breweries employ large family groups who stick together. An inspection of returned stock reveals that 'one bottle had leaves in the bottom, several contained only an inch of beer, and another was full but contained a large ball of adhesive tape ... I had a case of cans that were perfect – except that they were empty.' The label on one bottle of beer 'was dirty brown, frayed and wrinkled, and read SOY SAUCE'. The author attempts to pass new regulations in the workplace to deal with specific problems, including a ban on making insurance claims on behalf of the company and then keeping the proceeds, organizing gambling syndicates in the office, growing vegetables for personal use on factory sites and a new rule calling for dismissal for fighting with customers. None of it is any use. The Westerners eventually withdraw, rescuing a fraction of their investment.

After a long and complicated lunch we go to Pudong and visit the Jinmao tower observation galleries so we can truthfully say we've seen the whole city. Scores of tiny stars twinkle below us in the twilight. It takes a second to realize that these are blow torches. At dusk on a Sunday, work continues unabated. Tokyo Dave told us that when he had an office here, if he spent a week or so away the skyline would have changed entirely. 'They work twenty-four hours a day on building sites, and build in a quarter of the time we do in the West,' he said. 'You'd turn up and go, "Hang on, we had a river view last week; now we're two streets away."' I think back to a few months ago when a water main burst in Upper Street, Islington, and my bus was diverted for over three weeks until they got round to fixing it. We are in such trouble.

On the overnight flight home I watch *Supersize Me*, the documentary made by a man who eats nothing but McDonald's for a month, and horrifies his girlfriend and doctors with the effects. At this stage in my research I feel like I'm living in a curious hybrid of this movie and *Lost in Translation*. I'm living largely on a diet of beer and infinite variations on the theme of the ham sandwich, and am stuck deep in the otherwordly dislocation of long-haul travel to alien cities. I dream fitfully, images of Scarlett Johansson and Happy Meals colliding in ways you really don't want to know about.

I feel like I've seen the future in Japan and China, both economically and culturally. In both cases it's a future whose template has been set in train by the West and modified and run by the East. Everywhere I have ever travelled before (apart from Celbridge and Milwaukee) I've entertained thoughts of living there only to conclude that I would miss London, because that's where the action is, the front line. Now London feels quiet, because the new century will be shaped in Asia. Although nothing is certain, it does at least look like we'll be able to get a beer in this future.

If an alternative to Budweiser survives, it might not be that bad.

9

'Countless thousands of fattened creatures . . .'

Die Wies'n

'So, which do you think is worse: not being able to organize a piss-up in a brewery, or coming to the world's biggest beer festival and not being able to get a drink?'

I feel obliged to say what the others are thinking.

'Hmm . . .' replies one.

'I reckon they're probably about the same,' says the other, diplomatically.

Like Victorian urchins with faces pressed against a sweet shop window, the three of us stand just inside a tent in which 7,000 people are seated. From the sidelines, we're watching the biggest party in the world get under way.

The 'tent' is in fact an immense structure. For the first time I understand why people feel compelled to use a football pitch as the standard unit of measurement for large spaces. The ceiling arcs sixty feet above our heads. There's a mezzanine level halfway up. Who ever heard of a tent with a mezzanine?

In the centre of the main space rises a huge podium where a band dressed in traditional Bavarian costume is settling into its repertoire of traditional songs and cheesy Euro novelty hits. Surrounding the central podium, filling the acres, sit long trestle tables, people squeezed intimately onto their benches, roaring along to the songs, foaming litre steins swinging and smashing together. This is the crux of our problem: no one told us about the bloody tables.

Possibly the saddest, most predictable and pointless thing I could do at the start of this chapter is make some lazy, half-arsed comment reinforcing the stereotypes about Germans to which we Brits stubbornly cling. But I'm sorry; this tent runs like a machine. It's the most efficient thing I've seen in my life. Seven thousand people are served beer and food at their tables by an army of barmaids. Queuing at the bar would make the whole thing impossible. People crowding the aisles would make it impossible. So to make the system work, there's one simple rule: if you don't have a seat at a table, you can't order a beer. And on the first day of Oktoberfest, half an hour after the bars opened, there's not a seat to be had anywhere.

It's entirely my fault. The problem with squeezing so much international travel into such a short space of time – apart from the catastrophic effects on my health and bank balance – is that I haven't had time to research each trip as thoroughly as I would have liked beforehand. So far I've managed to work around this. Not here.

Oktoberfest starts each year at noon on the third Saturday in September. This could lead to confusion, but give me some credit – I did at least manage to get us here on the right day. The event is heralded by the Grand Entry of the Oktoberfest Landlords, a procession through town of the families of the festival hosts, the bands, the waitresses, the lord mayor and a young woman dressed as a monk. This entourage sits in magnificent carriages, adorned with flowers and pulled by magnificent horses. The procession arrives at the festival grounds, and on the stroke of noon, the lord mayor taps the first keg of beer and cries, '*Ozapft is!*' (It's tapped!) and the festivities begin.

I knew all this would be worth seeing, which is why I arranged for us to be here on the opening day. The problem is, I didn't check the exact timings until after I'd booked my hotel and flights. So despite getting up at 5.30 a.m. and catching the first flight from Heathrow, when the lord mayor and the transsexual monk were arriving at the parade ground we were still watching a procession of bags on a luggage carousel. When *Ozapft was*, I was checking in to my hotel. When people were piling like lunatics into the tents, we were thinking we'd better get a move on and make our way down here. And now here we are.

We're not alone in our sorrow; the chest-height partitions that separate the tables from the entrances to the tents, protecting them from hysterics launching themselves and landing in the pretzels and beer puddles, are lined with hundreds of peering heads, trying to look cheerful but with eyes betraying a desperate longing.

In our little group the silence grows uncomfortable. You tend to notice silence a lot more when you're only yards away from thousands of lederhosen-wearing Germans cheering and singing 'Is This the Way to Amarillo' with indecent gusto. I need to think of something.

'Oh well,' I say with forced cheerfulness, 'we're not here

just to drink beer. We need to take in the general ambience as well. Shall we go for a walk?'

John Harley and Luke Wade, my Oktoberfest companions, currently occupy that middle ground that exists between business colleagues, acquaintances and good mates. None of my real friends could come with me. Chris had to work; Liz said, 'Ha ha ha ha ha. No.' The other friends I phoned said, 'I'm going to a conference,' 'My wife won't let me,' 'I'm getting married,' and, 'Er, so am I then.' I phoned up John and asked him if he was going to Oktoberfest and he laughed and said, 'Well, I am now.' So these two people I really don't know very well came along, and I'm responsible for them being here, and there's still a residual politeness that you don't get with die-hard friends. So while they would have been entirely within their rights to respond to my suggestion along the lines of, '*What?* You force us to get up at the crack of a sparrow's fart, *on a Saturday*; you drag us over here with the promise of beer, and now there is none, and you're suggesting we follow you around "soaking up the ambience"? You know what, mate. You can fuck off. We're going to the pub. Without you,' as they might reasonably be expected to do, instead they nod and say, 'Sure,' in tight, high-pitched voices.

The festival ground is a vast space, over a hundred acres in total. We're in one of its main streets, the Wirtsbudenstrasse, where the beer tents dominate. There are fourteen of these, each devoted to a different beer brewed by one of Munich's six main breweries. We start off by checking out each one of them, just in case. Nothing doing. They're all packed. Efficient but packed. But they are still fascinating to observe; the interiors are reminiscent of forests, with vines and creepers growing up the trunk-like tent poles. The mounted heads of boars, stags and wolves glare at the revellers. Between them, these tents seat 100,000 people. I may have already pointed out that there isn't a seat to be had. And there are so many more people outside the tents, attendance must run into the hundreds of thousands.

So we wander down the Wirtsbudenstrasse and have every one of our senses assaulted. We manage to forget our thirst for a few minutes, as it becomes clear that beer is in no way the only attraction. The beer tents, or *Festhallen*, may be huge beyond our imaginings, but the Wirtsbudenstrasse is only one of two broad main streets, which are in turn criss-crossed by smaller avenues. A massive Ferris wheel dominates the skyline. Ghost trains, helter-skelters, shooting games, darts games and countless rides you really shouldn't go anywhere near with a stomach full of beer create a riot of sound and colour wherever we go. In total there are 41 fairground attractions and 17 sideshows here, including 5 roller coasters, 11 merry-go-rounds and 5 dodgems. Further down the list given to me by the Munich tourist office lurk 'one steep wand driver' and one 'humorous photographer'.

An American friend of mine who visited Oktoberfest a few years ago remarked drily that it was what Disneyland would have been like if Germany had won the Second World War. This is perfect not only because mentioning the war around Germans is always funny, but also because the similarities with Disneyland go a lot further than such a cheap shot might suggest. Bavarian culture has had an enormous influence on the whole Disney look and feel. The Brothers Grimm, who collected and wrote down hundreds of folk tales such as *Snow White* and *Cinderella*, were German. The iconic Disneyworld

Magic Castle is modelled on Neuschwanstein castle, built by King Ludwig II, the grandson of the king in whose honour Oktoberfest was first held. And Mickey Mouse was originally modelled on Adolf Hitler (OK, I made that last one up). Bavaria is real-life Disneyland. More than that, Oktoberfest forces a wholesale readjustment of the senses. It makes you feel childlike. Everything is oversized and in primary colours.

I'm also struck by the fascination with mechanical figures, clockwork toys again reminiscent of fairy tales. The Paulaner tent has a massive, foaming stein slowly rotating on top of a fifty-foot-high pillar. The Löwenbräu tent goes for a twelve-foot-high lion with a mug in his hand. Each time a new keg is tapped in the tent, the lion roars. The Spaten tent has the most eye-catching attraction of all though. The simple, doll-like figures in Bavarian traditional dress turning a giant hog on a spit roast are more than they seem: as the female figure bends over, the crowd on the street outside get a flash of her underwear.

In the gaps between the *Festhallen*, in any space too small for waltzers, dodgems or shooting galleries, there are stalls selling food and souvenirs. The importance of food at Oktoberfest is often overlooked: vast rows of whole chickens turn slowly on spits; lines of spikes hold smoked fish speared through the mouth. The smells of grilling meat and sugary gingerbread form an almost visible fug.

The statistics are so huge as to be almost meaningless, but I'm compelled to quote them anyway: six million people come to Oktoberfest every year from around the world, spending a billion euros between them. They drink over six million litres of beer, 200,000 litres of non-alcoholic beer, 36,000 litres of wine and 22,000 litres of sparkling wine. This helps wash down half a million sausages, nearly 700,000 chickens 60,000 pork knuckles, 50,000 fish and around a hundred whole oxen. No one even counts the huge quantities of burgers, candy floss and giant, ornately decorated gingerbread hearts. Then there are the pretzels hawked around the tables constantly by the serving women, twelve inches across and encrusted with salt, as if we needed any help stoking our thirst. Oktoberfest is the most popular festival of any description on the face of the planet. It has spawned at least 3,000 imitators worldwide and created the template from which any beer festival in the world is drawn.

If you look at these figures, Oktoberfest is much more than a celebration of beer. Perhaps wary of the appeal the event holds for the world's young backpackers and travelling hedonists, Munich tourist officials increasingly refer to it as a folk festival. But all that food and beer reveals that, first and foremost, this is a celebration of gluttony. It's late in the year and winter is approaching. Traditionally there was perhaps a need to fatten up at this time against the cold and austerity ahead. Until the twentieth century it might have been a long while before this abundance would be available again, and Bavarians had to enjoy it while they could. In his book *Planet Party*, Iain Gately describes the scene in suitably messy terms:

> Every stall, both inside and outside the beer tents, emphasises plenty – countless thousands of fattened creatures turn slowly on spits, dribbling grease and juices, whole pigs and oxen are stripped to their ribcages as flesh is hacked away and portioned out . . . Menus confirm that every animal has been plumped up before its slaughter.

Perhaps the traditional British harvest festival should be taking notes.

Gately argues that the human race, as a rule, loves to party. But we need an excuse. Festivals mean normal rules of behaviour and work are suspended, so we have to create a very good reason to have one. Otherwise we would have festivities breaking out all over the place, which wouldn't do. So as well as the usual religious festivals, weddings and birthdays, around the world there are scores of festivals still going strong where the original reason for the celebration has become a little tenuous, even all but forgotten, but still provides an underpinning justification for letting go.

Oktoberfest is a great example of this. Its origins have little to do with gluttony. In its first few years beer wasn't even sold. No, what we are doing today, in theory, is commemorating the ill-fated marriage of a randy duke and a fair young maiden. That, and – as far as I can see – a very dodgy horse race.

In 1810 Crown Prince Ludwig (soon to be King Ludwig I of Bavaria) married Princess Therese von Sachsen-Hildburg-hausen (perhaps her friends just called her Tee) and there was a grand celebration. What was the right way to mark such an event? A coachman and non-commissioned officer in the Bavarian National Guard by the name of Franz Baumgartner felt that a horse race would be the perfect thing. The excuse – sorry, rationale – was that this once-popular pastime was disappearing, and the wedding would be a great way to revive it. Ludwig's father, King Maximilian Joseph, felt this was a splendid idea. But where could they have it? There was no racetrack in Munich. Baumgartner modestly volunteered that, given a generous budget, he could perhaps design and build a worthy track, which was duly constructed in a meadow just outside the city of Munich. On 17 October, a week after the wedding, free refreshments were laid on, and 30,000 of Munich's 40,683 inhabitants gathered to watch the spectacle at the Theresienwiese (Theresa's Meadow), newly named in honour of the bride. And the winner of the race by a considerable margin was ... Franz Baumgartner!

Now, as you'd expect, given that a proficient horseman had had the idea for the race, designed and built the track and still been allowed to compete, Franz was something of a hot favourite. People betted heavily on his victory. When they all subsequently won there was much rejoicing, which carried on long after the royal couple had left for their honeymoon.

The whole thing smells very fishy indeed. You might say that Franz should not have been allowed to race. But now I'm here, on the site where that race was held nearly 200 years ago, I'm very glad that he was. The wedding celebration was such a success that everyone felt it was entirely reasonable to gather in the same spot and celebrate the royal couple's first anniversary. Once the routine was started, it developed a life of its own. The palace was hardly going to repeat its generosity with free food and booze, so by 1818 the first beer merchants were there, and the first rides and entertainments soon followed. The Theresienwiese was preserved as a permanent space for the festivities even after the city crept out to envelop it, and the locals soon began referring to the space, and even the event itself, simply as *Die Wies'n*.

Since then Oktoberfest has been cancelled twenty-five times, thanks to cholera, war or the total collapse of the German economy. The most telling fact is that it was celebrated with gusto even when the institution it purported to commemorate – the king of Bavaria's marriage – fell apart in spectacular fashion. The population that ultimately forced the king's abdication saw no problem with carrying on the celebration even as they ran his mistress out of town.*

Oktoberfest drew its first 100,000 crowd in 1860, in a city whose population then stood at 121,234. In the 1890s the *Festhallen* were first built, and the Bavarian brass bands were in place. Remarkably little about the festival has changed since then. In pictures from 1898 the beer tents look identical to the ones we currently can't get a seat in. The author Thomas Wolfe visited in 1928, and apart from the fact that he seems determined to be utterly miserable just for the sake of it, his account could have been written today:

> The beer tents are absolutely enormous and alarming –
> in one single tent there are four to five thousand people in
> one spot – you can hardly breathe or move. A Bavarian
> band with 40 players is producing a horrendous noise . . .
> and in these [tents] you discover the heart of Germany,
> not the heart of the poet and the thinker, but its real
> heart, which is really nothing but a monstrous stomach.
> They eat and drink and breathe themselves into a frenzy
> of animal-like apathy – the whole tent becomes a scream-

---

* Lola Montez, an infamous travelling dancer, thinker, actress and self-publicist, arrived in Bavaria in 1846 demanding to see the king. Lola was born to English and Irish parents, grew up in India and pretended to be Spanish for large parts of her life – as you do. She was a ravishing beauty who wanted a gig in Munich. She achieved this by dancing for the king and flashing her breasts at him during the performance. Ageing Ludwig was hooked. The next evening Lola was dancing at the Hof theatre, and soon after that she was the king's constant companion and main policy adviser. She was hated by the people of Bavaria for leading their king astray. In 1848 the king was compelled to abdicate, his marriage clearly now an empty shell, and Lola was forced to flee.

ing, roaring beast, and when the music plays one of their drinking songs, they all jump onto the tables, climb onto chairs, and sway arm in arm.

Perhaps the meaning of 'apathy' has changed over the years, but it's not a word I would normally use alongside 'frenzy', 'screaming' or 'roaring'. He even has a problem with the way they *breathe*. Why so miserable? I don't know; maybe he couldn't get a seat either.

Back in 2004, we start our own festival of gluttony in muted fashion, not being able to get any beer. It's lunchtime and we're surrounded by food, but as we've just arrived we're nervous about trying to communicate with the locals. None of us speaks much German,* so we dither for a while before John and Luke each get a croissant coated in congealed cheese (strangely, these seem to be what they actually asked for) and Luke and I each have a bun wrapped around a sausage that tastes a bit like a saveloy, only with meat in it. This is the last food we will eat all day, which may help to explain what happens to me later.

We spend a pleasant two hours soaking up the sights, the magnitude, the culture, the grease. When I say pleasant, it's possible I'm kidding myself. It's a beautiful day, and our thirst grows with every step. It's so hot. The beer looks so good. The people drinking it, every last one of the 100,000, look so happy. Perpetually, we're drawn in vain hope back to the *Festhallen*.

---

* Apart from being able to ask after someone's health and ask for directions to the town hall, my vocabulary extends little further than the phrases familiar to anyone who read war comics as a child between the 1960s and early 1980s, none of which would be very helpful here.

I've heard stories of the famous Bavarian barmaids, but they don't prepare you for the reality. People have whispered to me that they can carry four of five litres of beer at a time. We watch them go past carrying *ten* – seven or eight in one hand, two or three more balanced on top, the other arm curved around to keep them stable. Perhaps it's the antipathy the British invariably have towards anything German, but the image we have of these women is usually pretty close to the enormous Wagnerian Valkyrie. The truth is that most of the women carrying more weight than I could lift are young, slight and very pretty. Having gazed at them for a while, we no longer snigger at Bavarian national costume.

We're getting desperate. I have to do something. I clear my throat. 'You know, we didn't just come here to spend time at Oktoberfest.'

John raises an eyebrow, trying not to look as if he wants to punch me.

'What I mean is, there's a lot more to Bavarian drinking culture than Oktoberfest itself. Munich is world famous for its beer gardens as well. We could go and check those out today, and come back here tomorrow.'

Go on, I'm listening, say their faces.

I pull out *The Beer Drinker's Guide to Munich* from my backpack. ('Indispensable!' says *Travel Holiday* magazine.) 'Look, there are all these huge beer gardens. Some of them seat four or five thousand people. Er – this park, the Englische Garten, has several beer gardens. The Chinesischer Turm is the one that "wild and crazy people show up at". "Anything and everything is in season," it says here, and there's seating for seven thousand people. We'll definitely get a seat and a beer there. And we can sit and chill out in the sun.'

They start to nod.

'And it says there's nude bathing a couple of hundred yards away.'

'Taxi!'

For a long time, Bavarian brewing regulations did not allow beer to be brewed in the summer, so large quantities of winter beer had to be stored in a cool place. Large cellars were built, and shady chestnut trees were planted above to help keep them cool. Where *Bierkeller*s were built, so beer gardens followed. In Bavaria, if you visit one of the celebrated *Bierkeller*s, chances are you'll be doing your drinking in the garden.

Munich's population of 1.3 million shares around fifty beer gardens and cellars, with capacities ranging from a few hundred to over 8,000, and seats totalling 180,000. Not even counting the ordinary bars and pubs you see on the streets, 14 per cent of the total population can sit down for a drink at any given time, and that's during the brief periods when there are no festivals on. I wanted to be cynical about Munich's claim to be the beer-drinking capital of the world, but Oktoberfest is just the start of it. The Auer Dult festival, a flea market and beer festival combined, has been held three times a year for the last 600 years. Early spring sees the *Starkbierzeit* (strong beer time), and Frühlingsfest, which sometimes overlaps with the spring Auer Dult and is known to locals as a mini-Oktoberfest. Fasching in winter is compared to the New Orleans Mardi Gras. And all the time the people crowding into these gardens and events are drinking by the litre. The six massive breweries in Munich brew 580 million litres of beer a year between them, little of which is exported. Before I came here I questioned how Oktoberfest fitted in with the stereotype of Germans as calm, cold and efficient. Now I'm here it's obvious: this isn't Germany, it's Bavaria. And Bavarians are the biggest party animals in the world.

There's a curious stand-off between Bavaria and the rest of Germany. Bavaria, or Bayern, is home to many of the clichés we have about Germany: there's the beer-swilling, lederhosen-clad men who now surround us of course, but it's also responsible for sausage dogs, cow bells and Alpine villages, sauerkraut and wurst. It has half of Germany's 1,200 breweries. When Napoleon ruled most of Europe, he doubled Bavaria in size and declared it a kingdom. Even after German unification in 1870, it still retained a large degree of independence. It's part of a secret nation with Bohemia, a central European fellowship of hardcore beerdom.

Having said that, Germany as a whole has always had a reputation for serious drinking. The Romans found the Germanii fierce fighters, quite happy during winter to sled down snowy hillsides on their shields, nearly naked, to attack the invaders. But it seems the one deprivation they couldn't handle was beer. Tacitus, who seems to have something catty to say about drinking habits across the whole of Europe, observed:

> If we wanted to make use of their addiction to drink, by giving them as much of it as they want, we could defeat them as easily by means of this vice as with our weapons . . . They cultivate the grains of the fields with much greater patience and perseverance than one would expect from them, in light of their customary laziness.

Englischer Garten

Chinesischer Turm is so called because it has a huge Chinese tower in the middle of it. The reasoning behind this never becomes clear to us, but the tower is now used as a bandstand by Bavarian brass bands. Huge chestnut trees surround the bandstand, shading a sea of tables. The 7,000 seats are about two-thirds full. We negotiate a complicated glass deposit system, get our first *Maß*, the glass litre mugs in which beer is served, and sit down at a vacant table. We weep silently to ourselves, take photographs of our foaming mugs, pray to them, then take our first mouthfuls. It's now about four hours since we first went in search of a beer. Well, you can imagine, can't you? It's one of those moments when you taste not just with your mouth, but your whole body. The beer seems to shoot to every cell like cold fire, a moment of pure, unalloyed bliss.

The second round lasts long enough for some relaxed contemplation. The beer is darker than I expected, not the light or *helles* beer at which we gazed so longingly back at the *Wies'n*. I don't give it much thought: it's beer; it's the reason we came.

Some time later, John and Luke accompany me in a cab back to my hotel and make sure I get out of it OK before heading back off into the night. I've had four, maybe five beers, and I am every single one of the 1,250 euphemisms for being drunk that I have managed to collect over the years. True, they were four (maybe five) *litres* of beer, but still. It was spread over a whole afternoon and evening. I stand unsteadily and look at the hotel. My bed is mere feet away.

I start to walk towards the doors, then lurch violently to the right and find myself walking into the Taj Mahal Indian restaurant adjacent to the hotel. Call it a homing instinct. I know I need food, but my motives are even more primal than that – I have a stomach full of beer so I simply have to eat curry. I haven't had a pen all day but now I find one from somewhere, so I sit down, order a meal and take out my notebook with the intention of writing up the day's events.

I wake up in front of a half-eaten vegetable samosa. I try to write. I fall asleep. I wake up again. Various dishes appear and disappear each time I open my eyes. Those beers must have been very strong. Jet lag must have something to do with it. Yes, that's what it is. I only arrived back from China three days ago, and I had to get up early this morning. I can't have got this drunk simply as a consequence of the amount of beer I've had. Surely.

I wake up the next morning fearing the worst. Not only was that the most drunk I can remember being since the time I drank a litre of wine, two pints of Stella and several large Baileys the night a girlfriend finished with me at university fifteen years ago, this is also the last room in the world you would want to share a hangover with. I'm being churlish given that the Munich tourist office found the room for me a few months ago (no mean feat when many of the hotels are booked up a year in advance) and left a huge pack of information here for me along with passes for free public transport. But it's very unsettling. The hotel is about a mile and a half outside town. It feels like a small student hall of residence and smells like a wet dog. The room is basic: a bed and wardrobe, something shaped a bit like a desk, and a bathroom. For these comforts I am grateful. But the walls have been coated with swirling Artex which seems to have had insufficient quantities of red paint mixed into it. The result is a sort of pink, with white veins running through it.

'It sounds like a dead cock,' said John when I described it to him yesterday. Luke nodded sagely. 'You're in the Bobbit room.' These words run through my head again now. I'm not looking forward to taking my head off the pillow. When I finally do ... nothing happens. I stand up. A moment of dizziness, a slight gurgle from somewhere, and I feel fine. No hangover. People have said this about Bavarian beer and it has become one of those myths some enjoy demolishing. But it's true. I'm astonished by how good I feel.

I spend a couple of hours reading, and find a possible explanation for my shocking state last night. As well as *Helles*, Munich brewers make strong, dark beers for the March *Starkbierzeit* and for Oktoberfest. But they are no longer served at Oktoberfest itself, because they are 6 or 7 per cent. If this is what we were drinking at Chinesicherturm, it would explain a lot.

Die Wies'n

By midday I feel ready to brave the *Wies'n* again. The same cannot really be said of John and Luke, who stayed out drinking for several hours last night after I fell asleep in my curry, drinking all manner of stuff, but I think they feel honour-bound. Under several days' stubble, Luke's skin is waxy. John claims to feel awful, but he never shows any outward sign of a hangover. I think he's groaning just to keep

Luke company, in between chuckling and taking photos of him looking corpse-like.

It turns out there is a way of getting beer at Oktoberfest without having a seat in the *Festhallen* after all. The press release from my helpful friends at the tourist office provides lists of everything on the *Wies'n*. Under 'medium sized and small catering businesses', after the pork knuckle grilling stand, the six roast chicken stands and the '23 sausages snack halls, sausage grilling stands and delicatessen shops', it says, '2 wheat beer carousels'. This makes us all laugh because it is clearly an inaccurate translation that unknowingly makes it sound as though there are carousels that serve wheat beer to you while they (and you) spin around.

We stop laughing when we spot one.

We may all be hardened drinkers, but carousel drinking gives us pause. Admittedly, the white horses and fire engines have been replaced by a high bar with a few seats, but the damn thing is still slowly turning. We board hesitantly. It's an interesting feeling, particularly on such a scorching day. We rotate into the sun, fry for a bit, then back into the shade, doing about one revolution every ninety seconds. So this is how it feels to be a doner kebab.

Wheat beer (*Weizen*), or white beer (*Weissbier*) is something of a problem child in Bavaria. It's treated differently. It's the only beer that isn't served in a *Maß* – instead, it only comes in half-litre glasses. That's not because it's strong – it's weaker than many of the Oktoberfest beers – it's just separate. And at Oktoberfest you're only allowed to drink it if you stand on a carousel. I get the feeling they're taking the piss out of people who elect to drink it, but can find no direct evidence of this.

The Reinheitsgebot – Bavaria's famous brewing purity law – conspicuously excluded wheat from the acceptable list of brewing ingredients. This was not because wheat beer was felt to be inferior – quite the reverse; it was much more refined than the barley-based beers popular among the masses. But there were frequent wheat shortages in sixteenth-century Bavaria, so wheat beers were the preserve of the royal court. This was a frustration to the Degenburg family, who had the sole rights to brew wheat beer. Things changed in 1602, when the last of the Degenburgs died with no heir and their brewing privileges automatically defaulted to the royal court. Now they could profit from the sale of wheat beer, the court performed an astonishing U-turn. Wheat was now to be allowed in the manufacture of ales, but not lagers. These ales must contain exactly 50 per cent wheat, 50 per cent barley. And from not being allowed to sell them, Munich's beer halls were now *obliged* to sell wheat beer as a condition of their licences. In Bavaria the production if not the sale of wheat beer is still governed by these rules. The idea of being forced to drink it at Oktoberfest out of half-litre glasses on a rotating converted carousel now seems entirely reasonable.

From our questionable vantage point, we intermittently watch the last hour of the Riflemen's Parade. Having missed yesterday's big opening parade, I was determined to catch this one. It's a procession of 8,000 people dressed in historical uniforms. There are countless marching brass bands, huge brewery drays pulled by beautiful horses, and marching units of mountain riflemen. There are hundreds of flags and banners, floats with circus strongmen, hunting dogs, Napoleonic regiments, men on penny-farthings; in fact anything you can imagine is probably there at some point in the seven-kilometre parade. It takes over two hours to pass a single point, and ends up here at the *Wies'n*. The festival grounds, which were full when we arrived, simply absorb these costumed new arrivals into the fold as we watch.

Eventually the parade finishes, and we decide it might be a good idea to move on. Surprisingly, the carousel doesn't seem to have spoiled our drinking too much, but when we step off we are given a sneak preview of tomorrow's hangover, and we weave unsteadily through the crowd.

After a go (all right, three goes) on the dodgems, we pop our heads into the nearest *Festhalle*, just to check. The Spaten tent is almost as busy as it was yesterday, but not quite. We spot a row of empty tables and rush towards them, but they are protected by 'Reserved' signs.

And then we see it.

In the middle of a long table at the edge of the main seating area, between two groups of revellers, there's a space that would fit three people. No one is going for it because that would mean having to ask strangers to get up out of the way, squeezing past them and invading their personal space. We've been waiting for more than twenty-four hours for this. Our English reserve has disappeared. A tap on the shoulder, a gesture, a nod, some gangling limbs and we're in! We've done it! And here comes our very own young, pretty, buxom barmaid and she's not asking us to move – she's asking us what we would like to drink! Two minutes later she's back with three foaming *Maß* of Spaten clutched to her heaving bosom.

As soon as our beers are in our hands the four guys we squeezed past raise their glasses and toast us. They point at the barmaid and make thumbs up signs, and we toast them back. There's something about a woman with blonde pigtails, *that* costume and three litres of beer that makes you want to sing with gusto. On cue, Bruno Gress's Festkapelle take the stage. They start with a rousing traditional drinking song, and what I have always regarded as oompah music, a flatulent, cheesy racket, suddenly sounds so right. We cheer wildly. Something is happening. We've hardly drunk any beer yet, but this is euphoric.

Over the next hour or so we befriend our neighbours, communicating via sign language, pointing, clinking glasses, grinning and gurning like early 1990s rave casualties and saying, 'Whaay!' and, 'Aa-oo-ey!' a lot. It turns out that these are the only two words you need here. No, really. 'Whaay!' is a frequent and general toast, an exclamation of solidarity. 'Aa-oo-ey!' is more about gratitude, an acknowledgement of acts of reciprocal kindness, such as reaching out to support someone leaning back at a dangerous angle so he can take a photo of his whole table without slipping and smashing his brains on the edge of ours. It's amazing how much can be communicated using this simple system. We trade opinions with our neighbours on the beer (very good), the band (simply marvellous), the cast of characters surrounding us (crazy!) and the barmaids (buxom!). Each time we successfully communicate an idea or observation with this spontaneous beery Esperanto, we toast each other in celebration. Then we toast the spirit of fellowship that makes us want to toast each other in the first place.

Eventually though this is not enough for Luke, and he attempts to move things on. Adopting the classic tactic of speaking English slowly and loudly, he bellows, 'WHERE! ARE! YOU! FROM? WHERE! DO! YOU! COME! FROM?'

'North Carolina,' replies the guy sitting nearest to him. 'Say, this really is great, isn't it?'

High in the tent wall, maybe sixty feet up, a solitary window frames a panel of perfect blue, cloudless sky. Every thirty seconds a seemingly disembodied roller coaster car passes through it.

Bruno Gress's Festkapelle is far more talented than I would have thought possible. They mix in modern party hits with the traditional stuff, and when they play rockier songs, always at full tilt, the result often sounds surprisingly close to ska, which is never a bad thing. Lesser beer festivals often feel obliged to drag on an oompah band for the sake of appearances, and it's never anything more than an irritant, a reminder that the occasion is not exactly on the bleeding edge of the cultural landscape. At Oktoberfest, the band is an essential part of the enjoyment. The fact that the raised podium in the middle of every *Festhalle* resembles nothing more closely than a church pulpit is telling. Bands direct proceedings, creating the atmosphere and fine-tuning it throughout the day. They play songs which encourage people to drink and toast. And if it all gets too raucous, they play a slow number to calm things down. The band leader is by far the most influential person in any tent.

There's one short song that's already becoming familiar. Played at the beginning and end of a set, or when a message arrives from the bar saying that things are a bit quiet, the whole tent joins in with:

> *Ein Prosit, ein Prosit, der Gemütlichkeit*
> *Ein Prosit, ein Prosit, der Gemütlichkeit!*
> *Eins, zwei, drei, g'suffa!*

It forms a refrain to the proceedings, and in its three lines is the essence of Oktoberfest. *Ein Prosit* is a toast. The *eins, zwei, drei* bit is a countdown to taking a hearty slug of beer. *Der Gemütlichkeit* is a little harder to translate directly, but it's important to try. *Gemütlich* is German for warm, congenial, cosy, pleasant or friendly. *Gemütlichkeit* is a spirit, an atmosphere of congeniality that usually has beer at its heart. As with the *craic*, music is important. And like the *craic* there isn't a single English word that means precisely the same thing, but you can feel it everywhere.

The Americans have gone, leaving an inch of beer in the bottom of their mugs and pretzel debris scattered across the table. Bente, our barmaid, sweeps away the mess with one arm while depositing a group of camp Poles into the empty seats with the other. She really is a hell of a woman.

We're old hands at this now. As soon as the Poles' beers arrive we raise our glasses and toast them heartily. The one sitting nearest Luke, with a face that seems to have collapsed inwards like a deflating balloon, becomes very enthusiastic about this, crashing his glass into each of ours as hard as he can, seemingly trying to smash them, but to no avail. His friend next to him looks like Sean Pertwee with bleached yellow hair and a clit-tickler beard, a tiny vest and a very hairy back. Sean has no time for the toasting. He dangles a cigarette from his fingers, pouts whenever we shout a toast, and looks disgusted when we clink glasses. His sunken-faced friend tries to cheer him up by tweaking his nipples, but it doesn't work.

But, steadily, Bruno and his boys work their magic. They tear into a few particularly energetic numbers, one of which is very close to what Status Quo would sound like if they were any good. Sean begins to smile then clinks glasses with his friends, but he still smiles and looks away shyly when they turn to toast with us.

The Poles are to our left. To our right, the bored and miserable-looking family who were here when we arrived have left, finally figuring out that seven-year-old children not only hamper your own enjoyment of an event like this, but are probably having a miserable time themselves, especially with such a tantalizing array of rides so close outside the tent. In their place we get a family from Lithuania with whom we strike up an instant rapport. We like the twenty-something daughter very much indeed. So much, in fact, that her initially friendly father eventually feels the need to make it clear that he's actually her husband. We manage to stay on toasting terms with them, and the young 'wife' agrees to be photographed wearing John's bandanna, which gives us an excuse to take pictures of her. Several of these come out with a very pissed-off middle-aged Lithuanian man beside her, glaring into the lens.

Have I not mentioned the bandannas?

In Tokyo the touristy shops and market stalls all sell souvenir headbands bearing various inscriptions in Japanese characters such as 'Kamikaze', 'Samurai', 'Banzai' and so on.* Knowing I was coming here, when I spotted one design that was in lurid green, featuring a cartoon of a man drinking and punching the air, I knew I had to get one each for us. Of course we would never *wear* them; the *idea* of having Japanese

---

* This would sound like a racist joke at the expense of the Japanese were it not entirely true. I don't know; perhaps the joke is that they don't really say these things at all. Maybe like the tattoos some idiot travellers get in languages they don't understand, the script on the headbands really says, 'I am a total idiot; can you believe I paid five quid for this piece of crap?'

samurai drinking headbands was far funnier than the thought we might actually don them like some desperate stag party. But once again normal sensibilities are suspended at Oktoberfest. Everywhere you look there are people with specially designed group T-shirts depicting a team identity and individual nicknames. Our headbands are modest in comparison. Within minutes of arriving today, they went on.

There are brief menus on the tables and we decide a meal might be a good idea. I opt for half a roast chicken, because it's Sunday afternoon, and that means it's compulsory to have a Sunday roast if at all possible. But the meal that arrives is not what I expected. I know it *said* only roast chicken on the menu; no one lied. It's just that I assumed there would be gravy, vegetables and potatoes with it. I wasn't expecting them to be that tasty, but, you know, a few soggy peas, maybe a bit of mash, would have been nice. What arrives is half a roast chicken. Heavily salted. On a plate. With a lemon-scented wrap tucked under its solitary wing. I should have known. It's not a meal; it's the world's biggest salty bar snack.

The music never stops. Many of the bands from this morning's procession have ended up in here, their immaculate tunics now half undone, their uniforms compromised by an array of floppy novelty hats. They've settled in on the mezzanine level, and we can just see heads and the occasional brass instrument bobbing up and down. Whenever Bruno and the lads try to take a break, one of the off-duty parade bands picks up its instruments and plays an increasingly ragged impromptu set. This seems to have the effect of making Bruno's tea breaks shorter and shorter as the afternoon goes on. Festkapelle are Herculean. They must have been playing for five hours now and show no sign of wilting. They tear into

'Everybody Needs Somebody' and the tent goes apeshit yet again, people up on benches, dancing in long lines everywhere, roaring and – yes – breathing.

On the traditional numbers we use the *Beer Drinker's Guide* and attempt to sing along whenever we can. The Lithuanians have been scared away and replaced by a group of young Germans who are delighted and highly amused by our efforts. I show them the book, and they react in the way I imagine a group of English drinkers in London would if some German tourists handed them a book that said morris dancing was common in the city's pubs.

All that matters is that we are singing. Every one of us. The one that gets the most vigorous singalong is the cheesy Euro hit, which, with lots of 'eeys' and 'ooh-ahs', demands to know whether an unidentified 'baby' will be our girl. Perhaps everyone forgot to tell the British, but I'm becoming convinced that this is the new European national anthem. Its simple, some might say moronic, chorus is saying that wherever you go, you can relax; wherever you come from, you can all share in this kitschy communion. You're all happy. You're all a bit drunk. And the very idea of aggro is so far away as to be absurd.

And then the Festkapelle plays the 'Birdie Song'.

The 5,000-capacity tent is full. Fifty people jump up on their benches and flap along to the actions; 4,950 shuffle awkwardly, heads down, embarrassed not just for themselves, but for Bruno as well. It's the only bad call the band makes all afternoon.

Things start to wind down a little. There are gaps at some tables now. We move on to a different tent, dancing in the aisles in front of some Bavarians. Luke throws moves in a style that owes something to 1920s jazz, something else to Busby

Berkeley, a few nods to African-Americans and disco, and a large debt to Popeye the Sailor. It's just possible that this is entertaining rather than irritating our audience. You can never be sure with Germans.

At ten o'clock the tents close, and so does my notebook. I don't want the party to end, and it doesn't. The rides go on into the night. We shoot over the *Wies'n* in a tight corkscrew, indulge in drunken driving on the dodgems, and then head off into the night, into bars that are too dark for me to write in.

Munich, Bavaria, Germany

Munich has 40,000 tourist beds.

I struggle to write this down. I must keep my eyes open and carry on writing. This is not a hangover. It's sleep deprivation. Sunday night ended four hours ago, just before breakfast.

I can't think of anything else to ask.

I've been in the Munich tourist office for two minutes. Karoline Graf has very kindly taken time out of a busy schedule to talk to me about Oktoberfest, and if I can't stretch this out to at least half an hour it's going to look very rude. Karoline watches me patiently.

'Would you like some water?'

'Yes please.'

She brings me a bottle that is far too small. I drain it, attempt to focus on her and mumble, 'So why is Oktoberfest so popular then?'

Karoline smiles. She's being very kind. 'Oktoberfest and the beer gardens are very democratic. Anyone can be a star for the night on the *Wies'n*.' I think of Luke and nod. 'About ten years ago people started dressing up in traditional Bavarian dress in the Schottenhauer tent. There's always been a trend for young people to dress up at the *Wies'n*, and over the last ten years it has been traditional dress.

'Given such a high number of people and so much beer, it's very calm. There are a couple of fights, but not nearly so much as you would imagine. But then, beer drinking in Germany is very social. There's a very special atmosphere at the *Wies'n* and the beer gardens. It's very informal. You sit next to people on the benches and immediately you get to know them.' I think back, and nod again.

Karoline is keen to promote the beer gardens as well as Oktoberfest, which makes sense given they are open for so much longer through the year. From her point of view, it must be frustrating to see so much tourism crammed into a mere sixteen days. 'Beer gardens are a very Bavarian custom. We have a warm wind that comes down from the Alps – the *Föhn*. The *Föhn* can happen at any time of year, so Munich has warm and sunny days all year round. Munich is very different from the rest of Germany – it is very important that the beer is kept fresh. So we built cellars, and planted trees over them to keep them cool. Beer was served in the gardens fresh from the cellars. You bring your own food to the table, and beer is served by the litre—'

'Oh yes, why by the litre?'

'Because people are thirsty! We serve beer by the litre – they use much smaller measures in the Rhineland – and they bring you a new one automatically when you are finished. Men will drink maybe two or three mugs a day.'

My questions gradually dwindle to nothing, but we've been speaking for forty minutes now. I need to go back to bed before I do anything else today. I thank Karoline profusely, and leave.

I love the competitiveness that underpinned everything Karoline said. Munich is different, because here it is important that the beer is kept fresh. It's an outrageous thing to say in a country that takes its beer so seriously. But then, Bavaria has always considered itself above, if not apart from, the rest of Germany.

It was here in 1516 that the Reinheitsgebot decreed that the only permissible ingredients in beer were barley, hops and water. The law is still maintained and has long been celebrated as the earliest example of legislation promoting a fairer deal for consumers, but the European Court was closer to the mark in 1987, when it decided that the Reinheitsgebot was a restriction on free trade. I'm not suggesting it hasn't vastly improved the quality of beer, just that this wasn't the prime motivation.

Since prehistory, beer has been brewed from wheat, rice, rye, oats, even beans or peas, and flavoured with anything that would cover up the often foul taste that resulted. Any honest brewer with a passion for beer will insist that the ingredients stipulated by the Reinheitsgebot make the best beer, but the rulers of medieval Europe were not famous for their altruism. Beer was a vital part of German life. If quality fell, sales dropped, and therefore so did tax revenue. From the thirteenth century onwards, cities began to stipulate the ingredients that could be used for brewing inside their walls, the measures in which beer could be served, the time of year it could be brewed, and the prices that could be charged for it.

In 1447 the Munich council issued an ordinance stating that hops, barley and water were the only permissible ingredients for brewing.* On 23 April 1516 this ordinance became law for the whole of feudal Bavaria – the Reinheitsgebot. Gradually, it spread through some, but not all, of Germany. In 1919, with the formation of the Weimar Republic, what had until then been the Free State of Bavaria refused to join the new nation state until everyone else promised that the law would be enforced across the whole country.

That the Reinheitsgebot is so strongly associated with lager is also down to the rampant enthusiasm the Bavarians have for regulating beer production. Ale yeasts work best at 15–25 degrees Celsius, whereas lager yeasts prefer temperatures of 4–9 degrees. If they are too cold, ale yeasts fall asleep. This means that if you have little control over the yeast fermenting your beer, you are likely to end up with ale in the summer and lager in the winter. It also means that ale is harder to brew well, more likely to be affected by wild, airborne yeasts and other microscopic organisms that can foul the beer. The Bavarians solved the problem in 1553 by banning brewing in the summer, thereby effectively confining it to lager. These lagers could be dark or pale, but they were all lagers. Bavaria has since honed the style to perfection.

Wrapped up in this is another clue to the development of Oktoberfest itself. Faced with a summer of no new beer, large batches of dark beer, strong enough to survive months in

---

* This was before the existence of yeast had been rumbled. It was added later, as was a special dispensation to allow the brewing of wheat beers. This was carefully prescribed – an additional ingredient in top-fermenting *Kölsch*, *Alt* and *Weizen* beers.

storage, were brewed in March and kept in cool cellars throughout the summer months. Whatever was left towards the end of September had to be cleared out to make room for the new stuff when brewing began again.

Die Wies'n

John, Luke and I don't meet up back at the *Wies'n* until after 4 p.m., and even then there's a curious reluctance to head into the tents and drink more beer. It just feels wrong. Eventually we compromise by going into the Nymphenburg tent, a smaller affair than the rest of the *Festhallen*, which sells only wheat beer and wine. Embarrased to be doing so, we share a bottle of Pinot Grigio.

The band is smaller too, and marches around the gangways between the tables. At this point I notice that the vast majority of people are wearing traditional Bavarian dress, and looking very serious about it. The few tourists who venture in are asked to remove their humorous headgear at the door. Most of them look around sheepishly, holding their peasant/cow/beer barrel hats in both hands, before venturing out again.

Different *Festhallen* have different personalities. Oktoberfest has a reputation as a magnet for boozy Antipodean travellers who drink until they fall over. These people tend to say that the Löwenbräu and Paulaner tents are the best. Here in the Nymphenburg we're clearly at the other end of the scale: this is the locals' tent. When the singing starts, I get nervous. It's still celebratory, but it seems much more passionate, and there are no cheesy Euro hits. After my chat with the tourist board this morning, I'm very aware that Oktoberfest is first and foremost a Bavarian folk festival, and that we are outsiders. As the band gets closer and the singing around us rises in volume and intensity, I fight down the feeling that we should be grouping together in a corner and singing the 'Marseilleise' in competition. It's time to leave.

We wander among the rides. We throw darts and shoot guns. We pass a test your strength machine, which would probably be fun to try if it wasn't for a seemingly permanent crowd of around fifty, watching each contestant critically. A steady queue of men give it a go, almost hitting the bell, but not quite. Then one man who isn't that well built but clearly fancies himself as a bit tasty steps up. He swings the hammer and gives the bell a resounding ding. Just to show how easy it was, he does it again. And then again. And again. He's made his point, but he shows no sign of stopping. And no one looks willing to try to take the hammer away from him.

We move on, past a futuristic special effects ride that attempts to lure us in with music by Jean Michel Jarre and a spray-painted man body-popping, past a man in a tiny booth wearing a leotard and a hat selling Winky Worms, and finally, after witnessing all this, we feel ready for – no, make that in dire need of – a beer.

We walk up the Wirtsbudenstrasse and bump into Jon Mitchell (as opposed to John Harley), who works for Pan Macmillan, my publishers. He's in Munich for a few meetings and thought it might be a good idea to meet up. As he takes in our dishevelled appearance and slightly hysterical behaviour, it's possible he thinks he has made a dreadful mistake. We head into the Armbrust-Schutzen *Festhalle*, a Paulaner tent, to find out.

As a barmaid finds us half an empty table, Elvis takes the

stage with the band and the whole tent erupts. We're just across the aisle from a table of elderly and middle-aged people in traditional Bavarian dress. Two men in their late forties leap up and start jiving. A woman in her late sixties jumps onto the bench next to them, boogieing and swinging her *Maß*, pausing only to drink heartily from it. For a while we're quite muted in comparison, and then the bandannas go on. Immediately we're singing, dancing and toasting. Except Jon. He stares at the bandannas, his eyes wide and glassy. I don't have one for him. He doesn't seem to mind, but it troubles me. He has a lot of catching up to do, and surely the lack of a bandanna is going to hinder him.

Bandanna or not, he swallows his fear (and his beer) and catches up admirably. It's great to watch the magic at work. He suffers our German table neighbours crashing their *Maß* into his. He looks around the tent, possibly for an escape. Then slowly, over the course of several minutes, a smile creeps across his face, nervous at first, then sincerely joyful. His *Maß* begins to swing. By the second chorus of *Ein Prosit* I can see that *der Gemütlichkeit* is in him, and he's bellowing along with the rest of us.

Jon has drunk maybe a pint of beer by this time. From the outside this must look like drunken behaviour: people being loud, standing on their seats, singing raucously. It would have you barred from most British pubs. But that's because the British normally only behave in this way when they are already dangerously drunk. Here, people are getting up on the benches roaring along to the songs and waving their *Maß* in the air while still on their first drink. The band up on their podium, all-seeing and all-powerful; the long trestle tables and their enforced communality – this is about atmosphere first, drinking second. Drinking facilitates having a good time, provides the focus of it, but it plays a supporting role to the main event, which is singing, dancing and toasting. The point of being here is not to get drunk; it's to enjoy *Gemütlichkeit*. And that is why Oktoberfest is the biggest festival – of any description – in the world. A typical pub is going to seem quite dull in comparison from now on.

The German man sitting next to me takes out a small vial of white powder, lays out a line of it on the back of his hand, and snorts it. Our entire party is speechless. I've seen my fair share of drug-taking, but never quite as shameless as this. The German looks up, sees our incredulous expressions, and asks if we want some.

'What is it?' asks John eventually.

'Ground peppermint,' replies the German, offering the vial. John takes the vial and makes a show of chopping out a line with his credit card. The Germans laugh and clap at this, and I think they are honestly making the association with cocaine for the first time. We snort it. It really is ground peppermint. It's quite invigorating up the nostril, a bit of a livener. 'I only take it at Oktoberfest,' warns our new friend, 'They sell it here.'

An old bloke who if he were English could only be called Reg, comes over to our table with his own ceramic stein and his own form of dance. He approaches on flapping legs, toasts us, throws a few interesting shapes and moves on. After all, it's a big tent. He has a lot of work to do.

Then, Jon Mitchell suffers a setback. Just as he has fully relaxed, John Harley, sitting next to him, leaves the table for a toilet break. Immediately a young, smiling German with a very big chin and a very tight, white T-shirt slides into his space and starts talking to Jon. He's very excited, speaking English in a sharp yapping tone. He wants Jon to swap seats with him, because the boys at his table really want Jon to sit with them. He would like to come and sit with us.

Jon's face is a picture of slightly ruffled English reserve. 'I'm confused. And a little frightened.'

'Why? Is my English so bad?' His new friend pouts.

At this point Harley returns and gestures for his place back. The German yields his seat, then promptly sits back down on John's lap. He wags a finger in Mitchell's face. 'Think about what I said,' he scolds, before returning reluctantly to his table.

The band plays 'Rosamunde', one of our favourites. It's sung to the same tune as 'Roll out the Barrel' and we have the words in the back of the *Beer Drinker's Guide*. I'm teaching the song to Jon when our peppermint-snorting neighbours ask if they can have a look at the book. No one will tell me what's so funny about it. When the German sitting next to me finally recovers his composure, he sees me scribbling and asks if I am writing a book about Oktoberfest. I explain the idea. As the Germans understand, the usual jealous scowl appears. But they're delighted I'm here. 'Did you write this?' asks one of them, holding up the *Beer Drinker's Guide*. I shake my head. They cheer and toast me warmly.

Reg returns and insists we all stand on our benches. We lean over and link arms in a huge group with his table across the aisle, bellowing a song very loudly. I have no idea what it is. Pleased with the cross-aisle, mid-air group hug, Reg builds up to his finale: a conga line over the benches of each of our tables and across the aisle between.

When we sit back down, the big-chinned German is

waiting for us. He talks to each of our German neighbours until they disappear. He leans on me, digging his huge chin sharply into my arm, trying to see what I'm writing about him in my notebook. Mercifully, he can't read it. 'My English is so bad,' he says mournfully, before turning away. Jon Mitchell goes to the toilet. He's in there for a long time.

A few tables away, I spot four tiny Japanese girls wearing full traditional kimonos and huge, floppy comedy Bavarian felt hats. I'm watching them dance when they turn towards us and spot the bandannas. Within a second they're at our table, screaming at us, treating us like rock stars. They are so happy to see us, and insist on retying the bandannas properly with complicated triple knots. I've been dying to know, so I ask them what the Japanese script on them actually says. The picture of the drinking man is in the middle. There are two lines of text to his right. To his left are the numbers '1.2.3' and another line of text.

'It means one . . . two . . . three . . . *whaay*!' shouts the one girl who speaks a little English.

'Are you sure? Is that all it says? There does seem to be quite a lot of text there.'

She thinks for a second, nods, and says, 'It means one . . . two . . . three . . . *whaay*!'

I'm not at all sure about this. If anything, it confirms my paranoia that the real translation is something unkind. But I'm not going to get any further. 'Why are you here?' I ask.

She looks at me for a second, grins, holds her *Maß* aloft and says, 'We love beer!'

'But is this part of a tour of Europe?'

She doesn't understand.

'Are you visiting anywhere else?'

Her brow furrows.

'You go to London? Paris? Berlin?'

Each place name is met with a confused shake of the head.

'You're visiting Munich only?'

Finally, she nods.

'You came all the way from Japan just to visit Oktoberfest?'

'I love beer. I *love* beer!'

And that seems to be the end of it.

On the best night imaginable in Britain you would probably move on at some point, driven by the sense that you might be missing something better somewhere else. Here you're scared to leave because the atmosphere is so good, you resent missing a single second of it.

There are many different styles of drinking around the world, but common to all of them is the idea of sociability. It's about more than just alcohol lowering your social inhibitions: it's about pouring and toasting, giving you something in common to talk about, giving you something to do with your hands, even providing an excuse to get together in the first place. Raising your glass to a friend or stranger, you are saying, 'You drink like us; we are alike.' You bond. And at Oktoberfest this bonding is the whole point. Over the last two days we've sat at tables with up to sixty or seventy different people from all around the world, and toasted and subsequently chatted with every single one of them. It's not just scarcity of materials that led to Oktoberfest being banned during war years.

John Harley is telling a story about when he was introduced to Henry Kelly by Sandi Toksvig that finishes with Henry Kelly pointing at John and yelling, 'You are *fucked* in the *head*!' before storming off.

I'm now quite drunk. I have my photo taken with my

bandanna on. I look like someone who has been travelling for a long time through various time zones, eating nothing but sausage, ham and bread, drinking far too much beer and getting hardly any sleep.

John is telling another story. This time, it ends with Chris Boardman, the Olympic cyclist, pointing at John and saying, 'You're a cunt,' before storming off.

As we leave the *Wies'n*, walking just a trifle unsteadily, Jon Mitchell says, 'I'm glad I met you, Pete Brown,' lurching into me slightly. I never find out whether or not he still thinks this in his meetings the following day, or indeed later in the week when he gets back to the office in London and discovers that, in the spirit of *Gemütlichkeit*, I've emailed photos of him and his *Maß* to his colleagues.

We put him in a cab. For those of us who are now Oktoberfest veterans, the night is still young. Then I remember I have a train to Berlin at nine tomorrow morning, the first leg of my journey to Copenhagen.

I phone Chris. In that strange way that we all have after particularly heavy drinking, I describe in lurid detail all the most unpleasant aspects of the last few days, before telling him he really should have been here. The lemon-scented wipe which came with my salty chicken was the closest I've been to fruit and vegetables all weekend. My face is pale and bloated. My voice is a croak. 'My feet,' I moan. 'My soles are cracked and peeling.'

'That'll be your body desperately trying to suck up nutrients from your shoe leather,' replies Chris.

I need to get out of here.

Berlin, almost

I've hardly worked for four months. I'm in debt and have spent all my savings. My health is ruined. But I don't want this quest to end. I don't want to go home – not yet. There's one final journey I need to make from here, a pilgrimage north from Munich to Copenhagen, in the steps of the man whose obsession with quality ultimately resulted in modern beer as we know it, to the home of one of the world's most famous beers.

Of course, there are direct flights which take an hour or so, but I'm no longer the crap traveller I once was. I decide to go by train, and see a little more of Germany before I get to Denmark.

Bavaria has come to symbolize German brewing in general to such an extent that most of us assume that blonde lagers and lederhosen are all there is to German beer and the drinking of it. Munich is clearly the beer capital of Germany and, I'm prepared to admit now, possibly the world. But the rest of the country is famously passionate about beer and obsessive about its quality.

My plan was to spend two days drinking in Berlin so I could write about Germany from more than just a Bavarian perspective.* But I spend most of my time lying in my hotel room, whimpering, sleeping, tracking down fresh fruit and vegetables, and avoiding any sort of alcohol. It's a nice hotel

---

* Any beer expert will tell you that there are cities I could have visited which would have given me far greater insight into the story of German beer, but give me a break – I wasn't thinking straight.

room. There really is nothing else I can tell you about the rest of Berlin, or the rest of Germany, apart from the astonishingly violent history of beer there, which I read about in a book by a man called Horst.

Beer has been taken incredibly seriously in Germany throughout its history. Look at who was in charge of brewing at any given point, and you get a straightforward indicator of who had real power at the time. For centuries the ruling nobles granted brewing rights to the monasteries, then they realized how lucrative these rights were, and attempted to take them back. Feudal lords set up their own court breweries, or *Hofbräuhäuser*.* But while the nobles and the Church were bickering, they didn't spot the growth of the cities, and with them a new, prosperous merchant class. At first brewing happened in the home, but with city houses made of straw and wood packed closely together, if an unattended brewing fire got out of control whole districts could be lost. Brewing and baking were therefore soon only permitted in purpose-built communal brewhouses, which had the added advantage that brewing could be efficiently controlled and taxed. City brewers eventually formed powerful guilds – if you wanted to brew and sell beer within the city walls, you had to be a member. Neither the city council nor the Church were happy about this, and a three-way battle ensued.

Tensions over brewing came to a head in the Rhineland in 1288, in a spat that created an extraordinary local feud which still runs today. The brewers of Cologne were restricted in number by law. They were taxed on raw materials and the right to use brewing kettles by the Church, and on the finished

---

* Hofbräu remains the oldest of the big six breweries in Munich today.

beer by the city council. They had not been allowed to form a guild until 1254, a hundred years after forty-nine other professions in the city had come together. But when they finally won guild status, they became better organized, more militant, and eventually took drastic action to overthrow their oppressors.

The brewers recruited Duke Adolf V of Berg to get rid of the archbishop of Cologne, Siegfried of Westerberg. Adolf in turn recruited Jan Primus of Brabant and Flanders, a renowned knight,* and marched on the city. After a bloody battle, the archbishop was deposed, and the power of the Church to govern matters was ended. Adolf then decided Cologne needed a permanent check to its power, and travelled a few miles down the Rhine to a small farming village called Düsseldorf, and granted it city status. Düsseldorf grew rapidly,

---

* Jan Primus (John the First), became a legend in Flanders, and is a giant figure in the history of beer, better known via a corruption of his name, Gambrinus (hence the name of the beer). Often referred to as the King of Beer, he has been credited with the very invention of it, which we know is rubbish. The truth is that he was one of beer's biggest and most enthusiastic drinkers. He was a great supporter of the brewers' guilds in Leuven and Brussels, and was famed for spending his nights downing their products. Reputedly, at a single feast he could drink 144 mugs of beer. He was renowned for chivalry as well as revelry, and this combination helped him seduce a string of women around Europe. He met his end thanks to one such encounter which culminated in a duel. Gambrinus spent the whole night before the duel drinking and partying, and as was his wont still turned up for battle fresh and eager. He easily gained the upper hand, at which point his opponent, a French knight called Vasleneuve, resorted to the oldest, lowest trick in the book. Pinned back and about to die, he looked over Gambrinus' shoulder and exclaimed, 'What is this? Does the chivalrous knight need a second man to fight me?' The chivalrous knight turned around to see what second man this was, and Vasleneuve ran him through.

and within a few centuries was a fierce rival to Cologne in all things, not least in beer. Even now, Düsseldorf is famous as the home of *Alt* (old) beer, a top-fermented, full-bodied, copper-coloured ale. The Cologne brewers were not going to stand for being upstaged like this. They developed their own blonde ale and called it *Kölsch* (Köln being the German spelling of the city's name). Just as Bavaria effectively mandated that only lagers could be produced, Cologne passed a law in 1603 mandating that only top-fermented beers in this style could be brewed.

This is by no means the only example of beer-inspired warfare. The big guilds soon decided they didn't want brewers from other cities exporting beers into their turf, and many city-states prohibited sales of beer from their neighbours. Dortmund had a monopoly on brewing in Westphalia, in the northern Rhineland, and a tradition of exporting beer. When producers in other cities finally gained brewing rights, they objected to the Dortmunders' continued exports. The Dortmunders ignored these objections, so their rivals hired sharpshooters to ambush deliveries and shoot holes in the wooden kegs. The Dortmunders responded by hiring their own mercenaries, who drowned any sharpshooters they captured in vats of beer. While this practice has now apparently ended, Dortmunder Export remains a celebrated deep-golden lager, the best-selling style in Germany.

Bavaria was less bloody in pursuit of brewing supremacy, but just as serious. The town of Einbeck began producing a very fine strong, dark ale. This became so popular in Munich that it resulted in a serious drain on Bavaria's money supply. This was solved in 1612 when Duke Maximilian I lured a renowned Einbeck brewer to Munich, to brew Bavaria's own version of the beer. He was persuaded to make this beer a lager rather than an ale, brewed a successful product, and was never allowed to leave the city again. The name was corrupted to *ein Bock*, and another of Germany's celebrated styles was born.

Bavaria's vast range of lagers, wheat beer, Dortmund export lager, *Kölsch* and *Alt* from the Rhineland – to name but a few – Germany has a huge variety of beer styles. Developed amid intrigue and war, guarded throughout the centuries with hysterical fervour – is it any surprise that German unification is so relatively recent?

Before I arrived in Munich I simply couldn't understand how German beer had remained so singular, so regionally based, in a global beer market consolidating at such a rate. I have a better idea now. But as in so many other places, things are changing. Young Germans are turning away from beer in upsetting numbers. They consider it a drink for old men and yobs, and are starting to drink a lot more wine. Brewers are attempting to lure them back with some good ideas – improving the packaging and presentation of beer with corks and foil tops – and some disturbing ideas – a beer and cola mix, anyone? Global brewers are also moving in, gently nudging the German market, telling the brewers they have to modernize. But I can't imagine any of those wonderful styles disappearing, and I can't imagine Oktoberfest losing its appeal any time soon.

10

'. . . making themselves objects of derision . . .'

Copenhagen

I'm standing outside the Spunk Bar, wondering whether to go in. It looks like a cool place: a bit greasy spoon, a bit American roadhouse, the kind of bar Edward Hopper might have painted if he'd been a pervert. One persuasive reason for going in is that it is, of course, raining heavily out here. And there's a sign which explains that, despite the name, beer is the main drink on sale. The fact that this sign is bilingual robs me of any hopeful doubt that Spunk might be one of those accidentally humorous names that exists blissfully unaware of its meaning in English. They know what it means all right. That's why it's here.

Spunk sits in the heart of Copenhagen's Istedgade district. Like so many 'reclaimed' areas in old cities, Istedgade has become exceedingly fashionable by trading on the frisson of danger that still lurks in the streets, attracting the hippest bars and restaurants to sit alongside sex shops displaying enormous dildos matter-of-factly in their windows as if they were cream cakes or shoes.

Weighing against drinking in Spunk is the presence at the bar of a huge bald guy with a big moustache. He seems to be the only customer, and now he's glaring at me through the window in a very unfriendly manner. Maybe I'll come back tomorrow, when Chris is here. A couple of prostitutes stand across the road, pinched and desperate-looking, disguised by jeans and heavy coats against the regularly patrolling police cars. They make hopeful eye contact as I walk on, back around the corner on to Vester Farimagsgade, past a club advertising 'Madame Arthur and her Silicone Girls'. This sounds so unappealing I wonder if it really is a strip club, as I'd originally assumed. Perhaps it's the latest production from a small independent theatre. I'll still pass.

Since I realized I was on a global quest for the meaning of beer, I've known I had to come to Denmark, but up to now had no idea what I was going to look at, or write about, when I got here. The Danes are the eighth-biggest beer drinkers in the world, drinking more than the Australians per head. But as far I knew they all drank Carlsberg, the world's sixth-biggest brewer and one not noted for its diverse portfolio. While Carlsberg is a fine lager and has played an important role in the evolution of beer as we know it today, it's ... well, it's Carlsberg. We know it. It's familiar. It doesn't have any hidden depths. There are Vikings tucked away in the country's history, some of the greatest beer drinkers who ever lived, but I was fairly sure the story of modern Danish drinking would be flat and dull.

It doesn't take me long to find out how mistaken I was.

I journeyed here by train from Germany so I could sort of

follow in the footsteps of J.C. Jacobsen, Carlsberg's founder. In 1845 he travelled to Munich to visit his friend and mentor Gabriel Sedelmeyr at the Spaten brewery, to taste his beer and blag some of the special yeast helping to make it such a celebrated brew. Jacobsen was an uncompromising man: if he was going to brew beer it had to be great beer, and Bavarian beer was the best in the world. His journey from Munich to Copenhagen by coach took several weeks, and proved a painstaking process as the yeast had to be kept cool so it didn't spoil. Jacobsen kept it in a hat box, and stopped to chill it in any stream he passed.

My train journey was a little shorter and slightly more comfortable than Jacobsen's coach journey, but after missing my connection in Hamburg I had to board a succession of ever-smaller and slower trains across what seemed like most of Denmark's 500 islands.

Denmark was once a vast country, but through losing Norway – which it once owned – and Schleswig-Holstein – its richest, most fertile region – it has been reduced to a curious assortment of geographical odds and ends. Schleswig, now German, merges into Jylland (Jutland), a long peninsula which tapers off in a dramatic meeting between two seas, the Skagerrak and the Kattegat. Jylland consists of huge skies and stubbly harvested wheat fields, gently undulating like dunes. They give the impression that long, sandy beaches must be just over the next horizon, and much of the time they are. We made our way through the first fifty miles or so of this to the small port town of Kolding, where I changed trains yet again and headed east across the island of Fyn (Funen) and two consecutive five-mile-long bridges across the Storebaelt (Great Belt), a wide expanse of calm blue sea, and finally into

Sjaelland (Zealand), where Copenhagen sits on the east coast, nearer to Sweden than most of its own country.

Having finally made it to Copenhagen, Carlsberg is my obvious starting point. Early the next morning I head to the brewery and meet Nils Hauser, a Scandinavian secret agent. OK, he's not a secret agent, he's a brewery tour guide, but he's in his mid-fifties, has a short tidy grey beard, a worldly grave manner and a mackintosh neatly belted at the waist. He looks like someone Connery's Bond might have met to pick up a special gadget, or maybe get a tip-off that he'll be able to find this movie's baddie at eight o'clock tonight in the Spunk Bar.

Carlsberg holds a 70 per cent share of the Danish beer market. Although 51 per cent of Carlsberg's shares are owned by the Carlsberg Foundation, the remaining 49 per cent on the stock exchange are enough to make it one of the ten most traded stocks in Denmark. Apart from Carlsberg, the company owns Tuborg and Wiibroe, the other big beers in Denmark. Even though Carlsberg itself is synonymous with the country to many foreigners, Tuborg is the beer more commonly drunk by Danes.

Nils takes me to the world-famous Miranda gate, a majestic red-brick arch held aloft by four huge elephants which, legend has it, will speak to you if you drink enough Carlsberg. Each elephant is festooned with swastikas. J.C. Jacobsen's son Carl trademarked the symbol in 1881 and used it to distinguish his brewery from his father's, which employed a star symbol. Before its appropriation by the Nazis, this symbol had a 4,000-year history as an Indian signifier of the sun, and was associated with happiness. Of course, it became a problem in the 1920s and 1930s, and was finally dropped by Carlsberg in 1940.

You might be wondering why one Carlsberg would go to so much trouble to create a separate identity from another, particularly when the original was the most successful brewer Denmark had ever known. In fact, why did Junior have his own brewery at all? What's wrong with working your way up through the family firm? The family squabble behind these questions is one of the most dramatic stories in brewing history, a story that frankly I'm amazed hasn't yet been turned into a mini-series. Carlsberg is really – or was – two breweries, built by a father and son who were opposite in temperament and interests, fought almost for their entire lives, and shaped the modern beer market in Denmark and arguably the world.

Jacob Christian Jacobsen was born in 1811 and followed his father into brewing. By that time Denmark had gone from being a major European power to a shadow of its former glory. Similarly beer, once revered as 'Nordic wine', had become a low-strength, uninteresting table beverage often drunk with a shot of schnapps to give it enough of a kick.

J.C. Jacobsen was obsessed by scientific process, and spent much of his life regretting that he never received formal scientific training. The middle of the nineteenth century saw phenomenal leaps forward in brewing science, innovation following innovation at a dizzying rate comparable to the IT revolution of the late twentieth century. Europe's roads became congested with brewers jealously visiting whichever of their number had come up with the latest brilliant process or discovery, then rushing back home to use it in the search for their own moment of glory. On the surface it was all formal and polite, with letters of introduction and proud tours of new equipment. But visitors' luggage often included hidden thermometers and hollowed-out walking sticks with vent holes which they filled with stolen samples of beer for subsequent analysis. Sedelmayr from Munich and Dreher from Vienna visited England to witness the new strides forward in steam-powered brewing. In turn, Jacobsen went to study with Sedelmayr to learn about the lager he was producing in his new plant. The brotherhood of brewers I have witnessed on my travels was born.

When Jacobsen returned from Spaten with his yeast, he brewed his first lager in his mother's wash tub. It was a success, and soon he was brewing commercially at a site in Valby, then outside the city of Copenhagen. Valby had the only significant hill anywhere near the city, which meant Jacobsen could dig into it and build the cellars crucial for lagering before refrigeration came along. 'Hill' in Danish is *berg*, and Jacobsen named his brewery after his son Carl, then five years old. In 1847 Carlsberg was born.

J.C. Jacobsen was a driven, determined man. Few people could get close enough to him to spot the humanity beneath his harsh, disciplined exterior. As Carl grew, Jacobsen was adamant that his son would have the scientific education he had been denied. He planned the boy's life out in meticulous detail, subjecting him to a rigorous educational programme from the age of five. When Carl was seventeen he received an impassioned letter from his father, then on yet another European tour. In words that foretell the work Louis Pasteur would do with yeast a decade later, he wrote:

> The world does not stand still ... the metamorphoses during malting, mashing and fermenting are demonstrably not as simple as was previously supposed; there

now appear to be different substances and different
changes of substance that we had not dreamt of before . . .
He who possesses the most thorough knowledge of chemistry and its auxiliary sciences along with the necessary
practical proficiency and insight will be Europe's leading
brewer of the coming generation. This ought to be your aim.

J.C. seems never to have paused to ask Carl what he would
actually like to do. The boy was simply another of his scientific
projects.

I know it's easy to say now, but it was never going to work.
When J.C. returned from France, he learned that Carl was
engaged to be married – to his cousin Emilie.

The cousin part aside, J.C. didn't think that Emilie was
good enough. He also firmly believed that true love couldn't
exist in people so young. More to the point, marriage at this
stage just didn't feature in J.C.'s plans for his son. He was
aghast at the boy's audacious demonstration of free will. When
Carl flatly refused to end the engagement, it tore the family
apart. J.C. realized the only way he was going to sever the
engagement successfully was to move prematurely to stage two
of Carl's education: the European study tour. Carl described it
as being sent into exile. Four years passed before he was
allowed to return home.

Carl studied at breweries in Paris, Strasbourg, Marseille,
Munich, Vienna, London, Burton-on-Trent and Edinburgh.
Letters between the family are preserved by the Carlsberg
Foundation and quoted in Kristof Glamann's biography of
J.C. Jacobsen. When Carl refused to break off contact with
Emilie, J.C. thundered:

I had expected that your letters from Strasbourg would

breathe nothing but brewery ... if you think to be my
successor at Carlsberg, you must make yourself worthy of
that position ... Only a proficient and energetic brewer,
with the ability and the will to continue what I have
begun ... shall come into possession of this place after
me, which is dedicated to this undertaking. God forbid
that it should be anyone but my son.

Several times Carl asked his father if he might return to
Denmark. Each time, the reply was the same:

You must be 28 years old and have made good use of
your years of learning and rehearsing. I therefore cannot
under any circumstances give my consent to your making
a visit home before then.

Finally, in March 1870, the twenty-eight-year-old Carl received
a letter proclaiming:

You are now as fully equipped for the fulfilment of your
task as almost any young, or even older, brewer in Europe
can be, and with an interest in your calling which war-
rants the highest hopes. And what higher hope can there
be for me than to see the goal which has seemed to be
before me since my earliest youth, realised through you?

J.C. neglected to mention in this communication that Emilie
had finally married someone else.

The original plan had been that when the time came for
Carl's return, he would take control of the brewery as the son
and protégé created in his father's image to carry on his work.
But while Carl was away, J.C. decided that he would not retire;
he would set the boy up with his own place instead. As he was
producing lager, his son would brew top-fermented beer –

bitter or ale, a craft he would have perfected while studying in Britain. J.C. built a separate annexe brewery for Carl, which opened in 1871.

But Denmark was falling in love with the Bavarian lager J.C. had introduced. It was so popular that Jacobsen, now by far the country's biggest brewer, often had to ration supplies. Lagering took time, cellar space was limited, and he would never have considered compromising quality to meet demand. Carl took stock of the situation, ignored his dad's orders to brew English-style beer, and promptly went into competition brewing lager. If there was any doubt that this was a two-fingered salute, this was dispelled by Carl's decision to cut lagering time to meet demand. By the 1880s, he was selling more beer under the Carlsberg name than his father, beer that J.C. refused to even acknowledge as beer.

The two men became completely estranged. J.C. drew up a will that effectively disinherited his son. Carl barred the gate between the old Carlsberg brewery and the annexe brewery, now generally referred to as New Carlsberg. Carl called the road between the two breweries Pasteurs Vej. His father preferred Alliance Vej. Emil Hansen, J.C.'s gifted scientist, remarked, 'These two crazy people are putting up signboards bigger than the other's down there, because each of them is trying to cover the other's street name. They are making themselves objects of derision even to the workers, and the scandal has found its way into several newspapers, even in the provinces.' Hostilities endured until 1886, when Carl finally decided it was time to bury the hatchet. This was only six months before J.C.'s death.

Nils takes me into the stunning brew hall of Carl's New Carlsberg brewery, which is still used for special one-off beers.

We stand on a balcony with gold-painted rails, looking down at the four huge coppers rising from the black and white tiled floor. Behind us is a bust of Louis Pasteur, the godfather of modern brewing who became a personal friend of J.C. Jacobsen. It was a friendship that was to lead to another blazing conflict.

In 1876 J.C. hired Emil Hansen, a brilliant young scientist, to work at the Carlsberg laboratory. There, Hansen demonstrated that yeast was not a homogeneous substance but could be broken down into a number of strains, of which only a few were right for brewing. In 1883 he isolated and propagated single-strain yeasts for the first time, finally allowing brewers enough control over the fermentation process to guarantee a consistent product, brew after brew. It was beer's equivalent of splitting the atom.

You might think that J.C., the great scientific brewer, would be ecstatic at this development – it was precisely the kind of thing the laboratory had been set up to achieve. But he wasn't happy at all. If Hansen's work was right, then some of the tenets of Pasteur's work must be wrong. Pasteur was a friend and idol, Hansen a mere employee. Jacobsen refused to recognize the achievement, refused to patent it, and even as brewers like Heineken took the breakthrough and ran with it, Hansen received no recognition, financial or otherwise, from his employer. Things only changed when Pasteur himself came to the brewery to congratulate Hansen on his breakthrough. Lager yeast is still known as *Sacharromyces carlsbergensis* in Hansen's honour.

While J.C. Jacobsen was clearly as driven and egotistical as any member of that other great brewing dynasty, the Busches, in some ways they could not have been more different. When

Gussie Busch died in 1989 his estate was worth $1.5 billion. He left a total of $92,500 to the five staff who had nursed him through his long illness. The rest went to family members who were already multimillionaires. Not a cent was left to charity.*

By contrast, J.C. Jacobsen spent all his time outside the brewery working in public life. The laboratory he established in 1875 to study fermentation also encouraged scientists to pursue other lines of work which helped ensure Denmark was 'taking an honourable part in scientific progress'. In 1876 he established the Carlsberg Foundation to allow the laboratory to continue its work after his death, and to give a broader remit to the advancement of science and knowledge. In 1878 he endowed the Frederiksborg Museum of Natural History, and placed it under the foundation's care.

The brewery grounds still bear testament to the obsessions of father and son: the beautiful gardens (the father was a keen botanist) are full of sculpture (the son was passionate about art). When J.C. Jacobsen died in 1887 the Old Carlsberg brewery was left to the Carlsberg Foundation. In 1903 Carl donated his brewery to the foundation, and the two were finally united. He called it 'a reconciliation offering to eradicate every trace of an ancient disharmony between a father and his son'. Carl also established the New Carlsberg Foundation, which supported the Carlsberg Glypotheque, a public building to house the vast art collection which he donated to the city of Copenhagen. There's hardly a vista in the Danish capital that hasn't been improved by a spire or statue donated by Carl. He even bought the city its most famous landmark:

---

* 'Welcome to the world of Anheuser Busch, where . . .' Oh, you know it by now.

the Little Mermaid. Like the Busches, the Jacobsens were driven by a desire to keep their name alive after their death, but the two families proved that there are a variety of ways of achieving this.

Nils takes me into the banqueting halls built by Carl. The walls are lined with pictures of visiting dignitaries. 'A Scandinavian prince cannot become king until he has visited here – the current prince already has.' As well as every significant member of Scandinavian royalty, there's Yuri Gagarin, Charles Lindbergh, most British royals of the twentieth century and a smattering of Hollywood stars.

Next we visit the cellars that hold the world's largest collection of filled beer bottles. Over twenty-five years a rather overenthusiastic Dane amassed a collection of 12,000 bottles and cans. One day he phoned Carlsberg to say that he had been presented with a choice: either the collection went or his wife did, and would Carlsberg be interested in taking one of them off his hands. They chose the collection, which has now swollen to 15,500, all racked on long glass shelves, sorted by country. The oldest is a bottle of Bass Ale No.2, from 1869.

As we re-emerge into the light, I conclude that if you quite like your beer but are only going to choose to visit one brewery in your lifetime, it should probably be this one.

After the tour I meet Andrew Arnold, an English PR consultant who married a Dane and now works here for Carlsberg. He takes me for lunch in a Danish beer garden. It seems pleasant enough to sit outside, until we actually do so. Shivering but putting on brave faces, we eat a traditional Danish lunch of pickled herring, fried breadcrumbed fish, prawns, smoked salmon and cheese.

Andrew fills me in on the basics of Danish beer drinking. 'Seventy per cent of drinking happens at home – entertaining at home is a much stronger part of culture here than it is anywhere else,' he says. 'There's this massive Danish concept of *hygge*. I suppose it's best translated as 'Danish cosiness'. It's all about having a good time in your home with the people closest to you, your closest mates – who you've known since college days – and your family. The Danish sense of humour is very sarcastic – like the British. Beer's a big part of it, because you drink beer to loosen up and get in the mood. Wine immediately makes the occasion more formal. And if you stick to beer, there's a natural limit to how much you can drink because of the carbonation. You'll have six or seven bottles, so you'll feel the effect but not get totally pissed.'

It's fascinating how this concept keeps cropping up around the world. Like the Spanish *chispa*, Dwight Heath describes Danish cosiness brilliantly as an ideal state achieved by 'just enough' drinking – not enough to put yourself at risk, but enough to feel relaxed and happy. He compares it to the French concept of *ivresse*, which he defines as 'gaiety, spontaneity and zest', the very antithesis of the impairment caused by getting totally wankered, a kind of alcohol-induced rapture in a culture where clumsy or unseemly drunken behaviour is frowned upon.

Danish anthropologist Peter Schioler, writing in the *International Handbook on Alcohol and Culture*, finds it strange that there seems to be no Anglo-Saxon equivalent of *hygge*, which he describes as the 'first and lasting pleasurable effect of drinking alcohol':

All of the descriptive terms in English and German seem to be reserved for negative effects, which are not usually apparent until larger quantities have been drunk. There are many Danish words that describe various aspects of intoxication, for example to specify subtle degrees of change in behaviour, progressive lowering of inhibitions, and so forth. 'Intoxication' is too strong a term to be used for the primary exhilarating effect of drinking alcohol, a sensation that is the most usual for the great majority of Danish drinkers.

He also describes a recent survey of 2,000 Danes which showed alcohol was seen emphatically as a good thing. In Aarhus, Denmark's second-largest city, schoolchildren aged six to eight were asked to draw 'a person drinking alcohol,' a 'person not drinking alcohol', and 'children with adults drinking alcohol'. No drawing showed winos or alkies, or anyone displaying improper behaviour. Most were positive, and depicted people who were clearly happy.

'People do sometimes drink to get drunk,' concedes Andrew, 'but the Danes make happy drunks. It's not something that's frowned upon. Drunkenness is hardly ever the main aim – it's a consequence of being part of the group. It's strange really, because every other part of Danish culture – the films, the books and all that – are so depressing. And we've got the highest suicide rate in Europe.'

Andrew also tells me some surprising things about Carlsberg. I suppose that's his job, but I'm still impressed. The brewmasters are regularly given complete liberty to brew whatever style of beer they want. This usually results in eight or nine new beers that are a far cry from standard Pilsners. Let off the leash, Carlsberg's brewers prefer to create ales and stouts, or beers brewed with cherries or chocolate. The best ones are retailed as a range of limited editions under the name Semper Ardens (Always burning).

The first Semper Ardens beers were sold exclusively in the top thirty restaurants in Denmark, a hundred bottles each in each one. Carlsberg challenged the chefs to create dishes that went with the beers. They were priced like bottles of wine but sold out rapidly. Semper Ardens is now available more widely. Carlsberg asks the public to vote on which beer from each new collection should be launched properly. 'When we started we expected the bland, Pilsner-style ones to win every time,' says Andrew, 'but people seem to be voting consistently for the more interesting and unusual beers.'

After lunch, Andrew takes me to the Norrebro (North Bridge) brewery. Anders Kissmeyer used to be a Carlsberg brewmaster, and left to set up this microbrewery and brew-pub a couple of years ago. Norrebro just celebrated its first birthday, and Anders is buzzing with excitement. 'While I was away the guys brewed a special beer and kept it hidden from me. I have always been fascinated by other cultures, especially the US,' says Anders as we sit down with a beer, 'but I am not an entrepreneur. A friend of mine made a lot of money in biotechnology and was talking about opening a whisky distillery. I said it was more logical to do a brewery. We got someone professional to do the design and the PR. Many microbrewers feel the establishment has to look like a traditional German or English pub. I wanted to make mine more contemporary.'

Microbreweries can often be elegant, even beautiful, with compact brewing vessels polished until they gleam, fitted to take up as little space as possible. Cross this with Scandi-navian design expertise, and you get a pub-brewery that looks incomplete without supermodels pouting from behind the bar. Bare brick walls and metal girders provide the backdrop for glass staircases, bright red tabletops and those chairs that look a bit like the plastic ones we had at school but cost a lot of money and are very fashionable. 'People come in asking for tours,' says Anders. 'We get fifteen to twenty groups a week.'

'You can't get a table here for dinner,' says Andrew. 'It has good beer, nice ambience, but the restaurant has more to it than that. It brings people here who wouldn't have come just for the beer.'

'It's in the right location,' says Anders. 'This is an area that is currently gentrifying. Lots of students and new graduates. They don't have much money, but what they do have they spend.'

Just now the bar is home to a young, stylish crowd. The restaurant displays much more of a mix. 'This is very different from the *hygge*,' says Anders. 'People are learning something new – different tastes and experiences.'

We taste some beers, and immediately I spot the influence of the American micros. New York Lager is bitter and malty and has the pungent floral aroma of American Cascade hops, possibly now my favourite ever plant. Garrett Oliver helped Anders create Pacific Pale Ale, which puts lime and the aroma of pine needles in the back of your mouth. But there are also nods to German, Belgian, Czech and British traditions, with wheat beers, Pilsners, stouts and dubbels brewed frequently.

This is starting to become familiar: I'm in a country I thought brewed only fairly bland lager, in one of its most stylish bars, talking to a brewer who is passionate about different, eclectic styles and having huge success selling them to a smart young crowd. It must be time for the beer and food conversation.

Anders comes in on cue: 'Our food has its origins in traditional Nordic cuisine, which is all about the cheaper cuts, with heavy spices, lots of sugar and vinegar. It's impossible to eat with wine but is great with beer. The sugary, acidic fatty foods go well. The IPA is very popular because it cuts through fat so well. But our menu is not traditional food, and that's the whole point.'

He hands me a menu. 'Warm purée of parsley root with foam of lightly smoked shrimps, served with a salad of smoked shrimps, pears and hazelnuts with a reduction of La Granja stout' is top of the starters. You could follow this with 'Crisp fried grey mullet with ravioli, served with pickled chanterelles and bouillon of dill flavoured with Ceske Bohmer [Anders' Czech-style Pilsner], scallops from Beton, tomatoes and salsify'. And why not finish with 'Spiced pineapple tart with honey cake ice cream and spiced syrup with Chimay Bleu [a Belgian Trappist beer]', or 'Pear poached in Bellevue framboise and candied orange, served with truffle rolled in spicy cashew nuts'? Oh, this just isn't fair. You can only appreciate the lovely things being done with beer and food in countries like this for so long before your feelings turn to resentment and jealousy.

Chris arrives mid-afternoon. Later, Andrew meets up with us again and we're off on a tour of Copenhagen with Alan Milius Thomsen, local historian and beer enthusiast, and about forty locals who want to find out more about their town's beery history. Alan looks like Joss Ackland and chomps on a cigar the size of a baby's arm. He barks in Danish, which Andrew intermittently translates. Many of the streets and squares we visit were at one time directly on the seafront. Sailors provide the theme to much of the tour, and it seems that every corner was once a pub, every street a row of brothels. Alan seems as fond of the history of prostitution as he is of beer.

After an hour of this, we stop at a pub that still exists. Hviids Vinstue was established by a wine merchant in 1723. The wooden interior is almost black, which would be oppressive were it not for the stained-glass windows and the ancient photographs that cover the walls.

Alan comes over to join us, mercifully switching to English. 'This pub was badly damaged in World War Two,' he growls, sitting down. 'The Nazis threw bombs in through the door to punish the Danish resistance. They bombed all the popular places in Copenhagen, including the Tivoli.'

I ask him about beer.

'I have been interested in the history of my town since I was a child. In my forties I started writing a few articles. But beer and history are such a good match. I do this tour every day. Today I have done it twice. I've just made a Trivial Pursuit game called World of Beer. It has one thousand questions.

'In Denmark the pub is an extra living room, like you have in England. If someone doesn't come in for three days you're wondering where he is. Is he sick? Danish pub life is very close to *Cheers*. Everyone knows your name. You want to be the first one in the pub, because everyone buys you a drink when they arrive.'

He lights a new cigar.

'But the old pubs are closing down, and fewer new ones

are opening in their place. These new ones are bars, full of glass and mirrors. But now young people are rediscovering the old pubs. They start at eight, a little bit out of town, before coming in and going to the discotheque.'

Back out on the street, Alan switches back to Danish, and once again I'm relying on Andrew to translate, which he does selectively. I stare at Alan. Because I don't understand him, I'm trying desperately to read his body language and tone of voice, and they are just as impenetrable as his words. We're standing outside the Wessels Kro pub, and he's shouting at us, gesturing violently towards the bar. If my life depended on giving an approximate translation of what he is saying, I would guess it was, 'This is a shit pub. Don't go in here! The beer is fucking *awful*!' But it's a historical tour, and there's a sign above the door saying 1772, so he's probably not saying that.

We go through old districts that have been regenerated, and new districts that stand where even older ones haven't survived. 'There are a lot of old buildings still here,' says Alan. 'This is surprising really, given the city had three devastating fires at fifty-year intervals. The last of these was the bombardment by the British.'

During the Napoleonic Wars the Nordic powers made futile attempts to remain neutral. In 1801 the League of Armed Neutrality was smashed by a British raid that gently hinted you were either with us or against us. Six years later, when Napoleon devised the Continental System to isolate Britain from mainland Europe, King Frederick VI, still sore, readily agreed to join. It would perhaps have been better if he had mobilized properly equipped armed forces before he made his intentions clear. The British struck again, subjecting Copenhagen to three nights of constant bombardment, which finally stopped when the Danes agreed to hand over their entire navy and all its supplies. The British let them keep one flagship, possibly because it had been a present from them in the first place, and you had to have some standards of behaviour even in the middle of firebombing civilians out of their homes. Britain's actions were universally condemned at the time. The repeated references Alan makes to the bombardment, in every street that suffered damage – which, it turns out, is most streets – are the first Chris or I have heard of it. Strangely, it was never mentioned when we studied the Napoleonic Wars at school.

At the end of the tour Alan says goodbye to the rest of the group and shepherds them into a restaurant. They're in for a four-course dinner with beers matched to each dish, from a mild Pilsner moving up to a bock, which Alan helped put together. Then he takes Andrew, Chris and me back to his flat. He wants to give me a copy of his book on Danish pubs, which I'm very pleased about. We enter a seventeenth-century building and puff our way up four flights of stairs. 'No elevators back then,' grunts Alan. 'This is the old red light district. The last prostitutes moved out five years ago. They are tiny flats all being made into one flat. All the old working-class districts are being gentrified.'

Alan's place is moodily lit, definitely a bloke's flat. There are books everywhere, and posters of his football team, a socialist outfit with the slogan 'Forward'. He breaks out some rare beers from his collection, leans back and tells us more stories.

'Up until the 1950s people would drink fifty beers a day. They had no car; they worked hard. Then American companies came in – no beer, no smoking. No living. And we travelled to the Mediterranean and brought wine culture back with us. The wine lobby in the EU is so strong – the wine-producing countries were the ones who started it all. But now we are re-establishing traditional Danish culture. Take Christmas, for example. With a traditional Danish Christmas dinner you drink beer. Pork crackling, duck, red cabbage, goose and dressing made from vinegar. You don't mix vinegar with wine.'

It's great to be invited into this man's house and drink his beer, this man who only met us a few hours ago. Once again, I marvel at the international confederacy of beer. He shows me his study, which is dominated by a magnificent antique globe. 'A man's study is not really a study without a globe', he says, patting it. I realize he is absolutely right.

Much later, Chris and I sit in a bar on the corner of Studiestraede and Veste Voldgade in the centre of town, watching blondes go by on bikes. It's been a full, astonishing day. I was expecting Copenhagen to be a collection of beautiful people sitting in tasteful bars sipping Carlsberg, and for the brewing giant itself to be a corporate behemoth intent on turning its brand into the next Bud or Coke. I was absolutely right about the beautiful people and the tasteful bars, but Denmark is yet another country discovering a taste for different, eclectic beers. This bar is achingly stylish, but has huge car showroom-style windows so you don't feel intimidated about going in. A DJ spins decks in the corner, but not so loud you have to shout. The crowd is a broad mix of people, cool but not too cool.

Everything seems just a little more laid-back than it does in Britain, both more stylish and more relaxed, which is a curious combination. Beer, rather than wine or cocktails, is the drink of choice, and it has been incorporated into the culture as seamlessly as in Spain or the Czech Republic. This disproves the theory that chilled-out continental drinking is the result of the differences between sophisticated Latin cultures and boorish northern Europeans. These people used to be *Vikings*. And they make beer drinking look like the most stylish, civilized activity in the world.

Eventually we head back to the hotel to explore the contents of the minibar. I nick the whisky, and Chris decides to go for the bitter. This is not beer, but a little bottle of schnapps. It tastes like something your gran might have made you drink or, according to Chris, like the bile you throw up when there's nothing else left in your stomach. The Scandinavians drink this as a digestif. I can only assume that the point of it is to make you appreciate how nice your food really tastes.

Helsingor

Saturday morning dawns stunningly clear and blue, perfect weather for a day by the sea. Helsingor is half an hour up the coast by train. Last night Andrew described this coastline as a millionaire's playground. It's immaculate: small villages and tree-lined avenues, houses looking across the sea to Sweden, so close we can make out individual buildings on the far shore.

Helsingor is where Swedish drinkers come to buy beer at Danish prices. Andrew described Scandinavia to me as a place where everyone goes south. The Danes go to Germany. The

Swedes come here. Norwegians go to Sweden and Finns go to Norway. The further north you go, the more expensive and restricted the beer is, and the more mental the drinking is. There's an old Finnish joke. Two men are in a bar, drinking steadily and silently, pint after pint. After a couple of hours, when the tenth drinks are served, one of them raises his glass to his lips and says, 'Cheers,' to his friend. The second man stares at him, clearly upset, and says testily, 'Look, did we come here to talk or to drink?'

Here on Branstraede, a stone's throw from the ferry terminal, just outside the Hamlet Hotel and the Ophelia restaurant, drinking is the undoubted priority. Half the premises in the street are booze shops. Outside each, big green umbrellas shelter cases of Carlsberg, Tuborg and Harborg. Boris Yeltsin vodka sells by the litre. All prices are in Danish and Swedish kroner, and euros. People peruse the offers, dragging wheeled suitcases and trolleys behind them.

We wander away from the front, and eventually the beer shops peter out to be replaced by butchers and delicatessens. We find ourselves in Axeltov, a destination our guidebooks are pretty non-committal about, describing it as just a couple of cafes in an uninteresting town square. But when we get there, paradise slowly unfolds before us. First, there's a small market selling as many different types of *sild* as you can imagine: cured, pickled and seven shades of marinated. I'm sure you'll agree that that's enough to make any square a little special. But beyond the market is a small cafe, the kind of place that, if it were in Hyde Park in London, would sell ice cream and overpriced cans of warm cola. This one sells hot dogs, toasties and four different kinds of draught beer. People sit at the white plastic tables out front, beer in hand, faces turned to the sun, enjoying what may well be the last good day of the year.

Chris has disappeared up ahead while I take photographs of the most perfect thing I've seen since the kebab shop with the draught beer font in Madrid. 'Look,' I call after him. 'Come and look at this. It's perfect.'

'I know,' he calls back. 'Come up here.'

I walk up the steep cobbles, past a deserted makeshift stage which suggests just-missed summer festivals, past a statue surrounded by fountains, and into the top half of the square. It's a sea of umbrella-shaded tables, guarded by three or four more beer and hot dog bars. Blonde women in Danish national costume topped with denim jackets against the sudden chill wind serve mugs of beer. Men and women of all ages, all of them drinking beer, crowd the tables.

It feels Parisian, as we find seats on cobbles beneath a row of neatly planted lime trees. There is a surprising array of beers on offer: Wiibroe, Tuborg Guld Luxury Beer, Erdinger, St Fruillen Brune, Guinness and Kilkenny, as well as tiny bottles of bitters and, ruining the effect somewhat, a range of Bacardi Breezers. We're already liking Wiibroe very much. There's a contemporary variant, a light Pilsner, and Classic, a darker, amber brew, like a Bavarian lager.

Gaestgivergaarden has a decent menu but no tables on the terrace outside, so we head indoors. It's a nice, dark pub with sunshine pouring in through stained-glass windows. We find an empty table and sit down, and it's only now that I spot the Oktoberfest theme running through the place. Bunting everywhere promotes Spaten – *Spaten!* – Oktoberfest beer. The staff are wearing traditional Bavarian costume, and the PA is pumping out Bavarian brass band music.

It's a week since I arrived in Munich, almost to the hour. It's five and a half days since my last *Maß* in the Oktoberfest tents. But as soon as I hear that music, I'm back there. I can no longer see my immediate surroundings. As 'Rosamunde' swells, I'm inside a huge tent surrounded by noise and swinging steins. And I'm singing along, swinging my arms, toasting my new friends from around the world . . .

'You like oompah music now,' says Chris, matter of fact.

And I'm back in the room. I try to explain. Then I realize that, in an infinitely trivial way, I've had a glimpse of what it must feel like to be a Vietnam veteran suffering flashbacks. No one else here can feel it. No one understands. The waiters' outfits are clearly cartoon, fancy-dress versions, not authentic Bavarian costume. Our beers, when they arrive, are in 500 millilitre bottles; the litre steins depicted on the bunting are Spaten's Oktoberfest logo rather than an accurate representation of the how the beer is served. To everyone else this is simply an opportunistic promotion to flog a few bottles of guest beer. To me it's a brief, backward glimpse of what I now realize was one of the most intensely pleasurable weekends of my life. I sing along to *Ein Prosit*, somewhat louder than one bloke singing on his own in a pub really should.

But that marks the end of the Oktoberfest CD. Crappy MOR AOR swiftly takes its place. I calm down. The fog clears. I'm in Denmark. Not Bavaria. Denmark. It's a nice Danish pub which behind the Munich fluff has a typically Irish theme. I'm feeling disoriented, losing track of time. Munich was one week ago. The week before that I was in Shanghai. Three weeks ago was Sydney. Four: Tokyo. It's almost impossible to believe.

I have a *smorresod* for lunch, an open sandwich of black

bread, meatballs, lettuce, pickled gherkins and a fruit- or vegetable-based substance which I can't identify but am still very grateful for. Chris has something similar to the lunch I enjoyed with Andrew yesterday. He's unusually quiet, deep in thought, drinking his Spaten Oktoberfest. 'Is all the beer in Munich as nice as this?' he asks.

I nod. 'We should go there next year,' I tell him. 'We could fit in a trip to Barnsley's twin town of Schwabisch Gmund and see if there is any similarity whatsoever. Because, really, I think you shouldn't do more than a day or two at Oktoberfest itself.'

'That sounds like a challenge,' he replies.

'You fool. You don't understand.' I shake my head.

We emerge from the bar into the sunlight, blinking and pleasantly stewed, and make our way to the ferry terminal via a walk round Helsingor castle, better known as Elsinore, the setting for *Hamlet*. The castle is a brute hulk of a building that seems to sit in its own shadows even on a day as bright and sunny as this one. It's not difficult to imagine the troubled prince stalking the heavily fortified ramparts. The atmosphere is dispelled only when we end our circuit of the walls and reach the car park, where a smattering of elderly women sit with flasks and picnic baskets. Bronze statues of Hamlet and Ophelia guard them. Ophelia's breasts are uncovered, and whereas the rest of the statue is oxidized green, her boobs are shiny from being rubbed.

Ferries leave for Helsingborg, just across from Helsingor, every fifteen minutes. The terminal itself is little more than a vast off-licence, a last chance to stock up. Staff wheel trolleys full of cases of beer in a perpetual race to stock the shelves faster than they can be stripped by hordes of people who seem weighed down by sad, hatchet-faced desperation. There's no one who doesn't have at least a carrier bag or two. Families have driven onto the ferry, and our fellow foot passengers are students and teenagers, cases of beer under their arms, some of them already broken into, their owners swigging from bottles as we board. If there is a clearer illustration of the contrast between the effects of living under a regime that has a censorious attitude to alcohol and one that does not, I have yet to see it.

We're near the front of the queue, and we head up to the bar as soon as we're on board. But when we get there, it's already full. Some people are even nearing the end of their drinks. Others have already been served with meals. This can't be right, unless . . . *unless they never got off the boat coming the other way.* These people obviously board the ferry for its own sake, going backwards and forwards across the sound. Why they don't get off in Denmark as soon as they can is not clear; the prices on board are far more expensive than they are in Helsingor, so to stay on the ferry kind of defeats the object of leaving Sweden. But they seem happy enough in their perpetual transit.

Twenty minutes later we disembark, leaving the bar as busy as we found it. The people getting on this side, as you will have guessed, are carrying nothing but empty bags and full wallets.

Sweden

Helsingborg is closed. So emphatically, completely closed that we suspect the whole of Sweden has gone on holiday. The crowd leaving from the terminal melts away almost immediately, and we're alone on deserted city streets at four o'clock on a Saturday afternoon. Someone who might be Benny from Abba cycles past, which sounds like the most dreadful cliché, but you didn't see him. After he disappears, we don't see another living soul for about fifteen minutes.

Andrew told us there is a castle here well worth visiting. It probably is. We walk up a very steep hill and find the building shrouded in scaffolding and plastic sheeting. We've now done everything there is to do in Helsingborg on a Saturday afternoon. We look at the city. There's a good view from up here. The ferries move, but nothing else does. Now I understand why people get on the ferry. They probably hate Denmark and never get off there, but riding the boat is actually better than being here.

We descend the hill back into town, and find a solitary open bar. I ask for two Abrø beers. If the barman's mystified expression is anything to go by, Abrø is not pronounced *Ah-broe*. Extravagantly blond and unfeasibly handsome, he starts without invitation to tell me stories, in perfect English, of people who cannot pronounce their Os. Maybe they felt they didn't have to pronounce them, given you keep crossing them out, you smug git, I don't tell him. He regales me with tales from when he used to work in Ikea in France, and how stupid the people were who shopped there. Every day was a riot for him, a cavalcade of laughter in which his sides came tantalizingly close to bursting.

We sit down silently, as far away as we can from both the barman and Macbeth's witches, the only other occupants of the bar. 'What do people *do* in Sweden on a Saturday then?' asks Chris. I have no answer. Telling stories of French people struggling to pronounce Scandinavian words which are mostly made up anyway seems to be the height of Bohemia around here. As for vast numbers of Swedes before us, the call of the ferry to Denmark grows stronger. Chris doesn't mind: he's happy just to be able to tell everyone that he's been to Sweden *as well as* Denmark in the same weekend.

Back on board, we go to the dining room and consider joining the people sitting down to a three-course dinner as they shuttle backwards and forwards between the two countries. Eventually we decide against it. We've got a beer festival to go to.

Copenhagen

Nyhavn is one of those places that looks too good to be true. You see a picture of it in a travel guide, and the cynic in you just *knows* that it's twenty years out of date, or that the angle has been artfully chosen to omit the McDonald's or the chemical processing plant. But when we get back into Copen-hagen and walk across to the west of the city, there it is, perfect. Nyhavn is a short canal jutting a few hundred yards inland from the Inderhavnen River. It seems the criteria for allowing boats to moor here are that they must be pretty, or romantic, or ancient, or ideally all three. When I discover that this is where the Danish National Museum moors its collection of vessels, it makes sense.

Nyhavn was full of prostitutes in Hans Christian Andersen's day. Proving once again the rule that the sleazier a place once was, the more aspirational it is now, the former brothels lining both sides of the canal are now elegant, pastel-coloured restaurants and bars. But we're not here for that; by an extraordinarily good piece of fortune, today and tomorrow is the Nyhavn beer festival.

Except we can't find it.

We walk the length of both sides of the canal, straining our ears for oompah music and the clinking of glasses, hearing only polite murmurings of conversation. And then, finally, like that bit at the end of *Planet of the Apes* where Charlton Heston realizes he's on Earth, we stop in the small, deserted, sunken cobbled square at the end of the canal and look around with mounting horror. This is the beer festival. Or rather, it was. There's a trailer with a Carlsberg logo on the side. Two empty plastic glasses. And a leaflet, blown by an eddy of breeze against our legs. I pick it up. The beer festival was yesterday and today, not today and tomorrow as reported in the English-language newspaper back at the hotel. It ran from 4 p.m. till 8 p.m. yesterday, and 2 p.m. till 6 p.m. today. Not only has it finished, they've had time to tidy up afterwards. This is, without a doubt, the most rubbish beer festival I have ever failed to go to. Who finishes a beer festival at 6 p.m.? In a town where you can drink all night? It's like the beer shop in Bruges all over again. I sink to my knees and utter a steady stream of language that would make the sailors who used to frequent Nyhavn's brothels blush, until Chris pulls me gently away and offers to buy me dinner in one of Copenhagen's best restaurants.

One of Denmark's most infuriating features is the way a

population that regularly eats lard, chain-smokes and drinks beer like Yorkshire miners can be so beautiful. At the end of a fantastic meal in the the Peder Oxe (Peppered Ox) a younger, curvier Helena Christensen brings us a cheese plate. I decide to attempt some beer and cheese matching for Chris, and order a nice Pilsner for the light cheeses, and a dark Belgian beer with the heavy ones. Helena quite understandably starts to pour us one each. 'No, no.' I interrupt her. 'We're sharing this one first – can you not pour the other one just yet, thanks.'

'O-kaaaay . . .' she says warily, backing away, quite clearly thinking, it's a very liberal country we have here; you sick Brits just get on with whatever it is you have to do.

We roll out of the restaurant and on to one or two bars. The impending diet and detox waiting for me back home start to weigh heavily on my thoughts. Someone thrusts a leaflet into our hands for Klub Argot, which has performances tonight from bands including Bimbo Sons and Spaz Bitch. While we both enjoy discovering new music, we decide to pass on this, and instead drink steadily until we're reviving cruel childhood nicknames, before calling it a very long day.

Chris is good for me on these trips. He always insists on diluting the drinking with a bit of culture, and the visit is always much better for it. We spend Sunday morning at the Nationalmuseet, the national museum of Danish history and culture. Beer, of course, is a river running through Scandinavian history. The *Kalevala* (*Land of Heroes*) is a great Finnish epic poem, passed down by oral tradition for centuries until it was finally written down in the 1840s. It contains 200 verses about the creation of the world. And 400 verses about beer.

The Nordic peoples used to think of the sky as a giant brewing kettle. When Thor, the god of thunder, cleaned the kettle, all mortals knew about it. On days when he brewed, there were clouds in the sky.

The Vikings held sway between around AD 800 and 1250. Surviving literature from the time describes them as tall, bearded, aggressive and ruthless to their enemies. Beer fuelled this – they even brewed on board their longships. Beer-induced hallucinogenic stupors were part of the process of working yourself into a trance the night before a raid. And if Vikings died in battle, they knew their reward would be to spend eternity in the halls of the gods, drinking beer with their fallen comrades.

The museum prefers to emphasize the many more sedate aspects of Viking culture, which I suppose is understandable. They would never have conquered half of Europe and discovered North America centuries before Columbus if they had been drunk all the time.

We spend lunchtime and early afternoon strolling along the long, pedestrianized Stroget, Copenhagen's main shopping street, which is actually five streets laid end to end. It's late September now, and even though the sky is a cloudless blue there is a chill in the air whenever the buildings obscure the sun. And yet there's still a thriving outdoor cafe culture. Spare seats on the cobbled terraces are as hard to come by as they would be on a Mediterranean quayside. So it's cold. So what? People just wear coats. There are patio heaters. And if that's not enough, each chair outside each cafe has an orange woollen blanket draped over the back. The young, beautiful Danes sit with these blankets draped across their knees, sipping fortified hot chocolate.

When we finally find a spare table we order extravagant, elegantly tailored sandwiches for lunch. Chris has Carlsberg Special, dark and malty, and I order Carlsberg Hvede, a gorgeous wheat beer. The vast majority of beer drunk in Denmark is still blonde lager, but we're not sitting in a specialist beer cafe here and we're not the only ones drinking darker brews. I may have been right about most people drinking Carlsberg, but I was very wrong about it being uniform and bland.

And finally it's time to go home. These trips started in a spaced-out, random way, but over the last few months I have done little else other than travel and drink beer. I can't carry on any longer. My wallet, my health and my wife won't let me. There are so many other countries it would have been interesting to visit – Russians are the fastest-growing beer drinkers in the world; Nigeria would have been fascinating with its Guinness obsession; South America has an amazing carnival drinking culture. But I have been to each of the most important beer drinking countries in the modern world, the places that drink the most beer in terms of both total and per capita volume, those that make the most interesting and extreme beers, and those that really *celebrate* beer drinking as a way of life.

I need to go home and take stock. I need to visit the gym. I need to figure out what all this drinking means.

11

'Wi'aht it,
he's miserable'

London

My bus pulls into Euston station at 11.01 p.m. on a wet October night. It'll be about another twenty minutes before we reach Stoke Newington, and I've already missed last orders at the White Hart.

A short, blond-haired bloke sits at the bus stop, wearing only a tiny leopard-print thong. He's trying to pull on a pair of trousers and failing heroically, misplacing his legs, gathering himself and trying again. He may not have a hope of succeeding, but it's quite clear that he's not going to consider doing anything else until he does. His long-suffering mate sits beside him, making no effort to help, but patiently holding up a brown Carhartt T-shirt until such a time as it will be needed. Everyone on the bus watches them impassively, until we pull out and are on our way again.

The whole scene is quite distressing; why would anyone have a stag party in Euston? On a Wednesday?

And if it's not a stag party, what the hell is going on?

As we get closer to home the bus passes my local pubs and restaurants. I want to go to bed ... but not just yet. The springs and cogs in my body clock have long since given up the ghost and metaphorically boinged out in a mess of analogical metal, and for whatever reason, it doesn't feel like the end of the evening. But the White Hart is closed. Chickpizz is still open.* The Rose and Crown is closed. Millennium Kebabs is still open. Barracuda, the Asian–Irish fusion restaurant featuring top chef Ethel Minogue, closed an hour ago. And not only are all the pubs closed, they seem to have been for some time. Although I could no longer walk in and get served, we are still just within fifteen minutes' permitted drinking-up time after time has been called. But chairs are up on tables. Lights are switched off. People have been ushered out as quickly as possible. The whole culture feels half asleep. It feels like the 1930s.

It's now 11.40 p.m. In Spain there would still be another three and a half hours of drinking and playing Russian Roulette with a bowl of *pimientos de Padron*. There would be another couple of hours in Australia, Japan, China, Germany, Denmark or the Czech Republic. Even in boring Belgium, a place every true Brit delights in taking the piss out of, I could stay out drinking till dawn if I wished. You expect a capital city to be the most vibrant place in the country, and London is not just any capital city. Nine months on from this wet late-October night, it will beat Paris in the race for the 2012

---

* This is a shop that sells fried chicken, 'pizza's' and 'kebab's'. So it's called Chickpizz. There's a sign outside showing a fat little chicken eating a big pizza. Chickpizz.

Olympics. That aside, London has always fancied itself as a rival to New York as the most glamorous, sexy, vibrant metropolis on the planet. In New York I sauntered into a pub at half past midnight and got a meal.

I probably could have found another drink if I'd been in Soho after closing time. Before now I've drunk into the small hours in private clubs with people who are members. I've been to seedy drinking dens where you have to give a special knock on a sheet-metal door, have a word with the seven-foot bouncer who opens up, and be escorted to a bare cellar where you can drink cans of eastern European lager at three quid a pop. But in every other city I've visited on this tour I didn't have to do anything so absurd to get a late drink. Even as a clueless tourist and crap traveller, I was able to drink as late as I wanted, in pleasant surroundings. But in Britain in late 2004 this is not an option.

By the time you read this, new licensing laws will have come into effect and, local councils permitting, pubs should have much greater freedom to stagger their closing times according to what suits them and their customers, rather than what was suitable for munitions factories in the First World War (the basis for the current 11 p.m. curfew). If you've stayed with me this far, hopefully you'll agree that my quest has demonstrated that freer licensing, treating people like adults, leads to more chilled-out, responsible drinking. And yet the British press, from the *Daily Mail* right through to the *Guardian*, are currently united in the belief that later licensing will lead to the phenomenon of town centres as 'no-go zones for normal people'. Never mind the research presented to the government by people like Dwight Heath and Oxford's Social Issues Research Centre saying this will not happen; never mind the evidence of the six o'clock swill, or even the introduction of all-day opening and Sunday afternoon opening in the UK in the late 1980s and early '90s, which all led to drinking becoming more relaxed. It seems we're scared of a little liberty.

Let's be honest: since I've been back, I've been having trouble readjusting to normal life. I'm starting to piss Liz off by complaining about the licensing laws every time a pub closes and moaning about barmen every time they sullenly plonk a dribbling, unbranded, dirty pint glass of lager on the bar. I gripe about how great it would be if people just *gave a shit* every time I go into a pub that doesn't serve trick peppers, fresh squid or half a chicken with a lemon wipe stuck under its wing. I know it's better to have gone around the world drinking loads of beer in hundreds of different pubs and bars, and then lost it, than not to have gone at all, but right now it just feels crap. Is this parade of closed bars and lifeless alleyways really all that we, one of the world's proudest drinking nations, have to offer? And is this really the end of my journey?

Of course it's not. But I need to look at England the same way I looked at all those other countries, to see it with new eyes. I need to go somewhere that has country inns and a town-centre circuit of pubs within easy reach of each other. I need to go somewhere a bit more straightforward than London.

I need to go to Barnsley.

'Hello, *Barnsley Chronicle*!'

'Hi, I wonder if you can help me. I grew up in Barnsley but I don't live there any more. I write about beer now, and

415

I've just finished a book about beer around the world, and I wondered if I could talk to a reporter who covers the town centre and stories about drinking?'

'When did you last live in Barnsley?'

'About fifteen years ago. I still come up to visit my mum and endure the football. The thing is, I wanted to look at the town centre and—'

'And where does your mum live?'

'Sorry? Er ... Staincross. Do you have someone who specializes in reporting on the town centre or not?'

'What's your mum's name?'

'Er ... Pamela. Pamela Brown. Look, what does this have to do with—'

'Pam-el-ah ... Brown. And has Pamela always lived in Staincross?'

'Well, for about the last twenty years.'

'OK, I'll get someone to call you back. Bye.'

Barnsley

Barnsley is the kind of town that forms the butt of many jokes, particularly among people who have never been there and know nothing about it or its people. But the town itself does have to take a small part of the blame – it doesn't exactly invite people in to reappraise it.

Barnsley sits on top of a steep hill, a valley or two away from a stretch of the Pennines which offers some of the most bleakly beautiful moorland in the country. The peat bogs that cut across these moors give an unsubtle hint that there are rich coal seams under the hills. Even a majority of Barnsley's residents don't realize that it originally rose to prominence as a weaving town – famous primarily for its linen until around 1860 – because when coal mining and glass blowing took over, they redefined and rebuilt the place. Barnsley itself became a market town surrounded by a dense cloud of villages, each with its own pit, eventually merging into each other to form the big suburban sprawl where most of Barnsley's 75,000 inhabitants now live.

Nobody seemed keen to move into a community so focused around mining, and Barnsley people were encouraged not to move out – why go to university when you could have 200 quid in your hand a week after leaving school, and a job for life? Barnsley developed a tough, straightforward, plain-speaking character, and a mistrust of strangers. Barnsley's favourite son is Michael Parkinson, whose interview skills are all the more remarkable once you've encountered the sullen-ness of most of our fellow Barnsleyites. Barnsley's second-most-famous son is Arthur Scargill.

Despite 'King' Arthur's best efforts, in the 1980s every single one of Barnsley's twenty pits was closed (even the ones still making a healthy profit). The town lost its heart. There was nothing else for people to do – no other industries, no other skills. Hard drugs arrived for the first time. Then, in 1997, the football team, assembled for a grand total of £950,000, got promoted to the Premiership. Everyone said they would come straight back down again . . . and of course they did. But along a path of 6–0 and 7–0 defeats, they managed to beat Liverpool at Anfield and knock both Spurs and Manchester United out of the FA Cup in a way that was almost cocky. Pride was restored. The community believed in itself again. At the same time lottery and European investment money started pouring in, and the town even opened a tourist information office. Some architects visited and decided it resembled a Tuscan hill village, and proposed surrounding it with a wall of light. It was hard to tell who was more amazed by this: the amused, sneery broadsheet commentators or the bemused local population.

Barnsley still has an insularity to it that makes it by turns frustrating, scary and irresistible. People living in villages like Darton or Pogmoor or Athersley or Cudworth refer to Barnsley itself as simply 'the town', or 'Tarn'. And while village dwellers around the country may also go to 'the town', most of them probably realize that the implication in this phrase – that their town is *the* town, the only town – is obviously false. People in Barnsley, however, just like Newcastle's Toon Army, choose not to. It's been known for Barnsley people, on the rare occasions they venture darn south to 'that' London, when asked where they are from to simply reply, 'Tarn.' Once every few years, when Barnsley FC play the odd game that makes them look capable of getting promoted out of whatever division they languish in at the time, the chant on the terraces is, inevitably (to the tune of 'Three Lions'), 'We're goin' up/ We're goin' up/ We're goin'/ Tarn are going up.'

Barnsley in the twenty-first century is a town of call centres, Europe's largest market space, and a staggering collection of pubs and bars. In recent years the council have encouraged a new breed of super-bars with DJs and late licences to colonize the streets. This is where I first learned how to drink, and since then it has remained a popular and typical example of the British town-centre weekend drinking circuit. It is currently as good an example of tabloid 'Binge Britain' as anywhere else. And yet, at the same time, there's a heritage of traditional British beer culture here. Thanks to its insularity, both facets are relatively unknown to the national media, who probably wouldn't care anyway. But there is no better micro-cosm of the different aspects of modern British drinking.

I arrive in Barnsley very early in the morning, a while before my first meeting, so I head for the cafes above the vast market hall for breakfast. As I order a white roll the size of a pillow, crammed with several pigs' worth of bacon and sausages plus a pint of tea all for £1.70, I congratulate myself on avoiding the stereotypically Yorkshire trait of flavouring everything with slight exaggeration.

An old man standing next to me in the queue looks down at my overnight bag. 'Who's is t'suitcase?' He laughs, delighted at seeing something so unusual as luggage in Tarn centre.

I take a seat and wait for my order. 'Number thirty-eight!' shouts the waitress after a few minutes. That's my sandwich.

'Gi' o'er shartin!' yells the man amused by my bag, as the winching equipment on the bar grumbles into life and, creak-ing and groaning, hoists my sandwich over and drops it onto the specially reinforced table in front of me.

I manage the first few cubic feet of the sandwich before my stomach suggests my heart really isn't going to be very happy if I take another bite, and decide to walk the mile or so out of town to the Oakwell Brewery instead of taking a cab.

There are three different beers in Britain today called Barnsley Bitter, because you can't trademark a place name as a brand. One is produced by a microbrewery in Wombwell, a village to the south of Barnsley. One, for some reason, is brewed in Blackpool. But the one with the best claim to the name is brewed in the shadow of Oakwell Stadium, a shadow that has grown longer since Barnsley FC conned Blackburn into parting with five million quid for Ashley Ward, and built a new stand with the proceeds. The Oakwell Brewery grew up alongside the football club. They were founded within a year of each other, in the late 1880s, and both grew at an intoxicating pace. By the time Barnsley won the FA Cup in 1912,* the brewery had over 200 pubs, and Barnsley Bitter was revered as one of the best in the north of England.

A couple of years ago Madonna claimed she loved drinking Timothy Taylor's Landlord, a beautiful, hoppy pale ale brewed just over the Pennines in Keighley, which she discovered in the Dog and Duck in Soho. Landlord immediately shot to nationwide fame. Legend has it that when Timothy Taylor set up his brewery, his stated aim was to brew something as close to Barnsley Bitter as possible. Even though today's Landlord is probably very different from Taylor's first brews, I still like to think that Barnsley Bitter is Madonna's real favourite beer; she just doesn't realize it yet. I appreciate this may be a cumbersome and problematic approach to marketing the beer, and decide not to mention it to Jonathan Stancill, Oakwell's head brewer, when I meet him.

In 1957 the Oakwell Brewery entered into a trading agreement with John Smith's in nearby Tadcaster. Four years later, Smith's took complete control of the brewery and its 260 pubs. It was the pubs they wanted, and pretty soon they discontinued production of the 'justly famous' Barnsley Bitter amid howls of protest from locals and accusations that Smith's

---

* Barnsley won the FA Cup in 1912. We won it. We did. We won the FA Cup.

deliberately ruined the beer because they were jealous of how much better it was than their own. The brewery site was turned into a distribution depot and ultimately abandoned. When Barnsley Council issued a compulsory purchase order on the site in 1994, a couple of mysterious, highly secretive benefactors stepped in to revive the Oakwell Brewery as a going concern.

Today, beyond proud wrought iron gates, much of the site looks abandoned. The working brewery has a temporary feel about it, sitting in the corner of a huge warehouse building. The main buildings from Oakwell's prime are a complex of stately, majestic ruins. 'It's my ambition to get this lot all repaired and up and running again. Look at it; it's magnificent,' says Jonathan, a young bloke from Sheffield who sees himself as the inheritor of a great tradition.

The oldest employee is Sid, eighty-six years old. He wants to be buried here. He looks after the brewery pensioners who come down here to 'inspect' the beer once a week, drinking free pints to ensure the quality is as good as it was in their day. This is Jonathan's tasting panel. 'Judging the beer, all that matters is that they're satisfied with it,' he tells me before rushing off to ladle some Pontefract liquorice into a batch of Old Tom, the brewery's mild.

Barnsley Bitter itself is a 3.8 per cent dark bitter, 'against the trend towards light, hoppy beers', says Jonathan. In a dig at the people who once destroyed it, it was advertised on posters at the Great British Beer Festival a few years ago with a picture of a Barnsley Bitter hand pump and the line, 'Definitely not Smooth'. Great beer ads say something about the product, but also something about the brand character. To describe the beer, take a subtle swipe at John Smith's and say something about Barnsley's temperament and attitude in three words is nothing short of genius.

Barnsley Bitter is true no-nonsense beer. Jonathan refuses to compromise on anything that might affect its character. He won't use dried yeast: 'Yeast character is essential, and you can't replicate it with dried.' He uses full hops instead of the pellets or hop extract that most brewers now use. But he can't be bothered with any pretentious nonsense. The beer is not bland, but it doesn't have too much flavour either. It's about quality without showiness: a great-tasting beer, impeccably produced, selling in down-to-earth pubs on estates and working men's clubs for £1.50 a pint, to people who could not be described as real ale aficionados. If you were to tell them they were drinking real ale, many of them would raise their eyebrows and say, 'What's that then?' This is just decent beer, like they've always drunk.

This is a typical Barnsley trait. It's easy to believe that the 'Ooh no, luv, we don't have owt like that round 'ere' traditionalism signifies a lack of discernment, but beneath it the same quality I find at the brewery is evident in places like the fresh fish and meat market which, if it was in London, would be salivated over so much in the Sunday supplements that a restraining order would have to be issued against Nigel Slater. Abundance, cheaply available, is a signifier of quality here. There's a professional pride in pubs offering home-cooked meals for less than a fiver. The Barnsley chop, a double chop, is renowned as one of the finest cuts of meat in the world. Perhaps the only frustrating aspect of this is that so few people in Barnsley realize how high their standards are compared to everywhere else.

I leave the brewery with the promise to meet Jonathan

again for a drink in Sheffield, which he boldly claims is 'the beer capital of England'.* It's time to head over to my mum's flat in Staincross, a former pit village a few miles outside the town centre, where I grew up.

I hardly recognize Staincross these days. When I left, the pits were closing but they still defined the place. Now it's as if they were never here. The pit site itself is a housing estate, a supermarket and a Chinese restaurant. The slag heaps have vanished, levelled into rolling green hills. The infant school is also a housing estate. Just across the road, they've also demolished my old junior school, sold the land to build yet more houses, and built a new school on what used to be the playing fields with the proceeds. I can't really claim that 'This were all fields when I were a lad,' but every bit of space is now covered in tiny boxes. I can't understand why there is such demand.

But the saddest change is the demise of the working men's clubs. There used to be two within a couple of minutes' walk of our house: the Miner's Welfare and the Ex-Servicemen's Club or 'Tin Hat'. My dad was never what Northerners call a 'club man', but he was a passionate fisherman, and he joined the Tin Hat fishing club for its coach trips to Bridlington, Whitby and Staithes. He loved sea fishing, and often won the 'I'm tellin' thee, it were that big' trophies the club had for heaviest catch, biggest fish or most spectacular seasickness. These trophies looked incongruous in the house – no one in our family was ever much cop at anything that trophies were

---

* It may well be, but as many of the best pubs still close at three on a Sunday afternoon, I will eventually fail to meet him as planned.

given out for – but they started to pile up, and Dad began to enjoy the admiration of the regulars down at the Tin Hat. Not that this admiration was ever openly expressed of course.

There was a brief period in my late teens when Dad used to take me with him to the Tin Hat for a couple of pints while Mum was getting Sunday lunch ready. Watches were checked with increasing frequency, and no one – *ever* – took the piss out of anyone who said, 'Right, lads, I'd best be off,' even if it was his round. Very occasionally a small child would dash in some time between 1 and 2 p.m., run up to his dad and say something like, 'Mam says you've got to come home or you'll be eating your bloody dinner from t' dog's bowl,' and the man in question wouldn't be seen for the next few weeks.

When I was at university, if I went up to St Andrews on the train Dad would shake my hand at the station when we said goodbye. I'd never seen him shake anyone's hand before. Soon he started to drive me up there, a twelve-hour round trip, finding excuses such as the cost of the train ticket or the size of my bags or just, 'I might as well.' He'd prefer to drive through the night with our next-door neighbour as co-pilot, me in the back trying to get some sleep wedged against my rucksack. He wouldn't want to go home straight away, and he'd hang around, demanding tea and toast from my flat-mates, thickening his Yorkshire accent with added seasoning that I'd never heard before, just so I had to interpret for him. He became something of a folk hero among Luton Steve, Cath from Aberdeen and Alistair – or 'MacAlistair' as my dad called him because he came from Edinburgh.

So we became much closer than we had been when I was growing up, and sometimes, when I was home, he asked in an offhand way if I'd like to go to the club with him. Dad would wear the official working-class Sunday-best attire: shirt and tie, suit, sensible jumper. Because it was smart, yet practical. Only idiots went out just in their shirtsleeves with a thin suit jacket on – 'Tha'd catch thi death o' cold.' But Mum knitted all Dad's jumpers and she was very fond of big chunky patterns, and they always made his jacket look a little bulky and odd. I'd walk in with him, dressed head to toe in black, my hair in a rockabilly quiff dyed blond on top, sure the punters would appreciate that here I was, back from the outside world, the coolest man among them.

'What's tha do, then?' asked one, about the third time I was there, apparently having resigned himself to the fact that I was going to carry on coming and sitting at his table.

'I'm at college,' I said proudly (college being the catch-all term for any education after the age of sixteen; you just didn't say the word 'university').

'What's tha study?'

This was brilliant. A follow-up question. A real conversation. 'Management studies,' I replied grandly.

An embarrassed silence fell immediately around the table. After a while, one of the other blokes, without lifting his eyes from his pint of John Smith's, muttered, 'Tha can't *study* management.'

And that was the end of it.

I was never invited to the Tin Hat after that. Dad and I never mentioned it again. In the way only a university education can, even though I grew up three streets from here and was living on a fraction of what these men earned, I was already a middle-class wanker.

Working men's clubs were an institution in Britain through most of the twentieth century. Run by the drinkers, with beer sold at a far lower mark-up than in most pubs, they took the idea of a gentlemen's club and reinterpreted it for the working classes. Consequently, they were places where men would drink with other men, except at Christmas and Easter, when the whole family would be brought along and displayed while the 'turns' sang or danced or told jokes on stage. There are still working men of course, but they no longer seem to have the breadth of shared experience, the kinship that made these places the true hearts of communities such as Barnsley's pit villages.

My dad died of cancer in 1996. He was fifty-eight years old. Not long after that, the Tin Hat was demolished, along with the Miner's Welfare Club up the road.

Like its fictitious alter ego, Peter Kaye's Phoenix Club, the Tin Hat did rise from the ashes.* The new club is much smaller, standing in the corner of what used to be its car park. Where the old club used to be there is now a parade of shops and an Italian restaurant, Mezza Luna. Working men's clubs are something of an irrelevance now, while Chinese and Italian cuisine – food you would struggle to get in the centre of town last time I went out for a meal here – is readily available even in sleepy satellite villages.

Mum gives me tea and biscuits, and as I fight off Missy, the attention-deficit-disorder dog, she puts on a programme she taped for me when I told her I was coming. I don't get to watch much TV these days – I've only managed to catch two episodes of my favourite comedy this year – but I have nevertheless managed to see about five programmes on

---

* Or it would have done, if it had actually burned down. But I can't write 'rise like a phoenix from the council workmen and a big digger'.

Britain's binge drinking problem. These seem to be rivalling makeover shows, property shows and ten-morons-locked-up-together shows as our favourite kind of telly this year. The one Mum taped was filmed in Barnsley by the regional news people. As she puts the tape in, just before normal telly cuts off there's a trailer for yet another one, this time with Trevor MacDonald.

Barnsley police have launched Operation BROVAC, a new initiative to curb drink-fuelled violence and persuade everyone that Barnsley is safe, following a recent rise in assaults, public order offences and antisocial behaviour. The programme makers have gone out in Barnsley to find out just how bad the problem is. They begin by interviewing town-centre revellers about why they drink, how much they drink, if they are worried about their drinking. People say it's a release, it's good fun, they're young, they'll worry when they're older. They lose count of how many drinks they've had; they're out to enjoy themselves. One lad tells the reporter, 'It's not binge drinking, because I enjoy it.' His mate chips in, 'Wi'aht it, he's miserable.' The first lad nods in agreement.

These interviews are interspersed with footage of women running at the camera, screaming and flashing their tits, and blokes putting their arms around each other and roaring to the tune of 'Glory Glory Hallelujah', 'Barnsley, Barnsley, Barnsley, B*aaaaaarn-sleey*!'

The reporter then goes out with the police. From the back of the van, she gravely announces, 'It's 11.45 p.m., and we're getting our first reports of trouble,' seemingly unaware that this implies there has been no trouble whatsoever while most of the pubs were still open. We see one fight, one bloke who has been hit with a glass, and a couple of people getting shirty when they are not allowed into a club. At the end of the night the reporter turns to camera and asks, 'What else can be done to stop this binge drinking epidemic?'

The studio panel in the second half of the programme seem shaken by what they have seen. But I'm not entirely convinced. If you follow the police around, you are by definition going to see the worst of what happens – you're not seeing the typical night out from the average drinker's point of view. And programmes like this help create these events because the camera is there. The girls were walking down the street laughing and chatting, and only started screaming and flashing their tits when they saw the camera. Likewise, the boys were performing for an audience, for cameras that rarely trouble Barnsley's streets. And I don't like the way 'binge drinking' and 'antisocial behaviour' are used interchangeably, because I don't think they are the same thing.

To get a true picture, I need to go out round Tarn, binge drinking myself. Bravely, as if I'm going off to war, I kiss my mum goodbye, peel Missy off my head, and walk down to the bus stop.

The potential for making a tit of yourself is so much greater in a place not normally frequented by tourists. Staincross just knows there are no outsiders here – why would there be? Therefore, the only possible reason anyone would get anything wrong is that they must be a bit of an idiot. The stop where I used to catch the bus into town is no longer there: no sign, no shelter, no timetable. So I walk down the road to the next one. Here, I try to get onto school buses three times, because they don't say 'school bus' on the front, and to me they look like ordinary buses until they are close enough for me to see the demon children laughing at me for trying to get on.

I check the timetables. These have been placed here by Barnsley Transport Exchange, clearly a body with its sights set high, under the slogan, 'If it wasn't for us, you might not get there.' They don't have the confidence to go balls-out and boldly claim, 'Without us, you *wouldn't* get there.' They have to concede, in their most crucial piece of communication, the one slogan that goes on everything they do, that when it comes to the crunch, there's a chance they might not actually be that essential in people's lives after all. I'm looking forward to future ads using this strategy, with slogans such as, 'You should be grateful for buses, because we might just stop running them, and if we did you might have to drive instead, and you might be mildly inconvenienced by that. So there.'

A proper bus finally shows up, stopping where my old bus stop used to be back up the road – it clearly is still there, it's just invisible – and finally rumbles along. The driver lets me on – and can I just say to Barnsley Transport Exchange how *privileged* I feel at this – and takes me into Tarn.

It's 7.30 p.m. and the town centre is deserted. In bigger cities, where it is ludicrous to go all the way home from work before making your way back into town for a night out, this is the time at which the evening is limbering up nicely. In Barnsley the bars are deserted. I am the only person on the streets. As a whole, Barnsley town centre is a lot less – well – *Barnsleyish* than it was when I last spent serious time here. There are chains such as HMV and Subway. There are restaurants. And there are so many more pubs. They're vast, open and split-level. They advertise DJs and happy hours, late opening and cheap drinks. And they're very stylish, with short, cool names like Tempo, Seven and Bar 1 – 'Barnsley's No.1 pre-club venue'.

I imagine I'll be visiting plenty of these later, so I duck into one or two smaller, quieter pubs to see if they are like I remember.

The Chennels used to be a down and dirty pool hall. It's a little more salubrious now, and tonight is playing host to women in their forties in long evening dresses, immaculately made-up. I wonder if there's a private party before remembering that in Barnsley, where you dress in jeans and sweatshirts at work, you make one hell of an effort when you're going out at night.

When I was growing up, we used to drink fantastic real ale without even knowing that's what it was. I only realized much later I had been drinking cask-conditioned versions of John Smith's and Tetley's. Now they're replaced by John Smith's Extra Smooth, Carlsberg Extra Cold, Carlsberg Export, Guinness Extra Cold, Carling Extra Cold – every beer on the bar is a brand line extension rather than a fully fledged brand in its own right. There's even Tetley's Extra Cold Extra Smooth – a brand extension squared. In my day job as a beer marketer I have little time for real-ale flat-earthers who maintain that marketing is, by definition, evil. But looking at what's happened to the beer range in the Chennels, for the first time in my life I feel moved by the whining call of the real-ale *jihadi*. They used to sell perfectly decent beer here. If you found a pint of John Smith's or Tetley's anywhere outside Yorkshire it used to taste foul. If you were drinking it in London, the Extra Smooth stuff represented a big improvement. But up here you could walk into almost any pub and the beer was wonderful. People of all ages used to drink it happily. There was no reason to change it, or rather no reason of interest to the drinker rather than the Scottish & Newcastle plc shareholder.

Across the road, the Corner Pin is even worse. Whereas the Chennels is clearly an oasis from the main action, it seems this place has decided its future lies in being right at the centre. Still early, the echoes bouncing around the space draw attention to the fact that there is very little seating. Twenty-five feet of tiled space separate the bar and the wall opposite, and there are maybe fifteen seats in the whole place. The beers on the bar are familiar from the expat bars I've been in everywhere around the world: Stella, Heineken, John Smith's and Castlemaine XXXX. Boards behind the bar advertise special offers on jugs of cocktails: 'Hulk' consists of four shots of vodka, a bottle of Reef, a WKD Blue and a K Ice for thirteen quid; 'Red Rooster' is ten vodkas and two cans of Red Rooster for a tenner; 'Cut the Bull' is eight shots of vodka and two cans of Red Bull for a tenner. By law, pubs are supposed to refuse to serve people who are obviously extremely pissed. Yet these drinks serve no other purpose than to get people smashed. The fact they are being advertised on posters behind the bar means the owners are actively encouraging people to get as drunk as possible, as quickly as possible, and if they appeal to girls and to younger people whose palettes have not yet developed, well, that's just an extra-large bunch of drinkers to sell to. In black and white on this chalkboard there's Britain's drinking problem summed up.

The barman works his way towards me, steadily removing the few remaining tables and chairs to create one big, tiled empty space which will encourage people to drink their cocktails more quickly. The parallels with Australia's six o'clock swill are unavoidable.

The Walkabout is a chain familiar to any weekend city-centre drinker. The Barnsley branch is itself the size of a small town. I arrive at 7.55 for an appointment to meet Mark, a journalist from the *Barnsley Chronicle* who called me back following the inquisition about my local credentials. Street and bar are still deserted. I wait for a few minutes. There are bouncers on the door, waiting. Given that pubs are tradition-ally about sociability above all else, I can't help feeling that if you get to the point where you feel the need for several huge bastards with shaven heads on the door of your pub for the entire evening, something in our culture has died. But these guys seem cheerful enough, chatting away, three to each door, long black coats and a bit of diamante bling to give a slightly unnerving edge to their textbook hardness. Two kids sit on bikes watching them, as if waiting for something.

It's late November now. I start to get cold so I do up my coat. I look down at my buttons for maybe three seconds. When I look up again, the street is full of people. They're all coming from the direction of the bus station as if on some prearranged signal, travelling in single-sex groups of between four and ten. A steady stream of cabs begins dropping people off, queuing like limos at a movie premiere. They all head into Walkabout at the rate of about thirty a minute. It takes ten minutes for the bar to go from empty to heaving.

Gritting lorries wheeze past importantly, orange lights flashing. Apart from the bouncers, I'm the only person wear-ing a coat. The temperature is around minus five. The lads are dressed in T-shirts, one or two actually wearing sweaters, conceding that it might indeed be a bit nippy. I remember the conversations we used to have at school:

'Are tha cold?'

'Are tha?'

'No, I'm not. I'm just asking.'

'Oh. I'm not either, then.'

As for the women – boy, do they dress up. No matter what kind of job you do, you couldn't wear these tiny, strappy, don't-think-you're-leaving-the-house-dressed-like-that-young-lady dresses to work. If I wasn't freezing in my coat I'd think I was in Barcelona, not Barnsley.

Mark arrives, younger than I expected, looking a bit like Ant out of Ant and Dec (or is it Dec?) – about twenty-two, boy-band haircut all angular and spikily gelled. We meet Mark's friend Ryan inside, nineteen and similarly coiffed. A *Chronicle* photographer takes a few pictures of me holding a pint and looking fat at the bar, then leaves us to it.

'We come out every week,' says Mark. 'Friday night's all right. But Saturday'll be even busier than this. We normally come out Wednesday an' all. Student night. That's t' best night.' On my first pint, I'm too diplomatic to ask why this is.

'How long do you want to stay out for?' asks Ryan.

'Oh, as long as possible. How long do you usually stay out?'

'About two. Most pubs have got late licences now. After about one thirty you can pull whatever you want.' This is new – the licensing, not the pulling. Because the pubs now have late licences and DJs, you can stay out drinking without having to queue to get into the one night club we used to have to go to.

I tell Mark and Ryan about my agenda. Do they see much drinking-related violence in Tarn?

'If you wanna get into a fight you can, but you don't see it happening,' says Mark. 'We do get stories for the *Chronicle* about it, and about once a month there'll be something big. Thing is, we start here in Walkabout and we finish here. If you go over to Wellington Street it's a lot rougher. That's where all the trouble is. It used to be where you went, but it's moved over here. Most people just don't go to Wellington Street now.'

In a town oversupplied with pubs and bars, the best ones have to work to remain popular. Last time I came out in Barnsley, Wellington Street was the centre of the action. Now, as we move on around the town-centre circuit, we find it deserted. We go into the Shakespeare, a pub that had queues to get in when I drank here. Tonight there are seven of us in the whole place. Some pubs have closed down altogether, which seems almost impossible when there are so many people out drinking two streets away. But the scene has moved on. 'Everybody starts and finishes at Walkabout,' says Mark. 'Market Hill is where it's at now.'

It's much more cosmopolitan than I thought it would be. People are better dressed; the bars are more stylish. There is no longer a sense of Barnsley being cut off from the rest of the world, and a lot of what I was going to say about it is no longer accurate. I should have come back here more.

Treadle's is a small bar bursting at the seams. One side of the room is raised in a small stage which has a bench and then a table on it, creating ranked terraces for people of all ages (between sixteen and thirty), lined up one above the next, all facing out into the bar, screaming and yelling along to the

Grease and *Saturday Night Fever* medleys being played by the DJ. Everyone in the place has a grin on their face a mile wide.

There are plenty of words I could use to describe the scene. It's safe to say that it's not the picture I would paint if someone said to me, 'Describe how you would spend your last night if you were going to die tomorrow,' but only a person with no joy in their life, someone missing a soul, could even attempt to deny the intensely positive good time these people are having.

Amid all the recent talk about binge drinking, there has been very little attempt anywhere in the media to understand why people do it. Throughout history, significant drinking problems have happened at times of great anxiety and stress in society: the gin epidemic in the Industrial Revolution; the alcoholism among Native Americans as their culture was crushed by European settlers; the suicidal drinking among Russians as communism collapsed. I wonder if today's young drinkers are in a similar crisis: working in unfulfilling jobs with few prospects for people and organizations they do not respect, where the government's solution to any uncertainty in or outside the workplace invariably seems to be, 'Work harder.'

Mark tells me that Barnsley's main industry is the call centres. This makes sense: I've already seen research that claims a Yorkshire accent is regarded as trustworthy and plain-speaking. On the binge drinking documentary this afternoon a Tory MP from one of the posh bits of Yorkshire (yes, there are one or two, where the scenery gets *seriously* beautiful) said, 'Barnsley must take the biscuit as the worst place in Yorkshire for this type of thing.' Right now I want to grab her, force her to trade places with the fat lass on the table belting her heart out to 'Summer Nights', and live one week of her life. I want her to sit on the end of a phone for ten hours a day having people tell her to fuck off, in an office where her targets are displayed on banners wherever she looks, where her pee breaks are timed, where she is likely to be *penalized* if she tries to do her job well by staying on the phone until her caller is totally satisfied (thereby decreasing her total call volume per hour), where all the while she is made to feel grateful that the company hasn't yet decided she has so little intrinsic value that they would be better off relocating her function to India or China so people who work even harder for even less money can compete against her, and then attempt to convince me that she doesn't feel like getting utterly, completely and colossally *wankered* by the time Friday comes around.

It's possible that I'm pissed and sentimental. But there's more to the magic of Treadle's than that. The atmosphere is like your best friend's wedding reception, and it happens here every week. I phoned a couple of mates in Barnsley today and asked them if they would like to join us in town. They refused, saying things like, 'I hear it gets pretty rough. Why don't you come round for dinner on Sunday instead?' And here I am, in the midst of people snogging, dancing, singing, laughing. It couldn't be less menacing.

There are no draught fonts on the bar in Treadle's, just four coolers behind, above head height so you can see the brands more clearly. One is stocked with beer, the others with alcopops, and, er . . . Buckfast.

The absence of draught beer and the relatively low ratio of beer to other drinks in the coolers no longer surprises me. Earlier in the evening I asked Ryan how many pints he drinks on a big night out. He looked at me oddly, like I was an old-timer who was no longer with it. (Ha!) 'We don't drink *pints*,' he replied, emphasizing the word like I might if someone had asked me about my fondness for gramophone records. 'You can't get drunk on *pints*. Too filling. No, I'm on a couple of bottles of Bud to start, then I'll move on to Breezers and then maybe some Sambuca later on.'

He's right, and this makes me feel a little aggrieved on beer's behalf. There's a fly-on-the-wall programme on cable TV called *Booze Britain* which regularly shows footage of people drinking alcopops, shooters and slammers until they are sick. But when it goes to the break, what picture do they stamp 'Booze Britain' across? Yep, a lovely big pint of lager.

Ryan, Mark and I end up having to visit Cheadle's toilets at roughly the same time. As I walk in, a bloke at the urinal turns to Ryan and says, 'Are you in McFly?'

'Yeah,' replies Ryan, deadpan, 'I'm the lead singer.'

'Oh.' The bloke nods. He watches Mark and Ryan leave, turns his head back to his ablutions and says to no one in particular, 'Both on 'em out of *Back to t' Future*.' This is as perfect an example of Barnsley humour as I can imagine – obscure and yet literal, dry as a bone, and with a fifty–fifty chance that you might not get it.

As we finally stagger out of Treadle's, I remember something I wanted to ask Mark, the *Chronicle* journalist, my inside track on what's happening in Barnsley today. A few years ago a man called Peter Doyle became mayor of Barnsley. Peter eventually incurred the wrath of the townsfolk when he put together a consortium to buy the football club with money he didn't have and immediately mortgaged some of its assets, engendering the suspicion that he was interested in closing the club down and selling off the land for redevelopment. He didn't succeed in allaying such fears, in my house at least, by revealing himself at press conferences to be one of those people who, like Shabby back in the Stabbers, refer to themselves in the third person, saying to journalists things like, 'When Peter Doyle says he's going to do something, Peter Doyle sees it through.' He was eventually persuaded to sell the club to someone who was a fan (he freely admitted that he wasn't), and is no longer mayor. I'm curious. Is he still around?

'Yeah, he's still on the scene,' giggles Mark. 'We love him – he's a journalist's dream. He was invited to open this new Chinese restaurant, and he was there with a microphone doing a speech about how great it was that Barnsley was becoming so multicultural, and this firework display started behind him. He hadn't been warned about it or owt, so he ducks and yells "Fucking Chinky *bastards*!" right down the microphone. He's the mayor of Royston Vasey, man.'

We move on to a bar down a backstreet, an old courtyard moulded from the sandstone the town was built from a hundred years ago which has been recently glassed over. If it were in London it would be one of the most fashionable bars around.

'Is it all right in London then?' asks Ryan.

'It is. Busy and all that. Expensive. But I like it.'

He thinks for a bit. 'Do you know Abi Titmuss?'

I have to think for a second before replying. 'I don't. But I do know the kind of bars she probably drinks in.'

'Oh.' Ryan nods. He thinks hard for maybe ten seconds. 'Do you think it would be all right if we came down to stay with you and went out looking for her?'

Later, we're in yet another vast pub. This one's playing

very hip music but juxtaposing it with screens showing TMF's fifty worst videos ever. Curiously, with five decades of music to choose from, every single video seems to come from the same mid-1980s period, when I was out in Barnsley on a Saturday night by choice, doing the same thing that nineteen-year-old Ryan is doing now. I'm mesmerized by the video for 'Do the Conga' by Black Lace. I realize that Ryan is not only too young to remember this stuff; he was probably only born around the time we were all cringing to it. I've never been out drinking with someone so much younger than me. I suddenly take exception to him. 'You're so lucky not to have lived through this,' I tell him earnestly. I think some more. 'Your parents probably listened to this the night you were *conceived*,' I hiss.

Ryan nods, impassive. It doesn't seem to bother him as much as I think it should.

And then it's 1.15 a.m., and I'm standing in a taxi queue. Everyone is cheerful, well-behaved, queuing happily, chatting until the next cab comes. The only thing I can think about until I fall asleep is if the judges and newspapers are right, and our town centres are really 'no-go areas for normal people' populated by 'urban savages', can anyone explain to me exactly how Mark, Ryan and the other twenty thousand people out in Tarn tonight are not normal?

The Talbot Inn in Mapplewell is an unremarkable-looking building. Most visitors would say it was a pleasant enough pub but nothing amazing, but for me it sets the standard by which I've judged pretty much any pub for the last twenty years. Because it was in here that I first started drinking beer.

There are three rooms in an L-shape, which have been

knocked through into one large space. Upstairs there's a restaurant, which the slightly posher people in the village – the teachers, those who run their own businesses – dress up for and visit on Saturday nights. Until we were all finally of legal drinking age we always stayed downstairs, claiming the tables in the top corner of the raised section of the L, as far as you can get from the bar. Every Wednesday for the quiz night. Every Friday for the last hour after Youth Club. The Talbot is also the place where, if you were going out round Tarn, you'd get the first couple of pints in before the unofficial town centre start of 8 p.m.

I don't know how old the Talbot is, but it was listed as one of the pubs belonging to the Oakwell Brewery in 1898, which may explain why they always had excellent hand-pulled, cask-conditioned John Smith's on the bar in the 1980s. I'm delighted to see that they still do, given what's happened to all the pubs in Tarn centre. The food is also beautiful, and not in a trendy, pleased-with-itself gastropub way.

After visiting over 400 pubs and bars around the world in the last year, I realize I feel most comfortable in places like the Talbot, or the White Hart, my local in Stoke Newington. This is not about Englishness; wherever you go, however it might look, you can always recognize a real pub. It has a DNA impervious to local mutation, and I've found it in every country I've visited. It might look like an English or Irish pub, or it may think of itself as a bar. It might even be one of those pretend pubs you come across stuck deep inside big hotels – I found a perfect example in the corner of a terminal at Milwaukee airport. But underneath you can feel it's a pub. It's something to do with the role it plays. It's something to do with the smell. It's something about the staff, who are more relaxed and friendly than in any shop, bar or restaurant. Part of it is the bloke in his seventies sitting alone at the table that best captures the late-morning sun as he sips his half and stares into space, reliving his best times or simply waiting for them to get under way again inside a handful of telescoped hours. Visit a place like this for the first time, and within a few minutes you become aware of inside jokes that you don't get. But you can walk in, whoever you are, sit at the bar with the locals, and within a couple of drinks you'll have companionship and, if you want it, chat. Remember that rule about it being dodgy to drink alone? True pubs ensure you never have to if you don't want to. This is what separates real pubs from bars and restaurants that on the surface may look more like pubs, but which underneath pulse to a different rhythm – possibly the rhythm of global Europop rather than that of a living heartbeat.

After lunch I head back into town, and back to the Walkabout, to meet Mark so he can interview me for the *Chronicle*. Obviously it's different at this time of day, and it currently feels like a student union bar. Drinkers are casual, proprietorial, lounging.

Mark really wants to know about how Barnsley compares with all the other places I've been drinking in for this book. I think for a bit and am distracted by the final scores coming up on Sky Sports on the big screen. It's an agonizing situation we know only too well: Barnsley are 1–0 up with ten minutes to go. We both confidently predict a draw or 2–1 loss. The interview is forgotten for ten minutes. Outside, the winter twilight gathers. A cheer goes up across the whole pub when the digital tickertape changes colour to signify that 1–0 has solidified into the final score. I tell Mark that Barnsley is like all the expat bars, with the energy of Roppongi in Tokyo or some of the Irish theme pubs off La Rambla – people really going for it in a happy, hedonistic way. The only reason they are there is to enjoy themselves. We're interrupted by an even bigger cheer than the one that confirmed Barnsley's victory; Sheffield Wednesday have lost.

Many of my preconceptions about Barnsley have been proved wrong: it's much more outward-looking than when I left. When the pits dominated, both the employers and the nature of the job itself encouraged parochialism. You worked shifts with thirty blokes just like you, from families just like yours with histories like yours, who lived in the same streets. Call centre jobs may be terrible, but even if you're just saying, 'I'm afraid I'll have to go and check with my supervisor about that,' you're engaging with people from the world outside more than we ever had to do. In some perverse way this must have a positive effect.

I leave Barnsley with one final thing which delights me. As people travel and broaden their knowledge, it's increasingly common for cities to market themselves in direct comparison with somewhere else: Edinburgh is the Athens of the north; Copenhagen is the Barcelona of the Nordics. So I'm absolutely delighted when Mark confirms something I've already heard from more than one person: without the council's permission, Barnsley has unofficially been christened 'The Magaluf of Yorkshire'.

Staithes

I'm sitting outside the Cod and Lobster, a pub on the harbour front of a tiny North Yorkshire fishing village, drinking a pint of Black Sheep Bitter and eating a bag of Seabrook salt and vinegar crisps. The crisps themselves are a triumph: almost every pub in the country now has gone in for 'premium' crisps that start at fifty pence a packet, but Seabrook crisps are the real deal. Crinkly and far saltier than anything you put in your mouth should be, nothing has changed about them since we used to think of them as a special treat on holidays to the seaside. Foil-packed for extra freshness? You what? Sorry luv, we don't have owt like that round here. Seabrook crisps always seem to be just a month inside their best-before date, excessively greasy and more mashed up and broken than they should be. They set off the Black Sheep's rich fruitiness, and complement its refreshing dry finish perfectly. This beer and food matching lark? We've been doing it longer than we realize.

I've come to Staithes, one of my dad's favourite fishing haunts, for a couple of weeks' splendid isolation to finish the book off. This stretch of coastline consists almost entirely of hulking cliffs that just about manage to hold firm against the relentless bullying of the North Sea, one of those stretches of water that remain steely grey even when the sky above is a cloudless blue. About ten miles north of Whitby, Staithes Beck has carved a deep, sharp nick out of the cliff shelf, creating a small natural harbour and a slope down to it that manages to stay just the right side of steep hill and sheer, scrotum-shrinking drop. A hundred or so cottages cling to this hillside, and there's room for just one road at the bottom, which runs alongside the harbour. There are three pubs, a local shop for local people, a butcher that never opens and a world-class restaurant laden with awards. Seagulls outnumber humans by ten to one and never let you forget it. There's no mobile phone signal unless you wheeze up to the top of the hill, and no internet connection anywhere. Until a few decades ago Staithes men would go out on the boats; Staithes women would climb to the fish market at the top of the hill to sell the catch, and those were pretty much the only times most people left the village.

It's perfect.

I phone my mum to tell her I'm in Staithes and ask what she remembers about fishing trips with my dad. 'Oh, I never went with him to Staithes, love,' she says. 'He told me about that steep twenty-foot ladder you've got to go down to get into the boats, so I never fancied it.'

Later, I walk around the harbour and look at the low walls and promenades to which some boats are moored, while others lie lopsided on the low tide. There's no twenty-foot ladder anywhere. I imagine my dad out here with the lads – just lads – and laugh out loud, earning a pitying look from a passing Labrador.

I think about what I've learned, what's happened to me over the last year or so. I've drunk an awful lot of beer. I've put on a lot of weight, not just from the beer, but from the hotel, airline and bar food I've subsisted on for months.

It's safe to say that I'm now a more sophisticated traveller than I was. Chris, Liz and I went back to Barcelona a week or so ago, and on the Heathrow Express back into London I gave Chris a bad scare when I told him how much better the train's welcome video about meerkats is than the one about owls (though to be fair everyone must have realized this by now – they seem to be showing the meerkat one on every journey, whereas I haven't seen the owls since the America trip) and to watch out for the bit with the two staff telling you about the facilities at Paddington, where the middle-aged bloke standing behind the pretty young woman looks at her while she's talking like he's dreaming of eating her neck.

One thing I hadn't expected is how friendly the world's beer people are, but I shouldn't be surprised. Beer is without doubt the most sociable drink in the world. That's its role. We drink alcohol because we want to feel different; we want to feel happier, more up. If we do this with other people who are all doing it, we have a great time. Where people drink beer, fellowship is all. The curve of drunkenness is nice and gentle, and rituals abound that solidify the friendship and sense of good time. And most people whose lives revolve around beer are infused with its spirit.

Beer has proved a remarkable lens through which to look at the world. When I wrote *Man Walks into a Pub* I learned that drinking culture was a revealing and fascinating filter through which to look at history. Now I've learned that when you look at beer across the globe, it's similarly revealing about who we are, what we are like, and why we are like that. This book hasn't been about hops, barley, yeast and water. They've featured of course, but beer is what we do with our leisure time, and that's where we express our true selves. By asking about beer, I've learned about the Westernizing younger generation in Japan, the Australian male's struggle to define his evolving masculinity, the questing spirit that still defines modern America, and the great secret of modern Europe: that modern Belgium is wreaking its revenge on the neighbours that have torn it apart for centuries by being the world's most elaborate practical joke.

I've discovered the best drinking in the world; and where I've found it, it's been remarkably consistent in character.

Across the world, beer drinking is both different and the same. There is a common drinking culture. That's what makes beer important. But there are also differences. That's what makes beer interesting. The deep rhythms and currents of drinking, the motivations and essential behaviours, are universal. But the ways in which these truths are interpreted by supposedly very similar cultures remain infinitely varied. Whether this will continue to be the case is another matter, but I'm starting to suspect that whatever you do to beer, you can never remove it from the place it has in our hearts.

I'd like to say it's impossible to get *too* drunk if you stick to beer, but of course that's not true. Anyone who's been on the wrong side of someone fuelled by eight pints of Stella would guffaw at that. But Stella shouldn't really be drunk in pints the same way our dads used to drink bitter or mild that was effectively half as strong. Drink Stella in goblets like people do in its native country and, hey presto! It's no longer 'wifebeater'.

I'm not suggesting we do away with the pint – our national symbol – but we really do need to treat beer with a bit more respect, and celebrate its diversity and variety. If someone offers us a beer that's 6 per cent ABV and tells us that it should be drunk slowly in small measures, we should listen. Most of us have learned how to eat Chinese food with chopsticks instead of a knife and fork. We're increasingly trading mugs of Nescafé for cappuccinos and espressos, and drinking them the way the Italians do. Let's do the same with beer. Apart from anything else, it will make it more special.

But does the binge drinking problem go deeper into our culture? In *Man Walks into a Pub* I listed over a hundred words for being drunk; on www.manwalksintoapub.com there are more than 1,200. Most of these are attempts to describe oblivion, negation, total wankeredness. Anything else is a stage on the way to that.

Yet the best drinking is about a middle state. It's about having had too much to drive, feeling the effects, being more relaxed, loquacious and funny, but still being a long way off losing control of your faculties, doing anything you definitely wouldn't do sober, or forgetting your address, your pants or your belief in a basic level of decency and respect. In English, we'd usually describe this middle state as 'a bit pissed', defining it only in relation to the greater state of intoxication we soon hope to achieve. We might say 'tipsy', but that's a bit girly. We might say 'merry', but the only people who do are your parents when they have a second sherry at Christmas.

In most of the places I've visited this middle state is an end in itself, and comes with its own special name. The Spanish have *la chispa*. The Germans have *Gemutlichkeit*. The Danes have *hygge*. The Irish have the *craic*.* None of these words can be translated directly into English, but when people helpfully try to do it for us, they always use words like cosiness, friendship, warmth and buzz.

In most cultures, that lovely bit in the middle, the bit where all the banter, flirtation and laughter happens, the bit before conversation starts entering closed loops that seem hilarious and life-alteringly important only at the time, is not a stage on the way to oblivion, it's an end in itself. What might best be translated as 'the buzz' is a state that's separate

---

* This may end up in the same extremes of drunkenness we have, but a key part of the *craic* is music, and you can't play the *uillean* pipes or even a *bodhran* when you're blotto. Believe me, I've tried.

from sobriety but just as separate from drunkenness. 'Drinking responsibly' doesn't have to mean not drinking enough. It can mean having a bit of self-respect, a bigger, better laugh while you're drinking and a clearer memory of it the next morning. Maybe large sections of the British population really have forgotten how to drink like this. But if that is the case, surely the most successful way to persuade them that it would be a good idea to get back to it is to point out what a brilliant time you can have drinking this way, rather than simply telling them not to drink as much as they do now?

My journey has made me deeply frustrated with beer in Britain. Astonishingly, the average high-street pub in the UK is less likely to have a decent beer choice than bars in any other country I've been to. There are of course hundreds of great real-ale pubs if you know where to find them, and the beers available vary intriguingly across the country. The very best of them still struggle to achieve national recognition. There are brewers like St Peter's in Norfolk, making a broad range of interesting ales, porters and fruit beers and selling them in stylish, beautifully designed bottles. But tellingly 80 per cent of their output is exported. Quality brewers old and new – Samuel Smith's in Yorkshire and Meantime in Greenwich – make beers which are revered by thousands across the United States but are relatively unknown here.

The big brewers in Britain (none of them British any more, apart from Scottish & Newcastle, which no longer has any breweries in either Scotland or Newcastle) maintain that the only reason they push lager to the exclusion of all else is that it's what people want to drink. While true in a sense, this is also a little disingenuous. There's a thriving craft beer move-

ment in every single country I've visited, particularly in those
countries where you'd least expect it – the ones most like us –
the US, Australia and Denmark. I refuse to believe that Britain
is the only Western beer-drinking nation where a sizeable
proportion of the drinking population doesn't occasionally
fancy something different and interesting. People who only
drink generic beers like Foster's and Carling are buying better
wine and trading up to premium vodka and gin. They are
more obsessed with food and drink than ever before, buying
magazines and cookbooks, turning chefs into celebrities and
trading up to free-range chicken, freshly squeezed orange juice
and even Maldon sea salt. Surely they are ready to believe that
beer with flavour which has been lovingly brewed – real ale or
not – might be a good idea.

But, on the other hand, British beer drinkers need a better
champion than the Campaign for Real Ale (CAMRA) in its
current state. When CAMRA was founded the only beer that
tasted of anything was real ale; everything else was bland and
dodgy. If you were going to champion decent beer, it made
perfect sense to focus on cask-conditioned ale. But this is
simply no longer true. By getting caught up in how the beer is
made rather than how it tastes, CAMRA has become increasingly parochial. Bridgeport IPA is not real ale. James Squire
beers are not real ales. Most Belgian beers are not real ales.
CAMRA is now taking active steps to eradicate the image
of real ale as a beard-and-sandals hobbyists' ghetto, but it
remains strident, hectoring and defensive. If there's one thing
I've learned researching this book, it's that drinking beer is
supposed to be about having a laugh. Until CAMRA can
convince ordinary drinkers that crafted, flavourful beer –

whether real ale or the original blonde lager – is about enjoyment as well as appreciation, about socializing more than campaigning, Britain will struggle to accept quality beer.

It's late in the Cod and Lobster now. There were some traditional musicians in the corner earlier, but they've gone. There are apparently only two police vans to cover this stretch of the Yorkshire coast, so closing time is treated more as a guideline than a rule. The clock inches past eleven, and no bell rings. And I realize that despite all the problems with British drinking, if you know where to go, if you trust the landlord, there are places like Staithes, and pubs in towns like Barnsley and even London, with as much colour and character as Tokyo or Munich or Portland. I'm sitting in a perfect pub at the end of a perfect spring day, and it's as good as anywhere I've been.

I go to the bar and order another pint of Black Sheep.

Appendix:
Where to buy

Hopefully by now you have an urge to try something different. Here's a potted list of places you can buy some of the beers I discovered in this book, and hundreds more. It's by no means comprehensive – if you think there are any glaring omissions, please visit www.pete-brown.co.uk and let me know!

Restaurants and cafes

The following places all stock extensive beer lists and can give advice about the matching of beer with food:

Le Gavroche – 43 Upper Brooks Street, London W1. Tel: 020 7408 0881
Brew Wharf – 1 Stoney Street, London SE1. Tel: 020 7378 6601
Aubergine – 11 Park Walk, London SW10. Tel: 020 7352 3449
Quilon – St James's Court, 41 Buckingham Gate, London SW1. Tel: 020 7821 1899
The White Horse – 1–3 Parsons Green, London SW6. Tel: 020 7736 2115

Lowlander – 36 Drury Lane, London WC2B 5RR. Tel: 020 7379 7446

Anthony's – 19 Boar Lane, Leeds. Tel: 0113 245 5922

Any branch of **Belgo** or **Bierodrome** has a great list, is much cheaper, but possibly lacks the same level of personal expertise.

Shops

Utobeer – Borough Market, London SE1. Tel: 020 7394 8601, Website: www.utobeer.co.uk

The Beer Shop – 14 Pitfield Street, London N1. Tel: 020 7739 3701, Website: www.pitfieldbeershop.co.uk

Mail order

These websites all sell a huge range of beers, mostly from around the world (Cave Direct is a Belgian specialist). You can buy by the bottle or the case, and they'll deliver to your door:

www.beersofeurope.co.uk
www.cavedirect.co.uk
www.onlyfinebeer.co.uk
www.booze-uk.com

Trade

Stock fantastic world beers in your pub or bar! Build a beer list in your restaurant! Talk to these guys!

James Clay & Sons – Yorkshire-based importer and wholesaler with a great range of Belgian and German beers, a few

Dutch and US craft beers. Unit 1, Grove Mills, Elland, West Yorkshire, HX5 9DZ. Tel: 01422 377560. Website: www.beersolutions.co.uk, Email: info@jamesclay.co.uk

Vertical Drinks – Sole importers of the very fine Sierra Nevada craft beers, among many others, mainly US. Heritage House, 423 Otley Road, Leeds LS16 5AL. Tel: 01132 670565, Email: steveholt@manx.net

Fancy another?

More than any other aspect of this book, the breadth of background reading it entailed demonstrates the extent to which beer is many things: a drink, an intoxicant, a national symbol, a business proposition, a route around the world. You could get lost in the following list – I heartily recommend that you do.

General drinking behaviour, culture and history

Heath, Dwight B., *Drinking Occasions: Comparative perspectives on alcohol and culture*, Brunner/Mazel, 2000.

Heath, Dwight B. (ed.), *International Handbook on Alcohol and Culture*, Greenwood, 1995 (from which were taken essays dealing with drinking in the USA, Spain, China, Australia, Denmark, Ireland).

McGovern, Patrick, *Ancient Wine: The search for the origins of viniculture*, Princeton University Press, 2003.

Further reading

Nelson, Max, *The Barbarian's Beverage: A history of beer in ancient Europe*, Routledge, 2005.

Social Issues Research Centre, *Social and Cultural Aspects of Drinking: A report to the Amsterdam Group*, SIRC, 1999.

Wilson, R. G., & Gourvish, T. R. (eds), *The Dynamics of the International Brewing Industry since 1800*, Routledge, 1998 (from which were taken articles on Ireland, Denmark, USA, Australia).

The world of beer

Jackson, Michael, *Michael Jackson's Beer Companion*, Mitchell Beazley, 1997.

Protz, Roger, *The Ultimate Encyclopedia of Beer*, Prion Books, 1995 (reprinted as *The World Beer Guide*, Carlton Books, 2000, reprinted as *The Complete Guide to World Beer*, Carlton Books, 2004).

How to not be a crap traveller

De Botton, Alain, *The Art of Travel*, Hamish Hamilton, 2002.

McCarthy, Pete, *The Road to McCarthy*, Sceptre, 2002.

Spain

Williams, Mark, *The Story of Spain*, Santana, 2000.

Czech Republic

Hajn, Ivo, *Budweiser Budvar in the New Millennium*, Budweiser Budvar NC, 2002.

Further reading

Jalowetz, Edward, *Pilsner Beer in the Light of Practice and Science*, Pilsner Urquell brewery, 2001.

Ireland

McCrum, Mark, *The Craic*, Phoenix, 1999.

Malone, Aubrey, *Historic Pubs of Dublin*, New Island Books, 2001.

Molloy, Cian, *The Story of the Irish Pub*, The Liffey Press, 2002.

Belgium

Pearson, Harry, *A Tall Man in a Low Land*, Little, Brown, 1998.

Jackson, Michael, *Great Beers of Belgium*, MMC, 2001.

Webb, Tim, *Good Beer Guide to Belgium and Holland*, CAMRA, 1998.

USA

Baum, Dan, *Citizen Coors*, Perennial, 2000.

Burgess, Robert J., *Silver Bullets*, St. Martins Press, 1993.

Busch, August A. Jr, *Budweiser, a Century of Character*, American Newcomen, 1955.

Erickson, Jack, *Star Spangled Beer: A guide to America's new Microbreweries and Brewpubs*, Red Brick Press, 1987.

Hernon, Peter, and Ganey, Terry, *Under the Influence: The unauthorised story of the Anheuser Busch dynasty*, Avon Books, 1992.

Mosher, Randy, *Radical Brewing*, Brewers Publications, 2004.

Van Munching, Philip, *Beer Blast: The inside story of the brewing industry's bizarre battles for your money*, Times Business, 1997.

Further reading

Oliver, Garrett, *The Brewmaster's Table*, CCC, 2003.

Nachel, Marty, *Beer Across America*, Storey Publishing, 1995.

Palahniuk, Chuck, *Fugitives and Refugees – a Walk in Portland, Oregon*, Vintage, 2004.

Swiercczynski, Duane, *The Big Book of Beer*, Quirk Books, 2004.

Wells, Ken, *Travels with Barley*, Wall Street Journal Books, 2004.

Australia

Baglin, Douglass, & Austin, Yvonne, *Australian Pub Crawl*, Summit Books, 1977.

Bryson, Bill, *Down Under*, Black Swan, 2000.

Dunstan, Keith, *The Amber Nectar*, Viking O'Neil, 1987.

Pearl, Cyril, *Beer, Glorious Beer!*, Nelson, 1969.

Wannan, Bill, *Folklore of the Australian Pub*, Sun Books, 1972.

Japan and China

Clissold, Tim, *Mr China*, Constable & Robinson, 2004.

Germany and Oktoberfest

Dornbusch, Horst D., *Prost! The Story of German Beer*, Brewers Publications, 1997.

Gately, Iain, *Planet Party: A world of celebration*, Pocket Books, 2004.

Hawthorne, Larry, *The Beer Drinker's Guide to Munich*, 4th edition, Freizeit, 2000.

Further reading

Denmark

Glamann, Kristof, *Jacobsen of Carlsberg*, Gyldendal, 1991.
Thomsen, Allan Mylius, *The Humble Establishments*, Danish
 Hotel Porters Association, 1998.

And in all cities around the world, *Time Out City Guides*
provided the best context to help me find my around and
understand what was going on.

Tasting notes

Man walks into a pub

A sociable history of beer

Pete Brown

In *Man Walks into a Pub*, Pete Brown takes us on a well-lubricated pub-crawl through the amazing story of beer, from the first sacred sip of ancient Egyptian *bouza* to the last pint of lager on a Friday night.

It's an extraordinary tale of yeast-obsessed monks and teetotal prime ministers; of how pale ale fuelled an Empire and weak bitter won a world war; of exploding breweries, a bear in a yellow nylon jacket and a Canadian bloke who changed the drinking habits of a nation. It's also the story of the rise of the pub from humble origins through an epic, thousand-year struggle to survive misunderstanding, bad government and misguided commerce. The history of beer in Britain is a social history of the nation itself, full of catastrophe, heroism and an awful lot of hangovers.

'Like a good drinking companion, Brown tells a
remarkable story: a stream of fascinating facts, etymologies and
pub-related urban planning phenomena . . . hilarious'
Times Literary Supplement